Communications
in Computer and Information Science 223

W0227333

Ruay-Shiung Chang   Tai-hoon Kim
Sheng-Lung Peng (Eds.)

Security-Enriched Urban Computing and Smart Grid

Second International Conference, SUComS 2011
Hualien, Taiwan, September 21-23, 2011
Proceedings

 Springer

Volume Editors

Ruay-Shiung Chang
National Dong Hwa University, Hualien, Taiwan
E-mail: rschang@mail.ndhu.edu.tw

Tai-hoon Kim
Hannam University, Daejeon, South Korea
E-mail: taihoonn@hannam.ac.kr

Sheng-Lung Peng
National Dong Hwa University, Hualien, Taiwan
E-mail: slpeng@mail.ndhu.edu.tw

ISSN 1865-0929   e-ISSN 1865-0937
ISBN 978-3-642-23947-2   ISBN 978-3-642-23948-9 (eBook)
DOI 10.1007/978-3-642-23948-9
Springer Heidelberg Dordrecht London New York

Library of Congress Control Number: 2011935742

CR Subject Classification (1998): C.2.4, J.3, C.2, H.4, I.4, J.1, K.4, D.2

© Springer-Verlag Berlin Heidelberg 2011

This work is subject to copyright. All rights are reserved, whether the whole or part of the material is
concerned, specifically the rights of translation, reprinting, re-use of illustrations, recitation, broadcasting,
reproduction on microfilms or in any other way, and storage in data banks. Duplication of this publication
or parts thereof is permitted only under the provisions of the German Copyright Law of September 9, 1965,
in its current version, and permission for use must always be obtained from Springer. Violations are liable
to prosecution under the German Copyright Law.
The use of general descriptive names, registered names, trademarks, etc. in this publication does not imply,
even in the absence of a specific statement, that such names are exempt from the relevant protective laws
and regulations and therefore free for general use.

Typesetting: Camera-ready by author, data conversion by Scientific Publishing Services, Chennai, India

Printed on acid-free paper

Springer is part of Springer Science+Business Media (www.springer.com)

Preface

SUComS is an annual international conference on the emerging areas of security-enriched urban computing and smart grids, aimed at bringing together researchers and developers from industry and academia to present their latest research in the multifaceted aspects of urban computing and smart grids. SUComS 2011, held in Hualien, Taiwan, September 21 – 23, 2011, constituted the Second International Conference on the Emerging Areas of Security-Enriched Urban Computing and Smart Grids. It built upon the success of SUComS 2010 held in Daejeon, Korea.

Three workshops were held in conjunction with the SUComS 2011 conference:

- The First International Workshop on Mobile Social Networking and Cloud Computing (MSC 2011)
- International Workshop on Cloud Computing, Applications and Technologies (CloudCAT 2011)
- The 7th International Workshop on Mobile Commerce and Services (WMCS 2011)

The proceedings of these workshops are also included in this volume. In total, we received 97 submissions. The Program Committee finally selected 35 papers for presentation at the conference and inclusion in this CCIS volume. We would like to express our gratitude to all of the authors of the submitted papers and all attendees for their contributions and participation.

At SUComS 2011, we were very pleased to have two distinguished invited speakers, who delivered state-of-the-art talks on the conference topics:

- "Internet of Things and Cloud Computing for Future Internet" by Han-Chieh Chao (National Ilan University, Taiwan)
- "Building Next-Generation Massive Data Centers" by Mounir Hamdi (Hong Kong University of Science and Technology, China)

The conference would not have been possible without the support of many people and organizations that helped in various ways to make it a success. In particular, we would like to thank the National Science Council of ROC, Ministry of Education of ROC, Bureau of Foreign Trade of ROC, ACM SIG Mobility Chapter, and Taiwan Association of Cloud Computing for their financial support, and we therefore gratefully acknowledge their help in the realization of this conference.

September 2011

Ruay-Shiung Chang
Tai-hoon Kim
Sheng-Lung Peng

Organization

General Co-chair

Ruay-Shiung Chang — National Dong Hwa University, Taiwan
Adrian Stoica — NASA Jet Propulsion Laboratory, USA

General Vice Chair

Chenn-Jung Huang — National Dong Hwa University, Taiwan
Shin-Feng Lin — National Dong Hwa University, Taiwan

International Advisory Board

Tughrul Arslan — The University of Edinburgh, UK
Jianhua Ma — Hosei University, Japan
Sankar K. Pal — Indian Statistical Institute, India
Frode Eika Sandnes — Oslo University College, Norway
Xiaofeng Song — Nanjing University of Aeronautics and Astronautics, China

Workshop Chair

Der-Jiunn Deng — National Changhua University of Education, Taiwan
Hsing Mei — Fu Jen Catholic University, Taiwan
Chao-Tung Yang — Chung Hua University, Taiwan

Publicity Co-chair

J. H. Abawajy — Deakin University, Australia
Robert Ching-Hsien Hsu — Chung Hua University, Taiwan
Yang Xiao — The University of Alabama, USA

Program Co-chair

Tai-hoon Kim — Hannam University, Korea
Sheng-Lung Peng — National Dong Hwa University, Taiwan

Program Committee

Tatsuya Akutsu	Kyoto University, Japan
Jalal Al-Muhtadi	King Saud University, Saudi Arabia
Stuart J Barnes	University of East Anglia, UK
Luigi Buglione	ETS / Engineering, Italy
Yao-Chung Chang	National Taitung University, Taiwan
Chantana Chantrapornchai	Silpakorn University, Thailand
Hui Chen	Virginia State University, USA
Jiann-Liang Chen	National Taiwan University of Science and Technology, Taiwan
Paolo D'Arco	University of Salerno, Italy
Khalil DRIRA	Université de Toulouse, France
Schahram Dustdar	Infosys, Austria
Larbi Esmahi	Athabasca University, Canada
George A. Gravvanis	Democritus University of Thrace, Greece
Abdelwahab Hamou-Lhadj	Concordia University, Canada
Petr Hanacek	Faculty of Information Technology BUT, Czech Republic
Aboul Ella Hassanien	Cairo University, Egypt
Swee-Huay Heng	Multimedia University, Malaysia
Sun-Yuan Hsieh	National Cheng Kung University, Taiwan
Robert Ching-Hsien Hsu	Chung Hua University, Taiwan
Georgios Kambourakis	University of the Aegean, Greece
Farrukh A. Khan	FAST National University of Computer and Emerging Sciences, Pakistan
Hyun Sung Kim	Kyungil University, Korea
Brian King	Indiana University - Purdue University Indianapolis, USA
Chu-Hsing Lin	Tunghai University, Taiwan
Jose Manuel Molina Lopez	Universidad Carlos III de Madrid, Spain
Ami Marowka	Bar-Ilan University, Israel
Mohammad Riaz Moghal	Mirpur University of Science and Technology, Pakistan
Fionn Murtagh	University of London, UK
Tae (Tom) Oh	Rochester Institute of Technology, USA
Ai-Chun Pang	National Taiwan University, Taiwan
Witold Pedrycz	University of Alberta, Canada
Eric Renault	Institut National des Telecommunications, France
Matthias Reuter	Technical University Clausthal, Germany
Juha Jaakko Roning	University of Oulu, Finland
Biplab K. Sarker	PBM Consulting Services, Canada
Reinhard Schwarz	Fraunhofer IESE, Germany

Yannis Stamatiou	University of Ioannina, Greece
Hong Sun	University of Antwerp, Belgium
Agustinus Borgy Waluyo	Monash University, Australia
Ramin Yahyapour	TU Dortmund, USA
Toshihiro Yamauchi	Okayama University, Japan
Chao-Tung Yang	Tunghai University, Taiwan
Fangguo Zhang	Sun Yat-sen University, China
Wei Zhong	University of South Carolina Upstate, USA

Publication Chair

| Pao-Lien Lai | National Dong Hwa University, Taiwan |
| Shou-Chih Lo | National Dong Hwa University, Taiwan |

Registration Chair

| Guanling Lee | National Dong Hwa University, Taiwan |

Local Arrangements Chair

| Min-Xiou Chen | National Dong Hwa University, Taiwan |

Web Chair

| Chia-Ming Wu | National Dong Hwa University, Taiwan |

Table of Contents

Internet of Things and Cloud Computing for Future Internet

Kai-Di Chang[1], Chi-Yuan Chen[2], Jiann-Liang Chen[1], and Han-Chieh Chao[2,3]

[1] Department of Electrical Engineering, National Taiwan University of Science and Technology, Taipei, Taiwan
{d9807502,Lchen}@mail.ntust.edu.tw
[2] Department of Electrical Engineering, National Dong Hwa University, Hualien, Taiwan
chiyuan.chen@ieee.org
[3] Institute of Computer Science and Information Engineering,
National Ilan University, I-Lan, Taiwan
hcc@niu.edu.tw

Abstract. Currently, Internet of Things (IoT) and Cloud Computing are the hottest issues of Future Internet. The IoT is the most important concept of Future Internet for providing a common global IT Platform to combine seamless networks and networked things. Cloud Computing provides backend solution for processing huge data streams and computations while facing the challenges of everything will be connected with seamless networks in the future. However, there is a lack of common fabric for integrating IoT and Cloud. In telecommunications, the IMS (IP Multimedia Subsystem) based on the All-IP and Open Services Architecture has been regarded as the trend for Next Generation Network (NGN). We believe that the IMS communication platform is the most suitable fabric for integrating IoT and Cloud. In this study, we will provide the discussion of open challenges and possible solutions for Future Internet.

Keywords: Next Generation Network, IP Multimedia Subsystem, Future Internet, Internet of Things, Cloud Computing.

1 Introduction

The term of Future Internet is a collection of data communication network technologies in the future. The Internet of Things (IoT) is the most important concept of Future Internet for providing a common global IT Platform to combine seamless networks and networked things. In the future Internet, people will be connected Anytime, Anyplace, with Anything and Anyone, and appropriately utilizing Any network and Any Service. In other words, the IoT addresses the Convergence, Content, Collections, Computing, Communication, and Connectivity between people and things [1].

On the other hand, Cloud Computing [2] is regarded as the backend solution for processing huge data streams and computations while facing the challenges of everything will be connected with seamless networks in the future. Cloud technologies can provide a virtual, scalable, efficient, and flexible data center for context-aware computing and online service to enable IoT.

R.-S. Chang, T.-h. Kim, and S.-L. Peng (Eds.): SUComS 2011, CCIS 223, pp. 1–10, 2011.
© Springer-Verlag Berlin Heidelberg 2011

Both the IoT and Cloud Computing are the trends of Future Internet. However, the developments of IoT technology are diversity and are not interoperable. That results the service providers and operators have no definite specification to follow. On the other hand, the cloud computing solutions are depended on service providers. Since many international organizations are devoted to work out their specifications for providing a common architecture of networks and software. Thus, we regard the IP Multimedia Subsystem (IMS) is the ideal solution for fulfilling the requirements. However, there are still many challenges for IMS being the network and software fabric between IoT and Cloud. In this paper, we discuss the open challenges and propose the possible solutions for Future Internet. Finally, we construct an early IoT bootstrap platform to provide the discussion of those open challenges and solutions for deploying IoT in Future Internet.

2   Related Works

In this section, we will briefly discuss the backgrounds including the concept of IoT and IMS. According to the report of CERP-IoT[1], the Future Internet is defined as a dynamic global network infrastructure. It must have self-configuring capability based on standard and interoperable communication protocols to seamlessly integrate physical and virtual things in to information network. Besides the network and protocol, the Future Internet is composed of IoT (Internet of Things), IoM (Internet of Media), IoS (Internet of Services), and IoE (Internet of Enterprises).The IoT was proposed by the Auto-Id Labs more than ten years ago. It has been dedicated to using RFID to the logistics value chain. In the ITU Internet Reports 2005[3], the definition and applications are quite different from RFID (Radio Frequency Identifier) approach by Hancke et al.[4]. In recent years, the more communication technologies and applications [5-7] are developed to facilitate the concept of IoT[8].

The concept of IMS is to merge telecommunication technologies, wireless networks and wired networks under the All-IP environment to provide more extensible, real-time and interactive multimedia services for next generation networks[9]. IMS uses modified IETF SIP (Session Initiation Protocol) to establish the service session. In IMS, the contents are not limited by the access medium but become more extensible to offer more value-added services to users[10-11]. The IMS architecture can be divided into three tiers: the Media/Transport plane, Control/Signaling plane and Service/Application plane. The Media/Transport plane refers to a wide range of different access technologies. Within the IP transport layer, users go through Wireless LAN, GPRS (General Packet Radio Service) or UMTS (Universal Mobile Telecommunication Systems) to acquire network connectivity. Once connected to IMS, users can access a variety of multimedia services.There is a set of IMS core components in the Control/Signaling plane– CSCFs (Call Session Control Functions), which includes Proxy-CSCF (P-CSCF), Interrogating-CSCF (I-CSCF) and Serving-CSCF (S-CSCF). The SIP signaling will be processed and routed to the destination through this plane. In the Service/Application plane, there are various application servers. The application servers provide users a wide range of IMS service. Operators can use the standard IMS architecture to build up their application servers.

3   Discussion of Open Challenges

CERP-IoT has classified the IoT supporting technologies into 13 categories and discussed some possible technologies [1]. However, the possible technologies for enabling IoT are diversity and are not interoperable. Hence we propose the IMS-based possible solutions to fulfill the requirement of these 13 IoT supporting technologies as following Table 1. Furthermore, we also discuss open challenges with different aspects including Cloud Service Framework, Operation, Administration, and Maintenance (OA&M), and Application Services.

Table 1. IoT Supporting Technologies and Possible Solutions

Supporting Technologies	Possible Solutions
Identification Technology	IMS/SIP URI
IoT Architecture Technology	IMS Architecture
Communication Technology	IMS-SIP Protocol
Network Technology	IMS All-IPv6 Transport
Network Discovery	IMS Service Discovery
Software and algorithms	IMS Service Architecture
Hardware	SDR (Software Defined Radio) and CR (Cognitive Radio)
Data and Signal Processing Technology	IMS and Cloud Computing
Discovery and Search Engine Technologies	IMS and Cloud Computing
Relationship Network Management	IMS Architecture
Power and Energy Storage Technologies	SDR, CR, and CN (Cognitive Network)
Security and Privacy Technologies	IMS Security Architecture
Standardization	3GPP (IMS)

3.1   Cloud Service Framework

Cloud Computing can be regarded as an enabling technology for processing IoT Services. However, cloud computing solutions are depend on service providers and are not compatible with each other. Without a common service framework and communication interface, we need to implement different access methods between different clouds on IoT. IMS has provided a common service framework based on All-IP transport and SIP (Session Initiation Protocol) for telecommunications. Cloud Computing technologies can be utilized to improve the scalability and efficiency of IMS architecture. However, in order to support IoT services, the following issue should be addressed.

- Redesign the Home Subscriber Server (HSS) database schema for IoT environment.
- Improves the IMS service discovery and search function for IoT.

- Improves the original IMS-URI (Universal Resource Identifier) Naming Architecture for IoT.
- Enabling the 3GPP SCIM (Service Capability Interaction Manager) to achieve the Service Composition and Service Interaction.

3.2   Operation, Administration, and Maintenance (OA&M)

It's more challenging to use Quality-of-Service (QoS) technique in future Internet because the changing bandwidth and handoff of IoT device communications affect the trans-mission packet seriously. The existing network services can be divided into best effort service and real-time service. The best effort services like FTP and HTTP are just in the work can be completed within a period of time, and the real-time services like voice messages and video streaming are demanded for more real-time requirements so the real-time services are necessary to complete the work in the limited time. Under the current network environment, IoT cannot dynamically different requirements for the provision of appropriate services causes the mechanism cannot satisfy the user QoS requirements. In general wired networks, packet transmissions are in the "best efficiency" of the state, and the state means that the network will try to maintain the required Application bandwidth, but it's not based on band-width availability and network congestion situation to supply any guarantee. This design makes the Internet in the future IoT Real-time Applications Service cannot guarantee QoS

With the rapid development of the IoT, it will be a significant researching challenge to integrate the IoT and the next generation communication platform, such asIMS. In the next section, we stretch out our visions and suitable solutions to develop the IoT-IMS communication platform.

4   IoT-IMS Communication Platform

Figure 1 shows the evolution of telecommunication in simple concept. The All-IP architecture was planned promptly after R99 (the forerunner of IMS). Due to the architecture being too complex, the development work was divided into R4 (Release4) and R5 (Release5) in 2000. R4 was expected not to include IMS. It focused on the specification of IP transport, and was released in 2001. R5 was completed in 2002, and brought the IMS formally into the 3GPP standard. Further IMS related functions tend toward stability in R6 (Release 6) and were released in 2005. The follow-up R7 (Release 7) also adopted the concept of fixed mobile convergence. In the future, more access technologies and service frameworks will be integrated in to 3GPP specification. We believe that IMS will play an important role in Future Internet.

Based on the IMS concept to combine IoT and Cloud, we proposed a common framework for Future Internet as illustrated in the Figure 2 called IoT-IMS Communication Platform. The IoT-IMS can be divided into three layers: 1) Cloud Networks; 2) IMS Core Networks; 3) IoT Networks. We explain the possible solutions with different aspects as following.

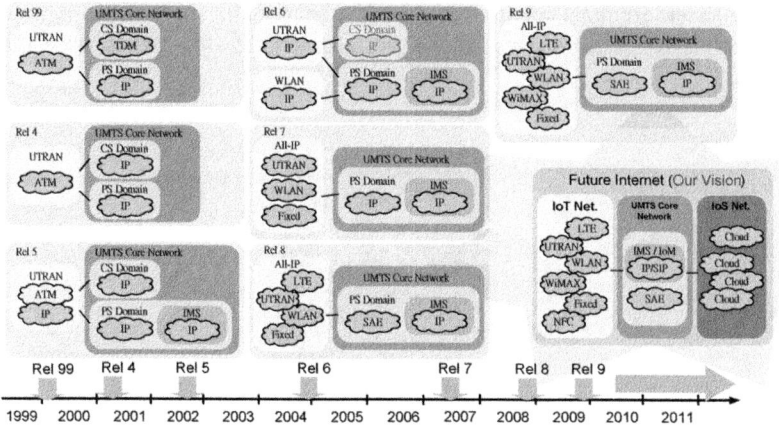

Fig. 1. The Evolution of Telecommunication

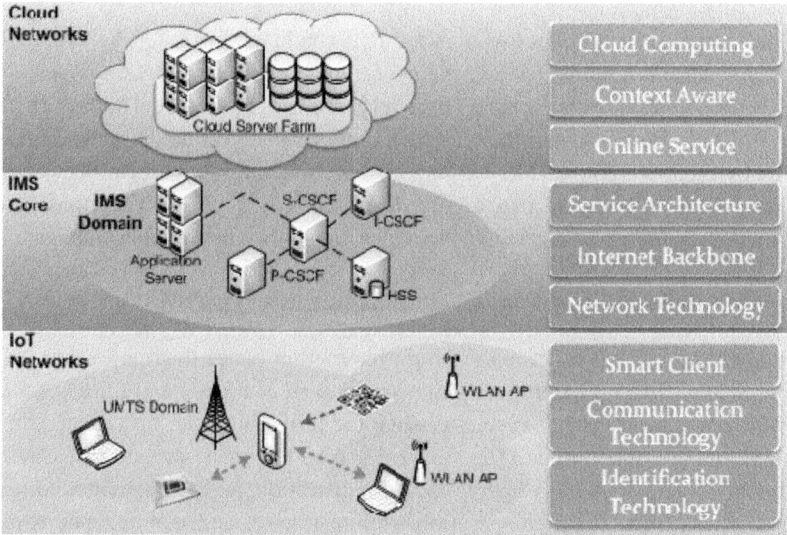

Fig. 2. IoT-IMS Communication Platform

4.1   Cloud Service Framework

In order to improve the IMS service framework by utilizing Cloud Computing technologies, the first step is the visualization as illustrated in the figure 3. Infrastructure
as a Service (IaaS) is suitable for IMS core network to improving the scalability and
performance. We can dynamic allocate the resource for IMS components based the
system load and component utilization. Furthermore, the IMS HSS database indexing
and searching technologies can also be improved by cloud computing technologies for

huge users/things and frequent accesses under IoT. The visualization of IMS-AS (Application Server) and Cloud business model are also suitable for IMS service third party providers.

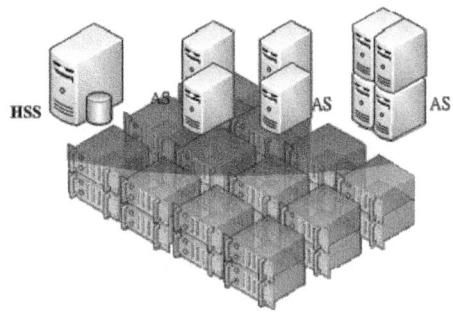

Fig. 3. Virtualization for IMS-AS (Application Server)

The Identification Technologies is the first challenge for IoT. The IMS-URI naming architecture is suitable for naming everything and every service under IoT, and is also fit for Context-aware Service Discovery and Context-aware Things/Devices Discovery. The Mapping, Grouping, and Searching of Real/Virtual/Digital Things can be solved by the hierarchical IMS-URI naming architecture. At present,Service Compositionand Service Interactionare rarely discussed in IoT. These functions have been specified by 3GPP and called SCIM (Service Capability Interaction Manager).

4.2   Operation, Administration, and Maintenance (OA&M)

With integrated operation of in the future Internet on issues that may occur, this study proposed an OA&M (Operation, Administrator, and Maintenance) framework to be as a bridge among the various layers to solve the problem of the operation, administration and maintenance issues. The figure 4 shows the basic structure of OA&M diagram that contains OA&M (Operation, Administration, and Maintenance) three layers to precede with the Internet operation, administration, and maintenance research of IoT-IMS communication platforms. The Operation Plane is responsible for IoT device or network bandwidth and other information and the traffic capture and dynamic bandwidth allocation, so that it ensures that the overall system object with the availability. According to QoS policies defined in Operation Plane, the Administration Plane proceeds with the packet delivery and network services for quality control and ensures that the services be dynamically adjusted according to demand to achieve the best performance system operation and the service with the reliability of the overall system. The Maintenance Plane is in charge of the monitoring and handling of IoTdevices and environment to ensure that services run smoothly. And the Charging system is for charging through the other information processing.

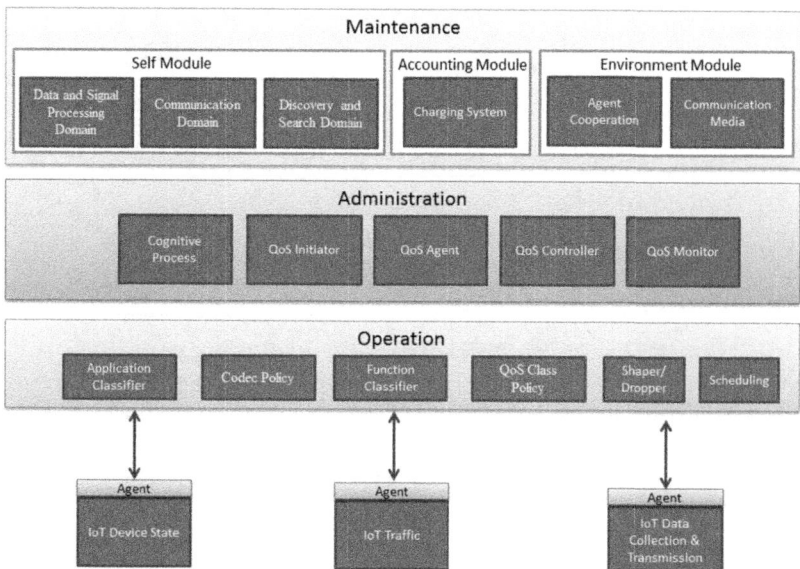

Fig. 4. OA&M Architecture

In order to build IoT-IMS communication platforms and defines related policy module in IoT Networks. With the policy previously adopted the definition of IMS intoCodec Policy, QoS Class Policy, Application Classifier and Function Classifier modules, this study integrated IoT Classifier module and IMS Policy to achieve the unity of the whole structure. Through defined QoS policies, importing relevant policy module in IoT-IMS communication platforms to meet the QoS control function related applications. This stage completesthe Operation and Administration Mechanism designs of Operation, Administrator, and Maintenance of IoT-IMS communication platforms.

As mentioned above, through our proposed methodology, it will provide a simple and direct mapping mechanism combining both features of the IMS and IoT to build the IoT-IMS communication platform and the corresponding IoT-enabled IMS application services in the future Internet.

5   EarlyIoT Deployment and Traffic Analysis

5.1   IoT Deployment Evaluation

In current environment, the main consideration of deploying IoT network is connecting low layer objects and Internet. Thus, we use the OPNet network modeler to evaluate the IoT deployment, construct a bootstrap platform and map it with Ning and Wang's Like Mankind Neural System [12]. The component mapping is described in Table 2, the object model and bootstrap platform are given in figure 5.

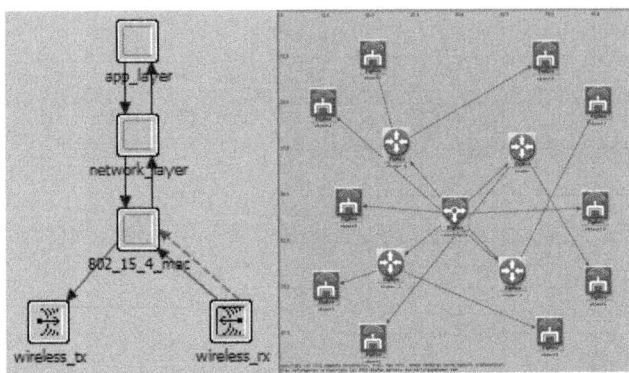

Fig. 5. Model for 802.15.4based IoT Object&IoT Bootstrap Platform Scenario

Table 2. IoT component mapping

In Ning and Wang's LMNS[12]	In our approach
M&DC	IoT Coordinator
Distributed Control Nodes	IoT Router
Sensors	IoT Object

5.2   Traffic Analysis

In our simulation, each object will send a 1024 bits packet per second, which stores sensed information, to coordinator in this IoT bootstrap platform. Then the coordinator handles those messages, feedback to each object. We measure number of hops, traffic to coordinator, router and object, and finally the average end-to-end delay.

The number of hops for data transmission is shown in figure 6. Most objects send their data to coordinator via one hop. However, some data is delivered via more than 2 hops. The reasons are the native limitation of IoT router and the distance from object to coordinator. That cause the information shall delivery through other objects.

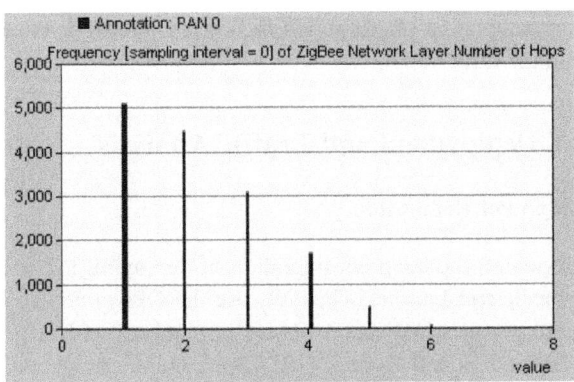

Fig. 6. Data transmission Hops

The traffic in bootstrap platform is drawn in figure 7. The IoT coordinator receives the most data from objects. The IoT router just forwards data from objects to coordinator, and vice versa.

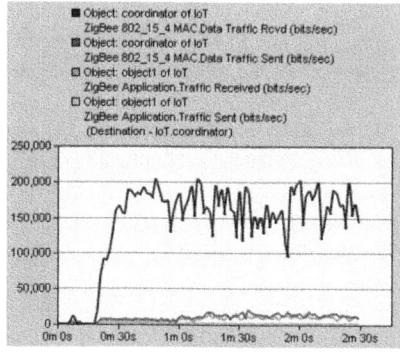
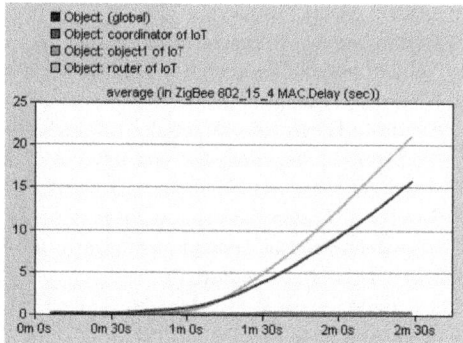

Fig. 7. Traffic in components' MAC layer   **Fig. 8.** Average E2E delay in each component

The average end-to-end delay is given in figure 8. In the beginning, the delay is quite small. However, the traffic is increase and then the delay raise violently. The reason is that the queue length in each router and coordinator is fixed. Thus, the delay time grow with the continually incoming traffic.

6   Conclusions and Future Work

The goal of IoT-IMS communication platform is to provide a common framework for Future Internet based on the existing IoT, Cloud Computing, and IMS technologies. IMS is the ideal solution to combine IoT networks and Cloud networks and maximize the benefit of each other. In this study, we not only discuss the integration issues of Cloud Service Framework and Data Sensing and Communication Technology but also include the Operation, Administration, and Maintenance (OA&M). Finally, we evaluated the early IoT bootstrap platform in the network modeler. We discover that the current Internet is insufficient to maintain the operation quality when constructing and deploying the IoT networks from traffic analysis results. In the future, we will integrate IoT objects with standardized IMS architecture as the fabric, and then continue the operation management and traffic analysis.

Acknowledgements. This research was partly funded by the National Science Council of the R.O.C. under grants NSC 99-2219-E-197-001.

References

1. European Research Projects on the Internet of Things (CERP-IoT) Strategic Research Agenda (SRA). Internet of Things – Strategic Research Roadmap (2009)
2. Armbrust, M., Fox, A., Griffith, R., Joseph, A.D., Katz, R., Konwinski, A., Lee, G., Patterson, D., Rabkin, A., Stoica, I., Zaharia, M.: A view of cloud computing. Communications of the ACM 53(4), 50–58 (2010)

10 K.-D. Chang et al.

3. International Telecommunication Union (ITU), Internet Reports 2005. The Internet of Things (2005)
4. Hancke, G.P., Markantonakis, K., Mayes, K.E.: Security Challenges for User-Oriented RFID Applications within the "Internet of Things". Journal of Internet Technology 11(3), 307–313 (2010)
5. Presser, M., Barnaghi, P.M., Eurich, M., Villalonga, C.: The SENSEI project: integrating the physical world with the digital world of the network of the future. IEEE Communications Magazine 47(4), 1 (2009)
6. Broll, G., Rukzio, E., Paolucci, M., Wagner, M., Schmidt, A., Hussmann, H.: Pervasive Service Interaction with the Internet of Things. IEEE Internet Computing 13(6), 74–81 (2009)
7. Hong, S., Kim, D., Ha, M., Bae, S., Park, S.J., Jung, W., Kim, J.: SNAIL: an IP-based wireless sensor network approach to the internet of things. IEEE Wireless Communications 17(6), 34–42 (2010)
8. Atzori, L., Iera, A., Morabito, G.: The Internet of Things: A survey. Computer Networks 54, 2787–2805 (2010)
9. Chang, K.-D., Chen, C.-Y., Chen, J.-L., Chao, H.-C.: Challenges to Next Generation Services in IP Multimedia Subsystem. Journal of Information Processing Systems 6(2), 129–146 (2010)
10. Wiljakka, J., Soininen, J., Sundquist, J., Sipilä, T.: IPv6 Enabling IMS-based Peer-to-Peer Services in 3GPP and 3GPP2 Cellular Networks. Journal of Internet Technology 5(2), 67–73 (2004)
11. Bari, F., Leung, V.C.M.: Architectural aspects of automated network selection in heterogeneous wireless systems. Int. J. of Ad Hoc and Ubiquitous Computing 4(5), 282–291 (2009)
12. Ning, H., Wang, Z.: Future Internet of Things Architecture: Like Mankind Neural System or Social Organization Framework? IEEE Communications Letters 15, 461–463 (2011)

Building Next Generation Massive Data Centers

Mounir Hamdi

Head and Chair Professor, Department Computer Science and Engineering
Hong Kong University of Science and Technology
Clear Water Bay, Kowloon, Hong Kong
hamdi@cse.ust.hk

Abstract. Data center infrastructure design has recently been receiving significant research interest both from academia and industry, in no small part due to the growing importance of data centers in supporting and sustaining the rapidly growing web-based applications including search (e.g., Google, Bing), video content hosting and distribution (e.g., YouTube, NetFlix), social networking (e.g., facebook, twitter), and large-scale computations (e.g., data mining, bioinformatics, indexing).

Today's data centers may contain tens of thousands of computers with significant aggregate bandwidth requirements. For example, the Microsoft Live online services are supported by a Chicago-based data center, which is one of the largest data centers ever built, spanning more than 700,000 square feet, and Google has more than 1 Million servers.

As a result, the architecture of the network interconnecting the servers has a significant impact on the agility and reconfigurability of the data center infrastructure to respond to changing application demands and service requirements. Traditionally data center networking was based around top of rack (ToR) switches interconnected through end of rack (EoR) switches, and these in turn are being connected through core switches. This approach, besides being very costly, leads to significant bandwidth oversubscription towards the network core. This prompted several researchers to suggest alternate approaches for scalable cost-effective network infrastructures, based on topologies including Fat-Tree, DCell, BCube, MDCube, and Clos network.

In this talk, we detail the trends and challenges in designing massive data centers. We will highlight the research efforts being undertaken by the academic and industrial communities to address these challenges. Finally, we present some of our own solutions by leveraging the key data traffic patterns and web-applications in achieving scalable and cost effective solutions to the design of massive data centers infrastructures.

R.-S. Chang, T.-h. Kim, and S.-L. Peng (Eds.): SUComS 2011, CCIS 223, p. 11, 2011.
© Springer-Verlag Berlin Heidelberg 2011

Charging Station Advertisement on Digital Multimedia Broadcasting Platform*

Junghoon Lee[1], Hye-Jin Kim[1], and Jason Cho[2]

[1] Dept. of Computer Science and Statistics
[2] Jeju National University, 690-756, Jeju Do, Republic of Korea
i SET Co., Ltd.,
Republic of Korea
{jhlee,hjkim82}@jejunu.ac.kr, jkboss@iset-dtv.co.kr

Abstract. This paper first designs and implements an advertisement management framework based on digital multimedia broadcasting facilities and then presents a status posting system for charging stations, aiming at facilitating a battery charging service to electric vehicles. The implemented system consists of advertiser interfaces, data service managers, and provincial broadcasting equipments, making it possible for an advertiser to create or change contents via Internet connection, while the update latency remains below 10 seconds. The charging station information on the queue length, waiting time estimation will be automatically sent to the telematics server via telematics networks to complement the absence of upload path in digital broadcasting. With the interaction between the telematics server and data service manager, this service can distribute electric vehicles over multiple charging stations, reducing the average waiting time.

Keywords: digital multimedia broadcasting, transport protocol experts group, advertisement information frame, update time, advertiser interface.

1 Introduction

DMB (Digital Multimedia Broadcasting) is a digital radio transmission technology capable of sending multimedia content such as TV, radio, and datacasting to mobile devices [1]. It can operate via T-DMB (Terrestrial DMB) and S-DMB (Satellite DMB) transmission. T-TMB works even in vehicles moving up to 120 kmh. In tunnels or underground areas, the broadcast is still available. S-DMB incorporates a high power geostationary satellite, extending its outdoor coverage. Through DMB, a variety of digital contents, generally consist of text, moving pictures, and location information, can be delivered to customers in a low price and updated in real-time. Being an instance of the digital content, the advertisement additionally has both location-dependent and time-dependent features.

---

* This research was supported by KIAT under the Regional Industry and Technology Development Project.

R.-S. Chang, T.-h. Kim, and S.-L. Peng (Eds.): SUComS 2011, CCIS 223, pp. 12–18, 2011.
© Springer-Verlag Berlin Heidelberg 2011

The advertisement on DMB can provide an online status update such as parking lot availability, seat availability, waiting time estimation, and the like, by means of an integrative cooperation of advertisers, content managers, and the system operator.

TPEG (Transport Protocol Experts Group) technology was developed to facilitate the delivery of information messages within the multimedia broadcasting environment from a service provider's database to an end-user's client device [2]. The key principle of TPEG technology requires hierarchically structured messages to be delivered to client devices, which is capable of decoding and filtering the content to provide language-independent presentation either directly for human use, or for agent systems. TPEG was founded in 1997 by the European Broadcasting Union. It is a group of experts coming from all areas of the Traffic and Travel Information businesses, as well as broadcasting. The group developed the TPEG specifications for transmission of language independent multi-modal traffic and travel information. Accordingly, TPEG is a good candidate for delivering advertisement messages in the DMB infrastructure.

TPEG transport also follows the layered protocol [3]. In addition, as shown in Figure 1, TPEG frame can be delivered on top of DMB layer synchronized with other images, sounds, and texts. Layer 7 is the top level and referred to in TPEG as the application layer. Initially, this layer includes the service & network information application and the road traffic message application. Layer 4 is the packetization layer, where components are merged into a single stream and encrypted and/or compressed. Layer 3 specifies how to synchronize and route, and this is the lowest layer belonging to the TPEG protocol. Layer 2 consists of a wide range of different bearers, which are suitable carriers for the TPEG protocol. An adaptation layer may be required in order to map the TPEG stream onto that bearer. Finally, layer 1 defines the transmission medium such as radio waves, wire, optical, and the like. A single bearer can make use of different physical layers.

In the mean time, many countries are making an effort to prompt the penetration of electric vehicles [4]. Even though many researchers and developers are working to improve driving range while decreasing charging time, weight,

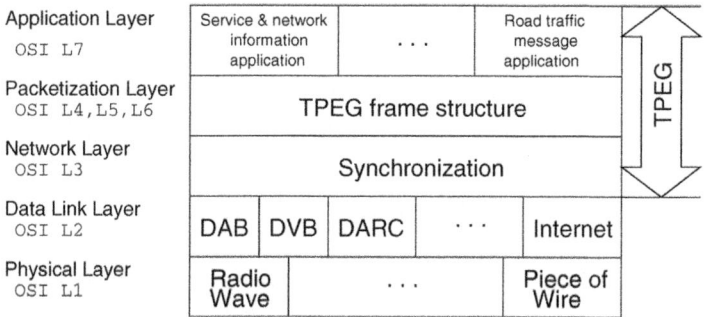

Fig. 1. TPEG and DMB

and cost of batteries, it still takes tens of minutes to charge an electric vehicle [5]. The drivers are highly likely to want to know where the available station is and how long he should wait in those stations. If this information is available to in-vehicle telematics devices, they can even make a new routing plan according to the charging station selection. However, the DMB receiver cannot expect such automation. Instead, drivers must select the charging station by themselves with the provided information on the DMB terminal. This service can distribute electric vehicles over multiple charging stations, reducing the average waiting time as well as helping electric vehicle to permeate into our daily lives.

2   System Design

Figure 2 illustrates the system we have implemented for advertisement broadcasting via DMB. Basically, the advertisement contents are uploaded to the data service domain via the Internet. As everybody can access the Internet, the membership management is important as other Internet services. The advertiser can purchase the right to create, modify, and delete the content. The price for the content transmission can be decided by the price plan for peak, mid-peak, and off-peak interval, respectively, while it can be paid on hourly, daily, and monthly basis [6]. After the operator endorses the advertisement content, it will be registered in the server system. This step is necessary to prevent illegal content from being displayed to the public clients.

The created contents are sent to the provincial DMB facility via the reliable and high-speed optical fiber network. The data service domain and provincial DMB stations can be spatially apart from each other. The DMB station decides the local schedule and converts the contents to the TPEG frame to transmit via the provincial DMB channel. The DMB receiver catches the DMB signal from the transmitter, decodes the TPEG frame, and finally plays the content to the in-vehicle monitor device according to the content type. It takes less than 10 seconds from the time the advertisement content is uploaded or modified until the modification is displayed in the DMB receiver monitor. It mainly includes the content upload delay via the Internet and the waiting time for the content to meet its turn in the local DMB carousel.

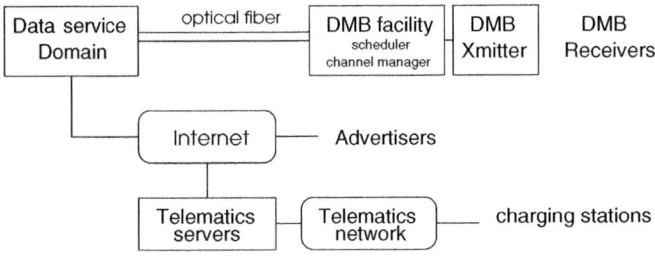

Fig. 2. Advertisement system

In addition to this basic advertisement scenario, charging stations want to announce their current queue status automatically. It's not possible for a human manager to keep uploading the waiting queue status every time a new customer arrives, a charging service is completed, or a new reservation is made. Hence, charging stations send this status message to the telematics server via the telematics network, which can be the Internet, cellular networks, WiFi, or sometimes vehicular ad-hoc networks [7]. The telematics server can either autonomously publish this status to the vehicles in vicinity or upload to the DMB data service. To this end, the telematics server and DMB advertisement manager must have agreement on the content upload fee and the right. The remaining procedure is identical to the ordinary advertisement content case. In addition, to estimate the waiting time, each charging station can schedule the requests having their own requirement [8].

3   Implementation Details

For more efficient management, each advertisement item has a common fixed field set by which most contents can be specified. Our authoring tool implementation provides a user interface for the advertisers to input title, contact phone number, address, latitude, longitude, detailed description, representative service menu, operation hour, and optionally a group of images and coupons. This interface easily converts the user input data to XML documents and stores in the data service domain. In our pilot implementation, the MS SQL server now contains now 41 restaurants, 44 tourist places, and 9 shopping areas.

TPEG can support frames on road traffic message, public transport information, and location referencing, while it is going to further include parking information, congestion and travel-time, traffic event compact, and weather information for travelers. As shown in Figure 2, we can extend a TPEG message to define an ADI (Advertisement Information) message. As an instance of the TPEG frame, the ADI frame must specify MID (Message Identifier) and VER (Version), along with encoding message management, event, and location containers. TPEG POI (Point Of Interest) for location containers consists of a variety of components. Basically, it includes components on classification, description, bi-directional service, time information, and parking information. Moreover, it can further have feature information, product information, relation information, and guide position components optionally. At last, the ADI table includes the ADI application primitives. The encoder converts the XML document created in the authoring tool to corresponding TPEG images and binary files.

The encoded contents are sent to the DMB transmitter system owned by YTN DMB, one of the major domestic broadcasting companies in the Republic of Korea. Broadcasting companies generally lease optical fiber line from the telecommunication companies or institutions. In the provincial DMB domain, the TPEG ADI caster module, implemented using Factum DBS100 5.2 API on the Microsoft .net framework, sends the encoded file to DBS100, which is the data broadcasting equipment. It also provides the monitoring interface through

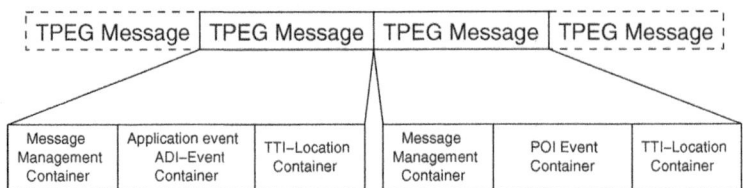

Fig. 3. Advertisement information TPEG frame

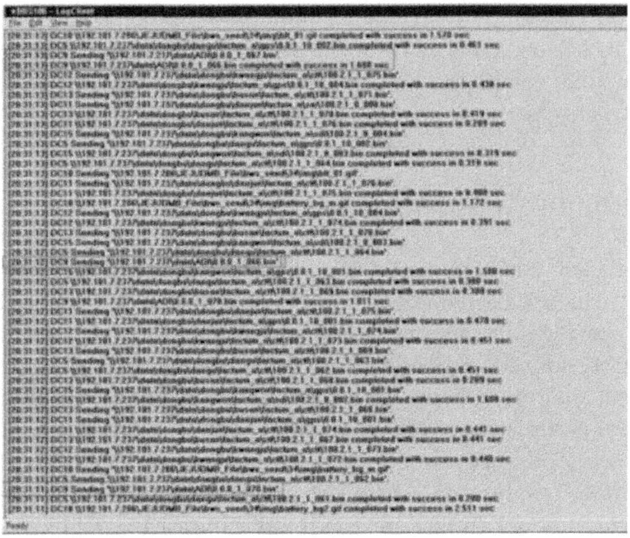

Fig. 4. DBS100 monitoring interface

which we can check the current operation status of the equipment as shown in Figure 4. In addition, Figure 5 also demonstrates the ADIcast interface implemented in our work. For sample data recording, our system employs the indoor transmitters such as DVU5000 DMB modulator radio frequency and DABAir-Multi recorders. In the receiver device, the decoder converts the TPEG-ADI signal into the text message. Here, it doesn't have to be XML format. In our experiment, the decoding time is less than 15 ms in the receiver module.

For the receiver side, the decoded content is displayed on the monitor. The receiver device stores the advertisement and displays one by one. Due to the carousel-style presentation, the update time depends on the number of contents. Here, we can optionally build a terminal side carousel [9]. For example, just the route-related information will be filtered. Receiving the DMB transmission, the receiver device decodes the message as usual. Then, the route match module analyzes the location tag to decide whether the content lies in the route of the vehicle. The A* algorithm can retrieve all the road segments along the path from the digital map, while the segment information includes the boundary box of the segment. Comparing the location tag and the boundary boxes, the route match

Fig. 5. ADI caster interface

module can decide the content is of interest or not. When the destination is not known, the route match module calculates the angular difference between the moving direction of the vehicle and the line segment consisting of the current position of the vehicle and the location tag of the contents. If it lies within the tolerance bound, the content is considered to be of interest.

4 Concluding Remarks

This paper has designed and implemented an advertisement management framework based on digital multimedia broadcasting facilities, defining the roles of advertisers connected to the Internet, data service managers in data service domain, and broadcasting facilities in the provincial area. The advertiser interface creates advertisement contents as XML documents in the data service manager. Then, the high-speed optical fiber network carries the TPEG frames converted from the XML files to the local broadcasting facility. In our system implementation, the content update latency is remained below 10 seconds, including the content upload time via the Internet, waiting time in the local carousel. In addition, test decoder device can decode the TPEG frame and display it within 15 ms.

Based on this framework, the charging station information on the queue length, waiting time estimation will be automatically sent to the telematics server via telematics networks to complement the absence of upload path in digital broadcasting. With the prearrangement on the purchase of right for content upload and the selection of the broadcast period between the data service manager and the telematics server, this posting can distribute electric vehicles over multiple charging stations, reducing the average waiting time as well as helping electric vehicle to permeate into our daily lives.

References

1. Manson, G., Berrani, S.: Automatic TV Broadcast Structuring. International Journal of Digital Multimedia Broadcasting (2010)
2. Paik, R., Chang, M., Kim, J., Choo, D., Jo, M., Bagharib, A., Tan, R.: On the Development of a T-DMB TPEG Traffic and Travel Service. In: Intelligent Transport System Asia Pacific Forum (2008)
3. ISO/TS 18234-2, Traffic and Travel Information (TTI), TTI via Transport Protocol Expert Group (TPEG) data-streams, Part 2: Syntax, Semantics and Framing Structure (SSF) (2004)
4. Kempton, W., Dhanju, A.: Electric Vehicles with V2G: Storage for Large-Scale Wind Power. Windtech International, 18–21 (2006)
5. Markel, T., Simpson, A.: Plug-in Hybrid Electric Vehicle Energy Storage System Design. In: Advanced Automotive Battery Conference (2006)
6. Lee, J., Kim, H.-J., Shin, I.-H., Cho, J., Lee, S.J., Kwak, H.-Y.: Design of an advertisement scenario for electric vehicles using digital multimedia broadcasting. In: Kim, T.-h., Stoica, A., Chang, R.-S. (eds.) SUComS 2010. CCIS, vol. 78, pp. 288–291. Springer, Heidelberg (2010)
7. Sato, K., Koita, T., Fukuta, A.: Broadcasted location-aware data cache for vehicular applications. EURASIP Journal on Embedded Systems (2007)
8. Mady, A., Boubekeur, M., Provan, G.: Optimised embedded distributed controller for automated lighting systems. In: First Workshop on Green and Smart Embedded System Technology: Infrastructures, Methods, and Tools (2010)
9. Lee, J., Park, G., Shin, I.: Design of a broadband multicast catcher in T-DMB services. In: International Conference on Convergence Content, pp. 229–230 (2010)

Security Encryption Schemes for Internet SCADA: Comparison of the Solutions

Rosslin John Robles, Maricel Balitanas, and Tai-hoon Kim[*]

Multimedia Engineering Department, Hannam University,
Daejeon, Korea
rosslin_john@yahoo.com, Maricel@sersc.org,
taihoonn@hnu.kr

Abstract. SCADA has now expanded as it utilizes the Internet as communication line. SCADA communications can contain sensitive data, it is also a core component of a SCADA Monitoring System. SCADA (Supervisory Control and Data Acquisition) communication can take place in a number of ways. Components that are designed to operate in safety-critical environments are usually designed to failsafe, but security vulnerabilities could be exploited by an attacker to disable the fail-safe mechanisms. This makes these devices must not only be designed for safety but also for security. Because of so many vulnerabilities, encryption Schemes are applied to secure the communication between the components. This work compares different Encryption Schemes for Securing Internet SCADA Component Communication.

Keywords: SCADA, Control Systems, Communication, Encryption, Security.

1 Introduction

SCADA Communication is a core component of a SCADA Monitoring System. Common misconception regarding SCADA security was SCADA networks were isolated from all other networks and so attackers could not access the system. As the industry grows, the demand for more connectivity also increased. From a small range network, SCADA systems are sometimes connected to other networks like the internet. The open standards also make it very easy for attackers to gain in-depth knowledge about the working of these SCADA networks.

The use of COTS hardware and software to develop devices for operating in the SCADA network also contribute to its lack of security. Devices that are designed to operate in safety-critical environments are usually designed to failsafe, but security vulnerabilities could be exploited by an attacker to disable the fail-safe mechanisms. This makes these devices must not only be designed for safety but also for security. Because of so many vulnerabilities encryption Schemes are applied to secure the communication between the components. This work compares different Encryption Schemes for Securing Internet SCADA Component Communication.

---

[*] Corresponding author.

R.-S. Chang, T.-h. Kim, and S.-L. Peng (Eds.): SUComS 2011, CCIS 223, pp. 19–27, 2011.
© Springer-Verlag Berlin Heidelberg 2011

The next sections discuss the related technologies such as the SCADA system, the Internet-based SCADA system, the Encryptions Schemes and the comparison of these Encryption Schemes.

2   Supervisory Control and Data Acquisition (SCADA)

Supervisory Control and Data Acquisition (SCADA) existed long time ago when control systems were introduced. SCADA systems that time use data acquisition by using strip chart recorders, panels of meters, and lights. Not similar to modern SCADA systems, there is an operator which manually operates various control knobs exercised supervisory control. These devices are still used to do supervisory control and data acquisition on power generating facilities, plants and factories [1][2].

Telemetry is automatic transmission and measurement of data from remote sources by wire or radio or other means. It is also used to send commands, programs and receives monitoring information from these remote locations. SCADA is the combination of telemetry and data acquisition. Supervisory Control and Data Acquisition system is compose of collecting of the information, transferring it to the central site, carrying out any necessary analysis and control and then displaying that information on the operator screens. The required control actions are then passed back to the process [3].

Typical SCADA systems include the following components: [4]

1. Operating equipment such as pumps, valves, conveyors and substation breakers that can be controlled by energizing actuators or relays.
2. Local processors that communicate with the site's instruments and operating equipment.
3. Instruments in the field or in a facility that sense conditions such as pH, temperature, pressure, power level and flow rate.
4. Short range communications between the local processors and the instruments and operating equipment.
5. Long range communications between the local processors and host computers.
6. Host computers that act as the central point of monitoring and control.

The measurement and control system of SCADA has one master terminal unit (MTU) which could be called the brain of the system and one or more remote terminal units (RTU). The RTUs gather the data locally and send them to the MTU which then issues suitable commands to be executed on site. A system of either standard or customized software is used to collate, interpret and manage the data. Supervisory Control and Data Acquisition (SCADA) is conventionally set upped in a private network not connected to the internet. This is done for the purpose of isolating the confidential information as well as the control to the system itself [2].

Because of the distance, processing of reports and the emerging technologies, SCADA can now be connected to the internet. This can bring a lot of advantages and disadvantages which will be discussed in the sections. Conventionally, relay logic was used to control production and plant systems. With the discovery of the CPU and other electronic devices, manufacturers incorporated digital electronics into relay logic equipment. Programmable logic controllers or PLC's are still the most widely used control systems in industry. As need to monitor and control more devices in the plant grew, the PLCs were distributed and the systems became more intelligent and smaller in size. PLCs (Programmable logic controllers) and DCS (distributed control systems) are used as shown in the next Figure.

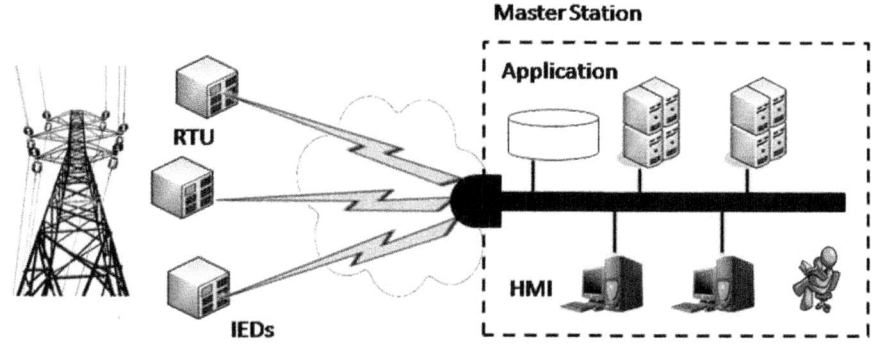

Fig. 1. Conventional SCADA Architecture

Data acquisition begins at the RTU or PLC level and includes meter readings and equipment status reports that are communicated to SCADA as required. Data is then compiled and formatted in such a way that a control room operator using the HMI can make supervisory decisions to adjust or override normal RTU (PLC) controls. Data may also be fed to a Historian, often built on a commodity Database Management System, to allow trending and other analytical auditing [2].

SCADA systems typically implement a distributed database, commonly referred to as a tag database, which contains data elements called tags or points. A point represents a single input or output value monitored or controlled by the system. Points can be either "hard" or "soft". A hard point represents an actual input or output within the system, while a soft point results from logic and math operations applied to other points. Points are normally stored as value-timestamp pairs: a value, and the timestamp when it was recorded or calculated. A series of value-timestamp pairs gives the history of that point. It's also common to store additional metadata with tags, such as the path to a field device or PLC register, design time comments, and alarm information [2].

3   Internet SCADA Technology

Conventional SCADA only have 4 components: the master station, plc/rtu, fieldbus and sensors. Internet SCADA replaces or extends the fieldbus to the internet. This means that the Master Station can be on a different network or location.

In the next Figure, you can see the architecture of SCADA which is connected through the internet. Like a normal SCADA, it has RTUs/PLCs/IEDs, The SCADA Service Provider or the Master Station. This also includes the user-access to SCADA website. This is for the smaller SCADA operators that can avail the services provided by the SCADA service provider. It can either be a company that uses SCADA exclusively. Another component of the internet SCADA is the Customer Application which allows report generation or billing. Along with the fieldbus, the internet is an extension. This is setup like a private network so that only the master station can have access to the remote assets. The master also has an extension that acts as a web server so that the SCADA users and customers can access the data through the SCADA provider website [5].

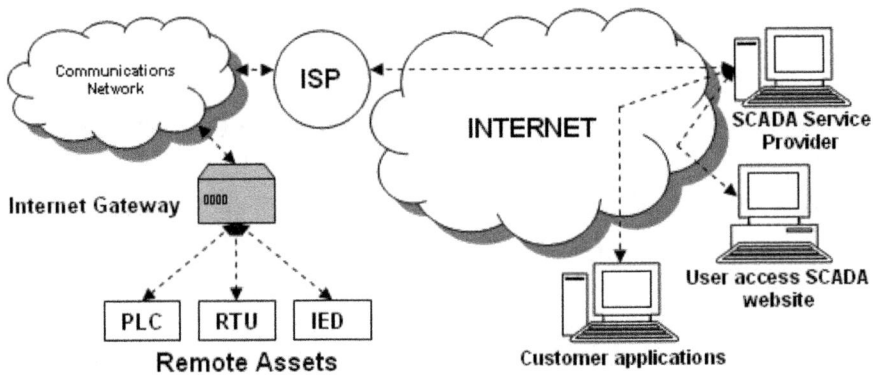

Fig. 2. Internet SCADA Architecture [6]

AS the system evolves, SCADA systems are coming in line with standard networking technologies. Ethernet and TCP/IP based protocols are replacing the older proprietary standards. Although certain characteristics of frame-based network communication technology (determinism, synchronization, protocol selection, environment suitability) have restricted the adoption of Ethernet in a few specialized applications, the vast majority of markets have accepted Ethernet networks for HMI/SCADA.

A few vendors have begun offering application specific SCADA systems hosted on remote platforms over the Internet. This removes the need to install and commission systems at the end-user's facility and takes advantage of security features already available in Internet technology, VPNs and SSL. Some concerns include security, [6] Internet connection reliability, and latency.

4   Encryption Schemes

In this Section, solutions to the issues and vulnerabilities in SCADA and Internet-based SCADA are discussed. The Encryptions Schemes and the comparison of these Encryption Schemes are highlighted.

4.1   Asymetric Key Encryption

The internet SCADA facility has brought a lot of advantages in terms of control, data generation and viewing. With these advantages, comes the security issues regarding web SCADA. In this section, web SCADA and its connectivity along with the issues regarding security will be discussed. A web SCADA security solution using asymmetric-key encryption will be explained.

Authentication will be required to access the data and reports so that only users who have enough permission can access the information. Quality system administration techniques can make all the difference in security prevention [7]. SCADA web server must always be secure since the data in it are very critical. Web server security software can also be added.

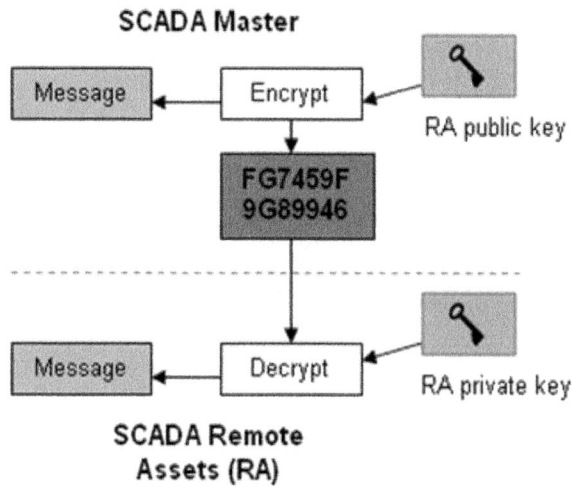

Fig. 3. Asymmetric-key encryption applied to internet SCADA

Communication from the customer or client will start with an http request to the master server. The client will be authenticated before the request will be completed. The SCADA master will then send back the requested information to the client. The information will also be encrypted using the same encryption that is proposed to be used between the SCADA master and the remote assets [7].

To test the usability of this scheme, it was tested using the web base Asymmetric-key Encryption simulator. Since there are many kinds of Asymmetric-key Encryption, in this simulator, RSA Cipher is used.

The following table shows the results of encrypted commands. The first column shows the command; the second column shows the key length; the third column shows the Modulo, the fourth column shows the key which is used for encrypting the command, the fifth column shows the encrypted data; the sixth column shows the key which is used to decrypt the data and the last column shows the actual command.

SCADA systems connected through the internet can provide access to real-time data display, alarming, trending, and reporting from remote equipment. But it also presents some vulnerabilities and security issues. In this section, the security issues in internet SCADA were pointed out. The utilization of asymmetric key encryption is suggested. It can provide security to the data that is transmitted from the SCADA master and the remote assets. Once a system is connected to the internet, it is not impossible for other internet users to have access to the system that is why encryption is very important [7].

Table 1. Asymmetric-key Encryption of SCADA commands

Command	Keylength	Modulo	Key 1	Encrypted data	Key 2	Decrypted data
command 1	2 bytes	110010100001	10001	KAqmOdXhpbh6	101011000001	turn on
command 2	2 bytes	110010100001	10001	9Ra8H"7TEXWLsc	101011000001	turn off
command 3	2 bytes	110010100001	10001	qS70fd_L"ti	101011000001	connect
command 4	2 bytes	110010100001	10001	bPWx5P_4o6JuC5B4	101011000001	disconnect
command 5	2 bytes	110010100001	10001	JLaO2p5HZXTHLS_7	101011000001	open valve
command 6	2 bytes	110010100001	10001	0XGvoFO4i7mIP3_M	101011000001	close valve
command 7	2 bytes	110010100001	10001	MNG1pMdWdR3nG6g	101011000001	half open
command 8	2 bytes	110010100001	10001	kRWkd7"nudFndww2	101011000001	half close

4.2   Symmetric Key Encryption

Symmetric cryptography uses the same key for both encryption and decryption. Using symmetric cryptography, it is safe to send encrypted messages without fear of interception. This means only the SCADA master and the remote assets can communicate with each other because of the said key.

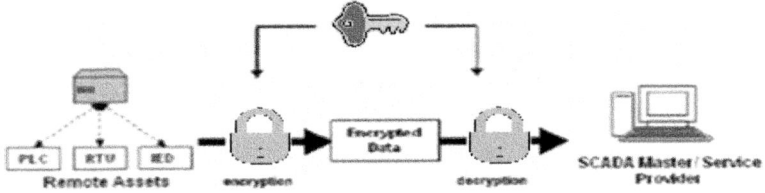

Fig. 4. Symmetric cryptography between SCADA Master Station and Remote Components

WEP was included as the privacy of the original IEEE 802.11 standard. WEP uses the stream cipher RC4 for confidentiality, and the CRC-32 checksum for integrity. It can be implemented to wireless SCADA as it is implemented to other wireless systems. Messages between remote RTU's can be converted to ciphertext by utilizing this mechanism. The next Figure shows how this is done [8].

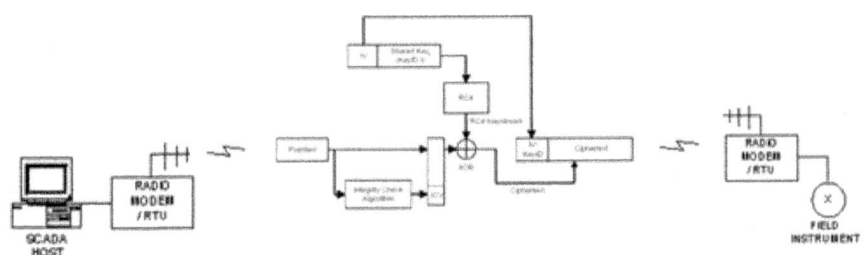

Fig. 5. Standard WEP Encryption in Wireless SCADA environment

The use of symmetric key encryption specifically the RC4 cipher was also is applicable in a wireless Web-SCADA. It can provide security to the data that is transmitted from the SCADA master and the remote assets and also communication between remote RTU's. Once a system is connected to the internet specially wirelessly, it is not impossible for other internet users to have access to the system that is why encryption should be implemented. Data and report generation is also in demand so the internet SCADA is designed to have a web based report generation system through http. And to cut off the budget for communication lines, SCADA operators utilize the wireless based SCADA. [8]

To test the usability of this scheme, it was tested using the web base Symmetric-key Encryption simulator. Since there are many kinds of Symmetric-key Encryption, in this simulator, RC4 is used. The simulator uses the following javascript function to encrypt the command:

```
function rc4encrypt() {
document.rc4.text.value=textToBase64(rc4(document.rc4.key
.value,document.rc4.text.value))
}
```

And the following javascript function is used to decrypt the command:

```
function rc4decrypt() {
document.rc4.text.value=(rc4(document.rc4.key.value,base6
4ToText(document.rc4.text.value)))
}
```

The following table shows the results of encrypted commands. The first column shows the command; the second column shows the key which is used for encryption; the third column shows the encrypted data and the last column shows the actual command.

Table 2. Symmetric-key Encryption of SCADA commands

Command	Key 1	Encrypted data	Decrypted data
command 1	10001	JqMgRYo7ca	turn on
command 2	10001	JqMgRYo7kig	turn off
command 3	10001	04NbRMk4ya	connect
command 4	10001	ZG3gMoA7ce2dCb	disconnect
command 5	10001	4ewdRYE9nGMgnb	open valve
command 6	10001	003b2M6OAugaEXa	close valve
command 7	10001	"ahbJYo7CeMa	half open
command 8	10001	"ahbJYo4aS2hnb	half close

4.3   Cross-Crypto Scheme

Figure 6 depicts the chain of operation in the proposed cipher scheme. The AES key which is used to encrypt the data is encrypted using ECC. The cipher text of the message and the cipher text of the key are then sent to the receiver. To ensure integrity of the data that is transmitted, the data is subjected to MD5 hash algorithm [49].

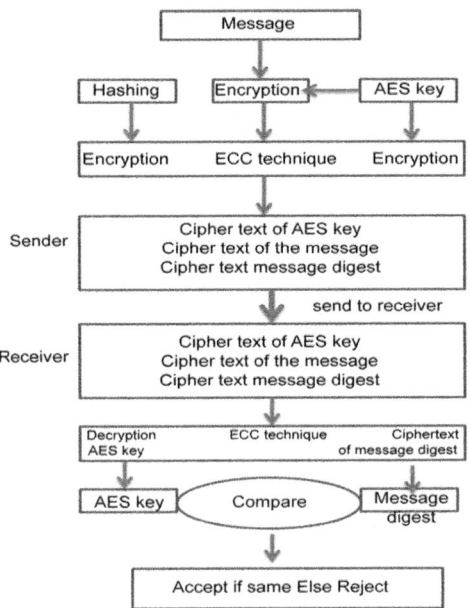

Fig. 6. Chain of operation

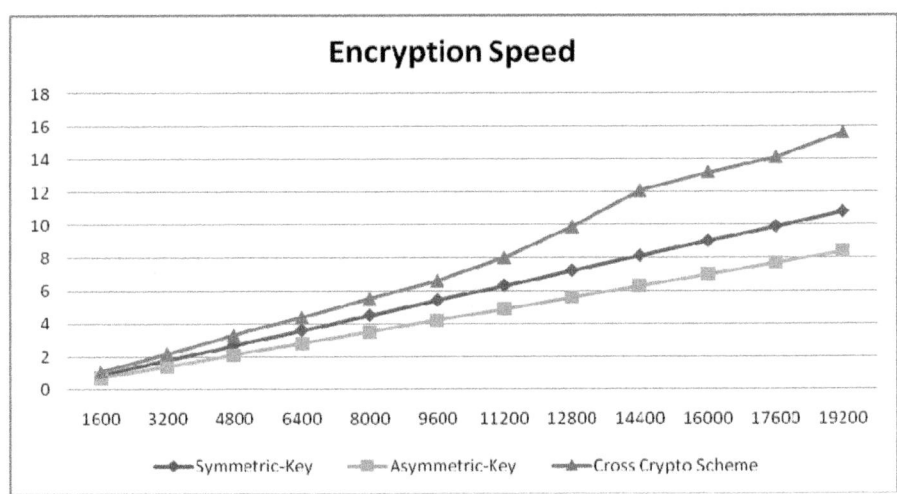

Fig. 7. Encryption Speed Comparison

The message digest obtained by this process is also encrypted using ECC technique. Thus the sender sends (1) Cipher text of the message, (2) Ciphertext of the AES key, and (3) Ciphertext of the message digest. The receiver upon receiving the Cipher text of the message, Ciphertext of the AES key, and Ciphertext of the message digest, first decrypts the Ciphertext of the AES key to yield the AES key. This is then used to decrypt the cipher text of the message to yield the plain text. The plaintext is again subjected to MD5 hash algorithm. This process yields a message digest. The ciphertext of the message digest is decrypted using ECC technique to obtain the message digest sent by the sender. This value is compared with the computed message digest. If both of them are equal, the message is accepted else rejected.

6   Conclusion and Comparison

SCADA (Supervisory Control and Data Acquisition) communication can take place in a number of ways. SCADA Communication is a core component of a SCADA Monitoring System. Early SCADA communication took place over radio, modem, or dedicated serial lines. The process of communication over a SCADA system involves several different SCADA system components. These include the sensors and control relays, Remote Terminal Units (RTUs), SCADA master units, and the overall communication network. Encryption is also an important part of communication. Solutions such as Application of Asymmetric-key Encryption to SCADA Security, Symmetric-Key Encryption for Wireless Internet SCADA and Communication Security for SCADA using a Cross Crypto Scheme are discussed in this paper.

An important thing to be considered is the Encryption Speed. Compared to Asymmetric Key Encryption, Symmetric Key Encryption appears to be slower. However, because of many processes, the Cross crypto Scheme seemed to be the slowest. It's important to note right from the beginning that beyond some ridiculous point, it's not worth sacrificing speed for security. However, the measurements will still help us make certain decisions.

Acknowledgement. This work was supported by the Security Engineering Research Center, granted by the Korea Ministry of Knowledge Economy.

References

1. Reed, T.: At the Abyss: An Insider's History of the Cold War. Presidio Press (March 2004)
2. Kim, T.-h.: Weather Condition Double Checking in Internet SCADA Environment. Wseas Transactions on Systems and Control 5(8), 623 (2010), ISSN: 1991-8763
3. Bailey, D., Wright, E.: Practical SCADA for Industry (2003)
4. Hildick-Smith, A.: Security for Critical Infrastructure SCADA Systems (2005)
5. Robles, R.J., Seo, K.-T., Kim, T.-h.: Communication Security solution for internet SCADA. In: Korean Institute of Information Technology 2010 IT Convergence Technology - Summer Workshops and Conference Proceedings, pp. 461–463 (May 2010)
6. Wallace, D.: Control Engineering. How to put SCADA on the Internet (2003), http://www.controleng.com/article/CA321065.html (accessed: January 2010)
7. McClanahan, R.H.: SCADA AND IP: Is Network Convergence Really Here? IEEE Industry Applications Magazine (March/April 2003)
8. Robles, R.J., Choi, M.-K.: Symmetric-Key Encryption for Wireless Internet SCADA. In: Security Technology. CCIS, vol. 58, pp. 289–297, ISSN: 1865-0929

Implementation of a Large Data Processing Method for Embedded System and CMOS SNR Application

Chien-Hung Chen, Tai-Shan Liao, and Chi-Hung Hwang

Instrument Technology Research Center, National Applied Research Laboratories,
Hsinchu, Taiwan
{cchung,tsliao,chhwang}@itrc.narl.org.tw

Abstract. The embedded system is the future trends of instrument and the larger memory capacity of embedded system is favor to different variety of applications. The commercial embedded systems are always restricted by their embedded memory capacity and required to be upgraded, especially in image application. This article reports a new design and development of an embedded system built in a CMOS image SNR measurement instrument. The new developed approach using the mix technique of large data processing (MLDP) method for CMOS SNR calculation is described. The MLDP method uses an external memory device as auxiliary memory in the regular embedded system to break the memory capacity limitation. The experimental results show the new method is applied successfully in CMOS SNR measurement and the calculated speed is increased almost 200 times compared to that of the traditional method even thought the processing data size is over the embedded system memory.

Keywords: Large data processing, Embedded system, External memory, CMOS SNR.

1 Introduction

Embedded system is a kind of application centric computing system designed for special purposes. Traditionally, an embedded system is implemented on a single microprocessor board with the programs stored in ROM. These kinds of embedded systems are used in various applications such as power plant, automobile control, house systems and information appliances etc.

The basic function of an industrial embedded system is to acquire and accumulate data about the status of the objects, and to control its operation. Besides, the images captured by most of the commercial image cameras are analyzed by embedded system [1-5]. The functions of image camera such as image data readout, image data compression, or image data storage, are easily implemented by embedded system. Furth more, some special functions such as dark current analysis [5,6], pattern noise (FPN) correction [7,8], or image signal-to-ratio (SNR) measurement are also integrated in embedded system applications of the cameras.

However, this kind of application usually needs large memory capacity to store the temporary data, which will be calculated later during sequent processing. For example, when the designer needs to know the SNR data of image sensor, the image data

R.-S. Chang, T.-h. Kim, and S.-L. Peng (Eds.): SUComS 2011, CCIS 223, pp. 28–36, 2011.
© Springer-Verlag Berlin Heidelberg 2011

are measured several times and the SNR results are calculated by the developed algorithm. In the Personal Computer (PC), this problem is easily solved because the designer can add the high memory capacity hard driver to PC memory. But in the embedded system, the system memory was fixed when it was produced. Therefore, memory issues are very important and often impact significantly the embedded system's performance.

The designer can choose the commercial embedded systems with largest memory capacity when the designer buys them and use them to analyze the large data. However, the data capacity is always not enough to feed the need when we are in the memory hungry era. For example, the CMOS image sensor size increases from 30,000 pixels to 100,000 pixels. The image data size of each figure will also improve almost 3.3 times. The other proposed methods are data and memory optimization [9-11]. There are many optimization algorithms in limited memory space, such as maximum a posteriori (MAP) algorithm [12], blocking [13] or tiling [14]. Those algorithms, originally described in the late 1980's, were generally used. However, those algorithms are seldom used in embedded systems. The reason is that the process speeds of embedded systems are not as fast as PC. The memory optimization algorithms are heavy loading for embedded system.

After paper surveying, we present a variety of optimization techniques for data and memory used in embedded systems. The main idea in this paper is to extend well-known techniques implemented in the paralleled processing and memory optimization techniques. We combine hardware and software to develop an algorithm and we call it the mix technique of large data processing (MLDP) method. The idea is that USB flash disk is used to extend memory capacity of embedded systems. Then the parallel processing method is used to read data and calculate the parameters of image.

In this article, we also propose a novel design for the NI CompactRIO embedded system built in the CMOS SNR measurement instrument. The embedded system incorporates industrial 400 MHz MPC5200 processor in order to support a real-time system. We also integrated field programmable gate array (FPGA) device to implement the digital logic control circuit. The FPGA can replace many digital logic parts, implement I/O control, as well as realize the large data processing algorithm that we propose in this paper. Finally, the CMOS SNR measurement instrument is well established and the SNR data is obtained successful by large data processing algorithm of this paper.

2   The CMOS SNR Measurement Algorithm

We propose a CMOS SNR measurement algorithm that is used to obtain the performance of CMOS images from the repeated image data measurements. The flowchart of CMOS SNR processing is shown in fig 1. At the beginning, the system parameters such as image exposure time, readout speed, as well as row data output is set. Then, the luminous of light source is controlled under the image pixel saturation state. The CMOS image data is measured and stored repeatedly. Those image data will be used to calculate the SNR of image data.

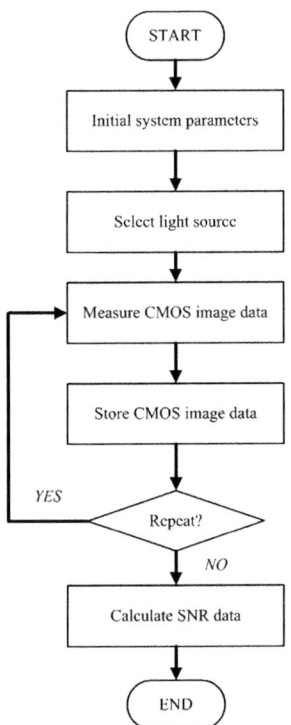

Fig. 1. Flowchart of SNR measurement

3   The MLDP Method Description

The MLDP method will be described in this paragraph. We divided the MLDP method into three steps. They are extended embedded system memory, processing data storing, and retrieving parallel data readout.

First, we use additional and external USB flash to expand the embedded system memory issue. Most of the commercial embedded systems have USB flash protocol and their kernel. We use this feature to add USB flash for extending memory of embedded system, wherein the additional memory space can store the temporary calculated data of CMOS SNR results.

Second, we store the temporary data in USB flash by hexadecimal numbering system. In order to save the extended memory space, we change the decimal numbering system to hexadecimal numbering system and store the information as Windows file system. This method can save one character space for each pixel. The CMOS image sensor which has 512 x 256 pixel size and 12 bits analog-to-digital converter resolution is demonstrated in this research. There are 131,072 total pixel numbers. In this normal state, the memory needs four character spaces to store the data, for example 1025 or 1513. If we use the hexadecimal numbering system, the row data will be shorter and $1025_{(10)}$ becomes $401_{(16)}$, $1513_{(10)}$ becomes $5E9_{(16)}$. Larger image pixel numbers will be saved more additional memory spaces.

Third, we need to read the data out and use those row data to calculate the SNR of CMOS image. The binary data readout technique was used in this part. After experimental test, the binary readout method is 3-times faster than the normal method. Then, those data will be processed by parallel method.

In memory structure, we create two-dimensional array to store the image row data individually and calculate the SNR parameter. The data status in the two-dimensional array is shown in fig 2. Each array stores the same pixel data between different frames. After image processing, we only use 256 arrays of system memory for data temporary storing, that also can predict the total system used and it also can significantly reduce the loading of embedded system memory in large data processing.

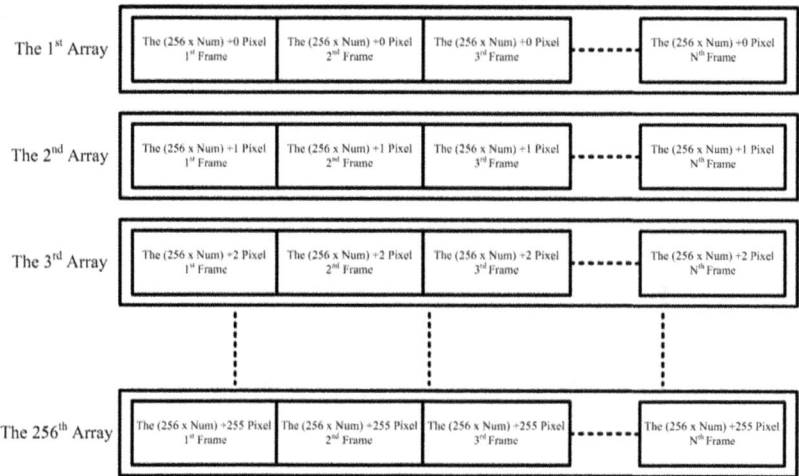

Fig. 2. The pixel data status in different array

4   System Implementation

The CMOS image SNR data is obtained by repeatedly measuring the image data difference between the different luminous of light sources. Generally, the SNR data of CMOS image need to be obtained in 3 status of luminous of light source. There are 25%, 50%, and 75% luminous. This is because that the traditionally SNR measurement methods are really complicated and waste the human resources.

A block diagram of the CMOS image SNR measurement is shown in fig 4. The hardware is composed of an NI CompactRIO embedded system, a 3M gate reconfigurable I/O FPGA, a CPLD component, CMOS image readout circuits, an integrating sphere, a light source controller, and a fluxmeter. The operating frequency of the embedded system is 400 MHz, 128 Mbyte system memory, and the input-output (I/O) interface is via a FPGA background board for the port expansion. The processing result can be transmitted to personal computer and display it later.

Initially, the integrating sphere functions a stable light source (shown as A in Fig. 3) to CMOS image sensor. The pixel numbers of CMOS image sensor are 512 x 256 (shown as B in Fig. 3). The image sensor, which includes 12-bits analog-to-digital

(A/D) converter, can be set some parameters, such as exposure time, or data readout mode. The time control and parameter setting of image sensor are via the CPLD (C) component, and then pass through the 12-bits image row data to the buffer (D). The digital image data is transmitted to embedded system via the high speed I/O ports (E). The maximum speed of I/O ports is 10 Mbyte/s. The FPGA (F) is used to control the sampling data in I/O ports and transmit the image row date to embedded system. The fluxmeter (I) can measure the luminous data of integrating sphere and transmit the luminous data to the embedded system. After all, the embedded system can modify the luminous of light source automatically or manually by the light source controller (H).

The embedded system (G) is the main core in this system. The embedded system function controls all the processes in real time and operates without any interruption. The NI CompactRIO real time embedded system was used in this research, and it can offer stand-alone embedded execution for deterministic real time applications. The NI CompactRIO is implemented by LabVIEW[15,16] graphical development software.

We also use the FPGA (F) to read the luminous data from fluxmeter (I), transmit the luminous data to embedded system, and sent the light source changed commands to light source controller. The development software was also LabVIEW [15,16] graphical program.

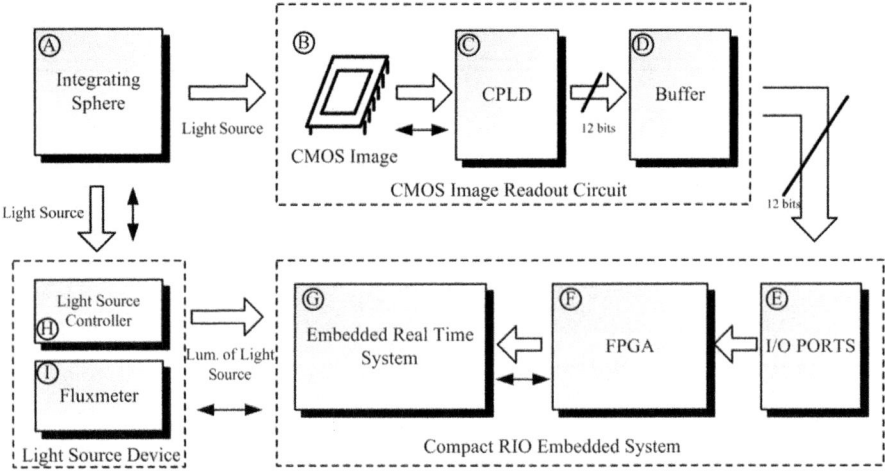

Fig. 3. The CMOS SNR measurement system block diagram

5   Results and Discussion

The accomplished CMOS SNR measurement system is pictured in fig 4. The complete system is composed of an embedded system & FPGA backboard, a fluxmeter, an integrating sphere, and image readout circuits with CMOS sensor. In fig 5, the screen clearly displays one array image row data. The X axis is pixel number and Y axis is gray level of pixel data. In the upper graph, there are 131072 (512 x 256) total pixels and 6 dead pixels are found. The dead pixels will affect the accuracy of SNR calculation. Therefore, the dead pixels need to be fixed before the processing. The bottom graph shows the pixel data, which the dead pixel has been fixed.

Table 1 shows the SNR results of 6 different frames measured using the same luminous light source. The SNR data designates the mean values and standard deviation (STD) of CMOS frames data during the different number frames. From table 1, we can observe that frame numbers of 250 or 300 are the most proper numbers for the CMOS row data measurement in this study. This experimental results show that the mean value and STD become small if the frame data are large enough. Basic on probability theory or statistics, the result is more significant for the applications if the data set or data population approach the normal distribution. A small standard deviation indicates that the data points tend to be close to the mean; therefore, the result will also be more precise. In addition, the high frame numbers will increase the processed data size and add the embedded system memory loading. Therefore, we purposed a new method which includes the extend USB memory for data storing.

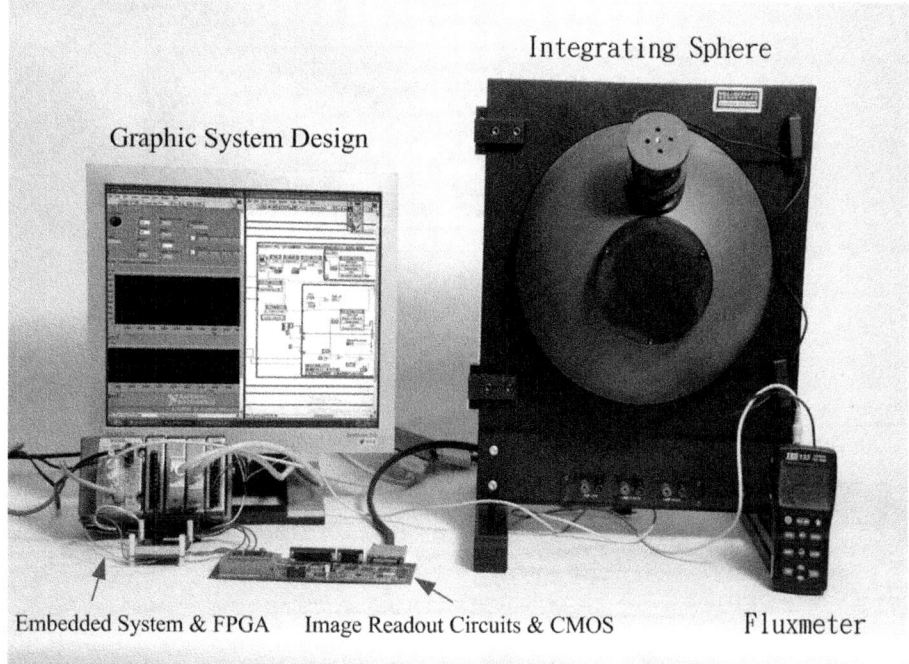

Fig. 4. The CMOS SNR measurement system

In data processing time experiment, we use 5 different frames to compare the normal method and MLPD method, and also test the processing speeds between inside memory and extended memory. The normal method of inside memory is that the image row data is stored into the memory of embedded system and calculated. In the normal method of extended memory, the image row data is stored to extended memory, then read them out and calculate pixel by pixel with regular methods. The MLDP is the large data processing method that we propose in this paper. The data sizes of

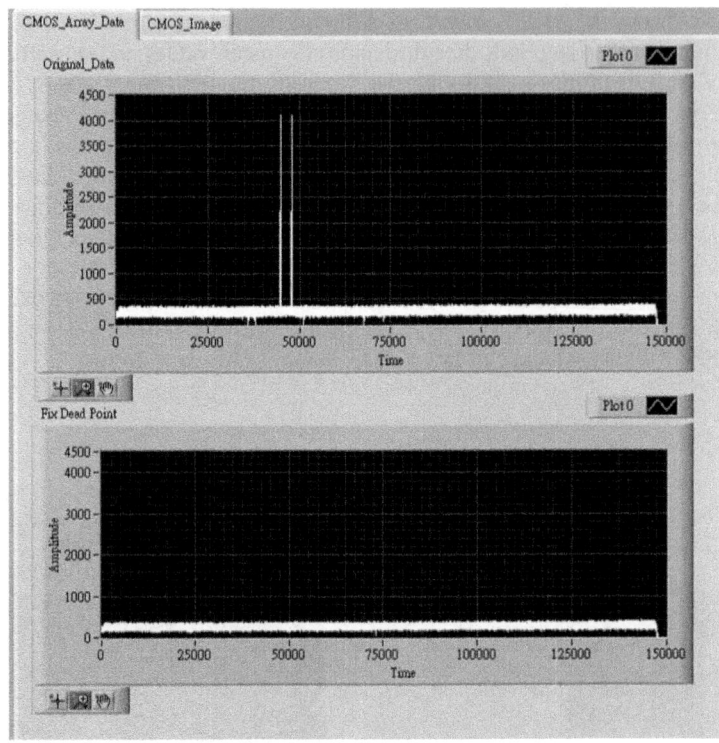

Fig. 5. The CMOS image row data

Table 1. The mean value and standard deviation between different measurement frames

FRAME NUMBER	50	100	150	200	250	300
MEAN	43.639	43.654	43.524	43.533	43.415	43.411
STANDARD DEVIATION	0.953	0.714	0.609	0.614	0.521	0.493

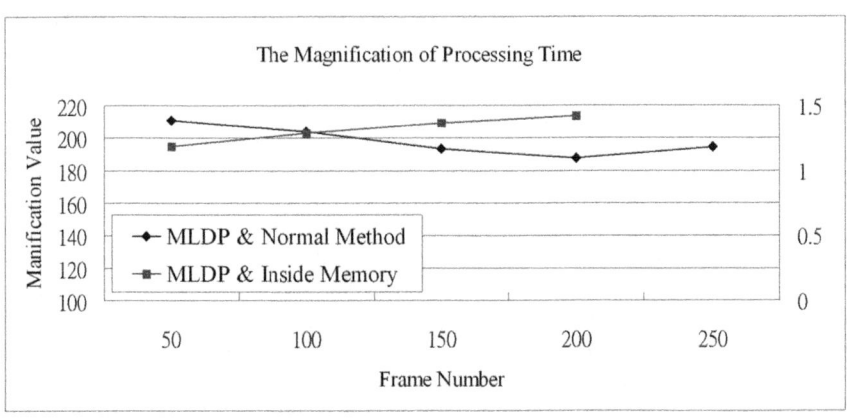

Fig. 6. The magnification of processing time

processing are 25 M(50 image frames), 50 M (100 image frames), 75 M(150 image frames), 100 M(200 image frames),, and 125 M(250 image frames), respectively. The 250 frames (125 MByte) data cannot process in inside memory because of overflow. The reason is that the system memory only carries 128 MByte, and the program of system and directive of program also need memory. We compare MLDP method with normal method of extended memory and with normal method of inside memory. The inside memory method uses the least processing time in the experimental results. But if the row data are lager than system memory, the embedded system cannot operate. The magnification values of processing time shows in fig 6. The X axis of fig 6 is frames number, the left side of Y axis is the magnification of MLDP and normal method, and right side of Y axis is the magnification of MLDP and inside memory. The processing time of MLDP method is almost 200 times faster than the normal method of extended memory. The performance of MLDP method still can have almost 80 % of the inside memory method. Those results verify that the MLDP method can process the large data in embedded system with considerable accuracy even thought the data size are higher than system memory.

References

1. Cheng, A.M.K., Wang, Y.: A dynamic voltage scaling algorithm for dynamic workloads. Journal of Signal Processing Systems 52, 45–57 (2007)
2. Smith, M., Miller, J., Daeninck, S.: A test-oriented embedded system production methodology. Journal of Signal Processing Systems 56, 69–89 (2009)
3. Talavera, G., Jayapala, M., Carrabina, J., Catthoor, F.: Address generation optimization for embedded high-performance processors: a survey. Journal of Signal Processing Systems 53, 271–284 (2008)
4. Pardo, F., Dierickx, B., Scheffer, D.: Space-variant non-orthogonal structure CMOS image sensor design. IEEE Journal of Solid State Circuits 33, 842–849 (1998)
5. Fossum, E.R.: CMOS image sensors: electronic camera on a chip. IEEE Transactions on Electron Devices 44, 1689–1698 (1997)
6. Correia, J.H., de Graaf, G., Kong, S.H., Bartek, M., Wolffenbuttel, R.F.: Single-chip CMOS optical microspectrometer. Sensor and Actuators A 82, 191–197 (2000)
7. Mühlmann, U., Ribo, M., Lang, P., Pinz, A.: A new high speed CMOS camera for real-time tracking applications. In: ICRA 2004 (New Orleans), pp. 5195–5200 (2004)
8. Schwarz, M., Ewe, L., Hauschild, R., Hosticka, B.J., Huppertz, J., Kolnsberg, S., Mokwa, W., Trieu, H.K.: Single Chip CMOS Imagers and Flexible Microelectronic Stimulators for a Retina Implant System. Sensor and Actuators A 83, 40–46 (2000)
9. Panda, P.R., Catthoor, F., Dutt, N.D., Danckaert, K., Brockmeyer, E., Kulkarni, C., Vandercappelle, A., Kjeldsberg, P.G.: Data and memory optimization techniques for embedded systems. ACM Trans. on Design Auto. of Electronic Systems 6, 149–206 (2001)
10. Catthoor, F., Wuytack, S., DeE Greef, E., Balasa, F., Nnachtergaele, L., Vandecappelle, A.: Custom Memory Management Methodology. In: Exploration of Memory Organization for Embedded Multimedia System Design. Kluwer Academic, Dordrecht (1998)
11. Byrd, R.H., Lu, P., Nocedal, J.: A limited memory algorithm for bound constrained optimization. SIAM Journal on Scientific and Statistical Computing 16, 1190–1208 (1995)

12. Schurgers, C., Catthoor, F., Engels, M.: Memory Optimisation of MAP Turbo Decoder Algorithms. IEEE Transaction on VLSI Systems 9, 305–312 (2001)
13. Golub, G., Van Loan, C.F.: Matrix Computations. Johns Hopkins University Press, Baltimore (1989)
14. Wolfe, M.: More iteration space tiling. In: ACM/IEEE Conference on Supercomputing, pp. 655–664 (1989)
15. Aspey, R.A., McDermid, I.S., Leblanc, T., Howe, J.W., Walsh, T.D.: LABVIEW graphical user interface for precision multichannel alignment of Raman lidar at Jet Propulsion Laboratory, Table Mountain Facility. Review of Scientific Instruments 79, 094502 (2008)
16. Blacksell, M., Wach, J., Anderson, D., Howard, J., Collis, S.M., Blackwell, B.D., Andruczyk, D., James, B.W.: Imaging photomultiplier array with integrated amplifiers and high-speed USB interface. Review of Scientific Instruments 79, 10F506 (2008)

The Design of Ubiquitous Learning System with Computing Context-Aware Function

Fu-Chien Kao, Wei-De Li, and Ting-Hao Huang

Dept. of Computer Science and Information Engineering,
Da-Yeh University, Taiwan
{fuchien,R9906031,R9606039}@mail.dyu.edu.tw

Abstract. This research proposes a context-aware computing ubiquitous learning system architecture design. The system integrates data grid, the ability to perform context-awareness computing, and Improved Ganglia Agent design, structuring an architecture that is able to perform context awareness mobile network, creating a ubiquitous learning environment. The improved Ganglia Agent server could provide context information on system network traffic, the CPU load of the content server, and hard disk capacity, and utilize the information to balance the load of back-end content server, providing a flexible expandability mechanism for the back-end content server. The framework of the proposed ubiquitous learning system that has context-awareness computing ability is consisted of 3 major parts: Learning Management System (LMS), Learning Content Management System (LCMS) and the Improved Ganglia Agent (IGA). LMS is responsible for managing the learners' basic personal information and studying records, LCMS is responsible for the management and storage of back-end learning contents, and IGA is responsible for the management network traffic, CPU load and hard disk capacity. With the three, the load of the back-end content server could be balanced, offering a flexible mechanism for the expansion of the server. Not only does the ubiquitous learning system architecture meet ADL's (Advanced Distributed Learning) SCORM standard, with the one-to-many distribution system architecture that allows flexible expansion mechanism, the shortcomings of traditional one-to-one SCORM system architecture is effectively improved, allowing a flexible expansion mechanism for back-end content servers.

Keywords: Context-aware, Data Grid, Ganglia, LCMS, SCORM.

1 Introduction

As information and internet technology advances, the popularization of Mobile Devices has made communication between people more multi and real time, also making the relationship between man and electronic devices more intimate. In the recent years, multi-media learning (e-Learning), with computers as the medium, has become an indispensable supporting method of learning. From the early periods of personal stand-alone learning, to learning using wired or wireless communication methods. The studying contents have evolved from simple text, figure, animation, to

R.-S. Chang, T.-h. Kim, and S.-L. Peng (Eds.): SUComS 2011, CCIS 223, pp. 37–46, 2011.
© Springer-Verlag Berlin Heidelberg 2011

three-dimensional virtual reality. The changes of digital learning methods and its' contents have once again proved the diversity and flexibility of digital technology when applied to learning methods.

With the widespread of wireless LAN and basic construction of mobile network, learners are now able to use their mobile devices as convenient devices of learning, without the restrictions of time and space. This kind of learning is called Mobile Learning. Mobile learning utilizes mobile devices that are highly mobile and convenient as supporting tools for learning, enabling learners to acquire the wanted information anytime, anywhere, therefore accomplishing their learning goals. With the increasing diversity of mobile learning devices (including Tablet PC, Pocket PC, PDA or mobile phones), the concept of ubiquitous computing is proposed. The technology of ubiquitous computing implements wireless network technology, enable people to acquire information without limits. Meanwhile, the differences comparing to mobile computing, is that it is context aware, which can decide the most effective and appropriate environment for learning according to the user's position, information about the surroundings, and personal studying conditions. Due to the fact that the sizes of mobile devices are getting smaller and smaller while becoming more powerful, the mobile learning method combined with context awareness is rapidly spreading. This kind of learning method that implements ubiquitous computing is called Ubiquitous Learning.

Lehner& Nosekabel thinks that ubiquitous learning is to provide digital information and contents without the limits of time and space, to help the learner acquire information [1]. With ubiquitous computing, the mobile device used for learning doesn't only display learning contents, but also detects the learner's surroundings, and apply it to display related information and interacts more with the learner. Ubiquitous computing integrates new types of computing such as Mobile Computing, Context Awareness, and Pervasive Computing, while hiding the technology and making it meld into our daily lives, so we could acquire all sorts of service and information without even noticing, without the help of traditional desktop computers. Ubiquitous learning has 5 features: (1) learning content (including studying content, useful resources, interaction with other learners etc); (2)The learning interface is no longer mouse and computer screen, but is provided with conversation and interaction in the surroundings; (3)The computer system that supports learning is more intricate, so the learner will not notice it, avoiding conflict with the process of studying; (4)Communication between learners and learning systems are made with mobile devices that has little burden on carrying and controlling; (5)The communication between man and machine will further more advance. In the future, a learner may not notice that he is using a computer device [2]. In order to construct an ubiquitous learning environment, the following 3 elements are required [3]:

(1) Wireless communication devices: With wireless communication technology, we can achieve ubiquitous learning that can avoid the limits of time and space, achieving interactive learning with teachers, peers and the system.
(2) Ubiquitous learning device: A ubiquitous learning device is an important element of ubiquitous learning. The device must have wireless network, small, lightweight and portable. Hand writing input is also a must for interaction.
(3) Learning activity mode: Other than wireless network and a ubiquitous device, the other important element is learning activity mode. With learning activity mode, the learner can complete a series of learning and establish his own learning style.

The reason why this research uses mobile phones as supporting tools is because not only are mobile phones light and convenient to carry. Mobile phones support wireless network abilities such as GPRS and WiFi and is also much more affordable than laptop computers so that almost everyone has one, making it suitable to be promoted to schools and users for ubiquitous learning.

2   Context-Aware Learning

Context means any information about a person, an event, time, location, things and all entities. The interaction of user, program, and environment is composed of the above mentioned elements, and is applied on the basics of context-awareness [4]. The concept of context-awareness was first proposed by Schilit and Theimer in 1994. Due to the rise of Mobile Distributed Computing, users are made able to interact with other mobile devices and computers using mobile devices, and mobile computing is no longer limited to a restricted position or environment, it can be spread to the office, home, air ports, bus stops etc [5]. For example, as a learner enters a classroom, library or meeting room, his surroundings, time, location, activity, and equipment he uses are all variables to the mobile computing device. The device has to be implemented with context-awareness in order to provide adequate service to the learner. Other than this, the mobility of the device makes the information of the current location very important, since with information of the location, the user can check out the devices and services in the area. The department of defense of USA proposed context-awareness in 1970 by utilizing GPS to acquire information about coordinates, traveling speed, time and etc. This accelerated the concept of Context-Aware Computing [6], which context-awareness program adjusts its' services according to the people, computers, the status of accessing equipment in the surroundings and adjust the services in real-time. This kind of application requires the help from sensors or mobile devices. Context-Awareness must fit the following 3 points: (1) Provide information or service to the user (2) Automatically executes the service for the user (3) Adds context information on the initial data, to enable advanced inquiries by the contents of the labels of context information. The types of context information can be sorted into Computing Context, User Context, Physical Context, and Time Context. Computing Context gathers information on network access, bandwidth and hardware; User Context gathers information on the users preference, location, people in the surrounding, the current social environment, or the user's current position or action etc. Physical Context takes care of the environment information such as lighting, sound, traffic, temperature. Time Context gathers information on time such as day, week, month, and season.

2.1   Architecture of Context-Awareness

Most of the early context-aware systems provide specific functions according to information based on the position. However, the development of context aware application is complicated work, leading to recent studies on Context-Aware Frameworks, providing all sorts of context-awareness development platforms [9]. The architecture can be divided into 5 layers, as shown in figure 1. Sensor Layer is composed of many different sensors. It not only captures the actual hardware but also capture all available information from different information sources. The types of sensors can be sorted as entity sensor, virtual sensor, and logic sensor. Raw data retrieval Layer can capture raw data of the sensor. Preprocessing Layer is not equipped in all context-awareness systems, but when the raw data is too rough, it could provide useful data. The preprocessing layer is used to interpret and inference the context data. Storage/Management Layer is to gather data in an organized way, and provide an open interface for the client to use. The client can choose to access the data with or without sync. Application Layer provides programmers a flexible and friendly way to manage and program for the needs of various contexts. The application layer can also provide tools for clients, or them to understand the condition of the sensors.

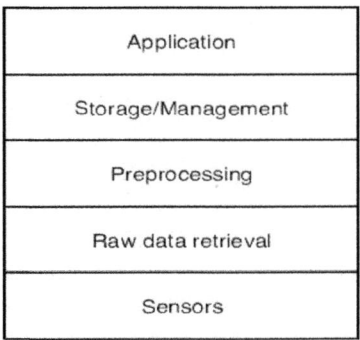

Fig. 1. Context-Aware Framework

3   The Learning Architecture of Ubiquitous Learning with Improved Ganglia Agent

The main objective of data grid computing is to divide huge amounts of calculations, storage or analyzing procedures, into smaller sections, and appoint them on to idle computers on the internet, achieving super-computer class processing speed with existing hardware, meanwhile also sharing data. All this can be done by releasing the processing capability and storage capability when the computer is idle. You could also say that grid computing is integrating scattered processing resources by implementing the correct routine, network bandwidth, and storage ability, to create a powerful virtual computer system. Grid computing can be seen as requesting resources to many computers in the network at the same time, using it to process problems that require a significant amount of time or data. Many organizations around the work have proposed many kinds of grids. They can be assorted into two categories, one is Computational Grid, and the other is Data Grid [10]. Computational grid places its focus on sharing the calculation resources to achieve fast data processing. Data grid focuses on sharing data, storage of data, quicker access to data and the transferring of scattered data.

Of the many organizations researching on grid, the Globus Alliance's Globus ToolKit is the more mature one. Globus was developed by the Argonne National Research Lab near Chicago, and there are 12 universities and research facilities participating in this project. Globus has fulfilled the theories and concepts of planning a grid, and researches on source management, data management, information management and grid security. The outcomes are now widely applied on many large scale grid platforms. This research utilizes RFT (Reliable File Transfer) for data management. The RFT works under the grid environment of GT4.0. It is set up on the GridFTP transfer mechanism, and therefore has the features of GridFTP, combined with GSI's accountable secure transfer, and uses the HTTP protocol and Third Party Transfer via standard SOAP information, to provide data about TCP buffer size, parallel data flow, confirmation of data routine and other parameter setting interface; The Third Party Transfer system can control two remote computers to proceed with data duplication or deletion, used with the data base to achieve monitoring of the process of transfer, as shown in figure 2 [10].

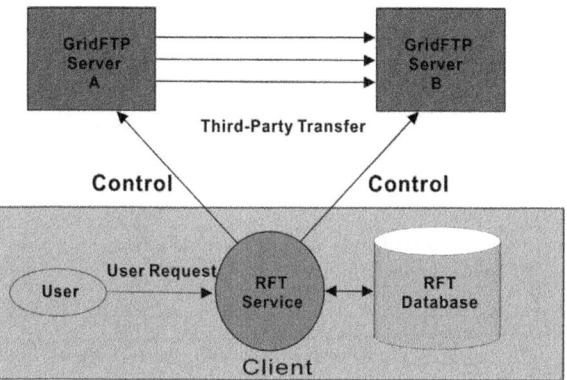

Fig. 2. RFT Supports Third Party Transfer and combines data base storage transfer condition

3.1 Ganglia Agent

Ganglia is an operation system with dispersion type context-awareness function. The information includes CPU, Memory, hard disk usage, I/O load and net traffic etc; This context-awareness software is often used with grid architectures, to monitor high spec cluster systems. Ganglia executes Gmond Daemon at every node, and Gmond will monitor the condition of the system. These daemons execute data exchange and communication with UDP broadcasting, and send all data via a tree map structure for Gmetad to organize all the monitored data. Cluster computers communicate with each other by XML via TCP. As figure 3 indicates, the whole architecture of Ganglia includes 5 cores that are Ganglia Monitoring Daemon (Gmond), Ganglia Meta Daemon (Gmetad), Gmetric, Gstat and Ganglia PHP Web Frontend. Gmond is a multi-threading daemon that monitors system data of nodes, while broadcasts by UDP to gather system data of other nodes, and sends all system status information in XML format to Gmetad; Gmetad will regularly require its' child nodes to provide context monitoring data, and analyzes the XML files collected, then send the organized context data to the client in XML format; Gmetric is a tool customized for clients. The client can input commands to request Gmond to combine the requested monitoring data; Gstat is a command line tool provided by Ganglia to acquire all the node's context data. The context data provided are those such as the number of CPUs of the cluster computer and its CPU load etc; Ganglia PHP Web Frontend provides a graphical monitoring interface. The client can monitor the contexts of all the cluster system's nodes.

This research integrates RFT components with Improved Ganglia Agent (IGA), and proposes a ubiquitous learning system architecture that is context-aware. The IGA provided could analyze the XML files the Gmetad has received, and acquire the network load context information of the LCMS server, to find the LCMS server with the lightest load, providing a convenient mobile learning environment anytime, anywhere, automatically.

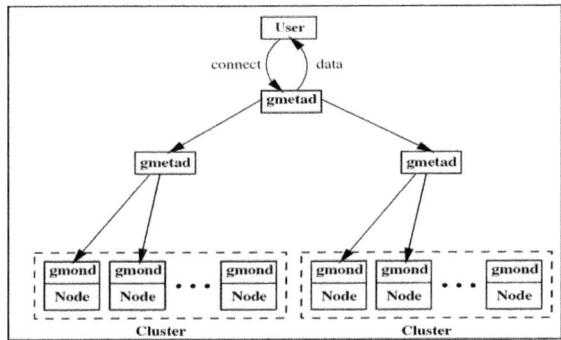

Fig. 3. Ganglia System Architecture Diagram

3.2   Proposed Improved Ganglia Agent

In order for many learners to smoothly access the LCMS contents, this research proposes the Improved Ganglia Agent design that collects and analyzes related back-end server context information. By analyzing context data, IGA will decide the adequate order of LCMS servers providing contents. When the monitored LCMS server is overloaded, the system activates the data transfer function of the RFT component of the grid, and automatically duplicates the content to an idle LCMS server within the grid, meanwhile guiding the learner to the LCMS server to proceed with his learning. The improved Ganglia Agent has Gmetad daemon implemented, and is capable of collecting back-end LCMS servers' context data (such as CPU load, memory space, hard disk capacity, network bandwidth etc). The Gmetad collects the system context data provided by Gmond in all back-end LCMS servers, and automatically organizes the data into XML format. The system is set that every 15 seconds Gmond will automatically transfer LCMS context data to the IGA server, and when the LCMS server's CPU load goes up to 40%, the grid RFT file transfer service will be activated, duplicating learning content to idle servers in the grid, effectively balancing the network load, achieving the flexible expansion mechanism of the LCMS. The following are explanations of executing grid RFT component services:

(1)   When the RFT service in inactivated, the LCMS network load stays below 25Bytes, and its CPU load below 15%.
(2)   With the increase in clients, the LCMS's CPU load increases. When the CPU load goes over 40%, the system will activate RFT file duplication function to copy the learning content on to an idle server in the grid, and the idle LCMS will begin receiving the content.
(3)   After flexibly expanding a LCMS, the LCMS network load will be relieved, and the CPU load will decrease.

4   Actual Implementation and Statistical Analysis

The system architecture proposed by this research mainly includes LMS, Improved Ganglia Agent server with context-awareness, and back-end learning content management system (LCMS) with flexible expandability. LMS is responsible for the management of students' personal information, learning log, and provides lesson catalogues for the student to choose from. LCMS is responsible for the management and storage of back-end learning contents. IGA is responsible for not only the sensory data of back-end LCMS server's network bandwidth, CPU load, hard disk capacity, but also integrates the grid RFT components for it to provide LCMS server with more effective flexible expandability, and by this information offers the clients the IP address of the LCMS servers with lower loads, thus effectively balancing back-end LCMS server's load; the actual implementations are as shown in figure 4.

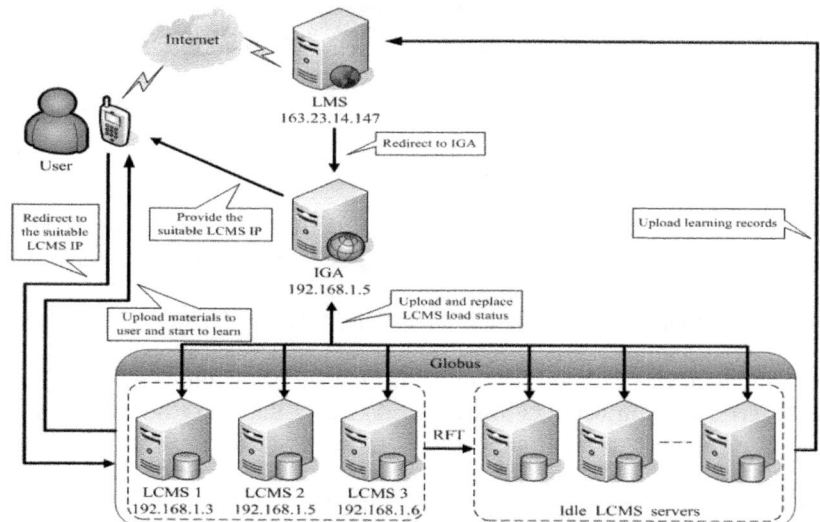

Fig. 4. Implementing IGA's ubiquitous learning system architecture

Related system design execution procedures are as follows:

(1) The client access the LMS learning web page via wireless network such as GPRS and WiFi, enter account name and password to log on.
(2) The client picks the lesson he wants (as shown in figure 5).
(3) After picking a lesson, the web page is automatically directed to Improved Ganglia Agent (as shown in figure 6).
(4) The IGA analyzes all the LCMS context data collected, and automatically redirects to a LCMS server with a lower load (as shown in figure 7).
(5) LCMS transfers the selected lesson contents to the client's mobile device and begins the related lesson studies (as shown in figure 8).

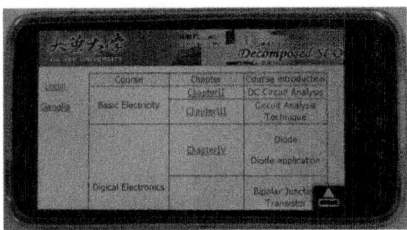   

Fig. 5. Lesson options   **Fig. 6.** Screen of connecting to IGA

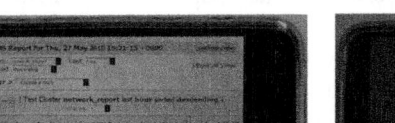   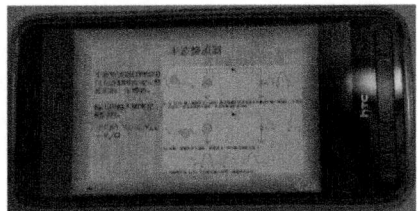

Fig. 7. Computing context data   **Fig. 8.** Learning contents

4.1   Survey Analysis

This research applies Likert scale as the standard of scoring in the survey. The options are: Strongly agree, agree, no comment, disagree, strongly disagree, which is 1 to 5 points for each of the options. 30 learners fill in the survey according to their own learning experience. The results are as shown in Tables 1 and 2. According to the survey, the ubiquitous learning management system scored around 3.43 to 4.2. The item with the lowest average is "I think this system can improve the interest toward the lessons"; the item with the highest average is "I think this system can provide a learning environment anytime anywhere." The survey on the satisfaction on download speed scored around 3.43 to 3.73, the item with the lowest average is "I am satisfied with the download speed of the contents "Diodes""; the highest average is "I am satisfied with the download speed of the contents "DC Circuit Analysis"". With the results of the survey, the item with the lowest average will be a basis of system and contents improvement

Table 1. Ubiquitous learning management system functionality survey

Assessments	Score	Average Score
1. I think the mobile learning management system's controls and explanations are easy to understand.	3.63	
2. I think the system's whole learning control interface is easy to understand and use.	3.73	
3. I think this system will be real help with my studies.	3.66	
4. I think this system will improve the convenience of acquiring lesson contents.	3.9	3.76
5. I think this system can improve the interest toward the lessons.	3.43	
6. I think this system can provide a learning environment anytime anywhere.	4.2	
7. Overall, I'm satisfied with this system.	3.76	

Table 2. Assessments on the download speed of learning contents

Assessments	Score	Average Score
1. I am satisfied with the downloading speed of SCORM learning contents using a mobile devise.	3.5	
2. I am satisfied with the browsing of mobile learning web sites with mobile devices.	3.43	
3. I am satisfied with the download speed of the contents "DC Circuit Analysis".	3.73	3.5
4. I am satisfied with the download speed of the contents "Circuit analysis techniques".	3.43	
5. I am satisfied with the download speed of the contents "Diodes".	3.43	
6. I am satisfied with the download speed of the contents "Diodes-application", "Transistor BJT", and "Embedded Systems".	3.53	

5   Conclusion

Most digital learning systems nowadays combine learning management system and content management system on a single high-end server. This kind of architecture is easier to design and implement, and is suited for a teaching environment for a less amount of learners. If there were to be a huge number of clients logging on the system to learn, the limits of network bandwidth and data access will become an obstacle to learning. This research proposes ubiquitous learning system architecture with context-awareness. With an agent server that has the capability to integrate load balancing, implementing many LCMS to provide learning services could be achieved. After the client logs on the learning management system and chooses a lesson service, the IGA will connect to a LCMS with lower load, and proceed with the lesson. This system utilizes dispersed low spec hardware equipment to build a high spec server system architecture. Not only does it effectively decrease the total cost of the system, but by the RFT component's file duplication function in the grid, the back-end LCMS server's flexible expandability mechanism could be achieved, thus effectively improving the total performance of the system.

References

1. Lehner, F., Nosekabel, H.: The Role of Mobile Devices in E-learning - First Experience with a E-learning Environment. In: Milrad, M., Hoppe, H.U., Kinshuk (eds.) IEEE International Workshop on Wireless and Mobile Technologies in Education, Los Alamitos, USA, pp. 103–106 (2002)
2. Sakamura, K., Koshizuka, N.: Ubiquitous Computing Technologies for Ubiquitous Learning. In: IEEE International Workshop on Wireless and Mobile Technologies in Education (2005)
3. Zhang, G., Jin, Q., et al.: A Framework of Social Interaction Support for Ubiquitous Learning. In: International Conference on Advanced Information Networking and Application (2005)
4. Ni, L.M., Liu, Y.H., Lau, Y.C., Patil, A.P.: LANDMARC: Indoor Location Sensing Using Active RFID. Wireless Networks 10(6), 701–710 (2004)
5. Schilit, B., Theimer, M.: Disseminating Active Map Information to Mobile Hosts. IEEE Network 8(5), 22–32 (1994)
6. Schilit, B., Adams, N., Want, R.: Context-Aware Computing Applications. In: IEEE Workshop on Mobile Computing Systems and Applications, Santa Cruz, CA, USA (1994)
7. Chen, G., Kotz, D.: A Survey of Context-aware Mobile Computing Research. Dartmouth Computer Science Technical Report TR2000-381 (2000)
8. Schiller, J., Voisard, A.: Location-based Services. Morgan Kaufmann, San Francisco (2004)
9. Baldauf, M., et al.: A Survey on Context-Aware Systems. International Journal of Ad-Hoc and Ubiquitous Computing 2(4) (2007)
10. Kao, F.C., Tsai, Y.S., Chiou, A.S., Wang, S.R., Liu, C.W.: The Design of Intelligent Sensor Network Based on Grid Structure. In: IEEE Asia-Pacific Services Computing Conference, pp. 623–630 (2008)

Carousel Scheduling of Advertisement Contents on Digital Multimedia Broadcasting*

Junghoon Lee, Hye-Jin Kim, Jin-hee Ko, and Youngshin Hong

Dept. of Computer Science and Statistics, Jeju National University
690-756, Jeju Do, Republic of Korea
{jhlee,hjkim82,litteltoamato7942,yshong}@jejunu.ac.kr

Abstract. This paper functionally designs a broadcast scheduler for the advertisement system built on top of a digital multimedia broadcasting system for fast moving vehicles. The design goals lie in improving the advertisement efficiency by giving a higher frequency to the advertisement item more users are likely to be interested in. To overcome the lack of upstream communication paths and limited bandwidth, path prediction and past history analysis techniques are exploited in estimating the current vehicle distribution. The inference engine periodically adjusts the broadcast frequency of each item so as to meet the bandwidth constraint, taking into account the estimated vehicle distribution along with the position associated with each advertisement. According to the assigned frequency, the periodic generator fills the carousel queue, from which broadcast item is taken one by one.

Keywords: digital multimedia broadcasting, advertisement content, carousel scheduling, path prediction, channel efficiency.

1 Introduction

DMB (Digital Multimedia Broadcasting) is a stable digital radio transmission technology for sending multimedia to mobile devices, especially those on fast moving vehicles [1]. Hence, DMB technologies are considered to be one of the most cost-efficient and easy-to-install wireless carriers for electric vehicles. In addition to the legacy digital contents such as TV and music, the advertisement can provide receivers or drivers with useful information having location-dependent and time-dependent features. In this regard, we have built a DMB advertisement framework consisting of an advertiser interface, a content manager, and local broadcasting facilities [2]. This framework focuses on the automatic integration of advertisers and the advertisement system, guaranteeing fast response to the content update from advertisers.

It is predicted that many ubiquitous computing applications will be supported by advertising, following the trend of ad-supported Internet sites as pointed

---

* This research was supported by KIAT under the Regional Industry and Technology Development Project and also by the MKE through the project of Region technical renovation, Republic of Korea.

R.-S. Chang, T.-h. Kim, and S.-L. Peng (Eds.): SUComS 2011, CCIS 223, pp. 47–53, 2011.
© Springer-Verlag Berlin Heidelberg 2011

in [3]. We can find an interesting example that the nearby friend finder application can be supported by an advertisement which suggests meeting places. DMB is a special case of ubiquitous networks and also able to carry advertisement. However, compared with the general mobile advertisement, it lacks an upstream communication path, so the server has no way to know the exact distribution of vehicles. In addition, as real-time images dominate the channel, the advertisement broadcast suffers from bandwidth shortage. Accordingly, it is necessary to make use of the channel bandwidth as efficiently as possible to overcome those difficulties.

The efficiency can be achieved by broadcasting more often those advertisements in which more drivers are likely to be interested. For constantly moving vehicles, the driver's interest in the advertisement is inevitably dependent on his or her current location. However, the unawareness of current vehicle distribution makes us rely on the statistics on the past history data. In some cases, a vehicle can restrictively report its location via another channel. For example, when an electric vehicle is being charged, it can temporarily connect to the charging facility via the standard V2G interface [4]. In addition, using the WiFi channel, which is very common in mobile devices, vehicles can report their locations just when they enter the WiFi coverage area. However, considering the long interval between the consecutive reports, real-time location tracking is impossible. In this case, the path prediction and location estimation is a reasonable policy to get the current distribution. According to this estimation, the broadcaster can give precedence to the advertisement contents close to more vehicles.

This paper is to functionally design a carousel scheduler which adjusts the broadcast period of each advertisement item according to the estimation of current vehicle distribution. To this end, we are to discuss useful path prediction strategies and exploit the history data analysis result for the case any estimation is not available at all. Specifically, the inference engine decides whether the period allocation can meet the bandwidth constraints considering the available DMB capacity, while the broadcaster takes the item one by one from the queue and transmits to the vehicles.

2   Related Work

Broadcast scheduling has been researched for a long time on the various system environments. First, [5] addresses a broadcast system that distributes a series of data updates to a large number of passive clients. The updates are sent over a broadcast channel in the form of discrete packets while the clients access the broadcast channel periodically to obtain the most recent update of interest such as traffic information and market updates. The design goal of this scheduling scheme is to minimize the waiting time, that is, the length of time duration a client needs to wait until it obtains the most recent update. This work assumes that each client has a different access pattern depending on the channel condition, computing power, and storage capabilities. It achieves those goals for all patterns universally.

Next, [6] handles the problem of scheduling in two separate channels, each of which has a different broadcast schedule. The multi-channel situation can be found when there are different types of receivers, some with better receiving capabilities than others. This work fixes the first channel with a schedule that is optimal for an average performance, and focuses on how to schedule the second channel, which is available only to some of the clients due to geography, power, or financial constraints. They propose the second channel be constrained to have equal number of packets for each item. Finally, their analysis discovers that schedules asymmetric in bandwidth and time domain are better than any symmetric schedules in terms of expected packet delivery time.

As a theoretical study on broadcast, [7] handles several scheduling problems. This work assumes that there are n pages of information, and clients request pages at different times. Multiple clients can have their requests satisfied by a single broadcast of the requested page. First problem is to minimize the maximum response time over all requests. Second problem is to maximize the number of requests that meet their deadlines when every request has a release time and a deadline. The authors reveal that both these problems are NP-complete, and use the same unified approach to give a simple NP-completeness proof for minimizing the sum of response times. Furthermore, this work gives a proof that FIFO is a 2-competitive online algorithm for minimizing the maximum response time and that there is no better deterministic online algorithm. After all, the main contribution of this work is a unified approach to prove NP-completeness in several different objective functions for broadcast scheduling.

3   System Design

3.1   System Architecture

For the DMB-based advertisement, it is necessary to connect advertisers, content creators, communication facilities, and clients. Figure 1 shows the framework we have built in the last project year. This architecture consists of an advertiser interface, an advertisement processing system, and a local broadcasting center. After the content manager endorses the advertisement content submitted by an advertiser via the Internet, it will be registered in the content server. This step is necessary to prevent illegal content from being displayed to the public clients. The leased optical line carries the contents from the server system to the local DMB facilities. Then, the scheduler encodes and multiplexes a group of items to a TPEG stream and corresponding DMB signals. The broadcast equipment transmits the signal through the DMB carrier [8].

According to our implementation, the advertisement item the advertiser creates or modifies will be present on the receiver display within 10 seconds. For advertisement broadcast, 8 *kbps* is allocated in our system. Actually, it's not sufficient for image transmission so large size contents are desirably embedded in DMB receivers. Then, the advertisement is broadcasted in text. This framework is very useful for instant coupons, hot deals, seat availability, and current gasoline price, in addition to the basic information on the contact point, menu, and location, for shops, restaurants, and the like.

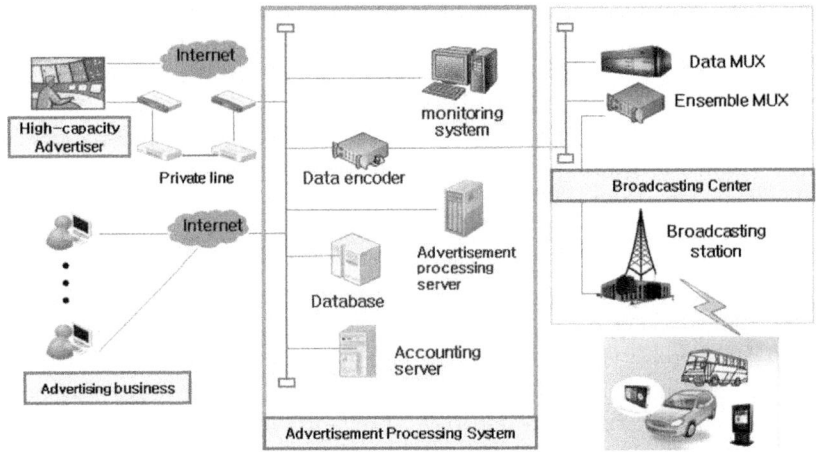

Fig. 1. Advertisement framework architecture

3.2 Availability of Vehicle Location Information

Even if restricted, when the location of each vehicle is given, we can estimate the location of vehicles using the prediction schemes for vehicle movement. First, according to J. Krumm's work, segmentation finds a total of 4300 discrete trips from their movement history data to compute statistics about the trips. This step finds out that the average temporal length of each trip is 14.4 minutes, while the average number of trips per day is 3.3 [9]. The assessment on driving behavior and destination prediction is conducted on the grid placed over the Seattle area, with each square cell equal to 1 km^2 [10]. The destination prediction is based on the assumption that drivers chose the efficient routes. They quantify efficiency using the driving time between points on the driver's path and candidate destinations. Between each pair of cells, the driving time is estimated. Then, using the spots sporadically reported to the center, particularly the combination of the last two points, the prediction module calculates the probability that a grid will be the destination of the vehicle.

In addition, [11] proposes a trajectory clustering scheme for objects moving on road networks to the end of efficient path prediction. From the viewpoint that a trajectory can be defined as a sequence of road segments a moving object has passed by, a similarity measurement scheme is designed based on the length of common road segments. Then, this work describes a clustering algorithm according to the similarity measurement criteria, modifying FastMap and hierarchical clustering schemes to implement the idea. Trajectory clustering identifies initial clusters of trajectories based on the similarity among trajectories, while the final clusters are built by iteratively changing the centroid of each trajectory cluster. This statistics can predict the future location of a vehicle by comparing the partial trajectory which the vehicle has taken from the start to the current position with the existing ones [12].

As the prediction is not always available, past movement history is important. Our previous work has conducted the analysis on the location history data for tens of vehicles in a real-time taxi tracking system [13]. From the 1.3 M location records accumulated for the 1.5 test month, we first select the locations and time instants of passenger pick-up and drop-off by sequentially tracing the change of the status field which indicates whether a passenger is one or not. According to the pick-up point, each session is classified to the respective area group. From the pick-up point, distances between the two points from the two consecutive records are added up to the last record to calculate the trip length. The travel pattern specific to each pick-up point allows us to estimate the vehicle distribution over the city area. For example, almost every passenger travels less than 10 km. The travel from the airport area takes relatively long route, compared with other areas, because the travel mainly needs to cross the multiple areas.

3.3   Carousel Scheduler

DMB is a kind of data broadcast system that distributes a series of dynamic data updates from a single information source to a large number of mobile clients. It is a push-based approach, where the server proactively transmits the data over the broadcast channel. As shown in Figure 1, the DMB facility gets advertisement items from the content manager and builds the broadcast schedule. At least, the contents are equally transmitted one by one, while the item is replaced independently. The modified item must wait by up to one cycle. On the contrary, with broadcast scheduling, the server divides a broadcast cycle into groups, each of which is broadcasted with a different frequency in a broadcast cycle. The broadcast frequencies of groups are in proportion to the probability of access in order to gain the optimal access time of the system.

For weighted broadcast scheduling, a mobile advertisement faces critical problems on how to target potential customers, how to evaluate the effectiveness of a specific advertisement, and how to ensure privacy [3]. The first step is to segment the population into different groups and find a better target for the advertisement item. Different segments will be exposed to different types of media and advertisement contents. In some scenario, street signs have sensors that detect which radio stations passing cars have tuned in to find the demographics group the driver belongs to. In DMB environment, the location information is most important. The advertisement for the location having many vehicles is more likely to change as the vehicles possibly make a new reservation. So this content must have a short period.

The scheduler adjusts the broadcast frequency periodically, considering the above-mentioned factors. Advertisement items, for example, restaurants, souvenir shops, charging stations, and the like, are necessarily bound to a location. The relative affinity between each pair of advertisements and vehicles is calculated by the network distance using the A* algorithm on the given road network represented by a cost matrix. For advertisement items currently included in the broadcast set, $A=\{A_1, A_2, ..., A_n\}$, the broadcast frequency is allocated

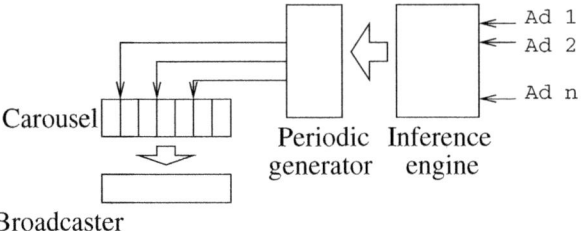

Fig. 2. Advertisement service scenario

according to the affinity to vehicles. Then, the utilization checker tests the following constraint every time a importance of an item changes and thus its period is to be shortened. Namely,

$$\sum \frac{L_i}{P_i} + O_v \leq 1.0, \tag{1}$$

where L_i is the time length for A_i to be broadcasted over the channel, P_i is the period assigned to A_i, and O_v is the overhead ratio for the unit time including frame overhead, mandatory idle time between the adjacent frame, and so on. Here, P_i can have a value in the set of permissible fixed periods, namely, $\{T_1, T_2, ..., T_v\}$, where $T_i \geq T_j$ for $i \leq j$.

Without any estimation, all $A_i's$ commonly have T_1. It is analogous to the simple carousel in which each advertisement is broadcasted equally. When the vehicle density for A_i increases by the predefined bound, its period will decrease by one level. If the current period allocation does not meet Ineq (1), the periods, if not T_1, will go down by one level for all A_i. When an item moves to the broadcaster, the carousel queue removes the entry. If the queue length reach the lower limit, the periodic generator refills the carousel queue.

4   Concluding Remarks

This paper has functionally designed a broadcast scheduler for the advertisement system built on top of the DMB technology, which is one of the most cost-efficient wireless carriers capable of delivering multimedia to fast moving vehicles. This design is aiming at improving the advertisement efficiency by giving a higher frequency to the advertisement item in which more users are likely to be interested. Here, we assume that the degree of interest for an advertisement is dependent on the network distance to each vehicle. To overcome the lack of upstream communication paths and limited bandwidth, path prediction and past history analysis techniques are addressed to estimate the current vehicle distribution. The inference engine periodically allocates and adjusts the broadcast frequency for each item, taking account into the estimated distribution along with the position associated with each advertisement. It also checks the bandwidth constraint, and if fails, the adjustment is repeatedly executed. According to the assigned frequency, the periodic generator fills the carousel queue, from which broadcast item is taken one by one. Finally, the transmitter broadcasts the DMB TPEG frame.

As future work, we are first planning to evaluate the performance of our design on the already-built advertisement framework, mainly in terms of hit ratio from the driver-side access, accuracy of content items on the broadcast, and the like. Next, more accurate model will be developed to quantify the interest to the advertisement item from drivers.

References

1. Manson, G., Berrani, S.: Automatic TV Broadcast Structuring. International Journal of Digital Multimedia Broadcasting (2010)
2. Lee, J., Kim, H., Shin, I., Cho, J., Lee, S., Kwak, H.: Design of an Advertisement Scenario for Electric Vehicles Using Digital Multimedia Broadcasting. In: Kim, T.-h., Stoica, A., Chang, R.-S. (eds.) SUComS 2010. CCIS, vol. 78, pp. 288–291. Springer, Heidelberg (2010)
3. Krumm, J.: Ubiquitous Advertising: The Killer Application for the 21st Century. IEEE Pervasive Computing Magazine 10(1) (2011)
4. Guille, C., Gross, G.: A Conceptual Framework for the Vehicle-to-grid (V2G) Implementation. Energy Policy 37, 4379–4390 (2009)
5. Langberg, M., Sprintson, A., Bruck, J.: Optimal Universal Scheduler for Discrete Broadcast. IEEE Transactions on Information Theory 54(9), 4365–4372 (2008)
6. Foltz, K., Xu, L., Bruck, J.: Scheduling for Efficient Data Broadcast over Two Channels. In: Proc. of International Symposium on Information Theory, pp. 113–116 (2004)
7. Chang, J., Erlebach, T., Gailis, R., Khuller, S.: Broadcast Scheduling: Algorithms and Complexity. In: ACM-SIAM Symposium on Discrete Algorithms (2008)
8. ISO/TS 18234-2, Traffic and Travel Information (TTI), TTI via Transport Protocol Expert Group (TPEG) data-streams, Part 2: Syntax, Semantics and Framing Structure (SSF) (2004)
9. Froehilch, J., Krumm, J.: Route Prediction from Trip Observations. In: Society of Automotive Engineers (SAE) World Congress (2008)
10. Krumm, J., Horvitz, E.: Predestination: Inferring destinations from partial trajectories. In: Dourish, P., Friday, A. (eds.) UbiComp 2006. LNCS, vol. 4206, pp. 243–260. Springer, Heidelberg (2006)
11. Won, J., Kim, S., Baek, J., Lee, J.: Trajectory Clustering in Road Network Environment. In: IEEE Symposium on Computational Intelligence and Data Mining, pp. 299–305 (2009)
12. Kim, S., Won, J., Kim, J., Shin, M., Lee, J., Kim, H.: Path Prediction of Moving Objects on Road Networks through Analyzing Past Trajectories. In: Apolloni, B., Howlett, R.J., Jain, L. (eds.) KES 2007, Part II. LNCS (LNAI), vol. 4693, pp. 379–389. Springer, Heidelberg (2007)
13. Lee, J.: Traveling Pattern Analysis for the Design of Location-Dependent Contents based on the Taxi Telematics System. In: International Conference on Multimedia, Information Technology and its Applications, pp. 148–151 (2008)

Achieving k-Anonymity for Associative Classification in Incremental-Data Scenarios

Bowonsak Seisungsittisunti and Juggapong Natwichai

Computer Engineering Department, Faculty of Engineering
Chiang Mai University, Chiang Mai, Thailand
bowonsak.s@gmail.com, juggapong@eng.cmu.ac.th

Abstract. When a data mining model is to be developed, one of the most important issues is preserving the privacy of the input data. In this paper, we address the problem of data transformation to preserve the privacy with regard to a data mining technique, associative classification, in an incremental-data scenario. We propose an incremental polynomial-time algorithm to transform the data to meet a privacy standard, i.e. k-Anonymity. While the transformation can still preserve the quality to build the associative classification model. The computational complexity of the proposed incremental algorithm ranges from $O(n \ log \ n)$ to $O(\triangle n)$ depending on the characteristic of increment data. The experiments have been conducted to evaluate the proposed work comparing with a non-incremental algorithm. From the experiment result, the proposed incremental algorithm is more efficient in every problem setting.

1 Introduction

Data sharing between business collaborators becomes a common practice currently. When collaborators share data to the others, the privacy issue must be addressed effectively. Typically all identifiers in the data such as ID or name must be removed. Unfortunately, there could be another dataset which can "overlap" to the shared data. The overlap can be established by the common attributes between the two datasets. If another dataset has the identifiers, then the overlap will revealed the identifiers again. Thus, the data must be transformed before the sharing. Once a dataset is transformed, the data quality issue in the transformation processes must also be addressed, i.e. the transformed datasets should have enough quality to be used by the designated data processing which is decided at the first place.

Since the transformation problem with optimal data quality has been proven as an NP-hard in [5]. There are a few heuristic polynomial-time algorithms have been proposed [1,2,7]. One of the prominent algorithms is Minimum Classification Correction Rate Transformation (MCCRT) algorithm proposed in [2]. The algorithm transforms the given datasets based on the k-Anonymity model in which the data mining task to be applied to the given dataset is associative classification [3,4]. The algorithm is guided by the Classification Correction Rates (CCRs) of the attributes in the given dataset. The experiment results have

R.-S. Chang, T.-h. Kim, and S.-L. Peng (Eds.): SUComS 2011, CCIS 223, pp. 54–63, 2011.
© Springer-Verlag Berlin Heidelberg 2011

shown in [2] that the algorithm can produce the transformed datasets with high data quality comparing to the exhaustive results. Also, such data quality can be achieved by only $O(n \log n)$ complexity.

In this paper, we present an improvement of the MCCRT algorithm for the data incremental scenarios. We start with studying of the characteristic of the MCCRT. Based on the studies, we propose a few observations which lead to the techniques to reduce the computational complexity for the problem setting in which the outputs remain the same. Subsequently, an incremental algorithm based on the techniques is proposed for the problem. Such incremental algorithm can transform datasets both effectively and efficiently, i.e. the transformed datasets can be used to build associative classifiers which are almost the same as the one built from the original dataset in polynomial-time complexity. Although the incremental algorithm was first proposed in [6], in this paper, the thorough experiment results are presented to see its performance in the real-life scenarios.

The organization of this paper is as follows. Basic definitions and the problem statement are presented in the next section. Section 3 explains the MCCRT algorithm and its observed characteristics in the data-incremental scenarios. Subsequently, we propose an algorithm based on the observations in Section 4. The experiment results of our work are presented in Section 5. Finally, we present the conclusion and future work in Section 6.

2 Basic Definition

In this section, we present the basic definition for defining the problem statement in the next section.

Definition 1 (Dataset). *Let a dataset $D = \{d^1, d^2, \ldots, d^n\}$ be a collection of tuples defined on a schema $\boldsymbol{A}$. Let C be a set of class labels, such that $C = \{c_1, c_2, \ldots, c_o\}$. The class label of a tuple d^i is denoted as $d^i.Class$.*

Definition 2 (Associative Classification). *A literal p is a pair, consisting of an attribute A_j, and a value v in domain of the attribute $dom(A_j)$. A tuple d^i will **satisfy** a literal $p(A_j, v)$ iff $d^i_j = v$.*

Given a dataset D, and a set of class labels C, let R be a set of classification rules, such that $R = \{r_1, r_2, \ldots, r_q\}$.

For all $l \in L$, a rule $r_l : \bigwedge p \to c_m$, where p is a literal, and c_m is a class label. The left hand side (LHS) of a rule r_l is the conjunction of the literals, denoted as $r_l.LHS$. The right hand side (RHS) of the a r_l is a class label, denoted as $r_l.RHS$.

*A tuple d^i **satisfies** a classification rule r_l iff it satisfies all literals in $r_l.LHS$, and has a class label c_m as $r_l.RHS$. The **support** of a rule r_l, denoted as $Sup(r_l)$, is the ratio between the number of the supporting tuples of r_l and the total number of tuples. The **confidence** of a rule r_l, denoted as $Conf(r_l)$, is the ratio between $Sup(r_l)$ and the total number of tuples which satisfy all literals in LHS of r_l.*

Definition 3 (Quasi-Identifier). *A quasi-identifier, or the linkable attributes, of the dataset D, written Q_D, is the minimal subset of the attributes* **A** *that can re-identify the tuples in D by using external data.*

Definition 4 (k-Anonymity). *A dataset D with a schema* **A** *and a quasi-identifier Q_D satisfies k-anonymity iff each tuple $d^i \in D$ there exist $k - 1$ other tuples $d^{i^1}, d^{i^2}, \ldots, d^{i^{k-1}} \in D$ such that $d^i_j = d^{i^1}_j = d^{i^2}_j = \ldots = d^{i^{k-1}}_j, \forall A_j \in$* **A**.

Definition 5 (Generalization). *Let a domain $dom^l(A_j) = \{v_{jl1}, v_{jl2}, \ldots v_{jln}\}$ be a lth-level generalization of an attribute A_j where $\bigcup_{t=1}^{n} v_{jlt} = dom^l(A_j)$ and $v_{jli} \cap v_{jlk} = \emptyset$, where $dom^0(A_j)$ is the original domain of the attribute A_j, or the no-generalized domain. For each attribute A_j, the height of its domain hierarchy is denoted as h_j. For a value v in $dom^l(A_j)$, its lth-level generalized value in a generalized domain $dom^l(A_j)$ is denoted as $\phi_{dom^l(A_j)}(v)$.*

Let $\prec_G$ be a partial order on domains, $dom^l(A_j) \prec_G dom^{l'}(A_j)$ iff $dom^{l'}(A_j)$ is a generalization of $dom^l(A_j)$.

Definition 6 (k-Anonymization). k-*Anonymization is transformation of D into D' where D' is a generalization of D which satisfies the k-Anonymity property.*

3   Observations on Data-Incremental Scenarios

3.1   Problem Statement

First, the MCCRT algorithm is discussed. The MCCRT algorithm begins with sorting all quasi-identifier attributes using their Classification Correction Rates (CCRs) increasingly (see [2] for more details). The result of the sorting and the current level of generalization are recorded in a generalization level defined as follows.

Definition 7 (Generalization Level). *Given a $dom(Q_D)$, a set of generalization domains for Q_D, let a generalization level of a Q_D, denoted as GL, be a sequence in which its elements are the pairs (A_j, l_j), where l_k is the level which the given dataset is generalized into for such A_j, $0 \le l_j \le h_j$.*

After the sorting, the algorithm selects an attribute to be generalized from the sorted sequence of the attributes. The generalization is performed in depth-first-search manner, i.e. it selects an attribute, subsequently, generalize the dataset until the dataset satisfies k-Anonymity. If the dataset has not been satisfied the condition, but the selected attribute has reached the height of its hierarchy, the algorithm will selects the next attribute from the sequence. The intuition behind this is to avoid excessive generalization of some important attributes, i.e. the attribute with higher CCR could generate the rules since its corresponding one-literal rules are satisfying the *minsup* and *minconf* thresholds. Therefore, such attributes will be more important for associative classification model building. If the algorithm has more than one choice of attributes to be generalized, it will generalize the attribute with less CCR.

The worst-case computational complexity of the MCCRT algorithm is $FULL \times (n + n\ log(n))$ where n is the number of the tuples in the dataset and $FULL$ is the number of the levels from the starting point of the generalization, i.e. the level 0 of the first attribute in the generalization level, to the generalization point that satisfies the k condition which be the last level of the last attribute in the GL, so called full generalization. The $n + n\ log(n)$ cost comes from the k-Anonymity verification which the dataset is first sorted by the attribute values in the Q_D. Subsequently, the dataset is scanned once for the anonymity verification. Therefore, re-applying the algorithm in the incremental data scenario will incur the complexity at $FULL \times (n + \triangle n + (n + \triangle n)\ log(n + \triangle n))$ where $\triangle n$ is the number of the tuples in the additional data $\triangle D$.

Then, our problem of incremental privacy preservation for associative classification as follows.

Problem 1. Given a generalized dataset D' with a set of class labels C, a k value, its generalization level GL which satisfied the k value, the $CCRs$ of the Q_D attributes, and an incremental dataset $\triangle D$, the problem is to generalize the appended dataset $(D + \triangle D)$ into $(D + \triangle D)'$ with regards to the MCCRT algorithm based on the GL and D' instead of generalization on $(D + \triangle D)$ from scratch.

3.2   Observations

Generally, when additional data, $\triangle D$, are added to an existing dataset D, we can re-apply the MCCRT to obtain a new generalization level, GL' which may be different from the original GL obtained before the new data are added. Meanwhile, in the incremental processing, the generalization can transform only the $\triangle D$ with the original GL, subsequently, the transformed $\triangle D'$ will be added to D'. Finally, the GL will be adjusted both in term of the generalized attribute order and the levels to obtain $(D + \triangle D)'$ which is exactly the same as the result from MCCRT re-applying approach. In order to allow this computing approach, in this section, we present our observations on the impact of the data increment which can be grouped into two main cases.

Case 1: No order-change in GL is required. Suppose there is no change required to adjust the transformation in term of the generalized attribute order in a given GL, we can categorized the characteristic of the $\triangle D'$ into two cases based on its generalized data. The first case is when all the generalized tuples in $\triangle D'$ have the same values as some tuples in D'. The latter case is when there is a new generalized tuples comparing with the existing generalized dataset D'.

Same-value Case: If all tuples in $\triangle D'$ have the same generalized values with some tuples in D', therefore, the $(D + \triangle D)'$ will already satisfy the k-Anonymity condition. Since adding $\triangle D'$, in this case, will only increase the number of the tuples in some satisfied k-Anonymity partitions of the D'. However, such GL can over-generalize the $D + \triangle D$, which the generalization decreasing can be applied.

New-value Case: When the additional generalized data, $\triangle D'$, are different from the existing data, D'. Given the pre-condition that GL is not changed, the only approach to generalize $(D + \triangle D)'$ in order to satisfy k-Anonymity with regards to MCCRT is to increase the generalization level along the GL sequence until the condition is met. However, $\triangle D'$ may already satisfy the k-Anonymity itself. In this case, we can simply add it to the existing data, and the existing GL can be applied without any further change.

Case 2: GL order change is required. In general, $\triangle D$ can change the CCRs of the attributes in Q_D. This will change the generalization level, GL, according to the MCCRT algorithm. We categorize such changes into 5 cases. In order to help the illustration in this section, we further denote the last attribute-level pair in a GL which is generalized as the current generalization point (which is already satisfied the k-Anonymity), **CGP**. For example, if a GL is $< (A_1, 2), (A_2, 3), (A_3, 2), (A_4, 0), (A_5, 0) >$, the **CGP** is $(A_3, 2)$.

Order change before CGP: If there is any change in the order before a **CGP**, the generalization of the attributes before the **CGP** will not be affected since such attributes have already been fully generalized. It means that the generalization process can re-begin from such **CGP**, i.e. from that point the generalization level can either be increased or decreased according to the cases in Section 3.2 Case 1 and Case 2.

Order change after CGP: Since attribute after a **CGP** has not been generalized, the new generalization order will not affect the previously-generalized data. Subsequently, we can re-begin the generalization in the same manner as the previous case.

After we present some observations in Section 3.2 Case 1 and Case 2, we summarize the complexity to deal with such previous cases as follows.

Observation 1. *If there is no order-change in GL or there is an order change before* **CGP** *or there is an order change after* **CGP** *in GL, and all tuples in $\triangle D'$ have the same generalized values with some tuples in D', the computational complexity in order to generalize $(D + \triangle D)'$ to satisfy a k-Anonymity with regards to the MCCRT algorithm incrementally is $START\_TO\_CGP \times (n + \triangle n + (n + \triangle n) \, log(n + \triangle n))$. Where $START\_TO\_CGP$ is the number of the levels from the starting point of the generalization to the* **CGP**, *and n is the number of the tuples in D, $\triangle n$ is the number of the tuples in $\triangle D$.*

Observation 2. *If there is no order-change in a GL or there is an order change before* **CGP** *or there is an order change after the* **CGP** *in the GL, and some tuples in $\triangle D'$ have the new generalized values comparing with all tuples in D', and some of them not satisfy a k-Anonymity, the computational complexity in order to generalize $(D + \triangle D)'$ to satisfy a k-Anonymity with regards to the MCCRT algorithm incrementally is $CGP\_to\_FULL \times (n + \triangle n + (n + \triangle n) \, log(n + \triangle n))$. Where CGP_TO_FULL is the number of the levels from the* **CGP** *to full generalization.*

Observation 3. *If there is no order-change in a GL or there is an order change before the* **CGP** *or there is an order change after the* **CGP** *in the GL, and some tuples in $\triangle D'$ have the new generalized values comparing with all tuples in D', and all of them satisfy a k-Anonymity, the computational complexity in order to generalize $(D + \triangle D)'$ to satisfy a k-Anonymity with regards to the MCCRT algorithm incrementally is $(n + \triangle n) + (n + \triangle n)log(n + \triangle n)$.*

We subsequently continue making the observations for the remaining three cases as follows.

CGP **move backward:** In this case, an assumption is that there is no change in the generalization order. However, the **CGP** attribute has been moved toward the beginning of the sequence. The new generalization level, GL', will not satisfy the k-Anonymity at the **CGP** $(A_j, l_j - 1)$. Therefore, we can use this **CGP** as the new re-beginning point of the generalization. Subsequently, the generalization level will be increased until the k-Anonymity condition is satisfied. The complexity in this case is presented in Observation 4.

Observation 4. *If there is an order change in a GL that is the* **CGP** *has been moved backward, the computational complexity in order to generalize $(D + \triangle D)'$ to satisfy a k-Anonymity with regards to the MCCRT algorithm incrementally is $NEW\_CGP\_TO\_FULL \times (n + \triangle n + (n + \triangle n) \, log(n + \triangle n))$ where $NEW\_CGP\_TO\_FULL$ is the number of the levels from the new* **CGP** *to full generalization.*

CGP **move forward:** The assumption in this case is the same as the previous case, i.e. there is no change in the generalization order. In contrary, the **CGP** has been moved toward the end of the sequence. In this case, the farthest generalization point (consider the beginning of the sequence as the starting point of the generalization) which does not satisfy the k-Anonymity is at $(A_j, 1)$ where A_j is the attribute which replaces the order of the previous **CGP**. At this generalization point, the k-Anonymity has not been satisfied, therefore, the generalization level will be increased until the k-Anonymity condition is satisfied. In Observation 5, the complexity in this case is presented.

Observation 5. *If there is an order change in a GL by moving the* **CGP** *forward, the computational complexity in order to generalize $(D + \triangle D)'$ to satisfy a k-Anonymity with regards to the MCCRT algorithm incrementally is $NEW\_CGP\_TO\_FULL \times (n + \triangle n + (n + \triangle n) \, log(n + \triangle n))$ where $NEW\_CGP\_TO\_FULL$ is the number of the levels from the new* **CGP** *to full generalization.*

Mixed cases: In general, the order changes of a GL can be complicated. However, it can be described as a combination of the four previous cases, or so called "mixed cases". The mixed cases can be coped using the procedures described in their mixtures. We categorize such cases as follows. Firstly, if the combination is between the order-change-before-**CGP** case and the order-change-after-**CGP** case, this means that the position of the **CGP** attribute in the GL does not move in GL', and the position of the first 0-level attribute in the GL is the same in the GL'.c In this case, we can further determine whether the generalized data in the $\triangle D'$ are the same-values or the new-values as discussed in Section 3.2 Case 1. Secondly, if the combination contains a **CGP**-move-forward case, or a **CGP**-move-backward case, or both of them. This means that the position of the **CGP** attribute in the GL, or the position of the first 0-level attribute in the GL, or both of them, must be changed in GL'. We can resolve this case by determining the new starting point of the generalization that satisfies the k condition. Such starting point of the generalization can be either the **CGP** attribute in the GL' or the first 0-level attribute in GL', depends on which attribute is closer to the starting point of the generalization.

4   Incremental Algorithm

Our incremental algorithm is based on the observation in Section 3. The algorithm begins with sorting GL into GL' using the new CCRs from $D + \triangle D$ increasingly. Then, it determines $\triangle D'$ using GL' and $\triangle D$. Subsequently, the $\triangle D'$ is added to the D'. After the appending, the algorithm considers the position of the attribute of **CGP** and the first 0-level attribute in GL, if they are not changed in GL', the data in the $\triangle D'$ are evaluated as presented in Section 3.2 Case 1 and Case 2. If the position of the **CGP** attribute or first 0-level attribute in GL is changed in GL'. The GL', the starting point of the generalization, can be determined by setting the attribute level after **CGP**, and setting the first 0-level attribute in GL' at 0. Such GL' can be used to find $(D + \triangle D)'$. If this $(D + \triangle D)'$ does not satisfy k-anonymity, the GL' can be increased by one level until the condition is met. However, if this $(D + \triangle D)'$ has already satisfied the k-anonymity, we can generalize the dataset as presented in Section 3.2 Case 1 (Reader can see more details in [6]).

5   Experiment

We present the evaluation of the incremental algorithm in this section. The experiments are conducted using two UCI repository datasets, i.e. the crx and the breast datasets. Both the datasets have 9 attributes. The crx dataset consists of 6710 tuples, while the breast dataset consists of 699 tuples. Note here that the crx dataset is quite dense, i.e. its original version has already satisfied 9-Anonymity. Meanwhile, all the tuples in the breast dataset are unique. The efficiency is evaluated in term of the execution time when the three parameters change, i.e. the k-value, the size of the quasi-identifier $|Q|$, and the size of the incremental dataset $|\triangle D|$. In each experiment, the dataset will be divided into two equal parts, the first part is used as the static part of the data, while the latter will be used as the incremental data. For the incremental part of a dataset, it will be divided further into twenty equal parts, unless specified (5% of the incremental part each), for appending to the the dataset. Once, all parts of the data are appended to the dataset, the execution time is subsequently reported.

In each experiment, the proposed algorithm will be compared with the MCCRT algorithm. The resulting numbers reported are five-time average.

5.1   Effects of k Value

In the first experiment, we evaluate the efficiency of the incremental algorithm when the k value is varied. Such value is varied from 2 to 30 to evaluate its effect. The $|Q|$ is fixed at 9 for both datasets.

In Figure 1 a), the experiment result is presented. First, the execution time of the incremental algorithm is much less than the MCCRT algorithm for both datasets. Clearly, re-applying the MCCRT algorithm to the dataset when each portion of data is appended requires much more time than processing the data in the incremental manner. For the crx dataset, the execution time of both algorithms is increased significantly when the k value is less than 10, subsequently, the execution time is stable for any k value. The reason behind the increasing is that the static part of the dataset at the beginning has not satisfied the k-Anonymity, thus, both algorithms require to transform the data until it satisfies the condition. When the k value is being increased, the more time is required to transform the dataset. After the k value is set at 10 or higher, the generalization level requires for such condition will transform the dataset up to the

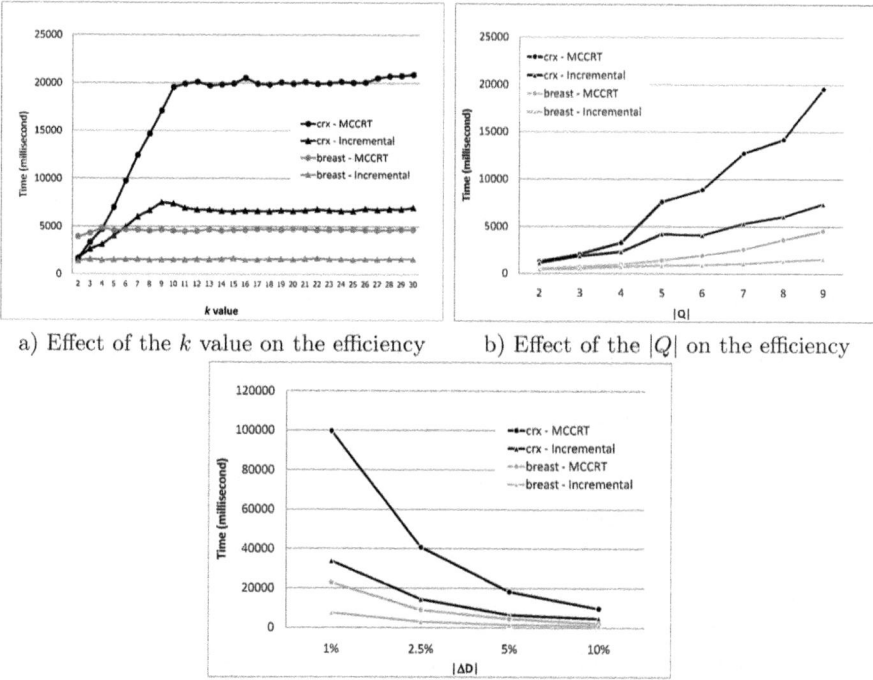

a) Effect of the k value on the efficiency   b) Effect of the $|Q|$ on the efficiency

c) Effect of the $|\triangle D|$ on the efficiency

Fig. 1. Effect of the 3 variables on the efficiency

highest generalization level. For the breast dataset, the execution time of both algorithms is stable for almost all k values because such dataset is very sparse. Even when the k value is set at 2 or 3, the high generalization level is required.

5.2   Effects of $|Q|$

In this experiment, we evaluate the efficiency of incremental algorithm when the size of the quasi-identifier attributes ($|Q|$) is changed. The $|Q|$ will be increased from 2 to 9 to evaluate its effect. We set the k value at 10 for both datasets.

The experiment result is presented in Figure 1 b). It can be seen from the result that when the $|Q|$ is increased, the execution time of both algorithms is also increased. The rationale behind this is that the lower $|Q|$ means the less number of the attributes to be verified whether the k condition is met. When consider the difference between the efficiency of both algorithms, it can be seen that the gap of the execution times is larger when the $|Q|$ is increased. This is because the low $|Q|$ means that the less generalization level to be transformed, thus, at a high value of $|Q|$, the difference between the starting point of the generalization in the incremental algorithm and the MCCRT algorithm becomes larger. Since the larger $|Q|$ is more preferable considering the more data quality can be obtained from the transformed dataset, thus, the proposed incremental algorithm is more desirable in the transformation processes.

5.3   Effects of $|\triangle D|$

In the last experiment, we evaluate the efficiency of incremental algorithm when the size of the incremental dataset ($|\triangle D|$) is varied. The variation is set at the percentage of the whole data to be appended, i.e. 1, 2.5, 5 and 10 %. We set the $|Q|$ at 9 attributes, and the k value at 10 for both datasets.

In Figure 1 c), the experiment result is presented. It can be seen from the result that when the $|\triangle D|$ is increased, the execution time of both algorithms is decreased. The reason is that the size of the whole incremental dataset is fixed, thus, the larger part to be appended to the dataset, the less time the algorithms will use. Also, it can be seen that the incremental algorithm clearly outperforms the MCCRT algorithm in every setting because its incremental feature. The difference between the efficiency of both algorithms becomes less when the size of the incremental dataset is increased. This is because of the number of time that the algorithms are applied is decreased, thus, the difference is decreased as well. Given that the size of the datasets in the real-world applications tends to be very large, the appended data can be considered only a small fraction.

6   Conclusion

In this paper, we address the incremental processing problem of the k-Anonymization under the circumstance that the transformed dataset are used to build associative classification models. The characteristics of a data-quality-proven heuristic transformation algorithm, MCCRT, in the incremental scenarios have been studied theoretically. The computational complexities of all possible cases are discussed. We have found that the complexities to cope with the increment are ranged from the size of the additional data ($|\triangle D|$) to the polynomial-time MCCRT complexity in the worst case, while the same outputs are always obtained. Subsequently, the incremental algorithm is proposed based on the studies. From the experiment results in term of the efficiency, the incremental algorithm can outperform the MCCRT algorithm in all experiment settings. Particularly, when the size of the quasi-identifier is large, which is preferable in the real-world applications, the incremental algorithm is significantly better than the MCCRT algorithm. Also, when the size of the stored dataset is large comparing to the appended data, our proposed algorithm is very efficient. In our future work, we will further investigate the problem where the data are stored in the distributed systems rather than a single repository.

References

1. Fung, B.C.M., Wang, K., Yu, P.S.: Top-down specialization for information and privacy preservation. In: Proceedings of the 21st International Conference on Data Engineering, pp. 205–216. IEEE Computer Society, Los Alamitos (2005)
2. Harnsamut, N., Natwichai, J.: A novel heuristic algorithm for privacy preserving of associative classification. In: Ho, T.-B., Zhou, Z.-H. (eds.) PRICAI 2008. LNCS (LNAI), vol. 5351, pp. 273–283. Springer, Heidelberg (2008)
3. Li, W., Han, J., Pei, J.: Cmar: Accurate and efficient classification based on multiple class-association rules. In: Proceedings of the 2001 IEEE ICDM International Conference on Data Mining, pp. 369–376. IEEE Computer Society, Washington, DC (2001)
4. Liu, B., Hsu, W., Ma, Y.: Integrating classification and association rule mining. In: Proceedings of the Fourth ACM SIGKDD International Conference on Knowledge Discovery and Data Mining, pp. 80–86. AAAI Press, Menlo Park (1998)
5. Meyerson, A., Williams, R.: On the complexity of optimal k-anonymity. In: Proceedings of the Twenty-third ACM SIGACT-SIGMOD-SIGART Symposium on Principles of Database Systems, pp. 223–228. ACM, New York (2004)
6. Seisungsittisunti, B., Natwichai, J.: Incremental privacy preservation for associative classification. In: Proceeding of the ACM First International Workshop on Privacy and Anonymity for Very Large Databases, PAVLAD 2009, pp. 37–44. ACM, New York (2009)
7. Wang, K., Yu, P.S., Chakraborty, S.: Bottom-up generalization: A data mining solution to privacy protection. In: Proceedings of the 4th IEEE International Conference on Data Mining, pp. 249–256. IEEE Computer Society, Los Alamitos (2004)

A Petri Net Based Model for Multipoint Multistream Synchronization in Multimedia Conferencing

Koninika Pal, Prajna Devi Upadhyay, and Animesh Datta

Dept. of Information Technology, National Institute of Technology, Durgapur, India
{koninikapal,kirtu26,animeshrec}@gmail.com

Abstract. Distributed multimedia application over IP network is an evolving paradigm for the researcher in the field of Information and Communication Technology (ICT). There are several applications of this technology —video conferencing, teleteaching and any collaborative application. Maintaining the satisfactory Quality of Service [1] and synchronization is a big challenge to the researchers in this field. In this paper, we extend our previous work [2] by ensur-ing multistream multipoint synchronization as an issue, involving the play out process of two streams (audio and video that were generated at the same time and bear temporal relationship) at different receivers at the same time and maintaining the temporal relationship between them to achieve fairness among the receivers. In this paper, we propose a distributed algorithm for achieving multi-stream multipoint synchronization and we also model the algorithm with Stochastic Petri Nets and verify its correctness.

Keywords: Multimedia, multipoint, petri net, synchronization.

1 Introduction

1.1 Media Synchronization

The real-time distributed multimedia systems are characterized by one or several sources transmitting (unicast or multicast) multimedia streams to one or several receivers, playing one or several of the streams. Continuous media, e.g. video and audio, have well defined relationships between subsequent Media Data Units (MDUs). In temporal synchronization we can distinguish between intra-stream synchronization, inter-stream synchronization and multipoint (or inter-destination) synchronization.

Intra Stream Synchronization. Intra-stream synchronization [3] refers to the temporal relationship between the MDUs of one time-dependent media stream i.e. between the MDUs of the same stream during their play out. Moreover, the play out process should be able to consume the MDUs with the same appropriate rate and sequence.

Inter Stream Synchronization. Inter-stream synchronization[3] refers to the synchronization, during the play out processes of different media streams (time-dependent or not) involved in the application.

R.-S. Chang, T.-h. Kim, and S.-L. Peng (Eds.): SUComS 2011, CCIS 223, pp. 64–73, 2011.
© Springer-Verlag Berlin Heidelberg 2011

Multipoint Synchronization. In multicast communications, another type of synchronization, called group or multipoint synchronization[3,4], involving the synchronization of the play out processes of different streams in different receivers, at the same time, to achieve fairness among the receivers. We can cite the example of teleteaching applications, network quizzes. We should guarantee that the initial play out instant should be the same for all the receivers. Once the play out processes have started simultaneously in each receiver, not only the temporal relationships between MDUs of the same stream should be maintained by the intra stream synchronization for that media stream but also temporal relationship between multiple stream should be maintained by inter-stream synchronization. Nevertheless, due to the difference between end-to-end delays, resynchronization processes will be needed to maintain the receivers synchronized (multipoint synchronization). The maintenance of temporal relationships within a stream or among the multimedia streams usually depends on network delay, network jitter etc.

In this paper, we present a novel approach for multipoint multimedia synchronization in a distributed environment. There must be some application layer mechanism that relies on the QoS guaranteed by the underlying network layer to synchronize multiple receivers. This approach specifically deals with audio-video conferencing applications. The algorithm used to provide multipoint multimedia synchronization is described in section 4. Our approach uses global time provided by clock synchronization protocol NTP and delay calculation provided by RTCP feedback messages.

1.2   Petri Net

Multimedia distribution systems are very complex, so it is required to model them for effective implementation. A common tool used to model concurrent sys-tems is a petri net [5], characterized by concurrency, synchronization, and mutual exclusion, which are typical features of distributed environment.

To satisfy the requirement to model the system more specifically new features are added to basic petri net. It is difficult to capture the synchronization behavior and precedence constraints through any model meant to depict random behavior. A stochastic Petri net [6] is a useful tool for modeling and performance analysis of stochastic systems. Generalized Stochastic Petri Nets (GSPN) is allow to classify the transition of SPN in two way, timed and immediate and also introduced inhibitor input arc [7]. CSPN uses the set of color token instead of normal token in GSPN to obtain more precise specification.

A CSPN is a 7 tuple $(P, T, W^-, W^+, W^h, \Lambda, C)$ where

- $P = \{P_i \mid 1 \le i \le |P| = n\}$; finite set of places.
- $T = \{ T_j \mid 1 \le j \le |T| = n\}$; finite set of Transitions, where $P \cap T = \emptyset$ i.e., the set of places and transitions are disjoint. $T_I \cap T_T = \emptyset$; T_I is a set of immediate transition and T_T is a set of timed transition.
- $W^-: P \times T \rightarrow N$; Input connection function.
- $W^+: P \times T \rightarrow N$; Output connection function.
- $W^h: P \times T \rightarrow N$; Inhibitor arc.
- $\Lambda: \{\lambda_k \mid 1 \le k \le | T_T |\}$; firing rates of timed transitions.
- C: finite set of colors.

In this paper we propose a CSPN to model our algorithm described in section 5, verification of the model in section 6 and lastly cite an example using our model in section 7.

2   Related Works

Data transmission in IP is connectionless. A connectionless data transfer mode is lightweight as no connection establishment is necessary. IP has a powerful mechanism, called IP Multicast, for conducting multipoint-to-multipoint communications. The Multicast Backbone (MBONE) has offered an IP Multicast service on the Internet for low-bandwidth video and audio conferences since 1992 [8].

There are some serious synchronization issues attached with this IP network based audio video conferencing [9], they are inter stream synchronization, intra stream synchronization and group synchronization. Numerous algorithms are developed for achieving intra and inter stream synchronization in different scenarios [10], [11]. An algorithm synchronizes the initial play out time for all receivers, subsequently a solution for group synchronization control with continuous media has been proposed in [12]. [13] proposes a media synchronization algorithm by enhancing virtual time rendering (VTR). Using virtual time expansion and contraction of the target output time[14], the algorithm skips the Media Units. [4] presents the comparison of the most known multimedia group and inter-stream synchronization approaches. A table is presented summarizing the main characteristics of each analyzed algorithm according to those techniques and other critical issues.

There are many papers which model and verify the Distributed Algorithm using Petri Nets [15]. Hierarchical Protocol [16] describe how simple protocol is turned into a Hierarchical protocol and describe CPN Model of sender and receiver behavior. [6] introduces stochastic petri net extension. GSPN is discussed in [7] with performance analysis and an example.

3   Scope of Works

The algorithm for achieving multipoint synchronization in the earlier works synchronize the media streams at the receiver's end by skipping or pausing the play out data arbitrarily without considering where some relevant data is being lost. In our previous work [2], we look for the silent zones and make necessary adjustments only on the silent zone and prevent the possible loss of significant information that may have been loss because of arbitrary skipping of data stream during play out at the receiver's end. The limitation of this work [2] is that it deals with only audio signal and we could analyze the signal in a deterministic way.

Here in this work, we extended the previous work [2] by incorporating the video signal with the audio signal. We analyzed both the signals, stochastically, which is more realistic and propose an algorithm for achieving multi-stream (audio and video) multipoint synchronization, with the minimum data loss to retain the quality of service. Also model the algorithm using CSPN and prove its correctness.

4   Proposed Algorithm

4.1   Delay and Expected Play Out Time Calculation and Initial and Periodic Synchronization

We consider a multicast scenario. Sender chooses the maximum of all delays (within threshold value) received from the receivers to calculate expected play out time is referred in [2]. Multimedia conferencing takes place in a distributed environment so clock synchronization which is done initially and at a regular interval by using NTP service is provided by the network of server located at the Internet referred in [2].

4.2   Multimedia Specification

The following specification represents the relationship that may hold between two frames of different streams. Here MDU is represented as a frame whose size may or may not be same for two different media stream.

A precedes B (A$\rightarrow_P$ B). This relationship holds when frame A finishes its playout before the start of the play out of frame B.

A overlaps B (A$\rightarrow_O$ B). This relationship holds when A and B have the following temporal relationship.

A During B. This relationship holds when frame A and B both start play out at the same time or frame A starts play out after the starting of frame B but finishes before the end of play out of frame B or frame A starts play out after starting of frame B but both finish together.

A Meets B. Frame A starts its play out after the start of B but ends after the end of B.

B Meets A. Frame B starts its play out after the start of A but ends after the end of B.

A succeeds B (A$\rightarrow_S$ B). This relationship holds if frame A starts its play out after the end of play out of frame B.

Table 1 represents all possible temporal relationships between two frames with logical specification. In diagram line represents the time duration of frame denoted by d^{frame} and ts_{frame} represents the starting time of generation of frame.

4.3   Synchronous Play Out Algorithm

For multipoint synchronization we take the audio stream as master stream and synchronize the audio stream at multipoint. The video stream is synchronized with audio stream using the relationship that they hold during the generation time at sender side. For multipoint synchronization all receivers play signal at expected play out time mentioned by sender. If audio reaches earlier then it block until the expected play out time otherwise it starts playing. Now expected play out time for video is calculated according to the presentation time of corresponding audio. Before processing a video frame we find out the temporal relationship of corresponding audio frame using the logical specification defined earlier. In following algorithm we describe how synchronization is done.

Table 1. Formal Specification

Relation	Diagram	Logical Representation
$A \rightarrow_p B$ A precedes B		$ts_a < ts_b$ && $ts_a \geq ts_a + d^a$
$A \rightarrow_o B$ A overlaps B Case I A during B		$ts_a \geq ts_b$ && $ts_a + d^a \leq ts_b + d^b$
Case II A meets B		$ts_a > ts_b$ && $ts_a + d^a > ts_b + d^b$
Case III B meets A		$ts_a < ts_b$ && $ts_a + d^a > ts_b$
$A \rightarrow_s B$ A succeeds B		$ts_a > ts_b$ && $ts_a \geq ts_b + d^b$

```
If (audio frame && video frame in the buffer) then
        If (audio precedes video) then
                process_audio_frame()
        elseif (audio succeeds   video)
                process_only_video_frame()
        else
                process_audio_frame()
                process_video_frame()
        end if
elseif (only audio frame in the buffer)
        process_audio_frame
else
        process_only_video_frame()
end if
```

Table 2. List of Variable

d^a, d^v	Duration of play out for audio frame and video frame respectively
ts_a, ts_v	Timestamp of audio frame and video frame respectively
R_a, R_v	Sequence no. of RTP packet for audio and video signal respectively
R_{ap}	Sequence no. of RTP packet which is most recently sent to play out buffer for audio
R_{ac}	Sequence no. of RTP packet that is currently processed for audio
S_{ap}, R_{vp}	Sequence no. of frame which is most recently sent to play out buffer for audio and video respectively.
S_{ac}, R_{vc}	Sequence no. of frame currently processed for audio and video
d_a, d_v	Delay for audio frame and video frame respectively
t_e	Expected playout time given in RTP audio packet
at_a, at_v	Actual arrival time in the receiving buffer for audio and video
t_p	Playout time of last processed frame for video
t_{pl}	Time at which frame is polled from buffer

Table 3 shows the functions that take the frames and calculate the delay that the frame should wait before presentation. Table 2 shows all the information used in three functions.

Table 3. Functions used to caculate presentation time

Process_audio_frame()	process_video_frame()	process_video_only_frame()

If ($R_{ac} = R_{ap}$) Then
    If ($S_{ac} = S_{ap} + 1$) Then
       $d_a \leftarrow d_a + d^a$
    else
       $d_a \leftarrow d_a + (S_{ac} - S_{ap})*d^a$
    endif
 else
 $d_a \leftarrow t_e - t_{pl} + (S_{ac} - 1)*d^a$
 endif
	$d_v \leftarrow d_a + (ts_v - ts_a) +$
	     $(at_a - t_{pl})$
	 If($d_v < 0$) Then
	    $d^v \leftarrow d^v + d_v$,
	    $d_v \leftarrow 0$,
	    $t_p \leftarrow at_v + d^v$,
	 endif
		If ($R_{vc} = R_{vp} + 1$) Then
		 If ($tp + dv > atv$) Then
		 $dv \leftarrow tp + dv - tpl$
		 else
		 $d^v \leftarrow d^v + (t_p + d^v - t_{pl})$,
		 $d^v \leftarrow 0$
		 endif
		 else
		 $dv \leftarrow t_p + (R_{vp} - R_{vc})* d^v - t_{pl}$
		 endif

5   Petri Net Model for Synchronous Play Out

The CSPN for synchronous play out consists of 11 places and 15 transitions. There are two types of transitions, timed (t_1, t_2, t_{12}, t_{13}, t_{14}, t_{15}) and immediate transition (t_3, t_4, t_5, t_6, t_7, t_8, t_9, t_{10}, t_{11}). Immediate transitions fire immediately whenever a token is available in input place represented by bars, while timed transitions take some time to fire represented by rectangles. Each place contains a set of markers called color tokens. Each of these tokens carries a data value which belongs to a given type to be distinguished from each other. To be able to occur, a transition must have sufficient tokens on its input place and these places must have tokens that match the arc expressions. The places P_1 and P_2 represent the receiving buffer for audio and video and carry tokens of type l and m respectively. From the buffer, the tokens are moved to places P_3 and P_4. The transition T_3 is enabled when we have a token at place P_1 and no token at place P_2. At place P_6 audio is processed. The transition T_5 is enabled when we have a token at place P_2 and no token at place P_1 and token moved to place P_{11} for processing. If P_1 and P_2 both hold token then T_4 transits. T_6, T_7, T_8 occur according to the temporal relationship hold between audio and video frame. Place P_9 and P_{10} hold the audio and video token respectively for the time it has to wait in the buffer before play out. Video frame is processed at Place P_7 if it has a temporal relationship with audio. Audio and video frames are played out after the time associated with transitions t_{12} and t_{13} elapses.

Declaration of data type:

l : (s, d_a , ts_a ,R_a ,S_a ,t_e , at_a, d^a) ; m : (s, d_v , ts_v ,R_v ,S_v ,at_a, d^v)
type float d_v , d^v; type int R_a ,S_a , R_v ,S_v; type time ts_a ,t_e ,at_a , ts_v , at_v ; type signal s

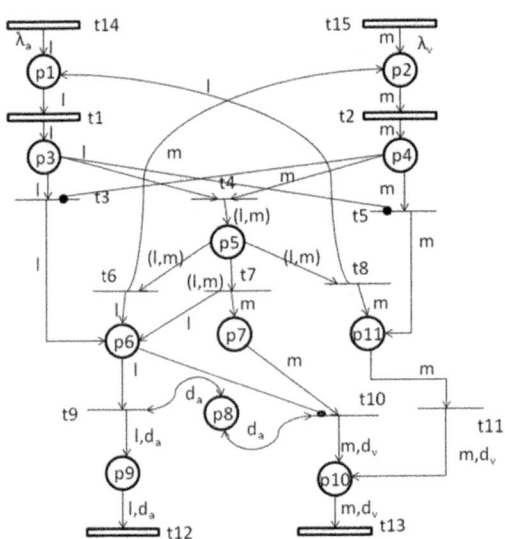

Fig. 1. CSPN Model

6   Verification of Model

Modeling power of a petri net has been examined by reachibility graph. It represents a part of transition system reachable from initial state. A state of a system represented by marking is a vector consists of positive number which represents the no. of token in all places in a net at that state. Reachibility diagram for our CSPN model is given below.

Now P and T represent place and transition respectively where P = (P₁, P₂... P_K) and T = (T₁, T₂...... T_m).

We define k × m incidence matrix [T] , [T]_(i, j)=Ø(T_j, P_i) - Ø (P_i, T_j) where,

Ø (T_j P_i) =no. of token added; Ø (P_i, T_j)=no. of token remove; [T]_(i, j)=Changed in place P_i when transition T_j fires once. Now if marking is reachable then the following equation is hold.

$$\mu_0 + [\ T\ ] \cdot \#\sigma = \mu_F \tag{1}$$

Where μ_0 =Initial marking, μ_F =Final marking, $\#\sigma$ =m-dimensional vector with its jth entry denoting the no. of time transition T_j occurs in σ.

If initial marking μ0 is $[0\ 0\ 0\ 0\ 0\ 0\ 0\ 1\ 0\ 0\ 0]^T$; Transition T14, T1, T3, T9, T12 occur then $\#\sigma = [\ 1\ 0\ 1\ 0\ 0\ 0\ 0\ 0\ 1\ 0\ 0\ 1\ 0\ 1\ 0]^T$. Putting the value of [T], μ₀, #σ in equation (1) we get marking $[0\ 0\ 0\ 0\ 0\ 0\ 1\ 0\ 0\ 0]^T$ which is also reachable through the reachibility graph. So we can establish the correctness of reachability graph for our petri net.

We represent verification of only one sequence of transition here. Other sequences of transition can be verified in similar way.

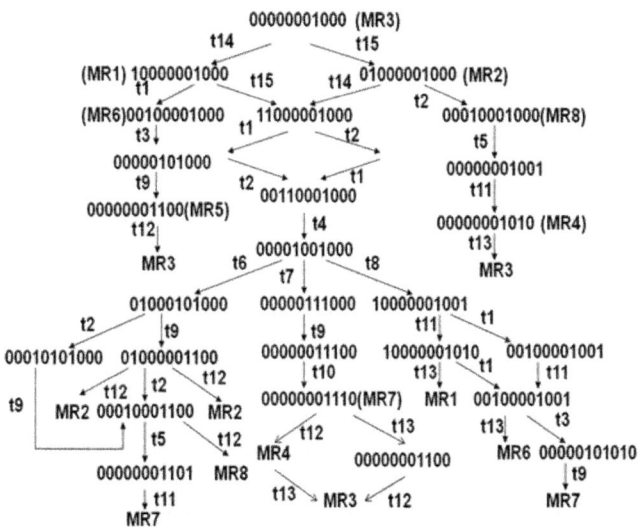

Fig. 2. Reachibility Graph

7 Discussion with an Example

The example in fig 3 shows how our algorithm works for different cases of asynchrony. It consists of audio and video stream at two receivers. Each stream is built with fixed length unit called frame. Here two audio frames of 2 time unit duration come together in one RTP packet and one video frame with 3 time unit duration come in one RTP packet. We recognize an audio frame with (sequence no. of RTP packet, sequence no. of frame within RTP packet), e.g., (1, 2), and video frame with sequence no. of RTP packet. We poll both buffers in receiver at unit time interval. Fig. 3 shows the original signal before sending, after receiving. After receiving the signal at rcv1 and rcv2 we apply our algorithm to synchronize the signal before playing out at each receiver. The playing out signal is also shown in Fig. 3.

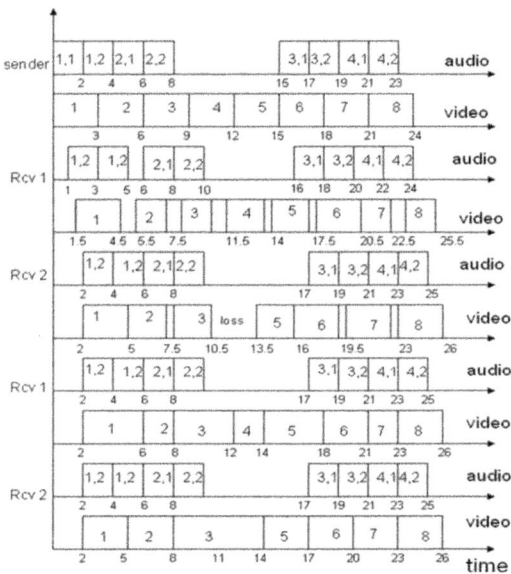

Fig. 3. Original, Received and Adjusted Signal

8   Conclusion

In this work we addressed a media synchronization issue called multimedia multipoint or inter destination synchronization which is required for designing any collaborative environment on distributed IP network. We suggested an algorithm for achieving this synchronization issue and modeled it using CSPN model and verified its correctness. The analysis of the CSPN model is not included in the paper. The future prospect of the work would be a detailed analysis of the CSPN model and implementation of the algorithm.

References

1. Quality of Service for Conferencing Reality or Hype? A guide to understanding and successfully deploying the appropriate level of QoS for conferencing. WainHouse Research (2003)
2. Pal, K., Upadhyay, P.D., Dutta, A.: A Petri Nets Based Model for Multipoint Synchronization in Audio Conferencing. In: Third International Conference on Communication Systems and Networks (COMSNETS), January 4-8 (2011)

3. Boronat, F., Lloret, J., García, M.: Multimedia group and inter-stream synchronization techniques: A comparative study. Information System 34, 108–131 (2009)

4. Cebollada, J.C.G., Mauri, L., Seguí, F.B.: Multimedia Group Synchronization Algorithm Based on RTP/RTCP

5. Yen, H.-C.: Introduction to Petri Net Theory

6. Bobbio, A.: System Modeling with Petri Nets

7. Marsan, M.A., Balbo, G., Conte, G.: A Class of Generalized Stochastic Petri Nets for the Performance Analysis of Multiprocessor Systems. ACM Transactions on Computer Systems 2(1), 93–122 (1984)

8. Casner, S.: Are you on the MBONE? IEEE Multimedia 1(2) (1994)

9. Weinstein, I.M.: The Universal IP Network for Video Conferencing A Manager's Guide to the Deployment of Inter-Enterprise Videoconferencing

10. Guerri, J.C.: Specification and performance evaluation of an adaptive multimedia stream Synchronization protocol based on global time and feedback techniques, with stream control Thesis. In: U.P.V. (June 1997)

11. Guerri, J.C., Esteve, M., Palau, C.E., Casares, V.: Feedback flow control with hysteresial techniques for multimedia retrievals. Multimedia Tools and Applications 13(3), 307–332 (2001)

12. Rangan, P.V., Ramanathan, S.: Performance of inter-media synchronization in distributed and heterogeneous multimedia systems. Computer Network ISDN System 27(4), 549–565 (1995)

13. Ishibashi, Y., Tasaka, S.: A synchronization mechanism for continuous media in multimedia communications. In: Proc. IEEE INFOCOM, pp. 1010–1019 (1995)

14. Tasaka, S., Ishibashi, Y.: Media synchronization in heterogeneous networks: stored media case. IEICE Trans. Commun. E81-B(8), 1624–1636 (1998)

15. Kindler, E., Reisig, W., ViSlzer, H., Humboldt, R.W.: Petri Net Based Verification of Distributed Algorithms: An Example. In: Universit zu Berlin, Institut ffdr Informatik, Berlin, Germany Fraunh

16. Jensen, K.: Hierarchical protocol. Aarhus University, Denmark, kjensen@daimi.au.dk

Summarizing Association Itemsets by Pattern Interestingness in a Data Stream Environment

Guanling Lee, Yu-tang Zhu, and Yi-Chun Chen

Department of Computer Science and Information Engineering
National Dong Hwa University, Hualien, Taiwan, R.O.C
guanling@mail.ndhu.edu.tw
m9821002@ems.ndhu.edu.tw
divien@gmail.com

Abstract. In the age of Knowledge economy, people are paying more attention to data mining. However, the number of the mined association patterns often exceeds the capacity of human's mind. Therefore, it is necessary for effectively present patterns according to their interestingness. This approach focuses on continuously differentiating interesting and valuable patterns from data stream and proposes a new data structure, Pattern's Interestingness Tree (PI-Tree) for discovering frequent patterns and helping to distinguish interesting knowledge. Performance Analysis indicates that the proposed approach is efficient for IOKD.

Keywords: Association itemsets, Knowledge Discovery, Data Stream, Data mining.

1   Introduction

Data mining has become a progressively important technology in recent decades, especially association patterns (rules) mining which was first investigated in [1]. Due to the number of association rules often exceeds the capacity of human's mind, it is necessary to effectively present the rules according to the *interestingness*. In general, the interestingness of a rule can be measured for different criteria. Among them are confidence and support, gain, variance and chi-squared value, entropy gain, gini, laplace, lift (a.k.a. interest or strength), and conviction [2]. Omiecinski also proposed the other three kinds of alternative measures, any-confidence, all-confidence, and bond [3]. Above mentioned approaches are *objective interesting measures*, because they are all based on the structure of discovered patterns and the statistics underlying them. However, "Your honey is my poison." The difference of users' knowledge should be considered as well. It leads the way for Interestingness Analysis System [4], which is the originator of *subjective interesting measures*. These kinds of measures are based on user beliefs in the data. As the length limit, more details and resembling approaches can be found on [4][5][6][7][8].

In recent years, emerging applications, such as sensor network data analysis, web-click stream mining, network traffic surveillance and ubiquitous computing, call for a study of a new kind of environment, named: *data stream*. When the data stream

R.-S. Chang, T.-h. Kim, and S.-L. Peng (Eds.): SUComS 2011, CCIS 223, pp. 74–83, 2011.
© Springer-Verlag Berlin Heidelberg 2011

growth over time, it is constantly changing with a variety of properties and quantities, which brings more challenge for analyzing because the tremendous amount of reformed knowledge. On the other hand, just as a Chinese proverb goes: "If you stay in a room for a long time where is full of orchids, their fragrance will disappear." People are interesting in revealing undiscovered truths, but also boring when they're familiar with them. By such observations, our approach focuses on continuously differentiate interesting and valuable knowledge from knowledge stream, which is the issue for Interestingness-oriented Knowledge Discovery (IOKD).

The rest of the paper is organized as follows. The foundation of IOKD from behavioral science and cognitive psychology is introduced in section 2. Section 3 defines the purposes of IOKD, data structure and algorithms. Performance analysis is discussed in section 4, and section 5 concludes this work.

2   Interestingness-Oriented Knowledge Discovery

Liu et al. in [4] elaborated there are two kinds of traits make knowledge become interesting: *Unexpectedness* and *Actionability*. Interestingly, similar arguments also appear in the research of behavioral science. In [9], Heath brothers generalized six principles of "Naturally Sticky" ideas, where is the "SUCCESs" : *Simple, Unexpected, Concrete, Credible, Emotional, and Stories*

From the view of language, "unexpected" is used to describe the things whose appearance or operation is not in accordance with what situation people have "expected". In other words, knowledge will be judged to noteworthy if it is dissimilar from pre-existing knowledge. This thought is extended from researches in cognitive psychology [10].

However, in spite of people have much interest in unfamiliar things; it could not be implicitly thought as a completely strange knowledge has the most attraction. Bauer [11] indicated that rare, unfamiliar and continuous behaviors particularly impress people, but the knowledge is desirable only while it's close to the world that they've experienced. Berlyne [12] also pointed out that whether a thing is too simple or too complicated, it can not draw peoples' attention on account of they can not realize what features should be noticed.

According to the studies noted in this section, the following key principles of interesting knowledge are deduced:

1. Interestingness of knowledge can be measure on the dissimilarity between it and pre-existing knowledge.
2. Interestingness of knowledge is relative to the dissimilarity within an upper bound and a lower bound.
3. The knowledge is regarded as "*unknown*" if its dissimilarity is not less than the upper bound, μ .
4. The knowledge is considered as "*static*" if its dissimilarity is not greater than the lower bound, λ .
5. The knowledge is differentiated as "*evolving*" if its dissimilarity is in the range of such bounds.
6. The certain upper and lower bound vary from person to person.

Our approach will use the foregoing principles as the guidelines for modeling IOKD and take root in the FP-Tree [13] and the DS-Tree [14].

3   Problem Definition and Algorithm

Let a data stream is decomposed for infinite batches, each batch consists of n transactions. After preprocessing, amounts of knowledge pattern P are generated, which is in the form of itemset: $P = \{i_1, i_2, ..., i_k\}$.

3.1   Problem Definition

In general, the purpose of IOKD is as follows:

Given a data stream, S ; a pre-existing knowledge pattern base, $\mathbb{K}$; two user-specific bounds, μ and λ. Calculates the dissimilarity of each undifferentiated knowledge $P \in B$, with $P' \in \mathbb{K}$, the most similar pre-existing knowledge of P, where B is the latest batch of S. Then according to Principle 3~5 in section 2, differentiates P into one of three states :{ Unknown, Static, Evolving}, by setting such dissimilarity as its interestingness. And finally, update $\mathbb{K}$ with B.

Since the naturally fluctuation of data stream, the knowledge it brings are always drifting as well.

To describe the degree of knowledge-drifting, two major dimensions: (i) Property and (ii) Age are considered to measure the dissimilarity among knowledge patterns in our approach.

i) Property of pattern
The property of an itemset can be represented by the composition of items it contains since it's the co-occurrence of potentially related items. If two itemsets are sharing the same common items, they are also sharing the same property for the subset of their intersection.

In behalf of measuring the dissimilarity for the pattern pair: P_1 and P_2 in the dimension of property, $DP(P_1, P_2)$ is defined as follow:

Definition 1. Dissimilarity of Property, $DP(P_1, P_2)$:

$$DP(P_1, P_2) = 1 - \frac{|P_1 \cap P_2|}{|P_1 \cup P_2|} \tag{1}$$

$DP(P_1, P_2)$ is an extended application of *Jaccard Distance*. It stands for the ratio of difference between P_1 and P_2.

ii) Age of pattern
The period (age) of validity for a knowledge pattern can be regarded as its subjective reliability. While a coming knowledge may be the evolving result of several pre-existing knowledge, people may subjectively associate it with the most senior one of them since it's more credible than others. Therefore, people also will be more interested if their prejudice has been evolved, which brings more unexpectedness.

Consequently, if the knowledge pattern P_1 may evolve to P_2, its interestingness is proportional to the relative distance of age between them. $DA(P_1, P_2)$ is defined to measure such distance:

Definition 2. Distance of Age, $DA(P_1, P_2)$:

$$DA(P_1, P_2) = \frac{|P_1.Age - P_2.Age|}{max\_age(\mathbb{K})} \tag{2}$$

$P_1.Age$ and $P_2.Age$ are the age of P_1 and P_2, respectively. $max\_age(\mathbb{K})$ is the age of the oldest pattern in $\mathbb{K}$. The relative distance of age for P_1 and P_2 can be reflected in $DA(P_1, P_2)$.

In the light of principle 1, above formulas are integrated in the form of linear algebra for completely measure patterns' dissimilarity:

Definition 3. Dissimilarity of pattern-pair P_1 and P_2, $D(P_1, P_2)$:

$$D(P_1, P_2) = \left\{ \begin{array}{ll} \alpha \cdot DP(P_1, P_2) + \beta \cdot DA(P_1, P_2) & , if \ P_1 \cap P_2 \neq \varnothing \\ 1 & , otherwise \end{array} \right\} \tag{3}$$

If $P_1 \cap P_2 = \varnothing$, $D(P_1, P_2)$ reaches its maximum: 1, because P_1 and P_2 are not sharing any items, and the maximum of both part in $D(P_1, P_2)$ are 1. If $P_1 = P_2$, $D(P_1, P_2)$ deservedly reaches its minimum: 0.

User may also give different weight of each part : α and β in $D(P_1, P_2)$, where $\alpha + \beta = 1$. For simplification, we let $\alpha = \beta = \frac{1}{2}$ in our approach. $D(P_1, P_2)$ can be extended to more dimension with suitable adjustment if necessary.

Then IOKD calculates $D(P, P_r)$ for all pre-existing knowledge patterns in $\mathbb{K}$, and set the minimum of it as $P.PIG$, the value of "Pattern's Interestingness Growth", which is the interestingness of P in our approach:

Definition 4. The value of Pattern's Interestingness Growth, $P.PIG$:

$$P.PIG = \min\{D(P, P_r) | \forall P_r \in \mathbb{K}\} \tag{4}$$

After $P.PIG$ is calculated, IOKD can differentiate P into one of three states according to the principle 3~5. The states transition of a knowledge pattern in IOKD can be depicted as Fig. 1.

Drifts of knowledge stream involve the maintenance and refinement of the pre-existing knowledge pattern base $\mathbb{K}$. On the other hand, even the knowledge of past may be valuable and interesting, it fades from peoples' memory if it becomes a stastill.

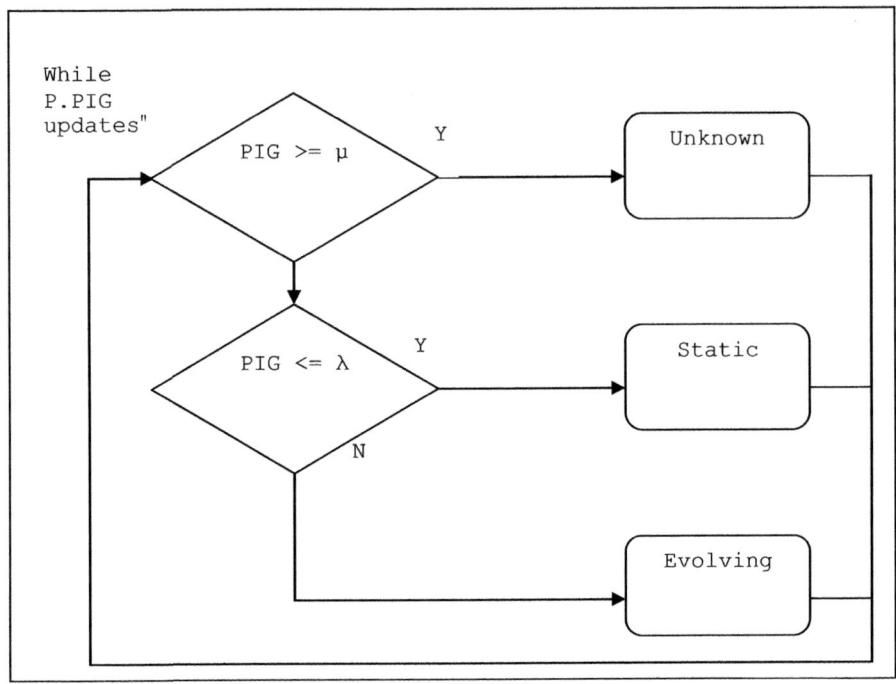

Fig. 1. The states transition of a pattern in IOKD

Thus for updating $\mathbb{K}$ efficiently and meaningfully, Definition 5~7 are defined:

Definition 5. Frequency of pattern Pr at time t, $Pr.Freq(t)$, can be formulated as

$$Pr.Freq(t) = Pr.Freq(t-1) \cdot \delta + Pr.Freq(t) \qquad (5)$$

Since the effect of past knowledge is fading though the time, Definition 5 is used as the accumulated frequency of every $Pr \in \mathbb{K}$ to keep both past and present frequency of Pr. δ is the decay factor, we let $\delta = 0.5$ for convenient in our approach.

Definition 6. Pr is *frequent* if $Pr.Freq(t) \geq min\_sup$.

And the definition for the age of pattern $Pr \in \mathbb{K}$ is presented as follow:

Definition 7. Age of pattern, $Pr.Age$:

$$P_r.Age = \begin{cases} P_r.Age + 1 & , \ if \ P_r \ is \ frequent \\ P_r.Age & , \ otherwise \end{cases} \qquad (6)$$

However, the naïve approach of IOKD — to calculate the dissimilarities between all coming knowledge with all pre-existing knowledge — may still suffer from a tremendous amount of redundant computation. To avoid this predicament, some observations of Definition 4 are very useful.

Let ρ be the current value of $\frac{1}{2}\left(\min(P.PIG, P_r.PIG)\right)$ because now we are focusing on the effect of one in two dimensions in our approach. In the process for finding the minimum of $P.PIG$, ρ will be replaced again and again on condition that $D(P, P_r) < 2\rho$. In other words, if $D(P, P_r) \geq 2\rho$, it affects nothing, thus two filtering lemmas are derived as follows:

Lemma 1. $D(P, P_r)$ should be calculated only if $\left|P \cap P_r\right| > \left(\dfrac{\alpha - \rho}{2\alpha - \rho}\right)\left(|P| + |P_r|\right)$.

Lemma 2. $D(P, P_r)$ should be calculated only if $\forall P_s \subset P_r, D(P, P_s) > \lambda$

Above lemmas will be cascaded together and work as an incremental and adaptive filter, which improves the efficiency of our approach.

3.2 Data Structure and Algorithm

We propose a new data structure named: PI-Tree (*Pattern's Interestingness Tree*), which is adopted the FP-Tree [13] and the DS-Tree [14]. The expatiation of node fields in PI-Tree is listed as Table 1:

Table 1. The fields' expatiation of node in PI-Tree

Field	Expatiation
P	The pattern, P, which N stands for.
$P.Freq$	The accumulated frequency of P in latest batch.
$P.Age$	The age for counting how many batch P survives.
$P.PIG$	A value which represents the interestingness of P at the moment.

PI-Tree maintains a header-table like FP-Tree for horizontal node-traversing; but it arranges the items of transaction with canonical order (ex: alphabetical order) instead of frequency, which is the same as DS-Tree. Such designs can fit the first issue by saving the time of node-swapping.

Considering the concept mentioned in [15] for the second issue, PI-Tree maintains an accumulated frequency and the age for each pattern by following Definition 5~7. With PI-Tree, the pre-existing knowledge pattern base $\mathbb{K}$ can be overlap with the patterns in the latest batch.

Global variable: a PI-tree, T; a minimum support, min_sup;
                     a lower bound, λ; an upper bound, μ.
Input: a data stream, S.
output: the lists of knowledge patterns of the latest batch for three states =
{Unknown, Evolving, Static}, respectively.
Algorithm IOKD(S)
{

```
(1)   while S has the latest unanalyzed batch do{
(2)       let B be the latest batch of S;
(3)       for each transaction I in B do{
(4)           insert I into T;} // update T.HT(header-table of T) if necessary
(5)       let L be the result list of all patterns in T;
(6)       for each node-list NL in T.HT do{ // descending order
(7)           for each node N in NL do{
(8)               let P be the pattern which N stands for;
(9)               let X be the result of P removes those whole-new items;
(10)              if |X| = 0 then{
(11)                  set P.PIG = 1;} // unknown pattern
(12)              else{
(13)                  for each item R in X do{
(14)                      let RL be the node-list of R in T.HT;
(15)                      for each node Q in RL do{
(16)                          check P,Q by using lemmas 1&&2;} } } }
(17)          run Maturate(N,L);}
(18)      sort L by PIG;
(19)      output three parts of L: Unknown, Static and Evolving; }
}
```

Fig. 2. IOKD algorithm

Input: a node, N; the result list, L;
output: null.

Procedure Maturate(N,L)
```
{
(1)              let P be the pattern which N stands for;
(2)              if P.freq is less than min_sup then{ // P is infrequent
(3)                      prune N and all its children in T;}
(4)              else
(5)                      P.Freq *= δ;
(6)                      P.Age += 1;
(7)              add a copy of P into L;
(8)              reset P.PIG = μ for next batch;}
}
```

Fig. 3. Procedure Maturate

4   Performance Analysis

In this section, a set of simulations was performed to present the efficiency and effectiveness of our approach. The testing data streams were generated by the IBM Synthetic-data Generator. Table 4.1 lists the parameters for generating the synthetic data streams. The efficiencies of naïve-IOKD and Filtered-IOKD were compared in each simulation.

Table 2. The parameters of performance analysis (for synthetic data stream)

Parameters	Default value	Ranges
Number of transactions (per batch)	4K	2K~10K
Average length of transaction	6	3~15
Number of distinct items	0.4K	0.2K~1K
Minimum support threshold	1.5%	-
Upper bound, μ, for the "Unknowns"	0.85	-
Lower bound, λ, for the "Statics"	0.15	-

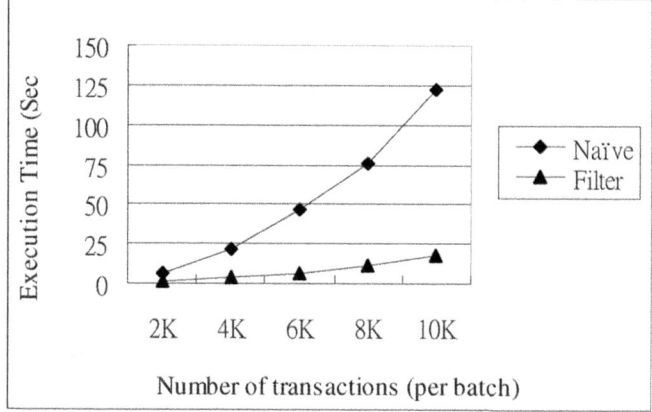

Fig. 4. Execution times vs. Numbers of transaction (per batch)

The effect of numbers of transaction (per batch) was investigated in the first simulation. As shown in Fig. 4, the time complexity is linear for Filtered-IOKD but exponential for naïve-IOKD. Filtered-IOKD clearly outperformed naïve-IOKD since the former can prune a large amount of redundant computation (it brings the same effect for all the later simulations in this section). The effect of average length of transaction was also compared, and since it brings more pattern while average length of transaction increase, the execution time of naïve-IOKD raises heavily. The execution times are shown in Fig. 5.

The following simulation examines the effect of number of distinct items, which can be regarded as the density of data stream. Fig. 6 indicates that while the stream is getting sparser, the relationship between patterns are weakening as well, which decrease the execution time.

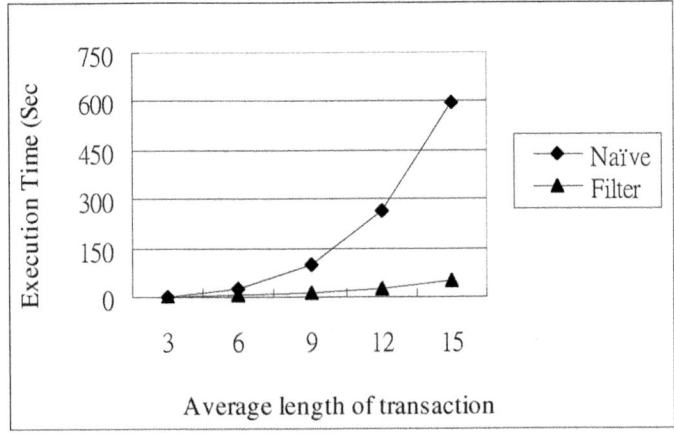

Fig. 5. Execution times vs. Average length of transaction

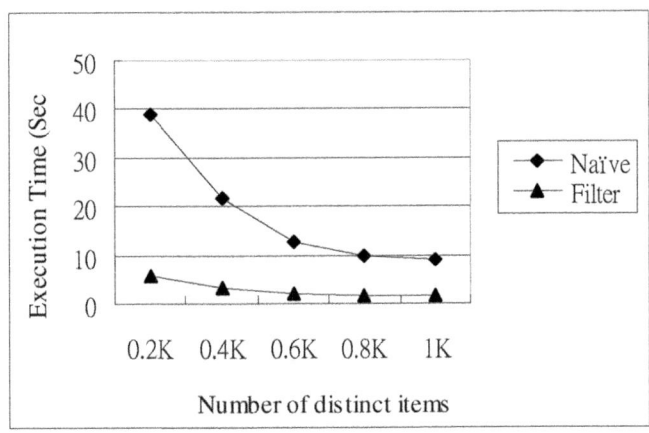

Fig. 6. Execution times vs. Number of distinct items

5   Conclusion

In this paper, a framework is introduced to solve the issue of interestingness-oriented knowledge discovery (IOKD) of knowledge stream. On the foundation of behavioral science and cognitive psychology, six principles are devised to define the interestingness of knowledge and model the knowledge stream. Two interestingness measures are proposed for measuring the interestingness growth of knowledge from different dimensions. A new data structure, *Pattern's Interestingness Tree* (PI-Tree) is presented for efficiently maintaining and refining the pre-existing knowledge base. Two filtering lemmas are derived for improving the efficiency of our approach. The results of performance analysis indicate that the Filtered-IOKD is efficient, effective and capable for real-time differentiating interesting knowledge from the knowledge stream.

References

1. Agrawal, R., Srikant, R.: Fast Algorithms for Mining Association Rules. In: VLDB, Santiago, Chile, pp. 487–499 (1994)
2. Roberto, J., Bayardo, J., Agrawal, R.: Mining the Most Interesting Rules. In: ACM SIGKDD, New York, USA, pp. 145–154 (1999)
3. Omiecinski, E.R.: Alternative Interest Measures for Mining Associations in Databases. J. IEEE TKDE 15(1), 57–69 (2003)
4. Liu, B., Hsu, W., Chen, S., Ma, Y.: Analyzing the Subjective Interestingness of Association Rules. IEEE Intelligent Systems and their Applications 15, 47–55 (2000)
5. Pohle, C.: Integrating and Updating Domain Knowledge with Data Mining. In: VLDB PhD Workshop, Berlin, Germany (2003)
6. Shin, S., Lee, W.: An On-line Interactive Method for Finding Association Rules Data Streams. In: ACM CIKM, New York, USA, pp. 963–966 (2007)
7. Wang, K., Jiang, Y., Lakshmanan, L.: Mining Unexpected Rules by Pushing User Dynamics. In: ACM SIGKDD, New York, USA, pp. 246–255 (2003)
8. Xin, D., Shen, X., Mei, Q., Han, J.: Discovering Interesting Patterns through User's Interactive Feedback. In: ACM SIGKDD, New York, USA, pp. 773–778 (2006)
9. Heath, C., Heath, D.: Made to Stick: Why Some Ideas Survive and Others Die. Random House, New York (2007)
10. Haviland, S., Clark, H.: What's new? Acquiring new information as a process in comprehension. Journal of Verbal Learning & Verbal Behavior 13, 512–521 (1974)
11. Bauer, J.: Warum ich fühle was Du fühlst (2009)
12. Berlyne, D.: Structure and direction in thinking. Wiley, New York (1967)
13. Han, J., Pei, J., Yin, Y.: Mining Frequent Patterns without Candidate Generation. In: ACM SIGMOD, Dallas, TX, USA, pp. 1–12 (2000)
14. Leung, C., Khan, Q.: DSTree: a Tree Structure for the Mining of Frequent Sets from Data Streams. In: IEEE ICDM, Hong Kong, China, pp. 928–932 (2006)
15. Lin, C.-H., Chiu, D.-Y., Wu, Y.-H., Chen, A.L.P.: Mining Frequent Itemsets from Data Streams with a Time-Sensitive Sliding Window. In: SDM, Newport Beach, California, USA (2005)

VoIPS: VoIP Secure Encryption VoIP Solution

Chiung-Yi Wu[1], Kuo-Ping Wu[1,*], Jason Shih[3], and Hahn-Ming Lee[1,2]

[1] Department of Computer Science and Information Engineering,
National Taiwan University of Science and Technology, Taipei, Taiwan
{m9815908,wgb,hmlee}@mail.ntust.edu.tw
[2] Institute of Information Science, Academia Sinica, Taipei, Taiwan
hmlee@iis.sinica.edu.tw
[3] Paysecure Technology Co., Ltd., Taipei, Taiwan
jason@paysecure.com.tw

Abstract. VoIP technology allows voice messages transmitted through the network, but it also encounters information security threats such as packet sniffering and authentication. In this research we propose an integrated algorithm - VoIPS (VoIP Secure). It conduct a secured VoIP communication which afforded confidentiality and message authentication. Furthermore, side-effect to performance is trival and able to eliminate the risk of well-known replay attack which used on VoIP system. According to our simulation experiments, the proposed system can be created to construct a secure VoIP communication system. A hardware prototype is created to verify the proposed system which practically feasible.

Keywords: VoIP, AES, SIP, embedded system.

1 Introduction

Traditionally, telecommunications are carried out through the analog method. Speeches are converted to analog signals and transferred to destination by wire. This is well-known circuit switch network. VoIP was proposed in 1995. Since 1997, related protocols and technologies are improved that makes VoIP applications popular. The sender transforms the voice data into digital data and encrypts the data to packets, while the receiver decodes the packets and restores the voice data. VoIP not only supports communication with circuit switching network but also can let its users talk on existed internet with no charge. It communicates with specific ports such as 5060 or protocols defined by manufacturers. For this reason, communication cost can be reduced.

VoIP technologies allow enterprises transfer the voice data through the data network, as for that communication cost can be reduced and more service can be offered. However, since VoIP transfers voice data on IP network, it unavoidably faces the same information security threats as IP network has, such as DoS, packet sniffing and authentication.[6,7]. According to the threat categories

---

* Corresponding author.

R.-S. Chang, T.-h. Kim, and S.-L. Peng (Eds.): SUComS 2011, CCIS 223, pp. 84–93, 2011.
© Springer-Verlag Berlin Heidelberg 2011

proposed by VoIPSA (VoIP Security Alliance)[12], the most significant problem of VoIP is that there is no proper information security content protection system to avoid social engineering, monitoring, interception and modification, abuse and malicious interrupt service and some other threats. In 2007, a concept software was proposed by Peter Cox, which can monitor, eavesdrop or record multiple network telephone. Once the political or enterprise secrets are leaked, the related consequences are very serious.

In this work we propose a light-weight algorithm incorporating authentication and encryption, named as VoIPS (VoIP Secure), for peer-to-peer usage and client-to-server usage. We use the proposed VoIPS algorithm to do authentication and message protection. According to the algorithm, key is replaced periodically and transmitting data are scattered and rearranged. In addition, we implement the proposed system as an embedded system. By this we can avoid the data stolen problem of software VoIP strategy, such as memory dump attack or packet sniffing before voice encryption and SSL transmission. The embedded system solution also alleviates the CPU consumption.

2   Related Work

Security issues of SIP voice service can be discussed in three layers: (1) SIP signaling: Instructions for A-B peers create communication (call management), state registration and presence, including Caller, Called party information, (2) RTP stream: packages transferring for A-B peers communication, ISPs widely use G.729a (out of north America area) and G.711(north America area), (3) Service blocking.

2.1   Security of SIP Signaling

There are security solutions based on SIP in the market, including SIP over TLS, SIP over IPsec, SIP over PPTP, SIP over SSL and so on. SIP over TLS bases on TCP, its connection oriented characteristic and can increase the loads, and three way handshake is a defect for real time phone call service. SIP over IPSec, similar to SIP over TLS, is high security while not economic when applied in practical operation. SIP over PPTP uses lightweight VPN solution, and its weakness is SIP/PPTP security and transmission efficiency since it uses Layer 2 tunneling such as UDP/IP/PPP/IP. SIP over SSL VPN uses SSL VPN to create a safe connection for the SIP communication. The construction cost of SSL VPN is high so that it is not yet popular in operation networks.

2.2   Security of RTP Stream

RTP stream is the packet stream of the coded and compressed voice data transferred over the network for communication. Peers creating the stream should use same voice data format to communicate successfully. There are several standards been widely used such as G.711, G.729a (simplified version of G.729) and GSM. In addition, Skype uses iLBC, ASTERISK open source IPPBX uses IAX, and

Microsoft proposes RTAudio as the format of UC platform. Voice data can be sniffered, reproduced or destroyed (such as modification of RTP packet serial number to make the playback intermittent) when they are transferred on the internet in plain format, so the security issues should not be neglected. IETF developments RFC 3711 sRTP (secure RTP, AES as default cipher) standard for RTP security. Skype, which owns more than 400 million registered users, uses 128bit AES based packet encryption [7].

2.3   Service Blocking

On public network, hackers detecting standard SIP and RTP packet formats to interfere VoIP services by sending fake SIP packets to denied the network voice service, blocking ISP traffic and disturbing SIP services with fake SIP message, RTP sequence disruption, etc. VoIPS does not transmits required packets in standard SIP, RTP, RTCP formats on internet, thus can avoid malicious denied of service attacks [2,3,13].

3   System Architecture

VoIP packet is consisting of RTP/SIP. The packet construction is presented in Figure 1. Logically, size of packet is increased and bandwidth may get congested when a VPN solution with extra headers such as AH,RSP, ect. is incorporated. However, we are concerning about potential risks due to the packet is not fully protected against the Man-in-the-Middle(MITM) attacks [15] based on its control message which comes from such RTCP and other for exploitation practice. The concept of VoIPS focuses on seamless protection on payloads and header. Furthermore, to avoid NAT services or firewalls blocking UDP/SIP/RTP packets according to the packet content signatures and thus leading VoIP communication fail, packet contents are obfuscated and encrypted to make sure that the data flow not only can be protected but also can pass through the gateways.

Figure 2 is the schematic diagram of VoIPS encrypted IP packet structure. The encryption part of VoIPS uses 128 bit AES (Advanced Encryption Standard).

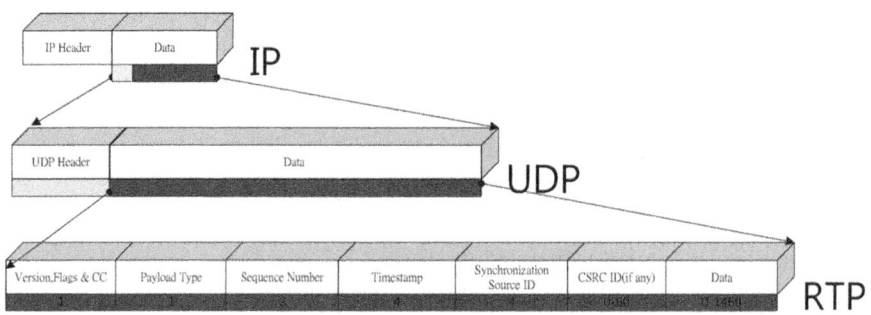

Fig. 1. VoIP packet construction

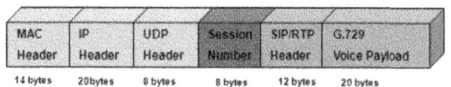

Fig. 2. Schematic diagram for VoIPS encrypted IP packet structure

AES was proposed by NIST in Nov. 26, 2001[9][10], it belongs to a symmetric block encryption algorithm [1]. VoIPS uses ECB mode to encrypt the data, and uses CBCMAC mode accompanied with initial vector computation to produce Message Authentication Code (MAC) according to the last block of eight bytes of ciphertext [1][14]. The encryption key, which behaves as session key, is substituted after every transaction be made to avoid hackers decrypt the contents by intercepting multiple ciphertext.

For cryptographic operation, it must satisfy the requirement of multiple of eight. We follow the PKC#7 Padding. The following is the definition.Let CB denotes Cipher Block, M denotes Message, P denotes Padding String and is composed of $8 - (||M||mod8)$ bytes. Then, $CB = M|P$, and CB must satisfy the following conditions:

$$CB = M|01, \; if \; ||M|| \; mod \; 8 = 7,$$
$$CB = M|02\,02, \; if \; ||M|| \; mod \; 8 = 6,$$
$$\ldots$$
$$CB = M|08\,08\,08\,08\,08\,08\,08\,08, \; if \; ||M|| \; mod \; 8 = 0.$$

The architecture of the proposed VoIPS is shown in Figure 3, and Table 1 is its Pseudo-Code.

VoIP packets are obfuscated by block arrangement and are encrypted by message encryption algorithm. Message Authentication Code (MAC) is generated and appended as the last two bytes of cipher message to avoid tampering before it is sent. With VoIPSP we design an interface on firmware level and allocate EEPROM to place the VoIPS object code and master key both with proprietary XORed mechanism. Hardware design of VoIPSP is shown in Figure 4. Its MPU is MIPS processor @ 400MHz, with 32MB memory and 4MB flash installed. The voice coders are G.729ab and G.723.1. Debian with Linux kernel 2.6.18 is the operation system. It uses IPv4 as the protocol stack and SIPv2 as the VoIP protocol. Its SLIC/SLAC is Zarlink 88266/88286.

Since VoIPS is implemented as an embedded system (VoIPSP), the system can avoid Trojan and malicious software threats. VoIPSP operates in the following steps:

1. Preparation stage
   Upload the object code of VoIPS and master key with XORed onto VoIPSP.
2. Operation stage
   (a) BootUp: Object code of VoIPS and mater key be loaded into memory after XORed.

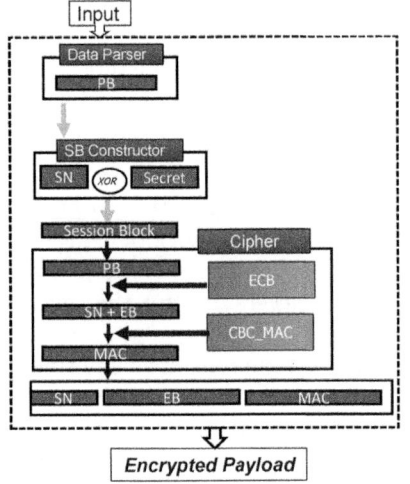
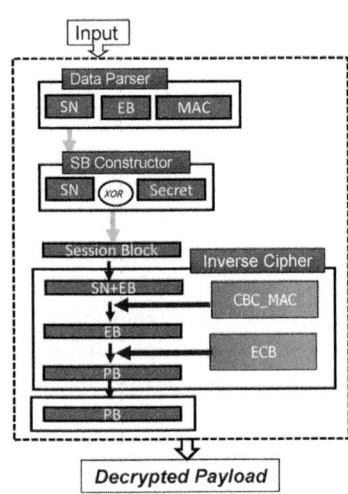

(a) VoIPS Cipher mode   (b) VoIPS Decipher mode

Fig. 3. VoIPS Architecture for Cipher/Decipher mode

Table 1. VoIPS Pseudo-Code

```
VoIPS(int OpsMode, unsigned char* ShareSecret, unsigned char* InputData,
    unsigned char* Static long SessionNumber, unsigned char* OutputData){
SwtichCase(OpsMode):
Case 0: //Encrption
  InputData= Parser(InputData);
  SB=GenSK(SessionNumber,ShareSecret);
  EB=ECB(InputData,SB);
  MAC=CBC_MAC(SN,EB,SB);
  Bulk=SN+EB+MAC;
  Output=Bulk;
  Return Output;
  Break;
Case 1: //Decryption
  InputData= Parser(InputData);
  SB=GenSK(SessionNumber,ShareSecret);
  MAC=CBC_MAC(SN,EB,SB);
  If(CompareMAC(OriginMAC,MAC )== 0 ){
  PB=ECB(EB,SB);
  Output=PB;
  Return Output;}else{
  MAC is wrong;
  }
}
```

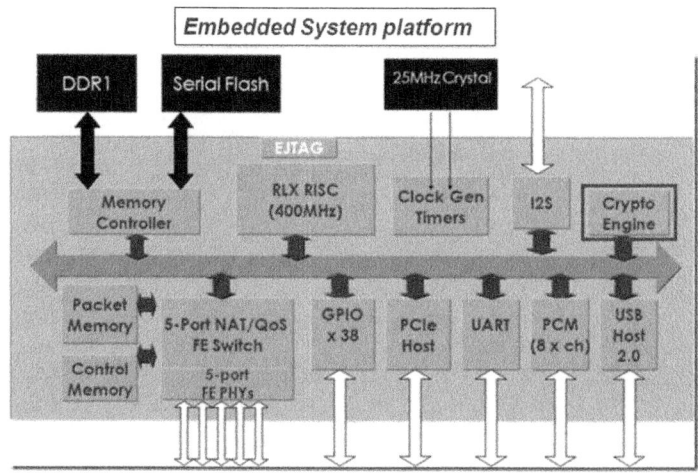

Fig. 4. VoIPSP Hardware Architecture

(b) SetupCall: Session Key be generated by master key with increment counter and ready for this transaction used.
(c) GetInput: Take the voicestream from DSP and feedback to VoIPS with session key.
(d) Packet Encapsulation: Transfer the output and encapsulate as UDP packet.
(e) Packet Transmission: Transmit the packet to destination.

4 Experiments

In this section we evaluate the proposed algorithm with software and hardware emulations for effectiveness and efficiency. According to the experiments, VoIPS is practical feasible and is able to eliminate the risk of various well known VoIP attacks. In order to avoid those kinds of attack for crypto analysis, a session block would be involved to ensure each packet is unique and unable for cloning. We realize the proposed infrastructure by implementing the VoIPS algorithm and the corresponding embedded system platform as known VoIPSP. We use the newest hardware platform from OCTTEL Communication Co., Ltd. as the embedded system development environment. Target platform is TravelMate 4720 which equipped with Intel Core2 Duo processor and 2GB memory for evaluation purpose.

4.1 Algorithm Effectiveness

At this section we want to demonstrate the effectiveness of our algorithm is cooresponding to the test vector provided by NIST. We use NIST test vector

Fig. 5. Output of VoIPS

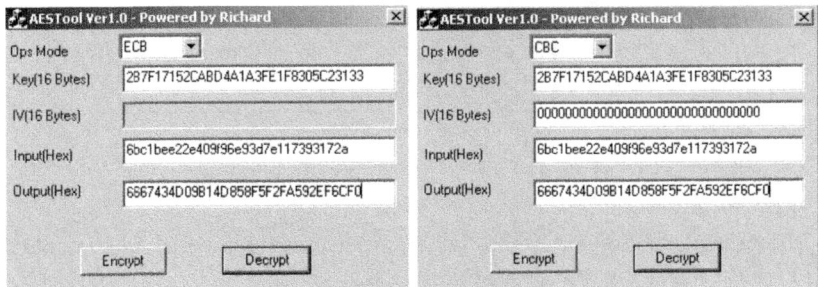

Fig. 6. Output of ECB and CBCMAC

for AES algorithm to verify the correctness of the VoIPS algorithm, make sure VoIPS can transfer data correctly.

Figure 5 demonstrates that session key generated by master and device session number. Then the session key is used to encrypt data and to calculate MAC. After that, we get the data 6667434D09B14D858F5F2FA592EF6CF06CF0 (18 bytes) which is cipher (16 bytes) | MAC (2 bytes).

Then we use ECB and CBCMAC respectively to see if we can get the same result. Figure 6 shows that, with ECB and CBCMAC method, the cipher data which encrypted is 6667434D09B14D858F5F2FA592EF6CF0 (16 bytes), which is identical to our cipher. For the MAC, it is generated with initial vector 0 and the last two bytes, so we have the MAC as 6CF0. Combining the above will have 6667434D09B14D858F5F2FA592EF6CF0 | 6CF0, which is identical to the output of VoIPS. So we show that VoIPS is effective and its encryption strength meets NIST request to AES algorithm.

4.2   System Usability

Here we intend to show that in a real scene the client side (VoIP embedded device) and server side (Proxy Server) can communicate with protection of VoIPS. We simulate the UDP transmission between two peers incorporated with VoIPS algorithm for feasibility assessment to show that the proposed system can offer encrypted voice communication service. There are three characters in the

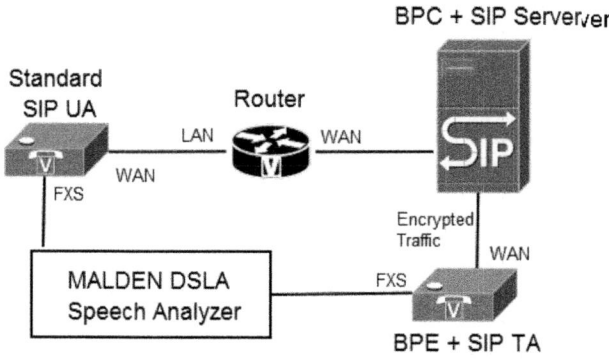

Fig. 7. VoIPSP Hardware Simulation

test case, including a Client (sends request to server side for authentication and transmission), a Server (processes client side request, does authentication, specify the target side to transmit) and a Sniffer (sniff packet to simulate the attack). Test program uses Socket language for UDP transmission. Simulated SIP/UDP data packet length is 16 bytes. WireShark is used to collect data to see whether VoIPS protects data. VoIPS plugin on Client and Server can be enable/disable when communicating.

Obviously, the transmission contents can be intercepted at receiving side easily if no protection is applied. When VoIPS enabled, the data can only be intercepted with its encrypted form. Sniffer (Wireshark) can easily acquire the data in the UDP packet. However, even the protected data are intercepted, the data cannot be recognized or analyzed, so the proposed system can offer a secured VoIP transmission service.

4.3 Hardware Implementation and Performance

Currently a prototype embedded system is implemented with the help of OCT-TEL Communication Co., Ltd. to realize our concept. Here we use MALDEN DLSA Speech Analzerto assess and measure the statistics between PPtP and VoIPS (Figure 7). In practice, our hardware VoIPSP peers can communicate continuously with protection.

Figure 8(a) shows that, with VoIPSP, the timeframe of transmitting packet sequence is stable at about 20ms. However, with PPtP, we can see that the timeframe of sequence of packet transmission is more unstable (Figure 8(b)).Also, in Table 2 we can see that VoIPS has much fewer overhead in comparison with PPtP (8.11% vs. 56.76%), and the overall performance of VoIPS is better then PPtP solution.

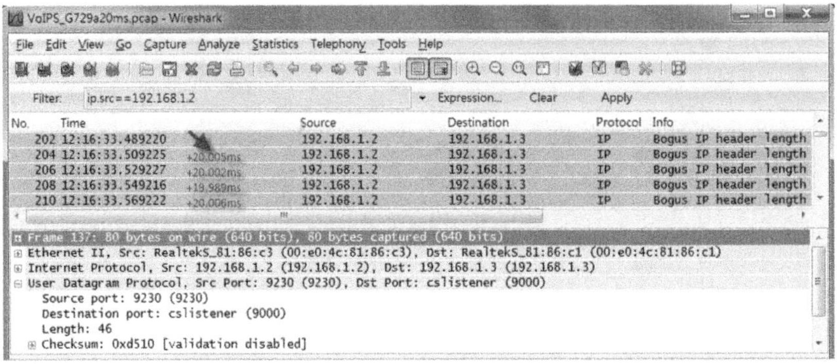

(a) VoIPS solution

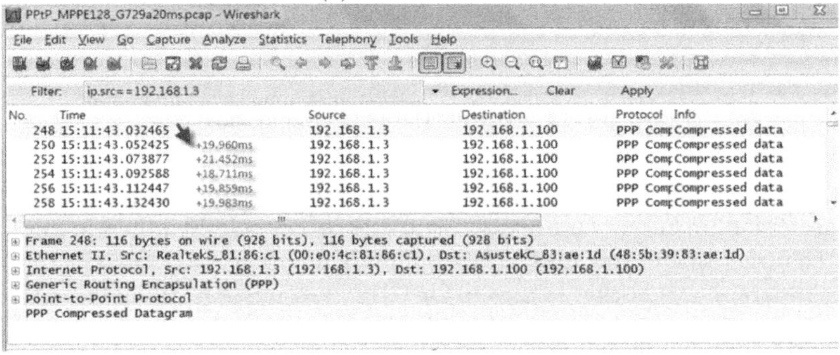

(b) PPtP solution

Fig. 8. Comparison of VoIPS and PPtP transmission behavior

Table 2. Measurement of MALDEN DSLA Speech Analzer

RTP 729a@20ms	Encryption Algorithm	Phone-PBX-Phone delay (ms)	CPU load (%)	Bandwidth (Kbps)	Additional overhead (%)
Generic VoIP	No	290	0.08	29.6	0.00
VoIPS	AES128bits	310	0.19	32.0	8.11
PPtP	MPPE128bits	316	0.24	46.4	56.76

5 Conclusion

This research proposes a novel approach that a secured VoIP communication system based on AES algorithm as known VoIPS. In order to implement a combined mechanism of authentication and secure communication, we integrate VoIPS with local manufacture's voice module embedded platform. The proposed system can become a hardware solution for peer to peer secure communication environment, encrypted VoIP communication. Effectiveness and Usability of VoIPS algorithm has been verified via simulations. Its security strength meets known standard, and implementation with embedded system can reduce the computation ability requirement.

Acknowledgements. This research is partly supported by Ministry of Economic Affairs ICT Security Industry Promotion Program under contract number B2-9916514 and by the National Science Council of Taiwan under grants number NSC 99-2218-E-011-018.

References

1. Dworkin, M.: Recommendation for Block Cipher Modes of Operation Methods and Techniques. NIST Special Publication 800-38A (2001)
2. El-moussa, F., Mudhar, P., Jones, A.: Overview of SIP attacks and countermeasures. In: Weerasinghe, D. (ed.) ISDF 2009. LNICST, vol. 41, pp. 82–91. Springer, Heidelberg (2010)
3. Gupta, P., Shmatikov, V.: Security Analysis of Voice-over-IP Protocols. In: 20th IEEE Computer Security Foundations Symposium (CSF 2007), pp. 49–63 (2007)
4. Handley, M., Schulzrinne, H., Schooler, E., Rosenberg, J.: SIP: session initiation protocol. RFC 2543, IETF (1999)
5. Jaberipur, G., Kaivani, A.: Binary-Coded Decimal Digit Multiplier. IET Computer & Digital Techniques 1(4), 377–381 (2007)
6. Keromytis, A.D.: Voice over IP: Risks, Threat and Vulnerabilities. In: Proceedings of the Cyber Infrastructure Protection (CIP) Conference (2009)
7. Keromytis, A.D.: Voice over IP Security: Research and Practice. IEEE Security & Privacy Magazine 8, 76–78 (2010)
8. Kuhn, D.R., Walsh, T.J., Fries, S.: Security Considerations for Voice Over IP Systems. Community Contributions (2005)
9. Lorch, M., Basney, J., Kafura, D.: A hardware-secured credential repository for Grid PKIs. In: IEEE International Symposium on Cluster Computing and the Grid, CCGrid (2004)
10. Nechvatal, J., Barker, E., Bassham, L., Burr, W., Dworkin, M., Foti, J., Roback, E.: Report on the Development of the Advanced Encryption Standard (AES). Journal of Research of the National Institute of Standards and Technology (2001)
11. Schulzrinne, H., Casner, S., Frederick, R., Jacobson, V.: RTP: Transport Protocol for Real-Time Applications. RFC 3550, Standard (2003)
12. VoIP Security Alliance: VoIP Security and Privacy Threat Taxonomy version 1.0 (2005)
13. Ja, W.K.: SIP Methodology Handbook. Unalis Press (2005)
14. Laih, C.S., Han, L., Chang, C.C.: Contenpory Cryptography and application. Unalis Press (1998)
15. Zhang, R., Wang, X., Farley, R., Yang, X., Jiang, X.: On the feasibility of launching the man-in-the-middle attacks on VoIP from remote attackers. In: Proceedings of the 4th International Symposium on Information, Computer, and Communications Security (ASIACCS 2009), vol. 69, p. 61 (2009)

Energy Cost-Effectiveness of Cloud Service Datacenters

Cheng-Jen Tang and Miau-Ru Dai

Graduate Institute of Communication Engineering,
Tatung University,
No. 40 Chung-shan N. Rd. Sec. 3, 104 Taipei, Taiwan
ctang@ttu.edu.tw, d9610002@ms2.ttu.edu.tw

Abstract. Cloud computing is a computation intensive service that clusters distributed computers providing applications as services and on-demand resources over Internet. Theoretically, such consolidated resource enhances the energy efficiency of both clients and servers. In reality, cloud computing is a panacea for enhancing energy efficiency under some certain conditions. For a user of cloud services, the computing resources are located at remote machines. Pioneers in exploring cloud computing, such as Google, AmazonWeb, Microsoft Azure, Yahoo, and IBM all use web pages as service interface via HTTP protocol. Through appropriated designs, sorting, one of the most frequently used algorithms, required by a web page can be executed and succeed by either clients or servers. As the model proposed in this paper, such client-server balanced computing allocation suggests a more energy-efficient and cost-effective web service.

Keywords: Energy Efficiency, Cloud Computing, Datacenter.

1 Introduction

Recently, datacenters have a significant growth in power density. Rapidly developing information and communication technologies (ICTs) and Internet elaborates establishment of datacenters. With the emergence of cloud computing, datacenters now also have to respond to the mounting computation requests. Modern datacenters usually equip with fully populated rack of blades to better use their limited spaces. Datacenters therefore become areas with the highest power density. The increasing power demand brings the rising energy costs together, thus improving energy efficiency becomes a key issue for the datacenter management. According to estimation from Amazons [10], expenses related to the cost and operation of their servers is responsible for 53% of the total budget, and energy-related costs for 42%, which consists of direct power consumption, about 19%, and the cooling infrastructure, 23%.

The energy demand of datacenters keeps growing due the emergence of cloud computing. Cloud computing is the newest Internet technology that evolves datacenters from information warehouses to information factories. The computation

R.-S. Chang, T.-h. Kim, and S.-L. Peng (Eds.): SUComS 2011, CCIS 223, pp. 94–103, 2011.
© Springer-Verlag Berlin Heidelberg 2011

oriented nature of cloud computing differs the power consumption patterns of datacenters from the traditional storage oriented model. This computation oriented model is likely to widen the difference between the amount of energy required for peak periods and off-peak periods in a cloud computing datacenter due to:

1. CPU: Intensive computation enlarges CPU utilization rate. Power consumption of modern server CPUs is proportional to their utilization.
2. DRAM: Increased computation needs bring up the required memory sizes. DRAM has been identified as one of the main contributors to energy consumption in a computer [13].
3. Hard Disk: Frequent computation requests raise the frequency of random disk accesses. Random disk accesses consume much more energy than sequential disk accesses [16].

That is, cloud computing broaden the gap between the peak energy demand and off-peak energy demand because of increasing needs for computation.

The way of how computation performed greatly affects the power usage of datacenters. There are numerous algorithms that are applied in computer applications. A reasonable first step to establish the relationship between energy efficiency and computation algorithms is to find the most energy-influential algorithm as a starting point. Among all the frequently invoked algorithms in a computer, sorting is one of the most applied computing procedures. According to Knuth [11], one quarter of the entire 1960s computer running time was consumed by the computation of sorting processes. Sorting also has been considered as the foundation of many other algorithms [15]. In other words, computers spend a great portion of CPU cycles on sorting data. Therefore, this paper uses sorting to demonstrate how locating computing processes on clients or servers affects energy efficiency from the perspectives of energy demand side and energy supply side.

Sorting has to be performed by computer CPUs. Therefore, the energy consumption pattern of a CPU is critical. With the development of dynamic voltage and frequency scaling (DVFS), CPUs now consume power in proportion to their utilization. Studies [5] show that current desktop and server processors consume less power at low-activity modes than at busy modes. The average dynamic range, which is the difference between peak power and idle power of a CPU, of these CPUs is more than 70 percent of the peak power. For example, if a CPU has a 150-Watt peak power and a 30-Watt idle power, the dynamic range of this CPU is 120 Watts. Within the dynamic range of a CPU, its power consumption is close to proportional to its utilization rate.

People rarely work on standalone computers nowadays. Many computation works require the involvement of Internet services. Sustainability and availability becomes the major factors for choosing Internet service providers. The number and the frequency of the web requests are important factors to the energy consumption of a web server. A report published by Forrester Research [1] predicted that there would be over one billion PCs in use worldwide by the end of 2008, and over 2 billion PCs in use by 2015. The projected number given by Forrester is probably a little underestimated. From another source [2], there were already 1,966,514,816 Internet users as of June 30, 2010. Based on the later number, if each Internet user spends one joule per second for a minute on computation tasks daily, the total consumed energy for one year is about 12 TWh. This amount of energy roughly equals to the energy generated by a nuclear reactor of Palo Verde, Arizona, which is the largest nuclear plant in U.S. [3] Obviously, how the computation tasks are handled is one of the important issues regarding the energy efficiency of datacenters. To effectively evaluate the energy efficiency of computation tasks need to consider the energy usage conditions on both client-side and server-side.

As mentioned above, cloud computing broaden the gap between the peak energy demand and off-peak energy demand because of increasing needs for computation. This paper discusses how computation task allocation, on clients or on servers, affects energy efficiency of datacenter from the perspectives of demand side and supply side. The findings help datacenter managers to improve the energy efficiency of computation-intensive web applications of cloud services.

2   Related Work

This section briefs some previous studies that address the energy efficiency issues, sorting performance issues, or related issues.

Besides designing a new energy-efficient hardware, existing researches mainly attack the energy efficiency issue regarding sorting algorithms from two different perspectives:

- Finds the most energy-efficient sorting algorithm by comparing different algorithms, such as Bunse et al.[8]
- Makes compilers to generate energy-efficient codes or use a energy-efficient library, such as Zhong et al.[17], Ayala et al.[4], and Segmund et al.[14]

Bunse et al. [8] define a set of trend functions that decides on which sorting algorithm to use under certain conditions. In their work, bubblesort, heapsort, insertionsort, mergesort, quicksort, selectionsort, shakersort, and shellsort are evaluated. Insertionsort is identified as the most energy-efficient sorting algorithm in this work, if the number of input items is large enough.

Zhong et al. [17] design a tool, AcovSA, Analysis of Compiler Options via Simulated Annealing that finds a good set of compiler options for a particular CPU and software. Although this tool is not particularly designed for optimizing the energy usage of a program, it is helpful for finding a set of compiler options that produces an executable image consuming less energy than other sets of options. Ayala et al. [4] tune the settings of register file with some code profiles. The main challenge of adopting such mechanism is the necessity of modifying ISA (Instruction Set Architecture). Segmund et al. [14] propose an energy feature library that is developed with many energy-saving techniques. These shared object libraries replace applications code with the code of the library or (de)activate the necessary hardware components.

Some existing approaches aim at building energy-efficient datacenters, such as Berl et al.[6], Rusu et al.[12], Bianchini, and Rajamony [7], and Elnozahy et al.[9]

Berl et al. [6] believe that Cloud Computing with Virtualization is a way to improve the energy efficiency of a datacenter. Rusu et al. [12] dynamically reconfigures a heterogeneous cluster to reduce energy consumption during off-peak hours. Bianchini, and Rajamony [7] identify the techniques for conserving energy in heterogeneous server clusters. Elnozahy et al. [9] show that using the dynamic voltage scaling (DVS) on each server node can achieve 29 percent energy saving. Moreover, by turning off certain nodes based on workload achieves 40 percent energy saving.

3   Energy Efficiency of a Datacenter

This paper uses the number of performed tasks, the power factor, and the cost of power generation to define the energy efficiency of a datacenter. The followings list the mathematical model of related factors.

Power factor is a ratio of the amount of real power to the apparent power. Real power is the capacity of datacenter machines for performing tasks at a particular time. Apparent power equals to the product of measured RMS (root mean square) voltage and RMS current of a datacenter, which is the supplied power. Suppose the amount of supplied power is P_s (the apparent power); the real power is P_u, which is the power consumed by working machines in a datacenter. The power factor PF of a datacenter is:

$$PF = \frac{P_u}{P_s} \tag{1}$$

- Suppose $PF_d(t)$ is the power factor of a datacenter d at time t.
- $P_{ds}(t)$ denotes the supplied power to a datacenter d at time t.
- n_d is the number of server machines in a datacenter d.
- K_d is a constant that represents the line loss and power consumed by other active electrically-driven devices in a datacenter d.
- $P_{di}(t)$ is the power consumed by a server machine i in a datacenter d, where $i = 1...n_d$.

$PF_d(t)$ is defined as:

$$PF_d(t) = \frac{K_d + \sum_{i=1}^{n_d} P_{di}(t)}{P_{ds}(t)} \tag{2}$$

The amount of supplied power must be larger than or equal to the demand. Therefore, power suppliers have to generate power based on some load forecasting. Due to the fact that electricity demand is not constant, different types of power generators are required to meet this fluctuating demand. Generators are usually divided into three different types according to their missions:

- Base load generators,
- Intermediate load generators, and
- Peak load generators.

Peak load generators usually cost most, followed by intermediate load generators, and then base load generators.

- $P_{Bd}(t)$ denotes the power generated for a datacenter d by base load generators at time t.
- $P_{Id}(t)$ denotes the power generated for a datacenter d by intermediate load generators at time t.
- $P_{Pd}(t)$ denotes the power generated for a datacenter d by peak load generators at time t.
- C_B denotes the unit cost of the power generated by base load generators.
- C_I denotes the unit cost of the power generated by intermediate load generators.
- C_P denotes the unit cost of the power generated by peak load generators.

The power generation cost for the datacenter d at time t is:

$$C_d(t) = C_B P_{Bd}(t) + C_I P_{Id}(t) + C_P P_{Pd}(t) \tag{3}$$

- Suppose the energy required for finishing a client request k on a server i of a datacenter d is E_{kdi}.
- Suppose a server i needs a period of time L_{kdi} to finish the request k.

The power requirement of the request k performing on a server i of a datacenter d is:

$$P_{kdi} = \frac{E_{kdi}}{L_{kdi}} \tag{4}$$

- Suppose the power usage of a server i at the idle state is $P_{idle_{di}}$.
- Suppose the server i performs one request at a time. Other requests are queued until the working request has finished.

Therefore,

$$\begin{cases} P_{di}(t) = P_{idle_{di}}, \text{ if there is no job at time } t \\ P_{di}(t) = P_{idle_{di}} + P_{kdi}, \text{ if there is a request } k \text{ at time } t \end{cases} \tag{5}$$

Energy Efficiency of a Datacenter

- Suppose the number of finished jobs in a datacenter d for a period t_0 to t_1 is J_d.
- Suppose the investigated energy suppliers have only one customer that is the datacenter d.

Therefore, the energy efficiency of the datacenter d for a period t_0 to t_1 is defined as:

$$Eff_d = \frac{J_d}{\int_{t_0}^{t_1} C_d(t) dt} \tag{6}$$

Investigation on Energy Efficiency. Suppose C_B, C_I, and C_P are constants, and $C_P > C_I > C_B$. From Eq. (3) , to determine $C_d(t)$ needs to find $P_{Bd}(t)$, $P_{Id}(t)$, and $P_{Pd}(t)$.

- Suppose P_{MAX_B} is the maximum output of base load generators.
- Suppose P_{MAX_I} is the maximum output of intermediate load generators.
- Suppose P_{MAX_P} is the maximum output of peak load generators.

$$\begin{cases} P_{ds}(t) = P_{Bd}, \; for \, P_{ds}(t) \leq P_{MAX_B} \\ P_{ds}(t) = P_{MAX_B} + P_{Id}(t), \\ \quad for \, P_{ds}(t) \leq P_{MAX_I} + P_{MAX_B} \\ P_{ds}(t) = P_{MAX_B} + P_{MAX_I} + P_{Pd}(t), \\ \quad for \, P_{ds}(t) \leq P_{MAX_P} + P_{MAX_I} + P_{MAX_B} \end{cases} \quad (7)$$

This paper does not consider the condition of $P_{ds}(t)$ exceeding P_{MAX_P}, which causes the circuit breaker of the datacenter to be tripped.

In order to simplify the calculations, this paper assumes the datacenter d uses homogeneous architecture, which means all server machines have the same hardware configuration. Furthermore, this paper also assumes all requests consume the same amount of energy, and P_j is the power requirement for performing a request. Therefore, for a period t_0 to t_1

$$\sum_{i=0}^{n_d} P_{di}(t) = n \times P_{idle_{di}}(t) + \frac{J}{t_1 - t_0} \times P_j \quad (8)$$

Suppose the datacenter d has a constant power factor PF_d. By substituting Eq. (8) in Eq. (2), $P_{ds}(t)$ is written as:

$$P_{ds}(t) = \frac{K_d + n \times P_{idle_{di}}(t) + \frac{J}{t_1-t_0} \times P_j}{PF_d} \quad (9)$$

From Eq. (9), the P_{MAX_B} of a carefully designed power generation system of a data center d is:

$$P_{MAX_B} = \frac{C + n \times P_{idle_{di}}}{PF_d} \quad (10)$$

The unit cost of the power generated by peak load generators C_P is always the highest among C_B, C_I, and C_P. Peak load generators are operated under some critical conditions. For most of time, the $P_{ds}(t)$ is:

$$P_{ds}(t) = P_{MAX_B} + P_{Id}(t) \quad (11)$$

The $C_d(t)$ is therefore:

$$C_d(t) = C_B P_{MAX_B} + C_I P_{Id}(t) \quad (12)$$

From Eq. (9), Eq. (10), and Eq. (11), the following equation is obtained:

$$P_{Id}(t) = \frac{\frac{J}{t_1-t_0} \times P_j}{PF_d} \quad (13)$$

By substituting Eq. (13) in Eq. (12), $C_d(t)$ is written as:

$$C_d(t) = C_B P_{MAX_B} + C_I \frac{\frac{J}{t_1-t_0} \times P_j}{PF_d} \qquad (14)$$

A well-known mathematical model for modeling request arrival is the queuing model. The probability of that there are exactly k arrivals of jobs is equal to:

$$f(k,\lambda) = \frac{\lambda^k e^{-\lambda}}{k!} \qquad (15)$$

where k is the number of occurrences of an event, λ is a positive real number that equals to the expected number of arrival jobs during the given interval, which is $\frac{J}{t_1-t_0}$. However, the number of arrival requests is not controllable in real world. From Eq. (6) and Eq. (14), the following equation represents the energy efficiency under normal condition, which is neither critically peaking nor completely idle.

$$Eff_d = \frac{J}{\int_{t_0}^{t_1} C_B P_{MAX_B} + C_I \frac{\frac{J}{t_1-t_0} \times P_j}{PF_d} dt} \qquad (16)$$

$$Eff_d = \frac{J}{(C_B P_{MAX_B} + C_I \frac{\frac{J}{t_1-t_0} \times P_j}{PF_d})(t_1 - t_0)} \qquad (17)$$

Let a constant $C_0 = C_B P_{MAX_B}(t_1 - t_0)$, a constant $C_1 = \frac{C_I P_j}{PF_d}$, the Eq. (17) is written as:

$$Eff_d = \frac{J}{C_0 + C_1 J} \qquad (18)$$

$$Eff_d = \frac{1}{C_1} - \frac{C_0}{C_1(C_0 + C_1 J)} \qquad (19)$$

From Eq. (19), to maximize Eff_d needs to maximize J. The upper bound of J in a period t_0 to t_1 is $\frac{t_1-t_0}{L_j}$. Therefore, an easy way to gain a better energy efficiency of a data center is to reduce the L_j, which is the period of time required for finishing a request.

4   Experiment Result and Analysis

The mentioned work in section 2 for enhancing energy efficiency of datacenters have their strength on certain aspects. However, to implement any of them either requires taking some major changes on systems, or needs to recompile existing code. Such modification might not be acceptable for some system operators; since system-level and code-level modifications often accompany with uncertainties, which lead to unexpected system failures. To avoid such risk, this paper proposes a new approach that is to make the required computation tasks of web pages swappable. In other words, this is to identify computation tasks of interactive web pages that can be performed by either the server or the client. If a server is more energy-efficient for performing the task than its client, let the server does the job. Otherwise, let its client does the job. This paper takes the sorting as a starting point to examine this concept. This section identifies some possible sorting-performing scenarios.

In considering the energy consumption scenarios of client computers, the power-saving CPUs and the ordinary CPUs are fundamentally different. Hence, there are two scenario groups: one is for the power-saving CPUs, and the other is for the ordinary CPUs.

Most of the content-sortable web pages perform sorting on servers. To make the sorting performed on a client, a sorting function is needed to be shipped with the web page. This sorting function is often written in Javascript or other client-side scripting languages. However, performing the sorting using an external application often offers a better performance than the browser-embedded scripting engine.

The workload of a server greatly affects the performance of a web server. In the surveyed scenarios, three workload levels are considered:

- light: 1 to 10 connections
- medium: 10 to 100 connections
- heavy: 100 to 1000 connections

For the power-saving CPUs, this experiment setup chooses Intel Atom processor N280 with 512KB Cache, 1.66 GHz, 667 MHz FSB. Intel uses clock gating to manage the power usage of Atom. This mechanism activates the clocks in a logic block only when they have work to do. Intel Atom N280 consumes 2.5 watts at the peak utilization, 100 mwatts at idle state. Acer Veriton N260G, which equips with Intel Atom N280, is used in the experiment. In the experiment, up to 4 Acer Veriton N260G PCs are used. The power supply unit (PSU) of Acer Veriton N260G provides up to 65 Watts. For the ordinary CPUs, Intel Pentium 4 2.4 GHz Northwood Processor with 533 MHz FSB, 512KB cache is used. 4 HP Compaq D330 Minitower PCs that equipped with Intel Pentium 4 2.4 GHz are chosen in this experiment. D330 uses a 240-Watt PSU. Intel Pentium 4 2.4 GHz Northwood has a 59.8-watt thermal design power (TDP).

The server used in this experiment equips with 4 Intel Xeon 2.4 GHz processors. Each processor in the server has a 65-watt TDP. Keep one thing in mind, this Intel Xeon 2.4 GHz processor is considered ancient, since it was first announced in March, 2002. The server has a CPU set of 260-watt TDP, and is equipped with two 500-Watt PSUs. This experiment assumes the CPU TDP is the power of a CPU at peak utilization, and PSU capacity is its maximum power.

In order to examine the finding of Eq. 19, there are three tests with f=8.33, 4.16, and 1.67 requests/sec in this experiment. Every run of each test is observed for 60 seconds. Each test uses two different web pages, sorted-by-client, and sortedVby-server. Each test runs either page 10 times. Table 1 shows the experiment result. From the result, there is an observable difference. This experiment is conducted on a single machine server. The process time has been reduced

Table 1. Experiment Result

	Sorted-by-client		Sorted-by-server		
	Ave. time(s)	Process time(s)	Ave. time(s)	Process time(s)	Improvement
$\lambda = 8.33$	0.026	13	0.029	14.5	10.34%
$\lambda = 4.16$	0.026	6.5	0.028	7	7.14%
$\lambda = 1.67$	0.02	2	0.025	2.5	20%

to some extent. For a datacenter that is with multiple machines and load balancing mechanism, the result implies a lessening of the difference between peak and off-peak demands.

5   Conclusion

Cloud computing regards applications (or software) as a service. A cloud computing datacenter must conduct huge amount of computations in addition to traditional server tasks. The energy cost of cloud computing datacenters are therefore staggering high. Recently, researchers try to resolve the energy-hunger problem for environmental purpose, or economical purpose etc. Most of the existing proposals focus on reducing the use of energy. This paper presents a different approach that levels the peak and off-peak demands to improve energy efficiency. In this paper, the definition of energy efficiency involves different types of power generation cost, and computation time. An experiment result shows this approach improves the utilization of the generated power. The proposed mathematic model suggests that consolidating computing resources altogether into a datacenter is not always the most efficient approach.

Acknowledgements. This study is funded by the National Science Council of the Republic of China under grant NSC100-2623-E-036-004-ET.

References

1. Forrester research - marketing and strategy data (2008), http://www.forrester.com/consumerdata/overview
2. Internet world stats - world internet users and population stats (2010), http://internetworldstats.com/stats.htm
3. Nuclear energy institute - u.s. nuclear power plants (2011), http://www.nei.org/resourcesandstats/nuclear_statistics
4. Ayala, J.L., Veidenbaum, A., Lpez-Vallejo, M.: Power-aware compilation for register file energy reduction. International Journal of Parallel Programming 31, 451–467 (2003), http://dx.doi.org/10.1023/B:IJPP.0000004510.66751.2e, doi:10.1023/B:IJPP.0000004510.66751.2e

5. Barroso, L.A., Hölzle, U.: The case for energy-proportional computing. IEEE Computer 40(12), 33–37 (2007), http://doi.ieeecomputersociety.org/10.1109/MC.2007.443

6. Berl, A., Gelenbe, E., Di Girolamo, M., Giuliani, G., De Meer, H., Dang, M., Pentikousis, K.: Energy-efficient cloud computing. The Computer Journal 53(7), 1045 (2010)

7. Bianchini, R., Rajamony, R.: Power and energy management for server systems. Computer 37(11), 68–76 (2004)

8. Bunse, C., Höpfner, H., Roychoudhury, S., Mansour, E.: Choosing the best sorting algorithm for optimal energy consumption? In: Proceedings of the International Conference on Software and Data Technologies (ICSOFT), pp. 199–206 (2009)

9. Elnozahy, E., Kistler, M., Rajamony, R.: Energy-efficient server clusters. Power-Aware Computer Systems, 179–197 (2003)

10. Hamilton, J.: Cooperative expendable micro-slice servers (CEMS): low cost, low power servers for internet-scale services. In: Conference on Innovative Data Systems Research (CIDR 2009), Citeseer (January 2009)

11. Knuth, D.E.: The Art of Computer Programming, Sorting and Searching, 2nd edn., vol. 3. Addison-Wesley, Reading (1998)

12. Rusu, C., Ferreira, A., Scordino, C., Watson, A.: Energy-efficient real-time heterogeneous server clusters. In: Proceedings of the 12th IEEE Real-Time and Embedded Technology and Applications Symposium, pp. 418–428. IEEE, Los Alamitos (2006)

13. Schmidt, D., Wehn, N.: Dram power management and energy consumption: a critical assessment. In: Proceedings of the 22nd Annual Symposium on Integrated Circuits and System Design: Chip on the Dunes, SBCCI 2009, pp. 32:1–32:5. ACM, New York (2009), http://doi.acm.org/10.1145/1601896.1601937

14. Siegmund, N., Rosenmüller, M., Apel, S.: Automating energy optimization with features. In: Proceedings of the 2nd International Workshop on Feature-Oriented Software Development, FOSD 2010, pp. 2–9. ACM, New York (2010), http://doi.acm.org/10.1145/1868688.1868690

15. Skiena, S.S.: The Algorithm Design Manual, 2nd edn. Springer, Heidelberg (2008)

16. Zedlewski, J., Sobti, S., Garg, N., Zheng, F., Krishnamurthy, A., Wang, R.: Modeling hard-disk power consumption. In: Proceedings of the 2nd USENIX Conference on File and Storage Technologies, pp. 217–230. USENIX Association (2003)

17. Zhong, S., Shen, Y., Hao, F.: Tuning compiler optimization options via simulated annealing. In: Second International Conference on Future Information Technology and Management Engineering, FITME 2009, pp. 305–308 (2009)

Solving the Sensitive Itemset Hiding Problem Whilst Minimizing Side Effects on a Sanitized Database

Guanling Lee*, Yi-Chun Chen, Sheng-Lung Peng, and Jyun-Hao Lin

Department of Computer Science and Information Engineering
National Dong Hwa University, Hualien 974, Taiwan
guanling@mail.ndhu.edu.tw

Abstract. Mining frequent itemsets from huge amounts of data is an important issue in data mining, with the retrieved information often being commercially valuable. However, some sensitive itemsets have to be hidden in the database due to privacy or security concerns. This study aimed to secure sensitive information contained in patterns extracted during association-rule mining. The proposed approach successfully hides sensitive itemsets whilst minimizing the impact of the sanitization process on nonsensitive itemsets. Our approach ensures that any modification to the database is controlled according to its impact on the sanitized database. The results of simulations demonstrate the benefits of our approach.

Keywords: data mining, frequent patterns, sensitive itemsets, sanitization process.

1 Introduction

The techniques of data mining [2] have been widely used in business applications to understand the behavior of customers and support decision-making. Some companies share their data in business collaborations in order to increase leverage profitability and market share or reduce production costs. However, in a cooperative project, some of these companies may want certain strategic or private data called sensitive itemsets to not be published in the database. Therefore, before sending database to other parties, these companies would like to transform their original databases into new ones that hide the sensitive itemsets according to some specific privacy policies.

The process of hiding sensitive itemsets is called *data sanitization* [1]. Verykios *et al.* considered the problem of hiding sensitive information to be an important issue of preserving privacy when data mining [14]. The sanitization process needs to ensure that the quality of the database is preserved by minimizing the impact on nonsensitive frequent itemsets. Therefore, the problem of determining the most

---

* Corresponding author.

R.-S. Chang, T.-h. Kim, and S.-L. Peng (Eds.): SUComS 2011, CCIS 223, pp. 104–113, 2011.
© Springer-Verlag Berlin Heidelberg 2011

effective method to protect sensitive itemsets whilst not hiding nonsensitive itemsets has been considered an important issue of privacy-preserving data mining.

Oliveira and Zaïane identified the transactions containing sensitive itemsets (named as *sensitive transactions*) in order to reduce the support of sensitive itemsets [8, 9, 10]. I the literatures [15, 16], the authors set the entries to appropriate values calculated and multiplying the original transaction database by a sanitization matrix in order to avoid the forward-inference attack. In [17], Wu *et al.* classified the valid modifications for hiding sensitive rules and represents each class of the modifications by three attributes that are used to increase the number of sensitive rules and reduce the number of modified entries. Sun and Yu proposed a border-based method to track the impact of altering transactions by greedily selecting those modifications whilst minimizing the side effects [12, 13].

Menon *et al.* [7] represented a transactional database as a binary matrix and mapped each sensitive itemset and nonsensitive itemset into a proper inequality so as to transform the sanitization problem into a constraint-satisfaction problem (CSP) [5, 11]. To ensure the quality of a sanitized database, Divanis and Verykios [3] extended the result of [7] by presenting an exact methodology to identify the smallest number of candidate items for sanitization and minimize the distance (*i.e.*, the number of variant bits) between the original and sanitized databases. Similar to [3], Divanis and Verykios [4] did not decrease the support of the sensitive itemsets but extended new transactions to the database based on minimizing the effects of the nonsensitive itemsets.

Following the work of [3], the sanitization problem can be transformed into a CSP. The benefit of this approach is that the sensitive itemsets can be successfully hidden whilst still allowing the nonsensitive itemsets to be mined from the sanitized database when the corresponding CSP is feasible. However, the approach may be infeasible for many real datasets. This paper extends the idea of [3] by presenting a method for relaxing the constraints when the CSP is infeasible. The side effects on nonsensitive itemsets are minimized by considering the relationships between sensitive and nonsensitive itemsets, and thereby increasing the feasibility of the solution. The presented approach first identifies the itemsets that may result in an infeasible CSP, and then the net profit to be gained by removing the inequalities corresponding to the identified itemsets is calculated. Finally, we determine which inequalities can be removed from the CSP in order to minimize the impact on nonsensitive itemsets.

The remainder of this paper is organized as follows. Section 2 introduces the primary concepts and background of the hiding methodology. Section 3 discusses the methodology of how to relax the constraint. Section 4 presents the experimental evaluations, and conclusions are drawn in Section 5.

2   Preliminaries

2.1   Problem Definitions

Let $I = \{I_1, I_2, \ldots, I_M\}$ be a set of items. An *itemset* X is a subset of I. A transaction $T = (tid, X)$ is a 2-tuple, where *tid* indicates the transaction ID and X is a pattern, and is said to contain pattern Y iff $Y \subseteq X$. A transaction database TDB is a set of transactions. Let $\Gamma(X)$ be the set of transactions containing itemset X. Given a database D, Sup_X denotes the support of an itemset X, which is the number of transactions in D containing X (*i.e.*, $|\Gamma(X)|$). An itemset X is called *frequent* in D iff its frequency in D is at least equal to a minimum threshold $minf$. Equivalently, X is frequent in D iff $Sup_X \geq msup$, where $msup = minf \times |D|$. In general, D can be represented as a binary matrix $D = T_{n \times m}$, where n is the number of transactions and m is the number of items in D. Entry t_{ij} in D is 1 if the j_{th} item (*i.e.*, I_j) appears in the i_{th} transaction; otherwise $t_{ij} = 0$. For convenience, we use T_i to denote the i_{th} transaction of D.

To hide the sensitive frequent itemsets, the original database (D) needs to be modified into the sanitized database, D'. Side effects of the process of hiding sensitive itemsets on the sanitized database need to be minimized, and can be evaluated from two aspects: (1) the *information loss*, which is quantified as the number of nonsensitive itemsets that become infrequent in D'; and (2) the *modification degree*, which is quantified as the number of variant bits between D and D'. This paper investigates how to hide sensitive itemsets from a database whilst minimizing the information loss and modification degree in the sanitized database.

2.2   Hiding Methodology

The concept of [3] is summarized as follows. The set of frequent itemsets in D is F and the set of sensitive itemsets is SI. According to the Apriori property, if a sensitive itemset X is hidden, any super-itemset of X is also hidden from F. Therefore, the set of nonsensitive itemsets, F', can be computed by removing each sensitive itemset and its super-itemset from F. The apriori property also allows us to focus on the *positive border* of F', denoted as $B^+(F')$, which consists of all the largest itemsets in F', *i.e.*, $B^+(F) = \{X | X \in F \text{ and } \forall Y \in F, X \subsetneq Y\}$.

The basic idea of [3] is that an itemset X is frequent in D' if its number of occurrences is no smaller than $msup$, which can be stated as

$$\delta_X = \sum_{i=0}^{n} \prod_{I_j \in X} t'_{ij} \geq msup, \text{ where } t'_{i,j} = \begin{cases} 1, & \text{if } I_j \in T_i \\ 0, & \text{otherwise.} \end{cases} \tag{1}$$

Equivalently, it is infrequent if $\delta_X < msup$. Therefore, each itemset in $B^+(F')$ and SI can be transformed into a corresponding inequality to represent that it should be frequent or infrequent in D'.

However, the CSP may be infeasible in many real datasets, in which case a relaxation procedure is repeated by removing the constraint corresponding to the largest and minimum-support itemset in $B^+(F')$ until the CSP becomes feasible. Removing the constraint indicates that the corresponding itemset and some of its subsets will be infrequent in D', and we name such itemsets as victim itemsets. How to minimize the number of victim itemsets (*i.e.*, the information loss) is an important issue in the sanitization problem. Therefore, the constraint should be removed carefully to reduce the number of victim itemsets. This paper considers the relationships between itemsets of SI and $B^+(F')$ to propose a heuristic approach for determining the set of inequalities that may cause the CSP to be infeasible. A constraint selection method is also proposed to select the victim constraints that will minimize the information loss.

3   Algorithm

The proposed approach successfully hides the sensitive itemsets whilst simultaneously minimizing the impact of the sanitization process on the nonsensitive itemsets. This is achieved by considering only the itemsets in $B^+(F')$ that may result in an infeasible CSP, named as *hazardous itemsets*, and removing them according to their gaining factor in a decreasing order. The gaining factor is a value associated with a hazardous itemset that reflects the net profit to be gained by discarding it. The approach can be divided into three phases: (1) identifying the hazardous itemsets, (2) calculating the gaining factor for each hazardous itemset, and (3) repeatedly relaxing the CSP by removing the inequalities corresponding to the itemset with the largest gaining factor until the CSP become feasible.

3.1   Identification of Hazardous Itemsets

The sanitization process is designed to hide the sensitive itemsets, which means that the support of sensitive itemsets in the sanitized database must be lower than $msup$. The fewest transactions needed to be modified for hiding sensitive itemset X is $Sup_X - \lceil msup \rceil + 1$. After the modification, some nonsensitive frequent itemsets may become infrequent due to the elimination of items belonging to X from the transactions. Lemma 1 shows that only the itemsets containing at least one item belonging to X would be affected by hiding X.

Lemma 1. *For $X \in SI$, only the support of those itemsets Y where $Y \cap X \neq \emptyset$ would be decreased by hiding X.*

Proof. To decrease the support of X, some item $x \in X$ must be eliminated from $\Gamma(X)$, where $\Gamma(X)$ is the set of transactions containing X. If itemsets Y and X do not have a common item, the elimination of any item $x \in X$ from $\Gamma(X)$ cannot affect $\Gamma(Y)$. Therefore, Sup_Y cannot be decreased by eliminating x from $\Gamma(X)$. □

Our approach establishes an *affected group* labeled as AG_X for each $X \in SI$. Affected group AG_X is the group consisting of the itemsets belonging to $B^+(F')$ whose support may be decreased by hiding X (*i.e.*, affected group $AG_X = \{Y \mid Y \in B^+(F')$ and $Y \cap X \neq \emptyset\}$). It should be noted that an itemset may be affected by multiple sensitive itemsets, since it can belong to multiple affected groups. After establishing the affected groups, we determine which group is *infeasible free* (where the class label can be successfully hidden without making the elements in the group becoming infrequent). Lemma 2 is used to identify the group that is infeasible free.

Lemma 2. *Affected group AG_X is infeasible free if*

$$Sup_X - |\Gamma(X) - \bigcup_{Y \in AG_X} \Gamma(Y)| - \sum_{Y \in AG_X} |overlap_Y| < msup,$$

$$where\ overlap_Y = \Gamma(X) \cap \Gamma(Y) - \bigcup_{Y' \in AG_X\ and\ Y' \neq Y} \Gamma(Y').$$

Proof. Assume itemsets $Y_1, \ldots, Y_n$ belong to affected group AG_X. It is clear that the set of transactions that can be modified to reduce the support of X without affecting the supports of $Y_1, \ldots, Y_n$ is $\Gamma(X) - \bigcup_{Y \in AG_X} \Gamma(Y)$.

Furthermore, some transactions that overlap between X and each itemset Y_i can also be modified without affecting the support of $Y_1, \ldots, Y_n$. We denote this set of transactions as $overlap_{Y_i}$, which can be calculated as $\Gamma(X) \cap \Gamma(Y_i) - \bigcup_{j=1 \sim n, j \neq i} \Gamma(Y_j)$. That is, $overlap_{Y_i}$ contains the transactions that support X and Y_i but do not support any other itemsets belonging to affected group AG_X. Therefore, for the transactions belonging to $overlap_{Y_i}$, some item x (where $x \in X$ and $x \notin Y_i$) can be eliminated to reduce Sup_X without affecting Sup_{Y_i}.

According to the above discussion, the total number of transactions that can be safely modified to decrease Sup_X is $\Delta = |\Gamma(X) - \bigcup_{Y \in AG_X} \Gamma(Y_j)| + \sum_{Y \in AG_X} |overlap_Y|$. Then, if $Sup_X - \Delta < msup$ (*i.e.*, then X can be successfully hidden without affecting any other itemsets belonging to $B^+(F')$), affected group AG_X is infeasible free. $\square$

The groups that cannot satisfy Lemma 2 are identified as *hazardous groups*, and the itemsets therein are identified as *hazardous itemsets*. For each hazardous itemset, a gaining factor is computed to determine the net profit of discarding it.

3.2   Measuring the Gaining Factor

The number of hazardous groups to which the itemset belongs is referred to as the *relaxation degree* of discarding it in the sanitization process. The relaxation degree of an itemset Y, denoted as RD_Y, can be regarded as the largest number of hazardous groups that may become infeasible free by removing the inequality corresponding to Y from the CSP. That is, RD_Y is the greatest benefit of discarding Y. However, because $Y \in B^+(F')$, discarding Y may result in some frequent itemsets Y' (where $Y' \subseteq Y$) becoming infrequent after the sanitization process. We denote the set of itemsets that may become infrequent after removing the inequality corresponding to Y as $Dis(Y)$, where $Dis(Y) = \{Y' \mid Y' \subseteq Y$ and $\forall P \in B^+(F') - Y, Y' \subsetneq P\}$. That is, if Y' is not a sub-itemset of any itemset belonging to $B^+(F') - Y$ (except for the inequality corresponding to Y), there are no other inequalities that can guarantee that Y' is still frequent in the sanitized database. Therefore, the highest cost of discarding Y is $|Dis(Y)|$. According to the above discussion, the net profit gained from discarding Y, denoted as GF_Y, can be calculated as $RD_Y - |Dis(Y)|$, with a larger GF_Y indicating that a higher net profit might be gained by discarding Y.

3.3   Relaxation Procedure

As discussed in Section 3.2, each itemset Y in $B^+(F')$ is associated with a value of GF_Y that can be regarded as the net profit to be gained by removing the inequality corresponding to itemset Y. Therefore, we employ a greedy approach to select the victim itemset as itemset Y with the largest GF_Y. The CSP is relaxed by removing the constraint corresponding to the victim itemset. The procedure is repeated until the CSP is feasible. It should be noted that the gaining factors of the remaining itemsets may be changed after removing the victim itemset, and hence the gaining factors are recalculated after removing the itemset.

The main algorithm is shown in **Algorithm 1**. In the algorithm, the initial values of sensitive itemsets and positive border of F' are set in Lines 1 and 2, and Lines 3 to 9 iteratively remove the inequality corresponding to the itemset with the largest gaining factor from the CSP. In each iteration, the *Hazardous_Groups_Identification* procedure is called first to identify the hazardous groups. The detailed algorithm is shown in **Algorithm 2**. In the Algorithm, an affected group is created for each sensitive itemset (Lines 1-10), and Lines 11 to 22 apply Lemma 2 to identify affected groups that are infeasible free–such groups cannot be infeasible inducers and do not need to be considered in the next iteration. After identifying the hazardous groups, **Algorithm 1** executes procedure *Gaining_Factor_Calculation()* to calculate the gaining factor for each hazardous itemset. After obtaining the gaining factor for each hazardous itemset, the inequality corresponding to the itemset with the largest gaining factor is removed from the CSP (Lines 14 and 15), and the positive border is also modified by removing the itemset from the current positive border (Line 18). The iteration is repeated until the CSP is feasible.

Algorithm 1. Relaxation($SI, B^+(F')$)

1: *affective_itemsets = SI*;
2: *current_PB = $B^+(F')$*;
3: **while** the CSP is infeasible **do**
4:    Hazardous_Groups_Identification();
5:    Gaining_Factor_Calculation();
6:    Find the itemset Y with maximal GF_Y in *current_PB*;
7:    Remove the inequality corresponding to Y from the CSP;
8:    *current_PB = current_PB − {Y}*;
9: **end while**

Algorithm 2. Hazardous_Groups_identification( )

1: **for** each $X \in$ *affective_itemsets* **do**
2:    Create *affected group* AG_X;
3: **end for**
4: **for** each Y in *current_PB* **do**
5:    **for** each X in *affective_itemsets* **do**
6:       **if** $Y \cap X \neq \emptyset$ **then**
7:          $AG_X = AG_X \cup \{Y\}$;
8:       **end if**
9:    **end for**
10: **end for**
11: **for** each affected group AG_X **do**
12:    *overlap*=0;
13:    **for** each $Y \in AG_X$ **do**
14:       $overlap_Y = \Gamma(Y) \cap \Gamma(X) - \bigcup_{Y' \in AG_X \wedge Y' \neq Y} \Gamma(Y')$;
15:       $overlap = overlap + |overlap_Y|$
16:    **end for**
17:    **if** $sup_x - |\Gamma(X) - \bigcup_{Y' \in AG_X}| - overlap < msup$ **then**
18:       *affected_itemsets = affected_itemsets* $-X$;
19:    **else**
20:       Identify AG_X as *Hazardous groups*;
21:    **end if**
22: **end for**

Table 1. Experimental parameters. The ration of sensitive itemsets is the number of sensitive itemsets divides the number of frequent itemsets.

Notation	Description	Default value	Range
N	Total number of transactions	10000	-
I	Number of distinct items	100	-
LEN	Average length of a transaction	10	-
RS	Ratio of sensitive itemsets $=$ $\frac{\text{number of sensitive itemsets}}{\text{number of frequent itemsets}}$	0.0003	$0.0001478 \sim 0.0007382$

4   Experimental Results

This section describes tests of the performance of our approach, and compares it with that of the Inline algorithm proposed in [3]. *Information loss* which means that some of the non-sensitive items are hidden in D' and *Modification degree* which means that the number of variant bits between the original and the sanitized databases are used to measure the quality of D'. Both our approach and the Inline algorithm ensure that the sensitive itemsets will be successfully

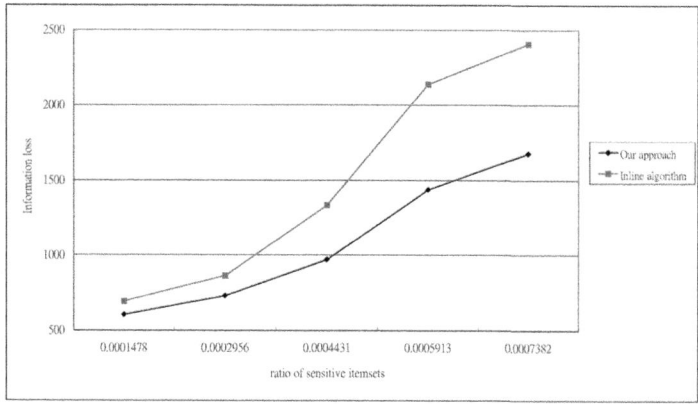

Fig. 1. Comparison of the variation in the information loss with the ratio of sensitive itemsets between our approach and the Inline algorithm

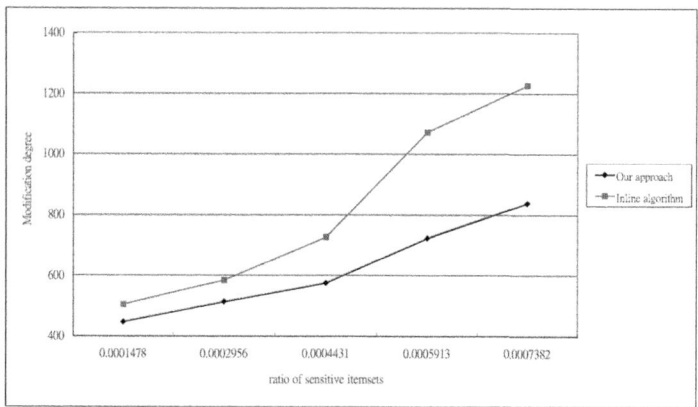

Fig. 2. Comparison of the variation in the modification degree with the ratio of sensitive itemsets between our approach and the Inline algorithm

hidden in D', and hence the hiding failure will be zero in both approaches. The test data were generated by an IBM synthetic-data generator. Table 1 lists the experimental parameters.

Fig. 1 and 2 show that the information loss and modification degree increase with the ratio of sensitive itemsets in both approaches. Our approach outperforms the Inline algorithm for both parameters since we remove the inequality carefully by considering the impact on nonsensitive itemsets, which results in fewer nonsensitive itemsets being hidden in D'. Moreover, fewer modifications are performed in D as the information loss decreases, resulting in a decreasing in the modification degree. The execution times of our algorithm and the

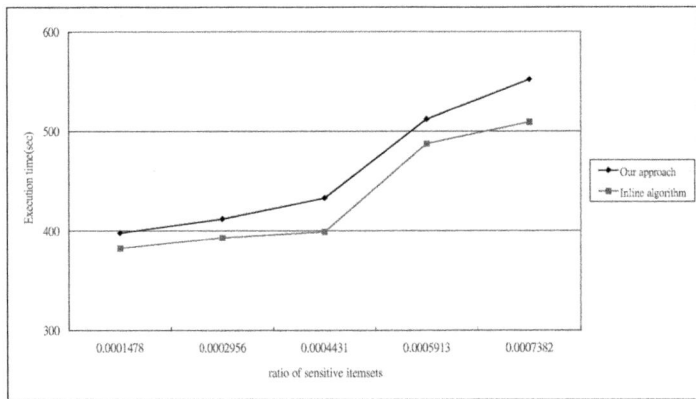

Fig. 3. Comparison of the variation in the execution time with the ratio of sensitive itemsets between our approach and the Inline algorithm

Inline algorithm are compared in Fig. 3. The focus of our approach on minimizing the side effects on the sanitized database increases the time needed to break the infeasible situation, which slightly increases the execution time.

5   Conclusion

This paper has addressed the hiding of sensitive itemsets in a database whilst minimizing the information loss and modification degree in the sanitized database. The approach involves transforming the sanitization problem into a CSP, with the side effects on the sanitized database being minimized when the CSP is infeasible. This is achieved by considering only the itemsets in $B^+(F')$ that may result in an infeasible CSP and removing the inequality according to the net profit to be gained in a decreasing order. The experimental results show that though the execution time of our approach is slightly longer than that of the Inline algorithm, the information loss and modification degree of our approach are both markedly lower than those of the Inline algorithm. This indicates that our approach preserves more nonsensitive itemsets in the sanitized database.

References

1. Atallah, M., Bertino, E., Elmagarmid, A., Ibrahim, M., Verykios, V.: Disclosure Limitation of Sensitive Rules. In: IEEE Workshop on Knowledge and Data Engineering Exchange, pp. 45–52 (1999)
2. Ayubia, S., Muyebab, M.K., Baraania, A., Keanec, J.: An Algorithm to Mine General Association Rules from Tabular Data. Information Sciences 179, 3520–3539 (2009)
3. Divanis, A.G., Verykios, V.S.: An Integer Programming Approach for Frequent Itemset Hiding. In: ACM International Conference on Information and Knowledge Management, pp. 748–757 (2006)

4. Divanis, A.G., Verykios, V.S.: Exact Knowledge Hiding Through Database Extension. IEEE Transactions on Knowledge and Data Engineering 21, 699–713 (2009)
5. Gueret, C., Prins, C., Sevaux, M.: Applications of Optimization with Xpress-MP. Dash Optimization Ltd. (2002)
6. Lee, G., Chang, C.Y., Chen, A.L.P.: Hiding Sensitive Patterns in Association Rules Mining. In: Annual International Conference on Computer Software and Applications, pp. 424–429 (2004)
7. Menon, S., Sarkar, S., Mukherjree, S.: Maximizing Accuracy of Shared Databases when Concealing Sensitive Patterns. Information Systems Research 16, 256–270 (2004)
8. Oliveira, S.R.M., Zaïane, O.R.: Privacy Preserving Frequent Itemset Mining. In: IEEE International Conference on Privacy, Security and Data Mining, pp. 43–54 (2002)
9. Oliveira, S.R.M., Zaïane, O.R.: Algorithms for Balancing Privacy and Knowledge Discovery in Association Rule Mining. In: Database Engineering and Applications Symposium, pp. 54–63 (2003)
10. Oliveira, S.R.M., Zaïane, O.R.: Protecting Sensitive Knowledge By Data Santization. In: IEEE International Conference on Data Mining, pp. 613–616 (2003)
11. Russell, S., Norvig, P.: Artificial Intelligence: A Modern Approach, 2nd edn. Prentice-Hall, Englewood Cliffs (2003)
12. Sun, X., Yu, P.S.: Hiding Sensitive Frequent Itemsets by a Border-Based Approach. Computer Science and Engineering 1, 74–97 (2007)
13. Sun, X., Yu, P.S.: A Border-Based Approach for Hiding Sensitive Frequent Itemsets. In: IEEE International Conference on Data Mining, pp. 426–433 (2005)
14. Verykios, V.S., Elmagarmid, A.K., Bertino, E., Saygin, Y., Dasseni, E.: Association Rule Hiding. IEEE Transactions on Knowledge and Data Engineering 16, 434–447 (2004)
15. Wang, E.T., Lee, G., Lin, Y.T.: A Novel Method for Protecting Sensitive Knowledge in Association Rules Mining. In: IEEE Annual International Computer Software and Applications Conference, pp. 511–516 (2005)
16. Wang, E.T., Lee, G.: An Efficient Sanitization Algorithm for Balancing Information Privacy and Knowledge Discovery in Association Patterns Mining. Data and Knowledge Engineering 65, 463–484 (2008)
17. Wu, Y.H., Chiang, C.C., Chen, A.L.P.: Hiding Sensitive Association Rules with Limited Side Effects. IEEE Transactions on Knowledge and Data Engineering 19, 29–42 (2007)

Retrofit to CAIN Issues for Critical Infrastructures

Maricel O. Balitanas, Rosslin John Robles, and Tai-hoon Kim[*]

Multimedia Engineering Department,
Hannam University
133 Ojeong-dong, Daeduk-gu,
Daejeon, Korea
maricel@hotmail.com, rosslin1@sersc.org, taihoonn@hnu.kr

Abstract. There is an increasing concern among both government officials and control systems experts about potential cyber threats to the control systems that govern critical infrastructures. The industrial control and SCADA systems that are responsible for monitoring and controlling our critical infrastructures and manufacturing processes historically have operated in isolated environments. These control systems and devices communicated with each other almost exclusively, and rarely shared information with systems outside their environment. As more components of control systems become interconnected with the outside world using IP-based standards, the probability and impact of a cyber attack will heighten. With the posted threats and listed vulnerabilities, a retrofit for these threats through the crossed cipher scheme is the main contribution of this study. To get the best of both types of cipher (symmetric and asymmetric) to address the Confidentiality, Authentication, Integrity and Non-repudiation issues in SCADA system.

Keywords: SCADA, Cryptosystem, Symmetric, Asymmetric.

1   Introduction

Major concern about cyber attack stems from the notion that the SCADA network is no longer an isolated network which prohibits outsiders from entering the network, nor is the specialized network based on private platforms and protocols, allowing only technical staffs with special knowledge to access to the resources. The reasons of claiming that the SCADA network is not a protected closed network is twofold. First, the communication architecture is more relying on the open standard communication protocols. The use of the open communication protocols renders the system more vulnerable to cyber attacks in many applications. Second, the SCADA network is moving toward being connected to corporate networks for convenience and other business reasons. Thus the SCADA network may open its doors to outsiders who can enter the corporate networks maliciously.

For the past several years a few of researches have been done on the SCADA security issues. Along with the works in the research community, the international standard bodies also have worked to derive the standard documents for the SCADA

---

[*] Corresponding author.

R.-S. Chang, T.-h. Kim, and S.-L. Peng (Eds.): SUComS 2011, CCIS 223, pp. 114–124, 2011.
© Springer-Verlag Berlin Heidelberg 2011

security. The purpose of this study is not only to define the challenges for a known isolated SCADA system, but also to organize the results that these isolated case is no longer isolated but is now vulnerable to cyber attack threats. The current results on these challenges will be summarized from the efforts of the international organization as well as research communities.

2   The SCADA Infrastructure Process

The evolution of SCADA system has been through 3 generations [11].

2.1   Monolithic: First Generation

Computing in the first generation was done with the help of Mainframe systems. When the SCADA was developed networks did not exist. Therefore the SCADA systems were without any connectivity to any other system hence were independent systems. Later on RTU vendors designed the Wide Area Networks which helped in communication with RTU. The usage of communication protocols at that time was proprietary. If the main mainframe system failed a back-up mainframe existed which was connected at the bus level hence the SCADA system of the first generation was considered redundant [11].

2.2   Distributed: Second Generation

The information between multiple stations was shared in real time through LAN and the processing was distributed between various multiple stations. The cost and size of the stations used reduced in comparison to the ones used in first generation as responsibility for a task was assigned to one station. The protocols used for the networks were still proprietary, which caused many security issues for a SCADA system that came under the eye of the hacker. Due to the proprietary nature of the protocols, the number of people who knew how secure the SCADA installation was apart from the hackers and developers is very few. Due to vested interest in keeping the issues of security quite, the security of the SCADA installation is overestimated, if security is ever under consideration [11].

2.3   Networked: Third Generation

The SCADA system used today belong to this generation, these systems instead of using a proprietary environment which is vendor controlled these systems use the open architecture system. For distributing functionality across the WAN instead of the LAN this system uses open protocols and standards. By using the open system architecture the connectivity of any peripheral device to the system like tape drives, printers, disk drives etc is very easy. The communication between the communication system and the master station is done by the WAN protocols like the Internet Protocols (IP). Since the standard protocols used and the networked SCADA systems can be accessed through the internet, the vulnerability of the system for cyber attacks increases. But by using security techniques and standard protocols it is assumed that the SCADA system receive timely updates and maintenance meaning that the standard security improvements are applicable to SCADA system [11]. Below, is a Remote Access via SCADA Service Provider.

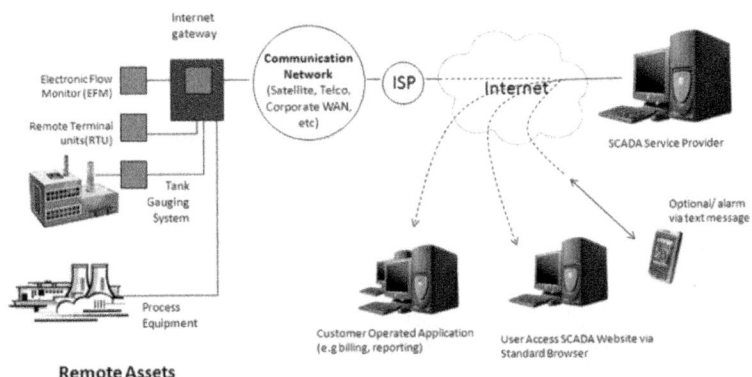

Fig. 1. Remote Access via a SCADA Service Provider [4]

The main advantage of this system is that it removes some of the cost associated with a traditional large scale SCADA system. The need for in house expertise to provide support and maintenance for the system is removed as this is all done by the SCADA Service Provider [12].

3   The Posted Problems

The complexity of modern SCADA systems leaves many vulnerabilities as well as vectors for attack. Attacks can come from many places, including indirectly through the corporate network, virtual private networks (VPN), wireless networks, and dial-up modems. Possible attack vectors on an SCADA system include:

- Backdoors and holes in network perimeter.
- Vulnerabilities in common protocols.
- Database attacks.
- Communications hijacking and 'man-in-the-middle' attacks.

All this listed attacks are threat to SCADA's Confidentiality, Authentication, Integrity and Non-repudiation aspects.

3.1   Known Attacks

2000 and 1982: Gas Pipelines in Russia (and the former Soviet Union). In 2000, the Interior Ministry of Russia reported that hackers seized temporary control of the system regulating gas flows in natural gas pipelines, although it is not publicly known if there was physical damage [6]. The former Soviet Union was victim of an attack to their gas pipeline infrastructure in 1982 when a logic bomb caused an explosion in Siberia [7].

January 2000: Maroochy Shire Sewage Spill [10]. The most well-known attack upon a SCADA system was the attack on the Maroochy Shire Council's sewage control system in Queensland, Australia. On January 2000, almost immediately after the control system for the sewage plant was installed by a contractor company, the plant experienced a series of problems. Pumps failed to start or stop when specified. Alarms failed to be reported. There were intermittent loss of communications between the control center and the pumping stations. At the beginning, the sewage system operators thought there was a leak in the pipes. Then they observed that valves were opening without being months of logging that they discovered that spoofed controllers were activating the valves. It took several more months to find the culprit: a disgruntled ex-employee of the contractor company that had installed the control system originally. The ex-employee was trying to convince the water treatment company to hire him to solve the problems he was creating.

The effect of the attacks was the flooding of the grounds of a nearby hotel, park, and river with approximately 264,000 gallons of raw sewage. In analyzing this attack, one of the insights was that cyber attacks may be unusually hard to detect (compared to physical attacks). The response to this attack was very slow; the attacker managed to launch 46 documented attacks before he was caught.

August 2005: Automobile plants and the Zotob Worm [9]. Zotob is a worm that spreads by exploiting the Microsoft Windows Plug and Play Buffer Overflow Vulnerability4. In August 2005, Zotob crashed thirteen of DaimlerChrysler's U.S. automobile manufacturing plants forcing them to remain offline for almost an hour. Plants in Illinois, Indiana, Wisconsin, Ohio, Delaware, and Michigan were also forced down. Zotob affected computers by slowing them down and causing them to continually crash and reboot. Infected Windows 2000 computers were potentially left exposed to more malicious attacks, while infected Windows XP computers can only continue to spread the worms. While the Zotob worm itself did not have a destructive payload, it left an open backdoor control channel that could allow attackers to commandeer the infected machine. The worm also added several lines of code into a machine to prevent it from accessing certain antivirus websites. Zotob and its variations also caused computer outages at heavy-equipment maker Caterpillar Inc., aircraft-maker Boeing, and several large U.S. news organizations.

4   The Scheme for CAIN Threats

4.1   Purpose of Cryptography

A cryptosystem consists of three algorithms: one for key generation, one for encryption, and one for decryption. Their application to industrial control systems may present design and operational challenges. This primer provides assistance to control systems security professionals to identify appropriate encryption techniques and determine whether to deploy a cryptosystem solution as a security feature in their specific control systems environment. This primer also presents examples of cryptosystem deployment solutions to assist users in identifying appropriate application for their specific system.

Cryptosystems have four intended goals:

- Confidentiality
- Authentication
- Integrity
- Non-repudiation

4.2   Symmetric

Symmetric-key cryptography refers to encryption methods in which both the sender and receiver share the same key.[12] With secret key cryptography, a single key is used for both encryption and decryption. As shown in Figure 5-1, the sender uses the key (or some set of rules) to encrypt the plaintext and sends the ciphertext to the receiver. The receiver applies the same key (or ruleset) to decrypt the message and retrieve the plaintext because a single key is used for both functions [13,14].

With this form of cryptography, it is obvious that the key must be known to both the sender and the receiver; that, in fact, is the secret. The biggest drawback with this approach is the distribution of the key.

Secret key cryptography schemes are generally categorized as being either stream ciphers or block ciphers.

Table 1. Summary of the Score of five replacement of DES

	Algorithm				
Category	**MARS**	**RC6**	**Rijndael**	**Serpent**	**Twofish**
General Security	3	2	2	3	3
Implementation of security	1	1	3	3	2
Software performance	2	2	3	1	1
Smart Card performance	1	1	3	3	2
Hardware performance	1	2	3	3	2
Design features	2	1	2	1	3

Stream ciphers operate on a single bit (byte or computer word) at a time and implement some form of feedback mechanism so that the key is constantly changing. A block cipher is so-called because the scheme encrypts one block of data at a time using the same key on each block. In general, the same plaintext block will always encrypt to the same ciphertext when using the same key in a block cipher whereas the same plaintext will encrypt to different ciphertext in a stream cipher.

In October 2000, NIST released the Report on the Development of the Advanced Encryption Standard (AES) that compared the five Round 2 algorithms in a number of categories. The table below summarizes the relative scores of the five schemes (1=low, 3=high): [15,16].

4.3   Asymmetric

In Asymmetric cryptography, one of the keys is designated the public key and may be advertised as widely as the owner wants. The other key is designated the private key and is never revealed to another party. This method could be also used to prove who sent a message and can address the Non-repudiation vulnerability of a system. Asymmetric cryptography is also known Public-key cryptography (PKC) which been said to be the most significant new development in cryptography in the last 300-400 years. Modern PKC was first described publicly by Stanford University professor Martin Hellman and graduate student Whitfield Diffie in 1976. Their paper described a two-key crypto system in which two parties could engage in a secure communication over a non-secure communications channel without having to share a secret key.

The significant smaller parameter used in ECC than with RSA is an advantage that can be gained from smaller parameters included in speed and smaller keys or certificates. RSA had been the mainstay of PKC for over a quarter-century. ECC, however, is emerging as a replacement in some environments because it provides similar levels of security compared to RSA but with significantly reduced key sizes. NIST use the following table to demonstrate the key size relationship between ECC and RSA.

Table 2. NIST guidelines for public-key sizes with equivalent security levels

Security (bits)	Symmetric encryption algorithm	Minimum Size (bits) of public keys		
		DSA/DH	RSA	ECC
80	Sklpjack	1024	1024	160
112	3DES	2048	2048	224
128	AES-128	3072	3072	256
192	AES-192	7680	7680	384
256	AES-256	15360	15360	512

4.4   The Integration

To this day there are lots of cryptographic schemes. A single type of cryptographic scheme is not enough with the escalating number of threats. Thus, a combination of this type of cryptographic scheme is used for this study. Each scheme is optimized for some specific application(s).

The algorithm presented here combines the best features of both symmetric and asymmetric encryption techniques. The data (plain text) that is to be transmitted is encrypted using the AES algorithm. The AES key which is used to encrypt the data is encrypted using ECC. The cipher text of the message and the cipher text of the key are then sent to the receiver.

Symmetric and asymmetric ciphers each have their own advantages and disadvantages. Symmetric ciphers are significantly faster than asymmetric ciphers, but require all parties to somehow share a secret (the key). The asymmetric algorithms allow public key infrastructures and key exchange systems, but at the cost of speed. So, in this study a combination of the best features of both symmetric and asymmetric encryption techniques is presented in the form of a crossed-cipher for SCADA system.

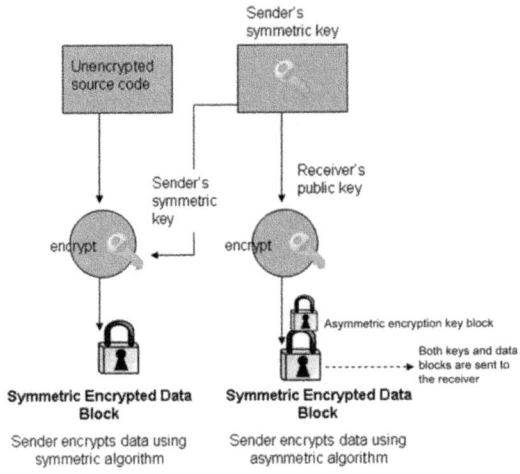

Fig. 2. Cryptography Scheme Chain of operation

5   Related Studies

Encryption fundamentally consists of scrambling a message so that its contents are not readily accessible while decryption is the reversing of that process [69]. These processes depend on particular algorithms, known as ciphers. Suitably scrambled text is known as cipher text while the original is, not surprisingly, plain text. Readability is neither a necessary nor sufficient condition for something to be plain text. The original might well not make any obvious sense when read, as would be the case, for example, if something already encrypted were being further encrypted. It's also quite possible to construct a mechanism whose output is readable text but which actually bears no relationship to the unencrypted original. A key is used in conjunction with a cipher to encrypt or decrypt text. The key might appear meaningful, as would be the case with a character string used as a password, but this transformation is irrelevant, the functionality of a key lies in its being a string of bits determining the mapping of the plain text to the cipher text.

It is desired to communicate data with high security. At present, various types of cryptographic algorithms provide high security to information on controlled networks. These algorithms are required to provide data security and users authenticity. This security protocol has been designed for security using a combination of both symmetric and asymmetric cryptographic techniques.

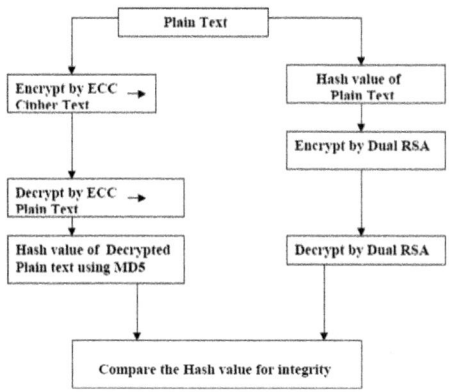

Fig. 3. Hybrid Protocol Architecture[17]

In the figure above, the Symmetric Key Cryptographic Techniques such as Elliptic Curve Cryptography and MD5 are used to achieve both the Confidentiality and Integrity. The Asymmetric Key Cryptography technique, Dual RSA used for Authentication.

Fig. 4. Cipher emulator

6   Implementation

The implementation was done using out in J2SE (Java 2, Standard Edition) v 1.4.0. J2SE has the built-in classes for AES, and MD5 Hashing. The code uses these packages and the header files have the following header. Using Java a method has been developed for elliptic curve generation, base point generation, keys (both public and private) generation and encryption and decryption. Below is the emulator used for this study [9].

6.1   Testing the Scheme

Testing the cipher scheme on a test data of various sizes, Figure 5 provides details on the time taken for encryption; decryption and calculation of MD5 message digest process. The following table depicts information on Encryption & Decryption of 128 bit AES key and MD5 message digest using ECC.

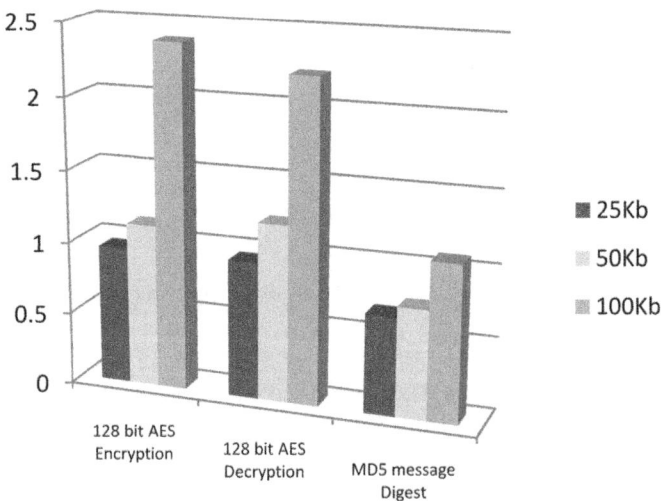

Fig. 5. Graphical analysis of AES and MD5

Since the ECC key sizes are so much shorter than comparable RSA keys, the length of the public key and private key is much shorter in elliptic curve cryptosystems. This results into faster processing times, and lower demands on memory and bandwidth. With any cryptographic system dealing with 128 bit key, the total number of combination is 2128. The time required to check all possible combinations at the rate of 50 billion keys/second is approximately 5 x 1021 years. Computational complexity for breaking the elliptic-curve cryptosystem for an elliptic curve key size of 150 bits is 3.8 x 1010 MIPS (Million Instructions Per Second years) [10] . While ECC may be relatively difficult to understand for the layman, it is nevertheless an important technology that has great potential to prosper in the future. The challenging and somewhat complicated nature of elliptic curve groups makes it harder to crack the ECC discrete logarithm problem. With less bits required to give the same security, ECC has fared favorably compared to RSA.

6.2   Comparison

Communication over the internet has impact the field of SCADA systems. It is desired to communicate data with high security. Security Attacks compromises the security and hence various Symmetric and Asymmetric cryptographic algorithms have been proposed to achieve the security services such as Authentication, Confidentiality, Integrity and Non-Repudiation. At present, various types of cryptographic algorithms provide high security to information on controlled networks. These algorithms are required to provide data security and users authenticity. To improve the strength of these security algorithms, a new security protocol for on line transaction was designed using combination of both symmetric and asymmetric cryptographic techniques in the study, DESIGN OF A NEW SECURITY PROTOCOL USING HYBRID CRYPTOGRAPHY ALGORITHMS [17]. This protocol provides three cryptographic primitives such as integrity, confidentiality and authentication. It uses Elliptic Curve Cryptography for encryption, Dual-RSA algorithm for authentication and MD-5 for integrity. This hybrid cryptography has been compared with the crossed cipher in this study.

Table 3. Comparison of Crossed-cipher and Hybrid Cryptography Algorithm

Block Size	Crossed-Cipher		Hybrid-Crypto algorithm [68]	
	Encryption	Decryption	Encryption	Decryption
10	0.951 sec	0.948 sec	1.079 sec	1.079 sec
50	1.126 sec	1.221 sec	2.040 sec	2.159 sec
100	2.38 sec	2.217 sec	4.020 sec	4.138 sec

Table 3 shows the comparison of the Crossed-Cipher as the proposed retrofit for SCADA systems CAIN threats and the Hybrid Cryptography Algorithm [17].

7   Conclusion

The move of SCADA system from proprietary technologies to more standardized and open solutions together with the increased number of connections between systems and office networks and the Internet has made system more vulnerable to attacks. The reliable function of SCADA systems in our modern infrastructure may be crucial to people. Attacks on these systems may directly or indirectly threaten public health and safety since SCADA control the sources of our daily necessities such as Oil and Gas, Air traffic and railways, Power generation and transmission, water and manufacturing.

The design and implementation of the scheme was done in Java combining the best of both symmetric (AES) and asymmetric (ECC) cryptography and to ensure integrity of the data, the MD5 hash algorithm was adopted. The design and strength of all key lengths of the AES algorithm (i.e., 128, 192 and 256) are sufficient to protect classified information up to the SECRET level. TOP SECRET information will require use of either the 192 or 256 key lengths. This symmetric cryptography AES was used along with ECC asymmetric cryptography. An important feature of these curves is that their points can be interpreted as part of a mathematical group and the challenging and somewhat complicated nature of elliptic curve groups makes it harder to crack the ECC discrete logarithm problem. With less bits required by ECC to give the same security compared to other existing asymmetric cryptography, ECC is indeed a reliable cryptographic scheme that will be important in the near future.

References

1. Ryu, D., Balitanas, M.: Security Management for Distributed Denial of Service Attack. Journal of Security Engineering 7(2) (April 2010), ISSN: 1738-7531
2. McClanahan, R.H.: SCADA AND IP: Is Network Convergence Really Here? IEEE Industry Applications Magazine (March/April 2003)
3. GAO-04-628T. Critical infrastructure protection: challenges and efforts to secure control systems. Testimony Before the Subcommittee on Technology Information Policy, Intergovernmental Relations and the Census, House Committee on Government Reform (March 30, 2004), http://www.gao.gov/new.items/d04628t.pdf
4. e-scada.com (2002), http://www.e-scada.com/why.html (viewed on October 15, 2005)
5. Bentek Systems, (n.d.), Internet and Web-based SCADA, http://www.scadalink.com/technotesIP.htm (viewed on October 15, 2005)
6. Quinn-Judge, P.: Cracks in the system. TIME Magazine (January 9, 2002)
7. Reed, T.: At the Abyss: An Insider's History of the Cold War. Presidio Press (March 2004)
8. Balitanas, M., Robles, R.J., Kim, N., Kim, T.: Crossed Crypto-scheme in WPA PSK Mode. In: BLISS 2009. IEEE CS, Edinburgh (2009) ISBN 978-0-7695-3754-5
9. Roberts, P.: Zotob, PnP Worms Slam 13 DaimlerChrysler Plants. eweek.com (August 18, 2005), http://www.eweek.com/c/a/Security/Zotob-PnP-Worms-Slam-13-DaimlerChrysler-Plants/
10. Stallings, W.: Cryptography and Network Security, 2nd edn. Prentice-Hall, Upper Saddle River
11. http://www.scadasystems.net/
12. e-scada.com (2002), http://www.e-scada.com/why.html (viewed on October 15, 2005)
13. Bauer, F.L.: Decrypted Secrets: Methods and Maxims of Cryptology, 2nd edn. Springer, New York (2002)
14. Spillman, R.J.: Classical and Contemporary Cryptology. Pearson Prentice-Hall, Upper Saddle River (2005)
15. http://csrc.nist.gov/archive/aes/
16. http://csrc.nist.gov/publications/fips/fips197/fips-197.pdf
17. Subasree, S., Sakthivel, N.K.: Design Of A New Security Protocol Using Hybrid Cryptography Algorithms. IJRRAS 2(2) (February 2010)

Performance Evaluation of BONET with PCI Express 2.0

Hide Nakayama, Kentaro Iwasawa, Chen Chi Wu, and Takuo Fugunaga[*]

AKIBSYSTEMS Inc. Taiwan
{hide,kentaro,timothy_wu,takuo}@akibsystems.com

Abstract. In this paper, the AKIBSYSTEMS presents a novel interconnect network system; the BONET system architecture, which provides sufficient bandwidth for cloud computing applications using purpose. We developed the BONET system architecture based on PCI Express (Generation 2) as network interface over Ethernet. By using PCI Express 2.0 (Generation 2), it not only improves the throughput and the latency, but also brings the power to parallel computing. The latency measurement will not be covered in this paper. Our evaluation results show that using the AKIBSYSTEMS's BONET systems can achieve significantly bandwidth performance results overall.

Keywords: BONET, Hermite, HPC.

1   Introduction

In HPC (High Performance Computing) and distributed parallel computing aspects, the bottleneck mostly appears in the network interfaces, handling data transmissions from nodes to nodes. Assume there are several computing nodes which have strong computing abilities, and these nodes have finished the designated computing data segment within a short duration. However, all of the computed data are queued in a Gbe (Giga bit Ethernet) network interface card, waiting for data transmissions. This limits the power of distributed parallel computing due to the network interface being the performance bottleneck. In BONET system, we unleash the limitation of bottleneck by providing higher bandwidth ability instead of other existing interconnect architectures. Moreover, the BONET system is fully compatible with all TCP/IP and UDP applications. In section 3, we are going to illustrate the measured bandwidth performance results on different platforms with different CPUs by using three kinds of benchmark evaluating applications. We gained over 12Gbps in AKIBSYSTEMS's HermiteI 4-lane network adapter and nearly 21Gbps in AKIBSYSTEMS's HermiteII 8-lane network adapter. The evaluation results reveal the excellent capability of BONET system, break the current network bottleneck.

2   Background

Before *PCI Express* has been adapted as a standard, PCI was widely used in PC (Personal Computer) architecture. PCI is a way to connect the peripherals such as

---

[*] Corresponding author.

R.-S. Chang, T.-h. Kim, and S.-L. Peng (Eds.): SUComS 2011, CCIS 223, pp. 125–130, 2011.
© Springer-Verlag Berlin Heidelberg 2011

sound card, network card, and video card. However, PCI has some shortcomings either. As the improvement of the power of CPU, the speed of network card and video card had gotten, the PCI still stayed in bus frequency of 33MHz or 66MHz at most, and only provides 32bits wide long instruction access. In 2002, the PCI-SIG and Arapahoe Work Group finished the 3GIO draft specification, renaming it "PCI Express" formally which its abbreviation is PCIe. The evolutions of PCI Express are described as follows.

PCI-SIG introduced PCIe 1.0a, with a data rate of 250 MB/s and a transfer data rate of 2.5 GT/s in 2003.

In 2005, PCI-SIG introduced PCIe 1.1. This was fully compatible with PCI Express 1.0a and updated some specification includes clarifications and several improvements. The data rate was still the same as PCIe 1.0a.

In 2007, PCI-SIG announced the PCI Express Base 2.0 specification. The PCIe 2.0 standard doubled the per-lane throughput from the PCIe 1.0 standard's 250 MB/s to 500 MB/s. This means a 32-lane PCI connector (x32) can support throughput up to aggregated bandwidth 16 GB/s. The base clock also doubled from 2.5GHz to 5GHz.

In addition, the PCI Express based systems I/O devices can connect to memory controller through I/O Bridge, naming as "Root Complex". PCI Express is still under development and improvement. The current PCI Express implementation is version 3.0. We are not going to describe the PCI Express them in detail. Further information can be found in [1].

2.1   BONET System

The BONET system architecture was proposed by AKIBSYSTEM in 2009. Among the current network interconnect system over Ethernet by PCIe slot, the common way to realize it is to develop chipsets which can transform the PCIe 2.0 protocol to Ethernet protocol on a specific carrier for transmission such as 1 Gigabit Ethernet and 10 Gigabit Ethernet. Therefore we; AKIBSYSTEMS think the packet transformation in both transmitting and receiving packets paths cost extra protocol transformation overhead. To eliminate such kind of overhead, we proposed a network interconnect system simply using PCIe 2.0 protocol to do the transmission instead of transforming to Ethernet or any other protocols. Compared to the 10 Gigabit Ethernet, packets which are coming from PCIe 2.0 slot through BONET system still PCIe packets. We realize the PCIe over Ethernet in BONET system without chipset managing protocol transformation. By BONET system, we can fully access the bandwidth that PCIe 2.0 brings. Further evaluations will illustrate the actual performance results in next section.

3   Performance Evaluation

3.1   Evaluating Applications

In this section, we evaluated AKIBSYSTEMS's BONET system using three different evaluation applications. First is Netperf version 2.4.5[2], which can be used to measure the bandwidth performance using different patterns in evaluating your network systems. The Netperf can not only measure the bandwidth of TCP and UDP streams but also latency of streams as well. Second is iperf 2.0.5 [3], which was developed by NLANR/DAST for finding maximal bandwidth of TCP and UDP. The latest one is NetPIPE version 3.7.1[4]. NetPIPE has several kinds of protocol evaluation tools. It can be used to measure the TCP, MPI and so on. In this paper we only focus on TCP performance by using NPtcp under NetPIPE categories. We didn't set any specific parameters while using these applications. The parameters settings of netperf, iperf and NetPIPE were almost set to default settings. Followings are the parameters and commands that we set to the applications.

1) iperf
   # iperf -c <IP address> -t 60 -i 30
2) netperf
   #netperf -H <IP address>
3) NetPIPE
   #NPtcp -h <IP address>

3.2   Prerequisites Testing Environment

Figure 1 shows the connecting method. We directly connected the client1 (CN1) and client2 (CN2) through a specific PCI Express cable. Each client equipped with AKIBSYSTEMS HermiteI 4-lane (x4) or HermiteII 8-lane (x8) network adapters. All data streams generated by the applications directly ran from peer to peer. The switch was not applied in this paper.

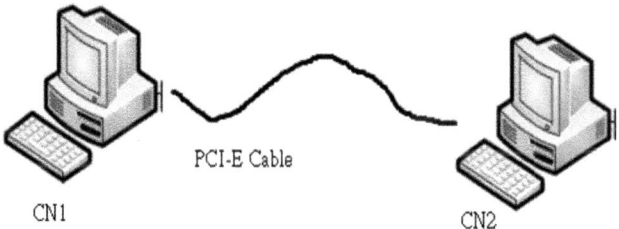

PCI-E Cable

CN1   CN2

Fig. 1. Connecting Method

Table 1 and Table2 show the detailed information about our hardware and software environment settings both.

Table 1. Hardware Environment Settings

Hardware	Type Name	Parameter
CPU	Intel Xeon 5570 2.93GHz	
Motherboard	Supermicro X8DTL-I	
Memory	DDR3 1333Mhz x 6G	
BIOS	AMI V2.0b(2010/10/25)	
BIOS Setting	IOH PCIe Max Payload Size	256

Table 2. Software Environment Settings

Software	Version	Variable
BONET Driver	0.6.3.2	mps=256, MTU=64096
OS	SLES11 64bit (SUSE)	
Kernel	2.6.27.19-5-default	

3.3   Evaluating Results

We have successfully tested a pair of HermiteI network adapter with PCI Express 4-lane width directly connecting each other and HermiteII network adapter with PCI Express 8-lane width on the same environment as described in Table 1 and Table 2. Figure 2 shows the result of NetPIPE of HermiteI and HermiteII network adapters in the testing environment described above. NetPIPE started to send from 0 byte message size to 8388611 bytes message size trying to probe the maximal bandwidth. Latency of each pattern was also measured in NetPIPE.

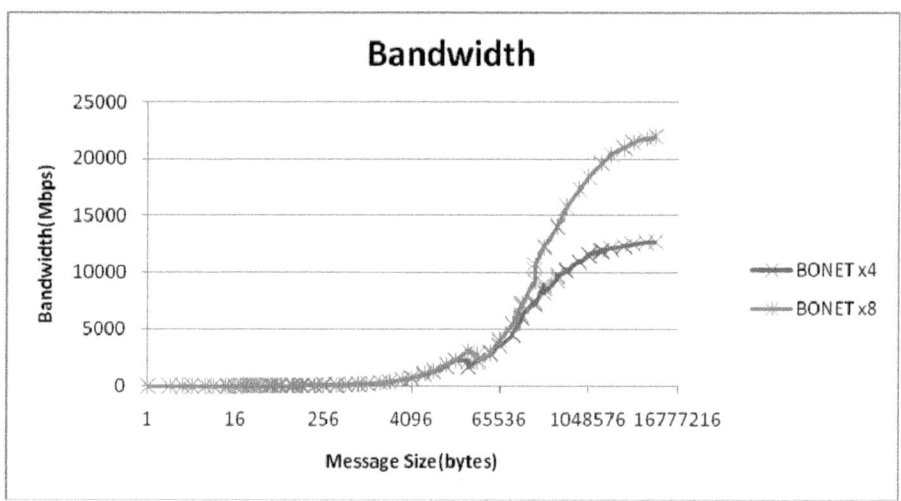

Fig. 2. NetPIPE of BONETx4(HermiteI)and BONETx8(HermiteII)

Table 3. HermiteI network adapter on Supermicro's X8DT-L

Iperf	netperf	NetPIPE
12.6Gbits/sec	12.622Gbits/sec	11.859Gbits/sec

Table 4. HermiteII network adapter on Supermicro's X8DT-L

Iperf	netperf	NetPIPE
20.4Gbits/sec	20.34751Gbits/sec	21.958Gbits/sec

In Table 3 and Table 4, we summarize the evaluation results as a list including iperf, netperf in the same testing environment like NetPIPE was in. The measured data listed in Table 3 shows that iperf and netperf have almost the same results as the measured result of NetPIPE. HermiteII network adapter delivers improved performance in bandwidth especially in large messages than HermiteI network adapter by around 66% because of HermiteII can fully use the resource of what the PCI Express brings.

Table 5. HermiteI 4-lane (x4) network adapter on different platforms

CPU Type	Motherboard	iperf Gbits/sec	netperf Gbits/sec	NetPIPE Gbits/sec
Xeon 5570	SuperX8DTL-L	12.6	12.622	11.859
E8400(2c)	Asus P5Q pro	9.22	9.21	8.75
E8400(2c)	Asus P5Q3	13.1	13.217	11.412
Core i5	Asus P7H55	12.9	12.870	11.914

Table 6. HermiteII 8-lane (x8) network adapter on different platforms

CPU Type	Motherboard	iperf Gbits/sec	netperf Gbits/sec	NetPIPE Gbits/sec
Xeon 5570	SuperX8DTL-L	20.4	20.3475	21.958
E8400(2c)	Asus P5Q pro	13.6	13.39	12.0
E8400(2c)	Asus P5Q3	17.7	17.192	14.616
Core i5	Asus P7H55	19.2	18.922	16.771

In Table 5 and Table 6 we list the collections of bandwidth performance of HermiteI network adapter with PCI Express 4-lane width and HermiteII network adapter with PCI Express 8-lane width on different platforms along with different CPUs that we have tested. We found that the ability of CPU would affect the bandwidth performance. Table 6 reveals that using Intel Xeon 5570 CPU gained better numbers than the numbers of Intel Core i5 and Intel core E8400. The Intel Xeon 5570 CPU with Supermicro's X8DTL-I has the best performance result among the evaluations. The Intel core i5 CPU has 13% improvement than the Intel core E8400. According to the experiments data, we suppose that if we apply more powerful CPU then we can achieve better performance result. By the evaluations above, the performance bottleneck is no longer be the network interface. It's depends on how strong that your CPU is.

4 Conclusions and Future Works

In this work, the AKIBSYSTEMS introduced a new interconnect network system naming "BONET" system. We applied some popular bandwidth evaluating applications for our evaluations. For large messages, the performance results showed that using HermiteII 8-lane (x8) network adapter could achieve excellent bandwidth performance. In HPC world, bandwidth is not the only factor needed to be considered.

Latency is an important factor as well. In the future, we plan to continue our evaluations seeking for low latency by using more evaluating applications. MPI over BONET system will be another interesting research aspect either.

References

1. PCI-SIG, http://www.pcisig.com/specifications/pciexpress
2. Netperf, http://www.netperf.org/netperf
3. iperf, http://sourceforge.net/projects/iperf
4. NetPIPE(Network Protocol Independent Performance Evaluator),
   http://www.scl.ameslab.gov/netpipe

Implementation of Image Watermarking Processes on Cloud Computing Environments[*]

Chao-Tung Yang, Chu-Hsing Lin[**], and Guey-Luen Chang

Department of Computer Science, Tunghai University, Taichung City 40704, Taiwan
{ctyang,chlin,g98357010}@thu.edu.tw

Abstract. With the faster Internet and data separation method were used widely and quickly, digital image watermarking becomes an important topic of intellectual property in the digital age. This paper proposes a method that can process image watermarking based on a robust method which combines the Singular Value Decomposition (SVD) and Distributed Discrete Wavelet Transformation (DDWT) over cloud computing environments. Hadoop system with the integrate functions, HDFS and MapReduce will play the key roles for this implementation.

Keywords: Hadoop, Watermarking, DDWT, SVD.

1   Introduction

Intellectual property of digital images has been a critical topic in the age of digitization. To enhance the security of digital images of large size such as those found in the National Digital Archives Program, we apply a watermarking technology [5-8-] based on DDWT [11][14] and SVD [1-2]. In order to efficiently process those digital images with large amount of data, we need high speed processors together with high throughput I/O.

DDWT with SVD as a novel digital watermarking method, in which robust watermarks is embedded into the cover image; and in this way, it can protect the ownership and also identify whether the source image is distorted. The intermediate frequency of DDWT and SVD are used to embed robust watermarks, and the spatial domain[3-5] is used to adaptively embed fragile watermarks. Results of simulation show that the proposed algorithm is very effective and can be widely used.

Hadoop, with reliable, scalable, and distributed computing characteristics, is open-source software and utilized heavily by Google. Here we take the advantage of these characteristics. HDFS[12], a distributed file system, provides high throughput access and low latency for data applications. And MapReduce[13], a software framework developed for distributed processing of vast amount of data sets on HDFS. In this paper, Hadoop is being used as a solution not only to provide the flexibility of

---

[*] This work is supported in part by the National Science Council, Taiwan R.O.C., under grants no. NSC 100-2622-E-029-008-CC3.
[**] Corresponding author.

R.-S. Chang, T.-h. Kim, and S.-L. Peng (Eds.): SUComS 2011, CCIS 223, pp. 131–140, 2011.
© Springer-Verlag Berlin Heidelberg 2011

computing ability, but also to offer a way to solve the high performance computing that needs a high throughput I/O.

This rest of the paper is organized as follows. Section 2 introduces the background for our implementation requirement. Section 3 describes the implementation details of system architecture and computing criteria. Section 4 shows the results of the experiments; and finally, Section 5 gives the conclusions and the future work.

2   Background Review

2.1   SVD, DDWT and Combined Scheme

2.1.1   Singular Value Decomposition
Singular Value Decomposition (SVD) method is based on linear algebra. Chadra [1] proposed a new digital watermark scheme using singular value decomposition in 2002 to enhance the robustness of watermark against geometric and non-geometric attacks. It is also used in image compression [2-7], watermarking technologies [8-10], signal processing fields [3-5], noise estimation [9], etc.SVD is described as follows:

- The SVD embedding process

Step 1 Input original image X (M × N) and watermark image W (P × Q), do SVD to the original image X and the watermark W to obtain:

$$X = U^x \Sigma^x V_x^T \tag{1}$$

$$W = U^w \Sigma^w V_w^T \tag{2}$$

Where Σ_x and Σ_w means the singular value of the original image X and watermark W, respectively.

Step 2 Embed the singular value of watermark into the singular value of the original image.

$$\sigma_{y_i} = \sigma_{x_i} + (\sigma_i \times \sigma_{w_i}) \tag{3}$$

Step 3 The stego-image Y is obtained by

$$Y = U_x \Sigma_Y V_x^T \tag{4}$$

- The SVD extracting process

Step 1 Input the attacked image Y', uses SVD to obtain:

$$Y' = U' \Sigma_Y' V'^T \tag{5}$$

Step 2 The singular matrix of extracted watermark is obtained as follows:

$$\Sigma_w' = \frac{(\Sigma_Y' - \Sigma_X')}{\alpha} \tag{6}$$

Step 3 Multiply the three matrices to obtain the extracted watermark $W^{'}$

$$W^{'} = U_W \, \Sigma^{'}_W \, V_W \qquad (7)$$

2.1.2   Multi-scale Distributed Discrete Wavelet Transformation (DDWT)

DDWT is based on Discrete Wavelet Transformation (DWT). As DWT is not resistant against cropping attacks, in 2006 Lin et a. [11][14] proposed the DDWT method. This approach use the multi-scaled DDWT to transform the image data from the space domain to the frequency domain, and then embed watermark information on the frequency domain. Process described as below.

- The DDWT embedding process

Step 1 Input original image $X_{M \times M}$ and watermark image $W_{N \times N}$;

Step 2 Using K-scale DDWT transform with X, where K is the number of scales and set scaling value t;

Step 3 Take the HL and LH from the K-scale DDWT transform and embed watermark into sub-band HL and LH using following equations:

The watermark extracting process

$$\text{If } W_{(i,j)} = 0; HL_{(i,j)} = t \times (2^k)^2 + HL_{(i,j)} \qquad (8)$$

$$\text{If } W_{(i,j)} = 1; LH_{(i,j)} = t \times (2^k)^2 + LH_{(i,j)} \qquad (9)$$

Step 4 Repeat step 3, until all of the watermark information were embedded;

Step 5 Do inverse DDWT to obtain the stego-image.

- The DDWT extracting process

Step 1 Input embedded image E and original image X (M × M);

Step 2 Compute the block length l of image data for a single extracting process:

$$l = \left(\frac{M}{2^{k-1}} \right) \qquad (10)$$

Step 3 Divide E and X with block length l into sub-blocks. Each image can be divided into s sub-blocks, $s = ((2^{k-1})^2)$ to obtain E_i and X_i, where $i \in \{1,2,3,\dots s\}$;

Step 4 Subtract corresponding subsections from E and X, resulting in elements of array V_i, where $i \in \{1,2,3,\dots s\}$;

Step 5 With each block of V, divide it into four square subsections with block length of (l/2). The sub-blocks are named as LL, HL, LH, and HH.

Step 6 Extract the individual pixel of the embedded watermark by equation

$$W_{(i,j)} = \begin{cases} 1, LL_{(i,j)} > 0 \quad and \quad LL_{(i,j)} > 0 \\ 0, LL_{(i,j)} > 0 \quad and \quad HL_{(i,j)} > 0 \end{cases} \qquad (11)$$

Step 7 Repeat until all of the pixels in the embedded image are processed.

2.1.3   Watermarking Scheme Combined with DDWT and SVD

Our proposed watermark scheme combines the merits of SVD and DDWT [14]. SVD will provide the robustness against geometric attacks and non-geometric attacks. DDWT will provide the robustness against cropping attacks.

- **Water marking embedding process**:

Step 1 Input the original image $X_{M \times M}$ and the watermark $W_{N \times N}$

Step 2 Apply SVD on X and W:

$$X = U_x \Sigma_x V_x^T \tag{12}$$

Step 3 Eigenvalues embedding processing:

$$\sigma_y = \sigma_x + (\sigma \times \sigma_w) \tag{13}$$

Where σ_x are eigenvalues of Σ_x, σ_w are eigenvalues of Σ_w, σ_y are eigenvalues of Σ_y.

Step 4 Use SVD to obtain Y' :

$$Y' = U_x \Sigma_y V_x^T \tag{14}$$

Step 5 Process Y', in the 3-scale DDWT then embed watermarks into sub-bands LL3 and HH3

$$If \, W(i,j)=0 \, then Y_{LL3}(i,j)=Y_{LL3}(i,j)+\alpha\,(2^k)^2 \,; \tag{15}$$

$$If \, W(i,j)=1 \, then Y_{HH3}(i,j)=Y_{HH3}(i,j)+\alpha\,(2^k)^2 \,; \tag{16}$$

Step 6 Apply inverses DDWT to obtain the stego-image Y.

- **Watermark extracting process:**

Step 1 Imports the stego-image Y, the original image X, the image Y', and the watermark W.

Step 2 Subtract Y' from Y to obtain Y_{Diff}, and apply the following equation to extract the embedded watermark

$$W_{DDWT}(i,j)=\begin{cases} 0, \, if \, Y_{DDWT}(i,j) < 0 \\ 1, \quad\quad otherwise \end{cases} \tag{17}$$

Step 3 Apply SVD on X, Y' and W to find their eigenvalues σ_{Xi}, σ_{Wi}, σ_{Yi}.

$$Y = U_Y \Sigma_Y V_Y^T \tag{18}$$

$$W = U_w \Sigma_w V_w^T \tag{19}$$

$$X = U_x \Sigma_x V_x^T \tag{20}$$

Step 4 Extract Σ_{SVD} by using equation

$$\sigma_{SVD} = \frac{\sigma_{Yi} - \sigma_{Xi}}{\alpha} \tag{21}$$

Step 5 Apply SVD to obtain the SVD watermark W_{SVD} :

$$W_{SVD} = U_W \Sigma_{SVD} V_W^T \tag{22}$$

2.2 Hadoop Infrastructure

2.2.1 HDFS
Hadoop Distributed File System (HDFS) [12] is the storage system developed by apache project and used by Hadoop applications. It creates multiple replicas of data blocks, distributes them on compute nodes and throughout a cluster for reliable, extremely and rapid computations. HDFS is created for distributed storage and commodity hardware was designed to use for distributed processing. With the above characters, HDFS is simple to expand, fault tolerant, and scalability.

HDFS has master/slave architecture. HDFS cluster included a single namenode, a master server for management the file system, and regulates files access by clients. HDFS create a file system namespace and let user data could be stored. Internally, a file split into one or more blocks and stored in a set of datanodes. The namenode response for the namespace operations of the file system, for instance, opening, closing, renaming files, directories, and determines the mapping of blocks to datanodes. The datanodes are responsible for reading and writing requests from clients of the file system. Also, the datanodes in charge of the creation, deletion, and replication which indicate from the namenode.

2.2.2 MapReduce
MapReduce is an integral part and well known for its Simplicity, applicability, and process a large set of distributed applications of Hadoop. Hadoop MapReduce [11,13] process lot amounts of data with it characters in-parallel on large clusters of commodity hardware with a reliable, fault-tolerant method. MapReduce jobs spitted the input data-set into the independent chunks, these chunks are processed by the map tasks under a parallel method. The framework sorts the maps' output, then input to the next step, reduce tasks. The input and output files of the job will be stored in HDFS, then framework will takes care the scheduling tasks, monitoring the task and re-executes the failed tasks. The cluster of storage nodes are the same with datanodes, it's means that the MapReduce framework and the HDFS are running on the same set of cluster.

3   Implementation

In this section, we introduce our system architecture and how we composed those components. The Hadoop infrastructure plays a key role in entire system. The entire system is according to official Hadoop manual. HDFS in charge of store the large data sets we need to process, offer the high throughput of data access rather than low latency. Mapreduce component in charge of the processes distributed. The master in charge of scheduling for the jobs' tasks on the slaves, and monitoring them. Our program specify (show in Figure 1) the input and output locations and supply map and reduce functions.

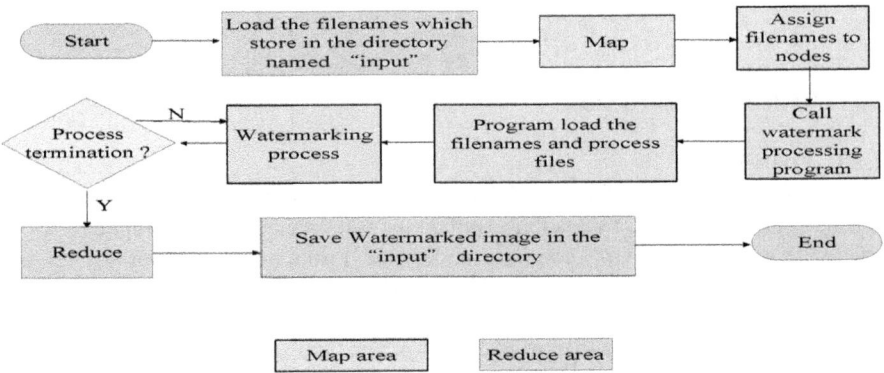

Fig. 1. Program flow

Table 1. Specification of hardware and software

Group	Node	Processor	Gflops	JAVA
Group 1	Node 1	Intel Xeon 2.0 G processor core x 4	1.22e+01	jre 1.6.0_24
	Node 2	Intel Xeon 2.0 G processor core x 4	1.23e+01	jre 1.6.0_24
	Node 3	Intel Xeon 2.0 G processor core x 4	1.22e+01	jre 1.6.0_24
	Node 4	Intel Xeon 2.0 G processor core x 4	1.24e+01	jre 1.6.0_24
Group 2	Node 5	Intel Xeon 3.2 G processor core x 2	6.37e+00	jre 1.6.0_24
	Node 6	Intel Xeon 3.2 G processor core x 2	6.32e+00	jre 1.6.0_24
Group 3	Node 7	AMD Opteron 2.8 processor core x 2	5.80e+00	jre 1.6.0_24
	Node 8	AMD Opteron 2.8 processor core x 2	5.82e+00	jre 1.6.0_24

Then the job client of Hadoop will submits the job (the JAVA program) from namenode and configure it to the jobtracker, then distributing the software to the slaves, scheduling the tasks and monitoring status of tasks, providing status and related information to the job-client. Job-client will take the job, execute the assignment and feedback to namenode. Results of each job-client will send to namenode and shown in the logs in the sub-directory named "logs" of Hadoop directory.

All the nodes were connected to Nortel ERS 8600, it offers 512 Gigabits per second backplane switch capacity. Bandwidth connectivity between hosts was 1 gigabits each Ethernet port. Different hosts get various transmission rates from 765 Mbits/sec to 924 Mbits/sec, and the average transmission rate in this HDFS cluster is 851 Mbits/sec. It means that the networking performance of the HDFS cluster was under the optimal condition.

We use 1000 images, import them to the "input" directory that will be processed by the watermarking job. The size of each image is 512x512 pixels. The proposed watermarking algorithm, DDWT combined with SVD, will be executed over Hadoop architecture, in which the watermark embedding process and extracting process are executed for eight times, each time using different number of datanodes for the performance measurement.

4   Experimental Results

4.1   Calculation with Images Distributed Evenly

This section shows the experimental result. There were two methods to measure the execution time. The first method divides the 1000 images evenly, in this way, each node will process the same numbers of image, result of time consumed will wait for the slowest host to finish job. The results are listed in Table 2. Each datanode will have a different loading, depending on how many datanodes are used. For example, if five datanodes are used, then each datanodes will have 200 image files to be processed. Table 2 shows the number of segments that each datanode must process, along with the segment size for each slaves. Obviously, If all the image were processed in a single node, it spend 2,182 minutes to finished the watermarking job, whereas the execution time for the cluster with 8 nodes was 392 minutes.

Table 2. Executing results

Node number	Loading per node (Image numbers)	Time consumed (minutes)
1	1000	2182
2	500	1003
3	333	718
4	250	523
5	200	592
6	167	525
7	143	445
8	125	392

Figure 2 shows the executing results of method 1. There is another point we generated from Figure 2. Because the result of time consumed of each calculation process will wait for the slowest host to return it's consumed time to program, when the slower one was added into the computing cluster, time consumed will increases and slope of the time-consumed line will becomes positive as Figure 2 since slower node 5 was added into computing cluster. The next experiment in section 4.2 shows how to resolve this issue.

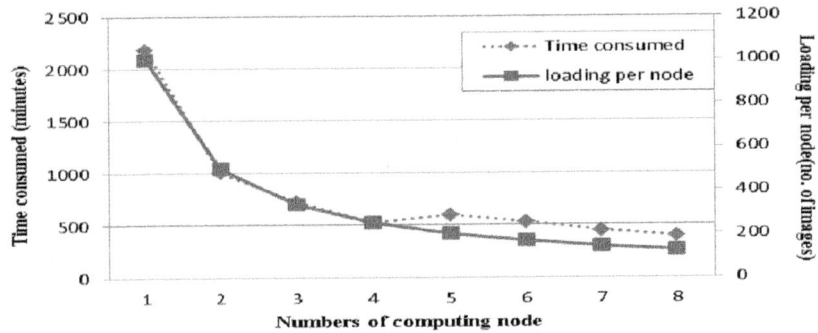

Fig. 2. Executing result chart

4.2   Calculation with Computing Ability Optimized

The second method distributes the 1000 images into different numbers to each host according to the HPC challenge benchmark, results will presents as gflops format (Please reference Table 1). Gflops or gigaflops represents a measurement in billions of floating-point operations per second (FLOPS) that a computer's microprocessor can handle. In this method that image numbers distributes by host's gflops, we optimized and sorting computing node from high to low for efficiency distribution.by their computing ability. The results are listed in Table 2. After the adjustment by gflops values generates from HPC challenge benchmark, node loading was optimized by their computing ability. Time consumed shown in Table 2 was better than Table 1 which distributed images evenly.

Obviously, in the first method, the computing group 1 (shown in Table 1, from node 1 to node 4) consumed the same period of time with second method to finish the watermarking job, whereas the best execution time for a cluster with 8 nodes is 392 minutes. From Table 2, distributed numbers of images were optimized by HPC challenge benchmark, the best execution time for a cluster with 5 nodes (shown in Table 3)will decrease from 592 minutes to 441 minutes, and the time consumed of the cluster computing with 8 nodes will decreases from 392 to 268, it means that image numbers distributed by the optimization of HPC challenge benchmark will enhances the efficiency of this implementation.

This implementation shows that when process these data with a single computer, it will consume quite a long period of time to complete this job. In the cloud environment, the impact will not be so much because all the jobs are distributed to multiple computing nodes.

From Figure 3, we deduce another interesting point, i.e., the curve of the execution time decreases slowly when the computing nodes are more than five. Due to the fact that the execution time of eight computing nodes are very close to the point of convergence, it is assumed that eight computing nodes give the optimal solution for the watermarking algorithm combining SVD with DDWT.

Table 3. Executing results

computing node	Node number	Node Loading (Image numbers)	Time consumed (minutes)
Node 3	1	1000	2182
Node 3,4	2	500	1003
Node 3,4,7	3	333	718
Node 3,4,7,8	4	250	523
Node (3,4,7,8),5	5	(221x4),116	441
Node (3,4,7,8),(5,6)	6	(198x4),(112x2)	372
Node (3,4,7,8),(5,6),2	7	(181x4),(94x2),88	301
Node (3,4,7,8),(5,6),(1,2)	8	(167x4),(79x2),(87)	268

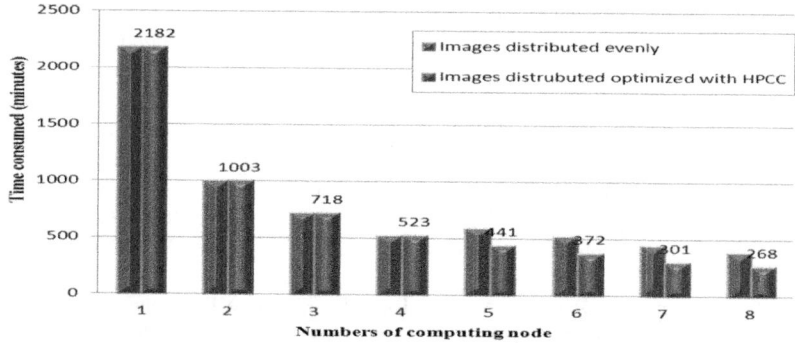

Fig. 3. Comparison chart

5   Conclusions and the Future Work

This implementation shows how to effectively process image watermarking based on a robust method which combines the Singular Value Decomposition and Distributed Discrete Wavelet Transformation over Hadoop computing environments. Through the implementation, we offer a better way to reduce the time consumed for such a heavy computing requirement.

Cloud environment is more and more popular and reliable. Issues of copyright infringement will accompany with the vast amount of personal files like pictures in Facebook or videos on YouTube. In the related social network website, the method we proposed can apply at all the digital files, such as pictures, videos, audios and also the documents in the cloud environment. Computation of digital watermarking technology over cloud environments will play a very important role for the protection of intellectual property in the age of digitalization.

Cloud environment is not only implemented for the public cloud, but also for lots of private cloud. Most of them are powered by Hadoop, which is the same cloud environment we used in this paper. In views of cost, performance and data security, business always chases on economies of scale for the balance of the lower cost, higher performance and more reliability. The proposed method and architecture will be helpful for enhancing data security in private companies, like online encryption for design drawing; and even more, be used to design a security gateway to detect if anyone trying to illegal upload the watermarked files to the Internet. So, the proposed method will play an important role in the future.

References

1. Andrews, H.C., Patterson, C.L.: Singular Value Decomposition (SVD) Image Coding. IEEE Transactions on Communications, 425–432 (1976)
2. Garguir, N.: Comparative Performance of SVD and Adaptive Cosine Transform in Coding Images. IEEE Transactions on Communications, 1230–1234 (1979)
3. Leary, D.P.O., Peleg, S.: Digital Image Compression by Outer Product Expansion. IEEE Transactions on Communications, 441–444 (1983)
4. Liu, R., Tan, T.: An SVD-based Watermarking Scheme for Protecting Rightful Ownership. IEEE Transactions on Multimedia, 121–128 (2002)
5. Tang, X., Yang, L., Yue, H., Yin, Z.: A Watermarking Algorithm Based on the SVD and Hadamard Transform. In: International Conference on Communications, Circuits and Systems, Hongkong, China, p. 877 (2005)
6. Ma, L., Li, C., Song, S.: Digital Watermarking of Spectral Images Using SVD in PCA-Transform Domain. In: IEEE International Symposium on Communications and Information Technology, Beijing, China, pp. 1489–1492 (2005)
7. Deng, T.B., Nakagawa, Y.: SVD-based Design and New Structures for Variable Fractional-delay Digital Filters. IEEE Transactions on Signal Processing, 2513–2527 (2004)
8. Redif, S., Cooper, T.: Paraunitary Filter Bank Design via a Polynomial Singular-Value Decomposition. In: IEEE International Conference on Acoustics, Speech, and Signal Processing, Quebec, Canada, pp. 613–616 (2005)
9. Karkarala, R., Ogunbona, P.O.: Signal Analysis Using a Multiresolution Form of the Singular Value Decomposition. IEEE Transactions on Image Processing, 724–735 (2001)
10. Vozalis, M.G., Margaritis, K.G.: Applying SVD on Item-Based Filtering. In: 5th International Conference on Intelligent Systems Design and Applications, Wroclad, Poland, pp. 464–469 (2005)
11. Lin, C.H., Jen, J.S., Kuo, L.C.: Distributed Discrete Wavelet Transformation for Copyright Protection. In: 7th International Workshop on Image Analysis for Multimedia Interactive Services, Incheon, Korea, pp. 53–56 (2006)
12. The Apache™ Hadoop™ project, http://hadoop.apache.org/
13. Jaliya, E., Shrideep, P., Geoffrey, F.: MapReduce for Data Intensive Scientific Analyses. In: Proceedings of the IEEE Fourth International Conference on eScience, Indianapolis, USA, pp. 277–284 (2008)
14. Lin, C.H., Liu, J.C., Shih, C.H., Lee, Y.W.: A Robust Watermark Scheme for Copyright Protection. In: Multimedia and Ubiquitous Engineering, Busan, Korea, pp. 132–137 (2008)

Uniform Disjoint Cycle Covers on a Hierarchical Multicomputer System*

Pao-Lien Lai** and Ming-Yi Chiu

Department of Computer Science and Information Engineering,
National Dong Hwa University, Shoufeng, Hualien, Taiwan 97401, R.O.C.
`baolein@mail.ndhu.edu.tw`

Abstract. The hypercube has been widely used as the interconnection network in parallel computers. The crossed cube is an variation of hypercube and preserves many of its desirable properties. The hierarchical crossed cube draws upon constructions used within the hypercube and also the crossed cube and is suitable for massively parallel systems with thousands of processors and owns many alluring features, such as symmetry and logarithmic diameter. Embedding cycles into interconnection networks is an important issue for the design of interconnection networks and cycle covering is a well-studied problem in computer science. In this paper, we propose a scheme for a variant of cycle covering problem in hierarchical crossed cubes which all cycles have the same length and each cycle contains the same number of vertices in each crossed cube. Furthermore, we obtain a lower bound for the number of uniform disjoint cycle covers in hierarchical crossed cubes.

Keywords: Interconnection networks, hierarchical crossed cube, hypercube, crossed cube, uniform disjoint cycle cover, Hamiltonian, Gray code.

1 Introduction

Hypercubes are the most well known of all interconnection networks for parallel computing, given their basic simplicity and their generally desirable topological and algorithmic properties. Thus, many practical parallel computer systems, such as Intel iPSC, the nCUBE family [11], the SGI's Origin 2000 [16], and the Connection Machine [17], employ hypercubes as their interconnection networks. The crossed cube proposed by Efe [8] is one of the most notable variations of the hypercube, but some properties of the former are superior to those of the latter. For example, the diameter of the crossed cube is almost the half that of the hypercube.

The hierarchical crossed cube [13] draws upon constructions used within the well-known hypercube and also the crossed cube. This topology is suitable for the design of massively parallel systems with thousands of processors. An interesting

---

* This work was supported in part by the National Science Council of the Republic of China under Contract NSC 99-2115-M-259-007-MY2.
** Corresponding author, Assistant Professor.

R.-S. Chang, T.-h. Kim, and S.-L. Peng (Eds.): SUComS 2011, CCIS 223, pp. 141–148, 2011.
© Springer-Verlag Berlin Heidelberg 2011

property of this network is the low vertex degree, which enhances the VLSI design and fabrication of the system. Other pleasing features include symmetry and logarithmic diameter, which imply easy and fast algorithms for communication.

A cycle structure is a fundamental network for multiprocessor systems and suitable for developing simple algorithms with low communication costs. Several efficient algorithms have been designed with respect to cycle-structures for solving a variety of algebraic problems, graph problems, and some parallel applications, such as those in image and signal processing [1,14]. To carry out a cycle-structure algorithm on a multiprocessor computer, the processes of the parallel algorithm need to be mapped to the vertices of the interconnection network in the system so any two adjacent processes in the cycle are mapped to two adjacent vertices of the network. A disjoint cycle cover of a graph G is a set of disjoint cycles which are subgraphs of G and contain all vertices of G. A targeted interconnection network possesses a disjoint cycle cover is a great benefit to efficiently execute parallel program(s).

With regard to the cycles embedding of interconnection networks, many interesting results have received much attention [3,5,6,9,10,12,15,18,20,21]. In particular, Zheng and Latifi [21] introduced the notion of the *reflected edge label sequences* and proposed a kind of codeword, termed the *generalized Gray code*. In this paper, we consider the problem of embedding a disjoint cycle cover in hierarchical crossed cubes. We adopt the concepts of reflected edge label sequences and cycle pattern in [5,21] and use them to propose an efficient algorithm for embedding a disjoint cycle cover in hierarchical crossed cubes.

The rest of this paper is organized as follows. Before introducing the heirarchical crossed cube, we present the background and definitions relating to the hypercube, the crossed cube, and the heirarchical crossed cube in Section 2 and introduce the reflected edge label sequence and the corresponding Hamiltonian cycles of the crossed cube in Section 3. Then, a constructive algorithm to generate a uniform disjoint cycle cover of a $HCC_{1,n}$ is provided in Section 4. Conclusions are given in the final section.

2   Preliminaries

We give here the basic graph-theoretic definitions relevant to this paper. The topology of an interconnection network is conveniently represented by an undirected simple graph $G = (V, E)$, where $V(G)$ and $E(G)$ are the vertex set and the edge set of G, respectively. Throughout this paper, the terms graph and network are used interchangeably. For graph terminology and notation not defined here we refer the reader to [14,19].

A walk in a graph is a finite sequence $\omega : \langle \lambda_0, e_1, \lambda_1, e_2, \lambda_2, \ldots, \lambda_{l-1}, e_l, \lambda_l \rangle$ whose terms are alternately vertices and edges so, for $1 \leq i \leq l$, the edge e_i has ends λ_{i-1} and λ_i, thus each edge e_i is immediately preceded and succeeded by the two vertices with which it is incident. In particular, a walk ω is called a path if all internal vertices, λ_i for $1 \leq i \leq l - 1$, of the walk ω are distinct. The first vertex λ_0 of ω is called its start vertex, and the vertex λ_l is termed the last vertex. Both are called end-vertices of the path ω. For simplicity, the path ω is also denoted by $\langle \lambda_0, \lambda_1, \ldots, \lambda_l \rangle$. If $\lambda_0 = \lambda_l$, then ω is called a cycle. A cycle traversing each vertex of G exactly once is a *Hamiltonian cycle*. A *disjoint cycle cover* of a graph G is a set of disjoint cycles which are subgraphs of G and contain all vertices of G. For a hierarchical graph G, a *uniform disjoint cycle cover* of G is a disjoint cycle cover satisfying all cycles have the same length and each cycle contains the same number of vertices in each component.

The n-*dimensional hypercube* Q_n is possibly the most ubiquitous interconnection network and the related research [2,4,7] is still active. Each vertex of Q_n can be distinctly labeled by a binary n-bit string and the vertex set of Q_n is $\{0,1\}^n$. There is an edge joining two vertices if and only if their labels differ in exactly one bit position. The n-*dimensional crossed cube* CQ_n is a variant of the n-dimensional hypercube. Like the n-dimensional hypercube, its vertex set is $\{0,1\}^n$. However, the definition of the edges of CQ_n is more involved.

We say that $x_1 x_0$ and $y_1 y_0$, where $x_0, x_1, y_0, y_1 \in \{0,1\}$, are *pair related* if $(x_1 x_0, y_1 y_0) \in \{(00,00),(10,10),(01,11),(11,01)\}$. The 1-dimensional crossed cube CQ_1 consists of a solitary edge. The n-dimensional crossed cube CQ_n is defined recursively and is built from two disjoint copies of an $(n-1)$-dimensional crossed cube, CQ_{n-1}^0 and CQ_{n-1}^1, where the name of any vertex in CQ_{n-1}^i is that of the corresponding vertex from CQ_{n-1} (that is, a bit-string of length $n-1$) prefixed with the bit i, for $i = 0, 1$. There are additional edges joining vertices in CQ_{n-1}^0 to vertices in CQ_{n-1}^1. The vertex $0x_{n-2}x_{n-3}\ldots x_1 x_0$ of CQ_{n-1}^0 is joined to the vertex $1y_{n-2}y_{n-3}\ldots y_1 y_0$ of CQ_{n-1}^1 if and only if

(*i*) $x_{n-2} = y_{n-2}$, if n is even;
(*ii*) $x_{2i+1}x_{2i}$ and $y_{2i+1}y_{2i}$ are pair related for all i such that $0 \leq i < \lceil \frac{n}{2} \rceil - 1$.

The *hierarchical crossed cube* $HCC_{1,n}$ has vertex set $\{0,1\}^{1+2n}$. Each vertex of $HCC_{1,n}$ is written as $(u, \mathbf{v}, \mathbf{w})$, where $u \in \{0,1\}$ and $\mathbf{v}, \mathbf{w} \in \{0,1\}^n$. The set of edges of $HCC_{1,n}$ is partitioned into 2 sets, E_{int} and E_{ext}. The set E_{int} is referred to as the set of *internal* edges, whilst the set E_{ext} is referred to as the set of *external* edges. In more detail,

$$E_{int} = \{((u, \mathbf{v}, \mathbf{w}), (u, \mathbf{v}, \mathbf{w}')) : (\mathbf{w}, \mathbf{w}') \text{ is an edge of } CQ_n\}$$

and

$$E_{ext} = \{((u, \mathbf{v}, \mathbf{w}), (\overline{u}, \mathbf{w}, \mathbf{v})) : \overline{u} = 1 - u\}.$$

In effect, $HCC_{1,n}$ is formed by taking 2^{1+n} disjoint copies of CQ_n, with $CQ_n(u, \mathbf{v})$ denoting the copy of CQ_n on the set of vertices $\{(u, \mathbf{v}, \mathbf{w}) : \mathbf{w} \in \{0,1\}^n\}$ (the edges of these copies of CQ_n form the internal edges). The vertices in these copies of CQ_n are then joined by additional edges (the external edges) whereby the vertices are partitioned into 2^{2n} sets of 2 vertices, with each set of 2 vertices joined by edges to form a copy of Q_1. Consequently, edges lie in the 'internal layer' or the 'external layer'. The graph $HCC_{1,n}$ can be visualized as in Fig. 1where the grey ovals are the copies of CQ_n and the black edges are the external edges.

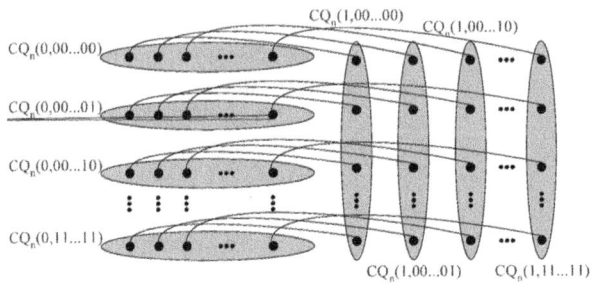

Fig. 1. Visualizing $HCC_{1,n}$

3   Hamiltonian Cycles in Crossed Cubes

For two adjacent vertices **x**,**y** (throughout the paper, bold type denotes a bit-string), the edge $(\mathbf{x}, \mathbf{y}) \in E(CQ_n)$ is labeled by i if $x_i \neq y_i$ and $x_j = y_j$ for $i + 1 \leq j \leq n - 1$, that is, **y** is the i-th dimensional neighbour (abbreviated as i-neighbour) of **x**. The edge $(\mathbf{x}, \mathbf{y})$ is also denoted by $\mathbf{x}[i]\mathbf{y}$.

A path in CQ_n might be specified by the source vertex and a sequence of labels detailing the edges to be traversed, for example, the path detailed as having the source vertex 000 and then following the edges labeled 1,2,1 (also denoted by [1,2,1]) is actually path $\langle 000, 010, 110, 100 \rangle$ (also denoted by $000[1, 2, 1]100$ or $\langle 000[1, 2, 1]100 \rangle$). Herein, a sequence $L = [d_1, d_2, \ldots, d_m]$ is termed an *edge label sequence* in CQ_n if two successive labels are not identical where $d_i \in Z_n$, $Z_n = \{0, 1, \ldots, n - 1\}$, for $1 \leq i \leq m$.

A walk, $\omega(L, \mathbf{x}) = \langle \lambda_0, \lambda_1, \lambda_2, \ldots, \lambda_m \rangle$, in CQ_n can be generated with respect to a given edge label sequence L and a given vertex **x** as follows: $\lambda_0 = \mathbf{x}$, and λ_j is the d_j-neighbour of λ_{j-1} in CQ_n where $1 \leq j \leq m$, that is, $\lambda_{j-1}[d_j]\lambda_j$ is an edge with label d_j. Thus, this walk $\omega(L, \mathbf{x})$ is also represented as $\lambda_0[L]\lambda_m$ or $\langle \lambda_0[L]\lambda_m \rangle$. In particular, the edge label sequence L is interesting when it generates a loop-free path $\omega(L, \mathbf{x})$ starting from any vertex **x** in CQ_n.

Herein, we focus on a special edge label sequence termed the reflected edge label sequence generated by a systematic method. A reflected edge label sequence of length $2^l - 1$ is generated from a permutation with l elements over on Z_n. Let $\pi_l = (d_1, d_2, \ldots, d_l)$, $1 \leq l \leq n$, be a permutation with l elements over on Z_n, and let $\pi_l(i) = (d_1, d_2, \ldots, d_i)$. The *Reflected Edge Label Sequence*, RL_{π_l} defined by π_l, is generated recursively as follows:

$$RL_{\pi_l(1)} = d_1,$$
$$RL_{\pi_l(i)} = RL_{\pi_l(i-1)}, d_i, RL_{\pi_l(i-1)}, 2 \leq i \leq l, \text{ and}$$
$$RL_{\pi_l} = RL_{\pi_l(l)}.$$

As a result, the RL_{π_l} defined by an arbitrary permutation π_l over on Z_n is a symmetry edge label sequence in CQ_n. For convenience, we use C_{π_l} to denote the specialized sequence $[RL_{\pi_l}, d_l]$ in the following; thus, C_{π_l} contains 2^l edge labels for any permutation, π_l, with l elements. We called an edge label sequence

L a *Hamiltonian cycle pattern* (HCP for short), of CQ_n if the walk $\omega(L, \mathbf{x})$ forms a Hamiltonian cycle for each vertex $\mathbf{x}$ in CQ_n. Moreover, π_n is termed a *Hamiltonian cycle pattern generator* (HCPG for short) if C_{π_n} is a HCP.

In particular, Chen et al. [5] shown that given a permutation π_n with n elements over on Z_n, the last two numbers d_{n-1} and d_n determine whether π_n can generate a HCP, C_{π_n}, of CQ_n.

Lemma 1. *[5] For $n \geq 3$, let $\pi_n = (d_1, \ldots, d_{n-1}, d_n)$ be a permutation with n elements over on Z_n. Then, π_n is a Hamiltonian cycle pattern generator of CQ_n if and only if*

(1) $min\{d_{n-1}, d_n\}$ *is odd, or*
(2) $|d_n - d_{n-1}| = 1$.

Given a HCP π_n and any vertex $\mathbf{x}$ in CQ_n, the walk $\omega(C_{\pi_n}, \mathbf{x})$ corresponds to a Hamiltonian cycle of CQ_n. Chen et al. [5] have provided a algorithm to construct several distinct Hamiltonian cycles with respect to the HCP in use so they pass through the same prescribed edge and given a lower bound for the number of Hamiltonian cycles by counting how many independent HCPGs there are in CQ_n.

Lemma 2. *[5] For $n \geq 3$ and a given edge $(\mathbf{x}, \mathbf{y})$ of CQ_n, there are at least m different Hamiltonian cycles in CQ_n passing through the edge $(\mathbf{x}, \mathbf{y})$ where $m = \frac{n^2}{4} \times (n-2)!$ if n is even; otherwise, $m = \frac{n^2-1}{4} \times (n-2)!$.*

4   Uniform Disjoint Cycle Covers in a $HCC_{1,n}$

Given a HCP π_n and any vertex $\mathbf{w}$ in CQ_n, we can construct a Hamiltonian cycle as $C = \omega(C_{\pi_n}, \mathbf{w})$. Let $\mathbf{w_0} = \mathbf{w}$ and $\mathbf{w_i}$ denote i-th vertex on C for $1 \leq i \leq 2^n - 1$. Each vertex $\mathbf{w_i}$ has two neighbours, the left neighbour is $\mathbf{w_{i-1}}$ and the right neighbour is $\mathbf{w_{i+1}}$, where "$-$" and "$+$" represent the modulo 2^n subtraction and modulo 2^n addition, respectively. For a vertex $\mathbf{x_j} = (0, \mathbf{w_0}, \mathbf{w_{2j}})$, $0 \leq j \leq 2^{n-1} - 1$, of $HCC_{1,n}$, we can construct a uniform cycle UC_j of length 2^{n+2} by Procedure $Uniform - cycle(C, j)$. In Procedure $Uniform - cycle(C, j)$, $UC_j[i]$ denotes i-th vertex on UC_j. A uniform cycle of a $HCC_{1,3}$ can be visualized as in Fig. 2where the grey ovals are the copies of CQ_n and the black edges are the external edges.

Procedure $Uniform - cycle(C, j)$
    {assume that $C = \omega(C_{\pi_n}, \mathbf{w})$.}
    {assume that $w_0 = w$ and $\mathbf{w_i}$ denotes i-th vertex on C for $1 \leq i \leq 2^n - 1$.}
    for $0 \leq k \leq 2^n - 1$ **do**
        $UC_j[4k] = (0, \mathbf{w_k}, \mathbf{w_{2j+k}})$.
        $UC_j[4k + 1] = (0, \mathbf{w_k}, \mathbf{w_{2j+k+1}})$.
        $UC_j[4k + 2] = (1, \mathbf{w_{2j+k+1}}, \mathbf{w_k})$.
        $UC_j[4k + 3] = (1, \mathbf{w_{2j+k+1}}, \mathbf{w_{k+1}})$.
    end for

$CQ_n(0,w_0)$ $CQ_n(0,w_1)$ $CQ_n(0,w_2)$ $CQ_n(0,w_3)$ $CQ_n(0,w_4)$ $CQ_n(0,w_5)$ $CQ_n(0,w_6)$ $CQ_n(0,w_7)$

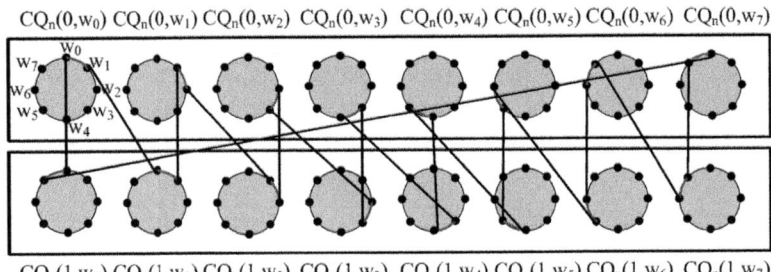

$CQ_n(1,w_0)$ $CQ_n(1,w_1)$ $CQ_n(1,w_2)$ $CQ_n(1,w_3)$ $CQ_n(1,w_4)$ $CQ_n(1,w_5)$ $CQ_n(1,w_6)$ $CQ_n(1,w_7)$

Fig. 2. Visualizing a uniform cycle of a $HCC_{1,3}$

Clearly, $UC_j[4k+1]$ are adjacent to $UC_j[4k]$ in $CQ_n(0, \mathbf{w_k})$ and adjacent to $UC_j[4k+2]$ by an external edge. Similarly, $UC_j[4k+3]$ are adjacent to $UC_j[4k+2]$ in $CQ_n(1, \mathbf{w_{k+1}})$ and adjacent to $UC_j[4(k+1)]$ if $0 \leq k \leq 2^n - 2$ or adjacent to $UC_j[0]$ if $k = 2^n - 1$ by an external edge. Since UC_j contains two vertices in each n-dimensional crossed cube, UC_j is a uniform cycle of $HCC_{1,n}$. Hence, we have Lemma 3.

Lemma 3. *Given a HCP π_n and any vertex $\mathbf{w}$ in CQ_n, Procedure $Uniform - cycle(\omega(C_{\pi_n}, \mathbf{w}), j)$, $0 \leq j \leq 2^{n-1} - 1$, can build a uniform cycle of length 2^{n+2} in $HCC_{1,n}$.*

We next prove UC_i and UC_j have no common vertices for $0 \leq i, j \leq 2^{n-1} - 1$ and $i \neq j$ as Lemma 4.

Lemma 4. *Assume that π_n is a HCP and $\mathbf{w}$ is a vertex of CQ_n, $\mathbf{w_{2i}}$ and $\mathbf{w_{2j}}$ are $2i$-th and $2j$-th vertices of $\omega(C_{\pi_n}, \mathbf{w})$, respectively, where $0 \leq i, j \leq 2^{n-1} - 1$ and $i \neq j$. Then the two uniform cycles UC_i and UC_j produced by Procedure Uniform-cycle respect to $C, \mathbf{w_{2i}}, \mathbf{w_{2j}}$ have no common vertices.*

Proof:

Let $0 \leq k, l \leq 2^n - 1$. Note, $\{UC_i[4k], UC_i[4k+1], UC_j[4l], UC_j[4l+1]\} \cap \{UC_i[4k+2], UC_i[4k+3], UC_j[4l+2], UC_j[4l+3]\} = \emptyset$. Hence, we only prove the following conditions.

Case 1: $\{UC_i[4k], UC_i[4k+1]\} \cap \{UC_j[4l], UC_j[4l+1]\} = \emptyset$.

SubCase 1.1: $UC_i[4k] \neq UC_j[4l]$ and $UC_i[4k+1] \neq UC_j[4l+1]$.

Without loss of generality, we only prove $UC_i[4k] \neq UC_j[4l]$. Note, $UC_i[4k] = (0, \mathbf{w_k}, \mathbf{w_{2i+k}})$ and $UC_j[4l] = (0, \mathbf{w_l}, \mathbf{w_{2j+l}})$. If $k \neq l$, $UC_i[4k]$ and $UC_j[4l]$ belong to $CQ_n(0, \mathbf{w_k})$ and $CQ_n(0, \mathbf{w_l})$, respectively. Clearly, $UC_i[4k] \neq UC_j[4l]$. Suppose that $k = l$. Since $0 \leq 2i, 2j \leq 2^n - 2$, the difference between $(2i + k)$ and $(2j + l)$ is not a multiple of 2^n. Hence, $UC_i[4k] \neq UC_j[4l]$.

SubCase 1.2: $UC_i[4k] \neq UC_j[4l+1]$ and $UC_i[4k+1] \neq UC_j[4l]$.

Without loss of generality, we only prove $UC_i[4k] \neq UC_j[4l+1]$. Note, $UC_i[4k] = (0, \mathbf{w_k}, \mathbf{w_{2i+k}})$ and $UC_j[4l+1] = (0, \mathbf{w_l}, \mathbf{w_{2j+l+1}})$. Suppose that $k \neq l$. $UC_i[4k] \neq UC_j[4l+1]$ since $UC_i[4k]$ and $UC_j[4l+1]$ belong to $CQ_n(0, \mathbf{w_k})$ and $CQ_n(0, \mathbf{w_l})$, respectively. Suppose that $k = l$. Since $0 \leq 2i, 2j \leq 2^n - 2$, the difference between $(2i + k)$ and $(2j + l + 1)$ is not a multiple of 2^n. That is, $UC_i[4k] \neq UC_j[4l+1]$. Hence, $\{UC_i[4k], UC_i[4k+1]\} \cap \{UC_j[4l], UC_j[4l+1]\} = \emptyset$.

Case 2: $\{UC_i[4k + 2], UC_i[4k + 3]\} \cap \{UC_j[4l + 2], UC_j[4l + 3]\} = \emptyset$.

Using the similar arguments in Case 1, we also can prove that $\{UC_i[4k + 2], UC_i[4k + 3]\} \cap \{UC_j[4l + 2], UC_j[4l + 3]\} = \emptyset$. Hence, UC_i and UC_j have no common vertices. □

Theorems 1 and 2 directly follow Lemmas 3 and 4.

Theorem 1. *Given a HCP π_n and any vertex* **w** *in CQ_n, a disjoint cycle cover can be constructed in a $HCC_{1,n}$ by Procedure Uniform-cycle.*

Theorem 2. *A $HCC_{1,n}$ can be decomposed into 2^{n-1} vertex disjoint cycles of length 2^{n+2}.*

Moreover, with respect to Lemma 2 and Theorem 1, the following result is immediately clear.

Lemma 5. *For $n \geq 3$, there are at least m different uniform disjoint cycle covers in a $HCC_{1,n}$ where $m = \frac{n^2}{4} \times (n - 2)!$ if n is even; otherwise, $m = \frac{n^2-1}{4} \times (n - 2)!$.*

5 Conclusion

In this paper, we introduce the concept of uniform disjoint cycle covers for hierarchical networks. The hierarchical crossed cube draws upon constructions used within the well-known hypercube and also the crossed cube. Herein, we extend the characterization of Hamiltonian cycles pattern from [5,21] to provide a systematic algorithm to generate uniform disjoint cycle covers for hierarchical crossed cubes. The algorithm is simple and interesting. Furthermore, it can be used in designing efficient parallel algorithms on the hierarchical crossed cube.

References

1. Akl, S.G.: Parallel Computation: Models and Methods. Prentice-Hall, Upper Saddle River (1997)
2. Bermond, J.C., Ferreira, A., Perennes, S., Peters, J.G.: Neighbourhood broadcasting in hypercubes. SIAM J. Discrete Math. 4, 823–843 (2007)
3. Chang, C.P., Sung, T.Y., Hsu, L.H.: Edge Congestion and Topological Properties of Crossed Cube. IEEE Trans. Parallel and Distributed Systems 11(1), 64–80 (2000)
4. Chen, M.S., Shin, K.G.: Processor Allocation in an n-Cube Multiprocessor Using Gray Codes. IEEE Trans. on Computers 36(12), 1,396–1,407 (1987)
5. Chen, J.C., Lai, C.J., Tsai, C.H.: A Systematic Approach for Finding Hamiltonian Cycles with a Prescribed Edge in Crossed Cubes. Proceedings of World Academy of Science: Engineering & Technology 64, 485–489 (2010)

6. Chen, Y.C., Hsu, L.H., Tan, J.J.M.: A Recursively Construction Scheme for Super Fault-Tolerant Hamiltonian Graphs. Applied Mathematics and Computation 177, 465–481 (2006)
7. Dvorak, T., Gregor, P.: Partitions of faulty hypercubes into paths with prescribed end vertices. SIAM J. Discrete Math. 4, 1,448–1,461 (2008)
8. Efe, K.: The Crossed Cube Architecture for Parallel Computing. IEEE Trans. Parallel and Distributed Systems 3(5), 513–524 (1992)
9. Fan, J., Lin, X., Jia, X.: Node-pancyclicity and edge-pancyclicity of Crossed cubes. Information Processing Letters 93, 133–138 (2005)
10. Fan, J., Jia, X., Lin, X.: Embedding of cycles in twisted cubes with edge-pancyclic. Algorithmica 3, 264–282 (2008)
11. Hayes, J.P., Mudge, T.N.: Hypercube supercomputer. Proc. IEEE 17, 1829–1841 (1989)
12. Kueng, T.L., Lin, C.K., Liang, T., Tan, J.J.M., Hsu, L.H.: Fault-tolerant Hamiltonian connectedness of cycle composition networks. Applied Mathematics and Computation 196, 245–256 (2008)
13. Lai, P.L., Hsu, H.C., Tsai, C.H., Stewart, I.A.: A class of hierarchical graphs as topologies for interconnection networksstar. Theoretical Computer Science 411(31-33), 2,912–2,924 (2010)
14. Leighton, F.T.: Introduction to Parallel Algorithms and Architectures: arrays, trees, hypercubes. Morgan Kaufman, San Mateo (1992)
15. Li, Y., Peng, S., Chu, W.: Hamiltonian cycle embedding for fault tolerance in dual-cube. In: The IASTED International Conference on Networks, Parallel and Distributed Processing, and Applications, pp. 1–6 (2002)
16. SGI: Origin2000 Rackmount Ower's Guide, 007-3456-003 (1997), http://techpubs.sgi.com/
17. Tucker, L.W., Robertson, G.G.: Architecture and applications of the connection machine. IEEE Computer 21, 26–38 (1988)
18. Wang, D.: On Embedding Hamiltonian Cycles in Crossed Cubes. IEEE Trans. Parallel and Distributed Systems 19(3), 334–346 (2008)
19. Xu, J.: Topological Structure and Analysis of Interconnection Networks. Kluwer, Dordrecht (2001)
20. Yang, M.C., Li, T.K., Tan, J.M., Hsu, L.H.: Fault-tolerant Cycle-embedding of Crossed Cubes. Information Processing Letters 88, 149–154 (2003)
21. Zheng, S.Q., Latifi, S.: Optimal Simulation of Linear Multiprocessor Architectures on Multiply-Twisted Cube Using Generalized Gray Code. IEEE Trans. Parallel and Distributed Systems 7(6), 612–619 (1996)

The Performance Impact of Different Master Nodes on Parallel Loop Self-scheduling Schemes for Rule-Based Expert Systems

Chao-Chin Wu[1], Lien-Fu Lai[1], Liang-Tsung Huang[2],
Chao-Tung Yang[3], and Chung Lu[1]

[1] Department of Computer Science and Information Engineering National Changhua
University of Education, Taiwan
{ccwu,lflai}@cc.ncue.edu.tw, m98612005@mail.ncue.edu.tw
[2] Department of Biotechnology, MingDao University, Taiwan
larry@mdu.edu.tw
[3] Department of Computer Science and Information Engineering, Tunghai University

Abstract. The technique of parallel loop self-scheduling has been successfully applied to auto-parallelize rule-based expert systems previously. In a heterogeneous system, different compute nodes have different computer powers. Therefore, we have to choose a node to run the master process before running an application. In this paper, we focus on how different master nodes influence the performances of different self-scheduling schemes. In addition, we will investigate how the file system influences the performance. Experimental results give users the good guidelines on how to choose the master node, the self-scheduling scheme, and the file system for storing the results.

Keywords: Parallel computing, cluster system, heterogeneous system, self scheduling, file system.

1 Introduction

A cluster system consists of multiple computers connected by network; it divides a big task into lots of small tasks and has them processed by different computers in parallel. Now most cluster systems use Local Area Network and Ethernet to connect computers, which are often cheap personal computers rather than expensive workstations. Thus, such cluster systems have a better cost-performance ratio.

Traditional cluster systems are homogeneous ones. In this kind of system, all compute nodes own identical system resources, including network bandwidth, I/O storage equipments, CPU clock speed, memory capacity, etc. On the other hand, a cluster system consisting of compute nodes with distinct system resources is called a heterogeneous cluster system. To this kind of cluster, assigning equal amount of work to each computing nodes is not proper. Nodes with better performance take less time to complete their jobs than those with weaker performance. The need of synchronization or data transmission would then have some nodes be idle and wait for

R.-S. Chang, T.-h. Kim, and S.-L. Peng (Eds.): SUComS 2011, CCIS 223, pp. 149–158, 2011.
© Springer-Verlag Berlin Heidelberg 2011

others to finish their jobs; the performance of the whole system deteriorates. Therefore, Load Balancing, to properly dispatch works to each node to achieve best system performance, becomes a significant issue to heterogeneous cluster systems.

MapReduce is one of the frequent referred technologies for cloud computing, which is a programming model introduced by Google Inc. for processing and generating large data sets [1]. Programmers use map and reduce functions to process data and merge results. Programs written based on the MapReduce model are automatically parallelized and executed on a large cluster of commodity machines. Data partitioning, task scheduling and inter-process communication are all handled by the run-time system. Programmers have no need to learn the complicated techniques for parallel computation for efficient resource utilization in a large distributed system.

We have proposed a method that can be easily parallelize FuzzyCLIPS-based expert system based on the MapReduce programming model [2, 3, 4]. The programmer only has to use our proposed directives to specify which facts can be parallelized, how to infer these facts, which inferred results should be sent back to the master and which rule has to be applied to infer the returned results. The modified inference engine will use a conventional well-known self-scheduling scheme to parallelize the inference. However, none of conventional scheduling schemes consider the matching feature of FuzzyCLIPS language. The unique feature of the matching of facts and rules for FuzzyCLIPS language is that allocating too many or too few data facts in a chunk cannot have the best processing efficiency. We use the feature to design a self-scheduling scheme especially for parallel FuzzyCLIPS-based expert systems. In addition to load balancing, the proposed self-scheduling scheme takes the processing efficiency into account and gives it the higher priority. The proposed $PC^{SL}SS$ scheme relies on a finite state machine to learn the proper chunk size for each worker node.

In a heterogeneous cluster system, different compute node has different compute power. Therefore, in this paper we investigate how different master compute node influence the execution time of applications. To alleviate the burden of the master node when the weak node is adopted, every worker node can writes the results of their allocated tasks directly to the output file via Network File System (NFS). Therefore, we also study how the performance is affected if every work node help write the results to the output file. Experimental results give the users and the system resources brokers a good guidance of how to select compute nodes from a heterogeneous cluster system.

2 Related Work

A parallel loop is a loop having no cross-iteration data dependencies. If a parallel loop has N iterations, it can be executed at most by N processors in parallel without any interaction among processors. However, because the number of available processors in a system is always much smaller than N, each processor has to execute more than one loop iteration. Static scheduling schemes decide how many loop iterations are assigned for each processor at compile time. The advantage of this kind of scheduling schemes is no scheduling overhead at runtime. However, it is hard to estimate the computation power of every processor in the heterogeneous computing system and to predict the amount of time each iteration takes for irregular programs, resulting in load imbalance usually. Dynamic scheduling is more suitable for load balance because it makes scheduling decisions at runtime. No estimations and predictions are required. Various self-scheduling schemes have been proposed to achieve better load balance with less scheduling overhead.

Chunk self-scheduling (CSS) assigns k consecutive iterations each time [5]. The chunk size, k, is fixed and must be specified by either the programmer or by the compiler. A large chunk size will cause load imbalance because the maximum waiting time for the last processor is the execution time of k loop iterations. In contrast, a small chunk size is likely to result in too much scheduling overhead. If k is equal to 1, CSS will be degraded to PSS. Thus, it is important to choose the proper chunk size.

Guided self-scheduling (GSS) assigns decreasing-sized chunks for requests [5]. Initially, the master allocates large chunks to workers and later uses the smaller chunks to smoothen the unevenness of the execution times of the initial larger chunks. More specifically, the next chunk size is calculated by dividing the number of the remaining iterations by the number of available processors. It aims at reducing the dispatch frequency to minimize the scheduling overhead and reducing the number of iterations assigned to the last few processors to achieve better load balancing.

Factoring Self-Scheduling (FSS) assigns loop iterations to processors in phases [5]. It tries to address the following problem of GSS. Because GSS might assign too much work to the first few processors in some cases, the remaining iterations are not time-consuming enough to balance the workload. During each phase of FSS, only a subset of remaining loop iterations (usually half) is equally distributed to available processors. FSS can prevent from assigning too much workload to the first few processors like GSS does. As a result, it balances workloads better than GSS when loop iteration computation times vary substantially.

Trapezoid Self-Scheduling (TSS) reduces the scheduling frequency while still providing reasonable load balancing [5]. The chunk sizes decrease linearly in TSS, in contrast to the geometric decrease of the chunk sizes in GSS. A TSS is represented by $TSS(N_s, N_f)$, where N_s is the number of the first iterations to be assigned to the processor starting the loop and N_f is the number of the last iterations to be assigned to the processor performing the last fetch. The two parameters, N_s and N_f, have to be specified in TSS either by the programmer or by the compiler. According to the values of N_s and N_f, the number of iterations to be assigned at each step is decreased in a constant ratio. Tzen and Ni have proposed $TSS(N/2p, 1)$ as a general selection, where N is the number of iterations and p is the number of processors.

3   Parallel FuzzyCLIPS

FuzzyCLIPS is an extended version of CLIPS (C Language Integrated Production System) [6] that is a tool for helping the developer to design the expert system. FuzzyCLIPS extends CLIPS by adding the concept of fuzzy logic, i.e. fuzziness and uncertainty. The extension let the FuzzyCLIPS inference engine be able to do the inference with the facts and rules with fuzzy expressions. Due to the rule-based characteristics of CLIPS, it makes the execution very time-consuming.

We proposed a SPMD-based programming model that hides message passing subroutine calls from the programmers [2, 3]. In other words, there are no Send or Recv function calls needed in the parallel code of a fuzzyCLIPS expert system. Instead, several simple directives are employed for parallelization. The programmers only have to identify the following information. (1) Which facts will be processed by worker processes in parallel? These facts are called the parallel facts and they will be stored in the input files. (2) Which rules will be applied to the parallel facts? These rules are called the mapping rules. (3) What kinds of facts should be sent back after each worker process finishes its work? These facts are called the intermediate facts. (4) Which rules the master process has to apply to the intermediate facts returned from worker processes? These rules are called the reduce rules.

The execution of a parallel FuzzyCLIPS program consists of the following four steps. (1) A master process and multiple worker processes will be created. The master process tells each worker process about the information about the assigned facts. The allocation is based on one of well-known self-scheduling schemes. (2) Each worker process reads assigned parallel facts from the input file and the uses the map-ping rules to match with these facts. (3) The intermediate facts are sent back to the master process by each worker process. (4) The master process matches the intermediate facts with the reduce rules and write the result to the output files.

We also proposed a self-scheduling scheme called $PC^{SL}SS$ especially for parallel FuzzyCLIPS-based expert systems [2]. In addition to load balancing, we also focus on the processing efficiency when designing a self-scheduling scheme. Furthermore, the processing efficiency plays more important role than load balancing in our design. In this way, the system can have better performance. In order to make each worker having better processing efficiency, the PCSLSS scheme was designed based on the following strategy. When the worker's performance with current chunk size is better than that with previous chunk size, the next assigned chunk size for this worker is increased, otherwise decreased. However, the adjustment of the chunk size is different depending on whether the worker has adequate workload or not.

In a heterogeneous cluster system, different compute node has different compute power. Consequently, which compute node acts as the master node might influence the application performance. We will investigate the issue in the next section.

4   The Impact of Different Master Node

We have constructed a cluster system with the configuration shown in Table 1 to evaluate how different master node influences the application performance. The cluster system consists of 16 compute nodes and 48 processor cores. The compute nodes are partitioned into five types and each type is labeled in Table 1.

In the cluster system, some of the compute nodes are multicore architecture and some are single-core architecture. To figure out how much performance difference between any two processor cores in different compute nodes, the compute power of each processor core in a compute node is normalized to the slowest processor core in the system, as shown in Fig. 1. The compute power of Type 1 compute nodes is 11.13 times than that of Type 5 compute node.

Table 1. The cluster configuration

Type 1: Intel Core Quad (2 Quad-core PCs)	
CPU	Intel Core 2 Quad-Core Q6600, 2394MHz
Cores	4
Memory	2048MB DDR2-553 × 1
Swap	2048
HD	SATA 160GB
OS	Slackware 12.1, kernel 2.6.24.smp
Type 2: AMD Quad-Core (8 Quad-core PCs)	
CPU	Phenom™ 9850 Quad-Core, 2499MHz
Cores	4
Memory	1024MB DDR2-533×1
Swap	1024
HD	SATA 300G
OS	Slackware 13.0, kernel 2.6.29.6.smp
Type 3: Intel Core Duo (2 Duo-core PCs)	
CPU	Inter Core 2 Duo E2160, 1809Mhz
Cores	2
Memory	512MB DDR2-667 × 1
Swap	1024 MB
HD	SATA 80GB
OS	CentOS 4.4, kernel 2.6.9-42.ELsmp
Type 4: AMD Athlon XP (3 single-core PCs)	
CPU	AMD Athlon XP 2800+, 2083MHz
Cores	1
Memory	256 MB DDR400 × 1
Swap	2048
HD	SATA 80G
OS	Slackware 12.0, kernel 2.6.21.5.smp
Type 5: AMD Athlon XP (1 single-core PCs)	
CPU	AMD Athlon XP 2800+, 1243MHz
Cores	1
Memory	256 MB DDR400 × 1
Swap	2048
HD	SATA 80G
OS	Slackware 12.0, kernel 2.6.21.5.smp

A human resources website has been implemented to evaluate the performance. Because users' query requirements are usually imprecise and uncertain, instead of matching the input phrases with the records in the database, the search engine uses fuzzy logic to find the records with different levels of fitness. The core of the human resources website is implemented by FuzzyCLIPS language and parallelized by our proposed method.

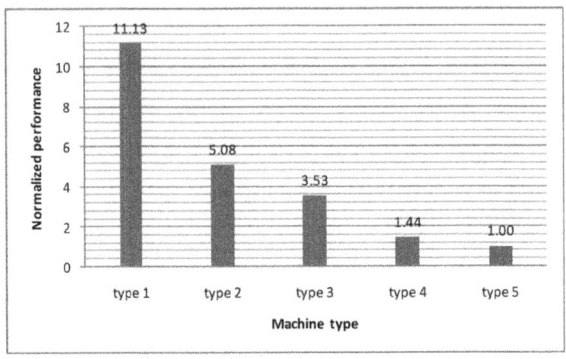

Fig. 1. The execution times normalized to Type-5 processor core

First, we evaluate the impact of different master compute node when we use five processor cores to run the application in parallel, as shown in Fig. 2. We select one processor core from each type of compute nodes and let each different processor core take turns running the master process. Fig. 2 shows that CSS(50), meaning CSS with the chunk size of 50, has the shortest execution time no matter which processor core runs the master process. The second best self-scheduling scheme is TSS, the third is GSS, and the last is FSS. The reason that GSS and FSS have poor performances is the chunk size is so large at the beginning of scheduling that the weakest processor core becomes the performance bottleneck if it is assigned a huge chunk of tasks. The situation is much severer if a fast processor core is responsible for running the master process because the fast processor core cannot help process the tasks. On the contrary, if a weak processor core runs the master process, fast compute nodes can accelerate the processing of tasks even though they are assigned large chunk of tasks, resulting in better performance.

Next, we evaluate the impact of different master compute node when we use eight processor cores to run the application in parallel, as shown in Fig. 3. Among the eight processor cores, at least one processor core from each type of compute nodes is selected. Each different type of processor core takes turns running the master process. Fig. 3 shows that CSS(50) still has the shortest execution time if Type-4 compute node is not selected to runs the master process. More importantly, it is better to choose a fast processor core to run the master processor because it can have better performance. When there are more processor cores to run the same application, the master process becomes busier because of more task requests from worker nodes. As for the performance ranking of the four kinds of self-scheduling schemes, both the cases of five-process and eight-process have almost the same results. However, it is hard to tell which kind of processor cores plays the role of the master can provide better performance. In particular, for GSS and FSS, the performance is more unpredictable because we cannot make sure if the weakest processor core will be assigned the largest chunk of tasks and then become the performance bottleneck. In other words, the request message from the weakest processor core might be the first one arriving at the master process.

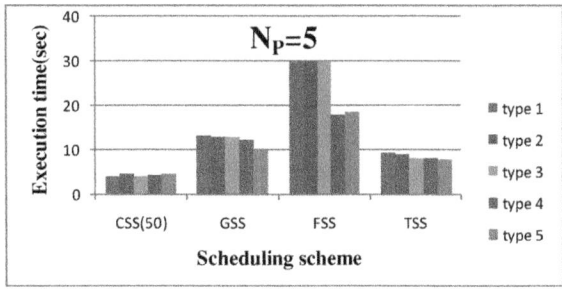

Fig. 2. The impact of different master processor core when the total number of cores is 5

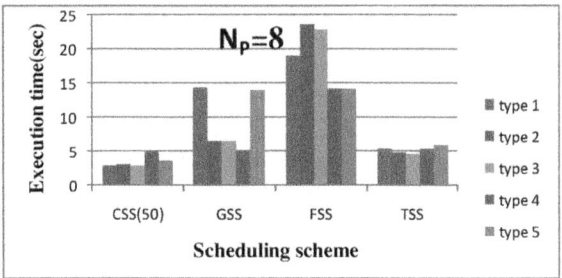

Fig. 3. The impact of different master processor core when the total number of cores is 8

When the total number of processor cores for running the same application in parallel becomes as large as 16, as shown in Fig. 4, the more powerful the master processor core is, the better the performance we have. The exceptions happen in two cases: when Type-1 processor core is adopted as the master core in GSS and FSS. However, when the total number of processor cores becomes as large as 32 or 48, as shown in Fig. 5 and Fig. 6, we can always have the best performance if the fastest processor core is chosen to run the master process. The only issue is which self-scheduling scheme can provide the best performance. For the application of human resources Website, CSS(50) can provide the best performance.

Since CSS(50) provides the best performance, we will investigate how much performance improvement CSS(50) can provide when different type of processor core is adopted as the master core and when the total number of processor core is increased, as shown in Fig. 7. For each specific total number of processor cores used to run the application in parallel, the execution time when each different type of processor core acts as the master core is normalized to the execution time when Type-5 processor core behaves as the master core. The impact of different master processor cores on the performance is increased when the total number of processor cores becomes larger. Although the compute power of Type-1 processor core is 11.13 times faster than Type 5, the performance improvement provided by Type 1 over Type 5 is as high as 2.9. Because the performance difference is very large, it is recommended to adopt the fastest processor core to be the master core, especially for the case when there are many worker nodes.

When an application needs many cores for its parallel execution, we have different core selection methods. For instance, if we need four cores, we can choose the four cores from the same compute node, or two cores from one node and two cores from the other node. To evaluate the impact of different core selection methods, we conduct the following experiment. We need 16 cores and they are from five types of nodes, where four cores are Type 1. For the configuration of one node, the four Type-1 cores are all form the same node while for the configuration of tow nodes, the four Type-1 cores are form two Type-1 nodes. Experimental result shows the configuration of two nodes is better and has speedup of 1.28. The reason is that each processor core can be allocated more system resources.

Because the compute power of the master core will influence the performance when the total number of cores is small, we are interested in whether we can alleviate the burden of the weak master processor cores by letting each worker node write the results of their allocated tasks directly to the output file via NFS. Fig. 8 shows the results when each worker nodes writes the results directly to the output file. Comparing the results with previous results shown in Fig. 3 to Fig. 6, letting worker nodes write results via NFS is not a good solution even though the total number of cores is small. Furthermore, how the master core influences the performance is not so regular. Adopting a weak core rather than a strong core to be the master core is better for GSS and FSS.

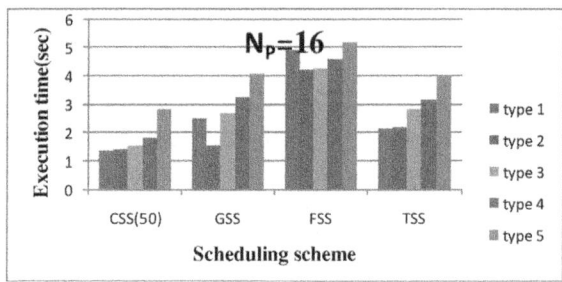

Fig. 4. The impact of different master processor core when the total number of cores is 16

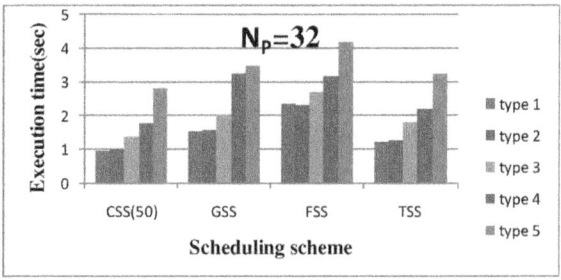

Fig. 5. The impact of different master processor core when the total number of cores is 32

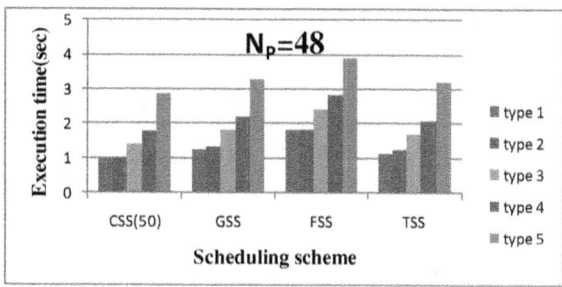

Fig. 6. The impact of different master processor core when the total number of cores is 48

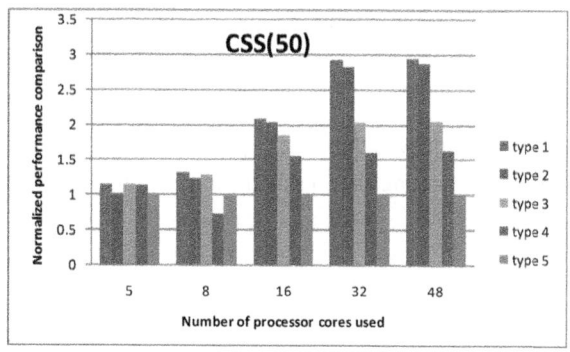

Fig. 7. Normalized performance comparison for different number of processor cores for CSS

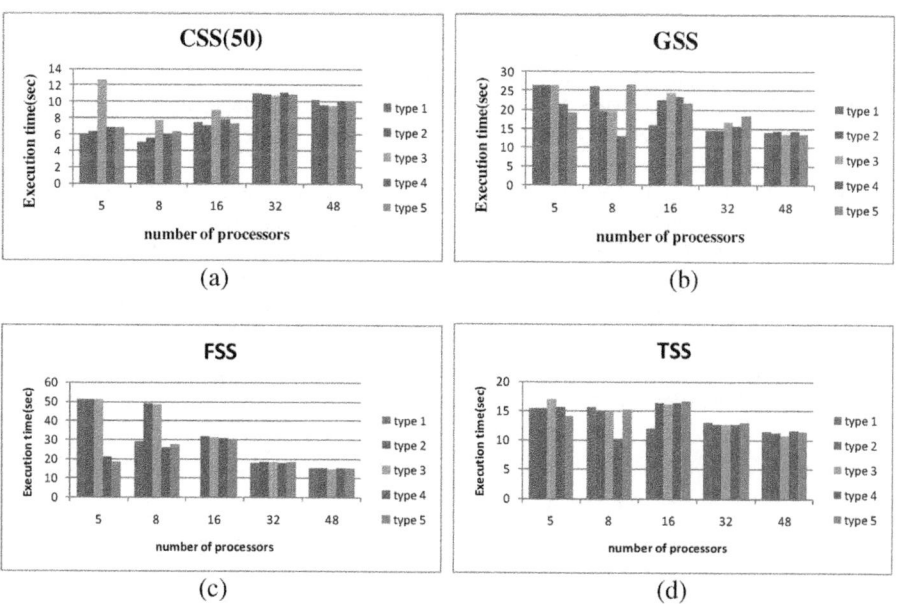

Fig. 8. The impact of different master processor core when each work writes results via NFS

5   Conclusions

In this paper, we study how different master cores influence application performance. When we need a large number of cores, a stronger master core always lead to better performance. On the other hand, if we need a small number of cores, adopting more powerful master nodes is recommended for only CSS and TSS. However, CSS is always the best choice for these two cases. Furthermore, if we need several processor cores of the same type, it is recommended to choose them from different compute nodes because each processor core can be allocated more system resources. Finally, it is better to let the master core be the only one writing the results to its local output file. Although allow each worker node to write their responsible results to the output file via NFS helps alleviate the burden of the master core, the performance is worsen because of write contention to the NFS. Experimental results give the users and the system resources brokers a good guidance of how to select compute nodes from a heterogeneous cluster system.

Acknowledgement. The authors would like to thank the National Science Council, Taiwan, for financially supporting this research under Contract No. NSC98-2221-E-018-008-MY2.

References

1. Dean, J., Ghemawat, S.: MapReduce: Simplified Data Processing on Large Clusters. In: Proceedings of the 6th Conference on Symposium on Operating Systems Design & Implementation, vol. 6, p. 10 (2004)
2. Wu, C.-C., Lai, L.-F., Ke, J.Y., Jhan, S.-S., Chang, Y.-.: Designing a Parallel Fuzzy Expert System Programming Model with Adaptive Load Balancing Capability for Cloud Computing. Journal of Computers 21(1), 38–48 (2010)
3. Wu, C.-C., Lai, L.-F., Chang, Y.-S.: Towards Automatic Load Balancing for Programming Parallel Fuzzy Expert Systems in Heterogeneous Clusters. Journal of Internet Technology 10(2), 179–186 (2009)
4. Wu, C.-C., Lai, L.-F., Yang, C.-T., Chiu, P.-H.: Using Hybrid MPI and OpenMP Programming to Optimize Communications in Parallel Loop Self-Scheduling Schemes for Multicore PC Clusters. Journal of Supercomputing (2009), doi:10.1007/s11227-009-0271-z
5. Wu, C.-C., Lai, L.-F., Chang, Y.-S.: Extending FuzzyCLIPS for Parallelizing Data-Dependent Fuzzy Expert Systems. Journal of Supercomputing, doi:10.1007/s11227-010-0542-8
6. FuzzyCLIPS, http://www.iit.nrc.ca/IR_public/fuzzy/fuzzyClips/fuzzyCLIPSIndex2.html

Implementation of a Smart Grid System with SOA-based Service on Cloud[*]

Chao-Tung Yang[**], Chung-Che Lai, Wei-Sheng Chen,
Jung-Chun Liu, and William C. Chu

High-Performance Computing Laboratory Department of Computer Science,
Tunghai University, Taichung, 40704, Taiwan
{ctyang,g98350006,g99350007,jcliu,cchu}@thu.edu.tw

Abstract. In recent years, with the rapid progress of information, and environment protection awareness is growing strongly now, people began to go for their living environment around carbon reduction, which is the most popular energy-saving. Starting from energy-saving and carbon reduction, with in information equipment and information technologies, many peoples will use applications for home and family to catch the wave of the Smart Home. Therefore, this thesis will play as electricity providers, which the devices they are actively developing which digital meter and its management system as the goal, and then to develop an energy management systems by using service-oriented architecture (SOA). The paper applies service-oriented architecture (SOA) approach to construct services and utilize commonly virtualization technologies on cloud infrastructure (IaaS). This work also applies distributed storage technologies to stored and distributed databases, to make sure the system can hold a lot of demand for services.

Keywords: AMI, SOA, Smart Grid, MySQL Cluster, Cloud Computing.

1   Introduction

In this work, based on perspective of electricity providers, we try to implement a smart grid system using SOA (Service-oriented architecture) and distributed techniques of MySQL Cluster technology to store short-term electricity consumption data. In addition to offer users with queries of related electricity information, controls of power supply, total electricity consumption of a public area is monitored, and through hand-held devices the region's population and the average power consumption or carbon emissions can be estimated.

Nowadays daily life resource management systems are gradually developing and their applications start to play active roles in our daily life. However, usage information of living resources, which are indispensible for modern life, such as water, electricity, gas, and the Internet, are often relatively huge. By analyzing these substantial data of the long-term storage of living resources, useful information can be deduced to offer resource providers for early plans for future production or early

---

[*] This work is supported in part by the National Science Council, Taiwan R.O.C., under grants no. NSC 99-2220-E-029-004 and NSC 99-3113-S-029-002.
[**] Corresponding author.

R.-S. Chang, T.-h. Kim, and S.-L. Peng (Eds.): SUComS 2011, CCIS 223, pp. 159–168, 2011.
© Springer-Verlag Berlin Heidelberg 2011

detection of safety issue of these commodities, and also to provide users a means to compute the amount of resources spending.

For storage in the database environment, developers must figure out how to store huge amount of information, and how to handle huge numbers of user inquiries, both of them will cause performance problems on the system. In this paper, we use distributed database: MySQL Cluster, and the industry-renowned cloud project: Gluster FS. In the system management level, developers need to consider methods to obtain the electricity information and backup mechanisms to deal with possible loss of information due to transmission failure. Furthermore, when the system detects abnormal use of resources, when, the system needs to send urgent notices to the user for emergency treatment. For system management, we use the MVC software engineering technology and SOA technology to do system test.

In section 2, we will review relevant technologies and background; in section 3, we introduce the structure of our experimental system; our experimental framework, method and data flow are presented in section 4; and finally section 5 concludes this article.

2   Background Review and Related Work

2.1   Smart Grid and AMI

The smart grid [4, 14, 15, 16] not just refers to the smart meter [2] or the digital meter, which may be part of the smart grid or not. The smart grid[3][4] is an intelligent monitoring system and contains several sensing devices. The smart Grid uses intelligent monitoring system continuously tracks all the digital sensing devices to obtain power usage data, and by extension, it may work with renewable energy systems and power generation systems.

Providers of the smart grid need to have access to information in the consumer's home via two-way communications, within the contract to help consumers manage electricity to achieve saving of energy and reduction of costs, and to provide consumers with all information related to electricity consumption to enhance the reliability and transparency. To achieve effective use and saving of electricity, via services provided by the smart grid, users can also set up power supply to appliances in their own house at any time.

Advanced Metering Infrastructure (AMI)[5] , not only data in electrical meters can be digitized and sent to computer systems for further processing, but also data in other kinds of meters, such as water, heat, and gas meters, used for many other living resources that come into our home through pipelines, can be digitized and include in the metering infrastructure. The electrical meter used in the meter infrastructure is commonly used for realization of the smart grid.

2.2   SOA

Service Oriented Architecture (SOA), an architectural model for software engineering, aims to allow service providers to create a flexible, reusable integration interface. Many people use SOA architecture, for example, by applying APIs of the SOA Protocol to allow cross-platform data exchange and processing. SOA has following technical characteristics [6]:

- Distributed architecture
- Loosely coupled
- Based on open standards
- Process centric

According to our experience, we adopt APIs provided by PHP with special SOA protocol support to implement our system in the latter part of this article.

There are currently three types of Web services, the more well-known implementations, one for SOAP, one for ReST, the other is the XML-RPC. In the framework of the concept of SOA, there is no particular use to which approach should be elaborated to implement the concept of SOA architecture, and ReST is because it was compared to the other two, more concise.

ReST (Representational State Transfer, someone write REST)[7] is a standing resource-based perspective, to observe the entire network, then use the URI to locate these resources, and allows users to access these resources by URI.

REST is often based on using HTTP, URI, and XML and HTML are widely popular. So he also has some specific needs and details, we will call him is in line with REST-style, and only meet the REST style of Web Service or Web API, we call ReSTful Web. The REST architectural style describes the following six constraints applied to the architecture, while leaving the implementation of the individual components free to design:

- Client and server architecture
- Connection agreement with the stateless
- Cacheable
- Hierarchical system
- Code On Demand – Javascript
- Uniform interface

And the uniform interface that any REST interface must provide is considered fundamental to the design of any REST service.

- Identification of resources
- Manipulation of resources through these representations
- Self-descriptive message
- Hypermedia as the engine of application state

2.3   MySQL Cluster and GlusterFS

MySQL Cluster [8][9] for MySQL [8] is a distributed computing environment of high practical, high-redundancy version. It uses the NDB Cluster storage engine, allowing a cluster to run multiple MySQL servers. The storage engine is provided in the binary version of MySQL 5.1, and RPM compatible with the latest Linux version provides.

There are three types of cluster nodes for the lowest MySQL Cluster configuration. These three types of nodes are:

- Management (MGM) node
- Data node
- SQL node(Query Node)

Cluster Configuration of the cluster engages configuring individual nodes in the cluster, and setting up separate communication links between nodes. For the current design of the MySQL cluster, its intention is to have homogeneous storage nodes, in terms of the processor capacity, memory space and bandwidth. Besides, to have a single point of configuration, all cluster configuration data are located in the same configuration file.

GlusterFS (Gluster File System), which is a distributed file system that uses a cluster computer hard disk space for each node, a combination of a large hard drive. It does not need to cut us another partition to give it, just give it the specified folder; it can be left for each node to make use of the space used.

And it provides a copy of the mechanism for damage after our files witch not be rescue. And it's not as Hadoop HDFS[10][11], will be on top of the file completely dispersed in each node biopsy, which uses the algorithm to the file it points on the different nodes to achieve the distributed storage. The GlusterFS features is that it can be a virtual machine (Virtual Machine) in the image file storage, and can operate normally use. In establishing a set of GlusterFS when it version 3.1, the friendly text provides a good set of interfaces, through the interface, you can easily set the entire file system.

3   System Architecture

Our system architecture is shown in Fig. 1, Fig. 2, and Fig. 3. Through ZigBee wireless network communications, meters will send information to the Server. We assume that in the future cost for wireless network transmission will be low, and battery power is sufficient to maintain a long time duration searching mode for the wireless networks. When a handheld device enters into designated areas of our system, it will find a particular Service Set Identifier (SSID). When a specific string is matched, an Access Point searching program running on the handheld platforms will remind users to login account of the wireless network.

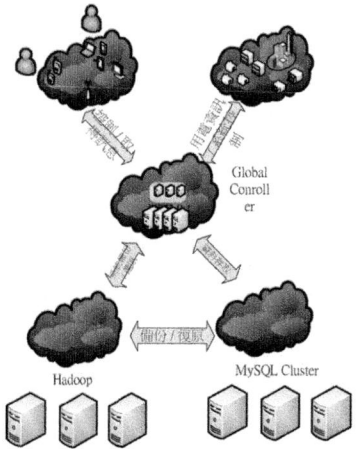

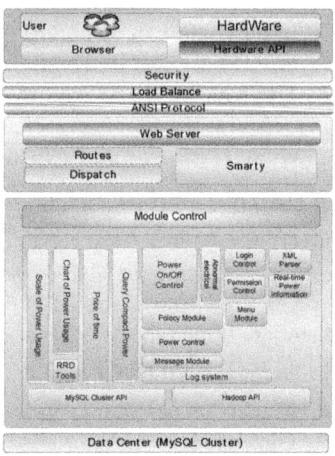

Fig. 1. Secondary environment system architecture   **Fig. 2.** System stack architecture

After logging in successfully, the user will be provided with an IP address for him to access the Internet. And the system will get the power information from the IBC (In-Home Building Controller), and then store the power usage information to system, the primary environment can get information from the global server like Fig. 3. User can control the air-conditioner from smart phone through the system in Fig. 1., Fig. 2, and the system can merge the information from sensor, weather form network, and power usage from global server.

3.1   Function Block of Global Server

As shown in Fig. 2, many functional modules are implemented in the system. We referenced American National Standards Institute (ANSI)[12] standards, ANSI C12-19, C12-22, when developing the system. We developed web pages for the system and adopted SOA-based approach and the Model-View-Controller (MVC)[13] separation development method. It also consists of distributed database system.

MVC architecture is important for developers in this feature. Sometimes the system will be modified by no particular reasons. In MVC architecture, modular modules are usually used in the program layer to develop programs. Programming in modular modules makes the administrator easy to delete functions in modules, without affecting functionality of the whole system. If some modules are fault, administrator can ask developers to fix it without affecting the whole system. In view layer, developers can arrange various themes to show when some special day is coming.

In this system, we used a smarty engine to make it easy to separate three parts of MVC: Modules, View, and Control. This engine makes the View layer easy to program and to combine with Control layer in the program layer.

For the data flow in the system, it uses a module controller to select the right module to deal with messages. Administrator can send emergency messages from the web service and stop or restart the power supply to users' appliances. From the system, user can query the information of power usage, set power supply rules for devices plugged on the socket, and the usage fees for individual device. The detail of the data flow will be described in next Section.

In Fig. 4, it shows the experimental of whole system environment architecture. In this paper, system uses the distributed file system and distributed database system to provide a service with high ability; it uses some replication method to make sure this issue.

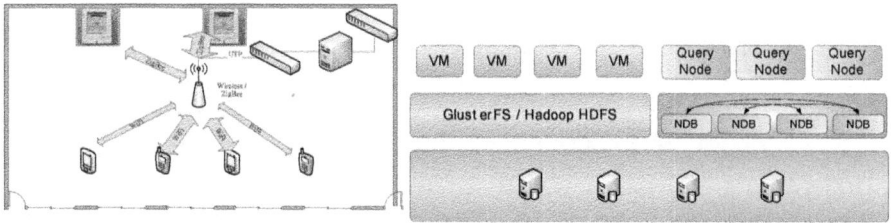

Fig. 3. Primary environment system architecture

Fig. 4. Hardware and Software architecture

4   Experimental Results

4.1   DataFlow

Fig. 5 shows the data transfer method in the system. We set the Linux time-based job scheduler, crontab, to send electricity consumption data, including values of voltage, current, power, from meter to the Global Server every 10 minutes. The communication method adopted by the meter follows the SOA protocol.

Before sending data to the Global Server, the In-Home Display (IHD) Server will process the data in the XML format with the communication protocol of SOA Service, since the data must follow the SOA protocol and SOA format. For the security issue, data are encrypted with SSL protocol before being sent to the Global Server. Then, the module controller will analyze messages packaged with the SOA protocol, and call the XML parser module to get data. After all, all data are stored in the MySQL Cluster, and written in a file to be stored in HDFS.

4.2   Distributed Systems

To store data and service image, the system uses two distributed systems. One for service image which uses GlusterFS the other one is for data which uses NDB file system. In system design concept, the old data should not be stored in the MySQL Cluster database. Since MySQL database is a relational database, it uses large amount of memory for indexing data. The system memory will be consumed too much when data become too large. It will bring down the efficiency of the distributed database system, when we select the data or update the data.

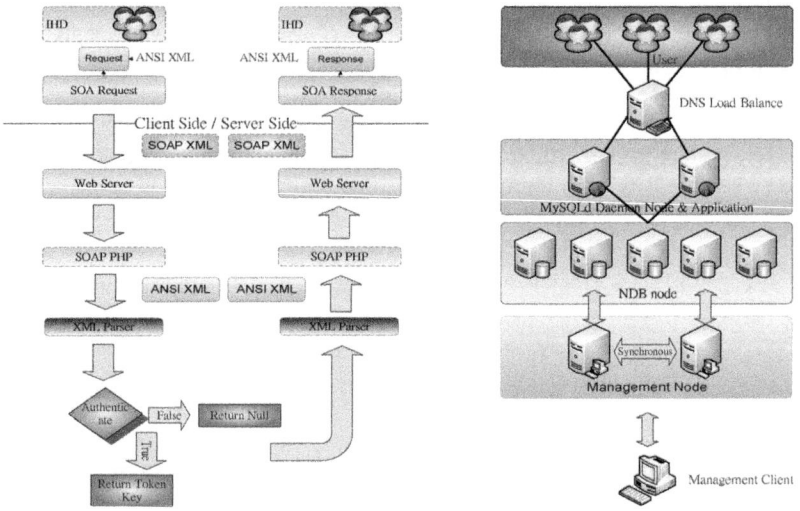

Fig. 5. Data format and transfer   **Fig. 6.** MySQL Cluster architecture

A better way to use the MySQL Cluster database is to store data in the database if the data are likely to be queried by users. So we use the database to store data collected in recent months, but not many years ago. The old, or long term data not stored in this database will stored in file system with XML format and backup with SQL format, not only for occasional queries from users, but also for prediction of electricity usage based on yearly data, for example, the electricity needed in next July.

The system architecture of MySQL Cluster is shown in Fig. 6. Five servers are used as cluster storage nodes, in which two nodes are Query daemons. To have better performance, we put our applications on the MySQL query node, rather than putting applications in other places and querying through networks.

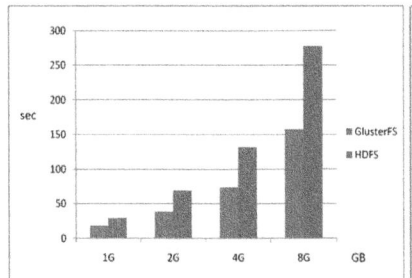
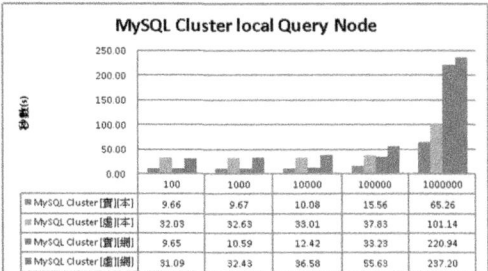

Fig. 7. Performance between GlusterFS and Hadoop

Fig. 8. MySQL Cluster Performance of local Query node and foreign Query node

Management work is done by using two servers. They synchronize the stored information. When data of one of the management nodes are damaged, the NDB node can get information from the other server. Administrator can communicate with management node to get MySQL Cluster service information and administrate the service to start or stop services.

Then, the Virtual Machine Image is used to be our service. We used the Virtual Machine with DNS load balance to serve among of user and IBC, these service are used to form the major components of Global Server. We used these components to build the AMI Cloud. The GlusterFS can help the service without broken by replication. And, GlusterFS performance in our experimental environment is better than with the use of HDFS's Hadoop Project, show with Fig. 7, this result is test both writing and reading to GlusterFS and Hadoop HDFS.

The Fig. 8 shows the performance of Query node in MySQL Cluster. This experiment will know the issue which the performance between our web application and Query node of MySQL Cluster. This paper find, when the application run on Query node, it can use less transfer from network, so it can get performance better than put the application on the other machine, and query data between networks. And the performance between virtual Query node and physical Query node, in this system, virtual Query node will worse than Physical Query node, although the Query node in virtual machine is a good way and an easy way to deploy the system, but it still worse than truly machine.

4.3   Carbon Reduce and Energy Saving

First, we estimate the number of users. IP addresses are used to estimate how many people are inside some specific area. We can query the DHCP service to know the number of IP addresses that are release to devices on the network. In our experiment, we assume that every IP address is used by a single wireless device, which is carried by one person. So, if 100 IP addresses are used, then there are 100 people in this area.

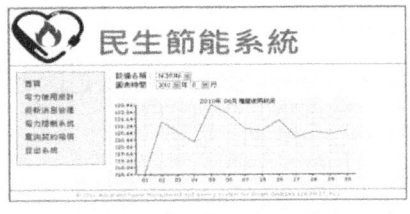

Fig. 9. Chart of power usage   **Fig. 10.** The oscilloscope and ZigBee Sensor

Second, we query the Global Server. Global Server obtains correct information of power consumption from IHD, which in turn obtains the power usage information from the meters and sockets. Third, we obtain information about location and size of this specific area. The power usage information looks like Fig. 9.

Based on power consumption information retrieved from system, we can estimate average electricity consumption per person in the area. The air conditioners in the experimental environment, the computer room, can be controlled by infrared rays remote control like Fig. 10. We use the oscilloscope to find the wave of the infrared ray, the wave like the Fig. 11, Fig. 12, and We use ZigBee Sensor infrared module to read out the frequency of infrared waves recorded in our Server-side, and the need for control, frequency of this wave to launch out, done by computer-controlled air-conditioning for a way.

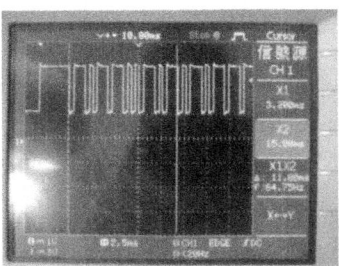

Fig. 11. The wave of the Air Condition Remote Controller   **Fig. 12.** Choose the device to enable/disable with manual control

So the system can send command to control the infrared ray to adjust the air conditioner. User can manual control, too. User can choose the location which they want to control and the device. We can preset the power usage policy for this area and automatically control the air conditioners (or other device) according to the estimated people in this area. When few people is detected in this area, the smart grid system will automatically adjust the air conditioners to operate in a saving mode; furthermore, the system can turn on more air conditioners in time if it expects more people will enter this area like Fig. 12.

4.4   User Control System

Advanced features can be implemented in the system. As mentioned in Section 3.3, we have already written a program to scan the wireless access point with a special SSID. Now we can write something for our users. And the system shows like Fig. 13 and Fig. 14.

Fig. 13. Change the temperature   **Fig. 14.** Scan for the AMI area

We develop a message response program with our scanner. When the user logs into our system, he should get the right to define his ideal temperature range. So he can vote the ideal temperature he prefers to the system. The system will gather all temperature preference information from people stay in this area, and after referencing with preset temperature policy it can dynamically adjust temperature according to the majority of people inside the room. Furthermore, the system can use the database to learn the policy of particular areas or rooms.

System can collect the data from temperature sensors and humidity sensors to improve this smart system. Since these environmental sensors are scattered in the real environment to collect vital environmental information in real time from different locations in the room, the system can based on these information to adjust wind strength of and directions of air conditioners fans. More importantly, the system can predict and smartly adjust electricity consumption for devices in the room based on information provided by these sensors.

5   Conclusions and Feature Work

To reach the aims of electricity energy saving and carbon dioxide reduction, we have implemented a smart grid system. Digital meters or sockets are used to send electricity consumptions information of appliances connected to them to servers that dynamically adjust and control power usage based on collected information.

In the near future, electric appliances will be tightly connected to and controlled by computers. Our smart system is a solution to interface conventional appliances with new computing power such as the cloud. The system detects total number of users in the area, collects electricity consumption data, manages power supply, and controls operation of electric appliances according to a decision mechanism based on an energy saving policy, which is dynamically tuned according to users' preferences and behaviors and environmental sensors information.

References

1. Rotem-Gal-Oz, A.: What is SOA anyway?
2. Wikipedia – Smart Meter, http://en.wikipedia.org/wiki/Smart_meter
3. Wikipedia – Smart Grid, http://en.wikipedia.org/wiki/Smart_grid
4. Depuru, S.S.S.R., Wang, L., Devabhaktuni, V.: Smart meters for power grid: Challenges, issues, advantages and status. Renewable and Sustainable Energy Reviews 15(6), 2736–2742 (2011)
5. Advanced Metering Infrastructure, AMI (2008), http://blog.udn.com/ctang/2324847
6. Service Oriented Architecture, SOA (2007), http://www.cc.ntu.edu.tw/chinese/epaper/20070620_1008.htm
7. Muehlen, M.z., Nickerson, J.V., Swenson, K.D.: Developing web services choreography standards—the case of REST vs. SOAP (2005)
8. http://twpug.net/docs/mysql-5.1/ndbcluster.html
9. A MySQL® Technical White Paper: MySQL Cluster Architecture Overview (2004)
10. http://hadoop.apache.org/
11. Hadoop Cluster Setup, http://hadoop.apache.org/common/docs/r0.18.3/cluster_setup.pdf
12. National Electrical Manufacturers Association, American National Standards Institute, Inc.: American National Standard Protocol Specification For Interfacing to Data Communication Networks (2009)
13. Model–view–controller, http://en.wikipedia.org/wiki/Model-View-Controller
14. Galli, S., Scaglione, A., Wang, Z.: For the Grid and Through the Grid: The Role of Power Line Communications in the Smart Grid. Proceedings of the IEEE 99(6), 998–1027 (2011)
15. Järventausta, P., Repo, S., Rautiainen, A., Partanen, J.: Smart grid power system control in distributed generation environment. Annual Reviews in Control 34(2), 277–286 (2010)
16. Olmos, L., Ruester, S., Liong, S.-J., Glachant, J.-M.: Energy 36(7), 4396–4409 (July 2011)

Gate Opening Effect:
Toward Understanding Mobile-Specific
Service Evolution

Toshihiko Yamakami

Toshihiko Yamakami ACCESS
Toshihiko.Yamakami@access-company.com

Abstract. There is an increased presence of Internet business players on the mobile Internet, such as Apple and Google. The different players are exploring different business models in the emerging mobile Internet. With increased convergence toward the Internet, the mobile business engineering is involved in a new type of business model engineering. The author compares the business models of mobile platform software. The author describes the role of enabler in mobile business model engineering. Then, the author proposes a gate opening effect in deploying the enabler from the viewpoint of the enabler's role in business model engineering in the emerging new Internet.

1 Introduction

The mobile Internet has become increasingly visible in the mobile industry and in the Internet industry. The mobile Internet has taken steady steps into the mainstream of the Internet. This represents a global landscape change on the Internet and in business model engineering.

This increasingly visible change has attracted major players in the computer and communications industries to mobile business engineering. Major Internet players such as Apple and Google have triggered ecosystem changes in the mobile industry. Sometimes, it has been seen as another attempt to dominate the emerging new business arena.

When NTTDOCOMO launched its i-mode service in Japan with a walled-garden business model-based carrier-portal, its ambition was considered to be to become the center of the mobile Internet. When Google announced its Android project, it was considered to be extending its realm into the mobile Internet. From the point of view of business model engineering, these are not accurate analyses.

The author presents a high-level view of business model engineering on the mobile Internet. Then, the author discusses the role of enablers in the business model engineering. In this context, the author proposes a new type of business model engineering, a so-called gate opening effect-based engineering, which is important for facilitating landslide transitions on the mobile Internet.

R.-S. Chang, T.-h. Kim, and S.-L. Peng (Eds.): SUComS 2011, CCIS 223, pp. 169–177, 2011.
© Springer-Verlag Berlin Heidelberg 2011

2   Purpose and Related Works

2.1   Purpose of Research

The mobile Internet continues to converge to the PC Internet even with multiple mobile-specific constraints. The aim of this paper is to identify convergence-specific business model engineering to facilitate a large-scale transition of mobile business model engineering.

2.2   Related Works

As mobile business including the mobile Internet business has expanded its coverage and demonstrated its growth opportunities, mobile business issues have caught the increasing attention of researchers.

Natsuno discussed the win-win relationship in the i-mode success [6].

Raivio discussed new business opportunities for mobile operators [8] from the STOF model. STOF stands for 'service', 'technology', 'organization', and 'finance'. This model suits mobile service engineering, which requires both technological and financial considerations. The author considers the limitation of this model in terms of mobile service evolution with a landslide effect on the mobile Internet.

Infrastructure changes and their accompanying business model changes also have attracted attention of researchers.

Regional differences on the mobile Internet have also captured attentions from researchers. Barns discussed the Japanese specific factors on the i-mode success [1]. Zhao discussed the integration of mobile business in China using an entertainment business case [9]. Lu discussed the mobile business value chain in China [5]. Bouwman discussed the barriers and drivers in mobile data services based on a survey [2].

Dhamdhere discussed the Internet ecosystem from the point of view of the links among Autonomous Systems [3]. Kim discussed the "keystones" and "flagships" in the business ecosystem in regards to the role of IT in the business ecosystem [4].

In the IT context, a shared platform is key for business ecosystem engineering. Quaadgras discussed the platform role in business ecosystems using an RFID case [7].

To the author's knowledge, little has been addressed to analyze the underlying principle of driving mobile services during a transition period.

The originality of this paper lies in analyzing business model engineering from the viewpoint of an indirect landscape transition on the mobile Internet.

3   Landscape

Google launched Android in November 2007. Apple launched the App Store in July 2008. Symbian launched OSS-version Symbian^3 in February 2010.

NTTDOCOMO launched i-mode, a Japanese mobile Internet service, in 1999. NTTDOCOMO is a Japanese wireless carrier. It should be noted that i-mode is an enabler of the mobile Internet. NTTDOCOMO invested a lot in i-mode content. NTTDOCOMO had the early feedback data from users, and weekly content subscription statistics. It used this quick feedback with content providers in order to improve the early content. It was sometimes viewed as a content aggregator with a carrier portal site. We can see i-mode as an enabler on the mobile Internet. Apparently, the major revenue stream for carriers is network traffic revenue. The business model of wireless carriers is to maximize network traffic revenue.

Google created OSS-based Android and a third-party application market, Android market. Here, we can see another example of an enabler. The major revenue stream of Google is search engine-based advertisements. Their business model is to maximize their search engine-based revenue. They have no intention to make a revenue stream out of Android, a mobile software platform. Android is an enabler to leverage a departure from SMS and the closed mobile Internet. Google is confident that end users will use their services once they get into the open Internet. There is no need to bundle any of their services or advertisements into the software platform.

The current business model analysis is presented in Table 1.

Table 1. Business model analysis

item	Carriers	Apple	Google	Microsoft	Vendors
Services and content	Sub revenue		Main revenue		
Portal and billing platform	Sub revenue	Sub revenue			
Network	Main revenue				
Client OS			Engaged	Main revenue	
Client device		Main revenue	Sub revenue	Sub revenue	Main revenue

4   Enabler Analysis

4.1   Definition

An enabler is a mechanism used to implement the prerequisites for a certain outcome. An enabler is a component that through its capabilities or actions allows something else to achieve something. Usually the outcome is a revenue generating mechanism. An enabler is the underlying infrastructure or condition for deploying transitions. In the software domain, an enabler is often the infrastructure or user agent software used to produce web content.

4.2   Importance of Enabler in Mobile Business

The mobile business needs to address multiple constraints on the mobile Internet. The layers involved in managing mobile-specific business components and their issues are

Table 2. Issues in Mobile Constraint

Eco-system management	Allocate the role and revenue relationships among stakeholders. Create new revenue opportunities for coming stakeholders to enhance the eco-system.
Constraint management	Manage multiple constraints such as CPU, memory, network bandwidth, battery life, display real estate.
Enabler Deployment	Manage deployment underlying infrastructure, mobile-specific content, and client capabilities

depicted in Table 2. An enabler is important in this domain because it is difficult to one killer application in the mobile constraints. THe mobile constraints make the aggregation of context-specific applications the best solution for end users.

The business structure is depicted in Fig. 1.

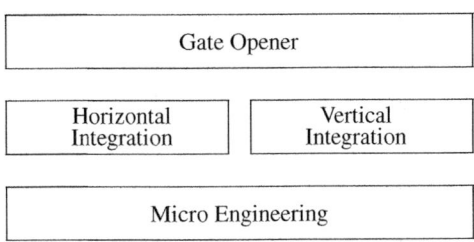

Fig. 1. Mobile Business Architecture

An example of each business structure is depicted in Table 3.

Table 3. Examples of each business structure

Gate Opener	Enable opening boundary gate in order to ensure the ultimate core revenue streams while facilitating enablers on the mobile Internet.
Horizontal Integration	Aggregate a wide range of applications.
Vertical Integration	Integrate services from lower layers to higher layers.
Micro Engineering	Transform the current business models into different business models to ensure future revenue generation.

Table 4. Comparison with enabler

Item	description
Enabler	In IT, it is a component (hardware, software) to allow something (content) to achieve its goal.
Value-chain	It is a chain of activities for a firm operating in a specific industry. Products or services pass through all activities of the chain in order, and at each activity the product or the service gains some value. The chain of activities gives the products more added value than the sum of added values of all activities.
Core competence	It is a specific factor that a business sees as being central to the way it, or its employees, works. The three criteria are: a) It provides consumer benefits, b) It is not easy for competitors to imitate, and c) It can leverage many products and markets.
Ecosystem	In business, it is a set of businesses functioning as a unit and interacting with a shared market, together with relationships among them.

4.3   Comparison with Other Approaches

Value-chain analysis is similar to enabler analysis. The difference is that the value-chain is a shared relationship among stakeholders to create value, and that the enabler is a unidirectional relationship with a final result. Whether the enabler is built into the value-chain relationship depends on the power structure or business contexts. In some cases, enabler analysis is similar to value-chain analysis.

The comparison is depicted in Table 4.

The core competence focuses on the uniqueness of the business position for capturing revenue. The value-chain focuses on the explicit interactions among stakeholders. The ecosystem also focuses on the positive and interrelated relationships among players with different roles. The ecosystem is the closest to the enabler, however, the enabler focuses on the pre-requisites and on facilitating relationships.

The important point of the enabler discussion is that the utilization of an enabler can generate mainstream revenue in an indirect manner in the end.

4.4   Gate Opening Effect

The wireless telephony industry has two different landscapes, one in developed countries and one in emerging countries. In the developed countries, the telephony service is saturated and data services penetrated quickly. In the emerging countries, the large-scale incoming users enable any type of region-specific service development, which may be different from that of developed countries.

In the former case, we can see increasing visibility of the Internet players. Microsoft wanted to create a Microsoft network in 1990's, but they gave up. With more than 90 % share of operating system and browsers, Microsoft could not stop the penetration of the Internet to PCs. The same situation is occurring with the mobile Internet. The increasing presence of service providers and decreasing presence of wireless carriers is something that happened with the fixed line Internet a decade ago.

When a closed market is replaced by an open market, we can see the gate opening effect. In the gate opening effect, it is more important to accelerate dynamism than to build each business model. It is true in the case of i-mode, and the Android case. The exception is Apple iPhone case which includes branding and marketing issues, however, it is beyond the scope of this paper to include discussion about this exception.

5   Business Models

5.1   Vendors and Carriers

Apple's business model is based on vertical integration. The core business is handset sales, however, vertical integration to enclose end users is key. Vertical integration and enclosure of end users with special computing tastes was the success of Macintosh in the 1980's. For this purpose, Apple does not license their technologies to competitors Marketing to persuade end users to become devoted Apple fans is a crucial part of this business. The total taste and flavor of computing are sold with a high price tag. Therefore, the ceiling for this kind of marketing share of this kind is 10 % or so. Apparently, Apple is not interested in the dominant market share, but in a high profit margin.

Google Android is quite different from the Internet Explorer of Microsoft. Microsoft competed with Netscape communications, fearing that browsers could come to act as replacements of the client OS. Google's core business is the advertisement revenue of Internet search engines. Therefore, whether Android occupies a major share of mobile handsets or not is not a critical issue for Google. There are a billion PCs worldwide, at the same magnitude as the number of TVs. There are 5 billion mobile handsets worldwide, with increased connectivity to data networks. With increased capabilities to connect to the Internet, Google cannot ignore the size of this mobile market. Google has confidence that users will come to Google search engines when they are connected to the non-walled garden mobile Internet. Departures from SMS and the walled garden mobile Internet is key. For example, Google maps is one of the killer services for iPhones.

Microsoft has a strong influence on PC software using its flagship Windows OS and popular Office software suites. Microsoft provides wide coverage of enterprise computing as a client platform. It is a natural extension to provide client software that is similar to a PC to mobile devices including mobile handsets. In the past, this was a challenge due to the restrictions of CPU and memory restrictions.

Nokia has marketing channels and a worldwide brand. Nokia has a competence for integrating a wide range of mobile-handset engineering skills and knowledge covering weight, wave interference, battery life, various device drivers, and real-time processing. Unlike Apple and Google, it is not a service-business company, which has 24-hour service operating skills.

Wireless carriers are under a regulated business. With the emergence of the mobile Internet, wireless carriers acted as the most influential stakeholder, with control over handsets. Even though, many wireless carriers took the role of mobile content aggregator seriously in the early days, the wireless carrier's main business model is traffic revenues. It is the most important interest of wireless carriers to maximize their traffic revenue. The mobile content business is just a side interest for them considering the size of their traffic revenue.

5.2   Business Model Engineering

The patterns of business model engineering are depicted in Table 5. All of the services, except gate opening, are also applicable to other business domains. These services can be applied to the PC Internet. The gate opening business model engineering is crucial in the era of device convergence. This model only applies to the industry-leading players. Although the scope of application is narrow, this business model engineering appears to be crucial on the mobile Internet, especially during the landscape-level changes.

The number of users of wireless telephony worldwide reached 5 billions. The number of mobile Internet users is expected to quickly catch this number in the future. Despite this high rate of penetration worldwide, the mobile Internet has a large gap between service design and user acceptance. This is partly because the screen real estate is limited and services are forced to be context-specific.

It should be noted that the mobile Internet services were largely focused on this gate opening effect in the early stages. Current mobile service engineering is also heavily impacted by this effect, as witnessed by Google mobile service engineering.

There are two reasons for this:

- The number of wireless telephony subscribers (potential mobile Internet users) is too large, therefore, the landslide effect of gate opening has a significant impact on business model engineering, and
- Since the penetration rate is high, it is difficult to satisfy the end users with content made from scratch. Therefore, the landslide effect of gate opening has a significant impact on business model engineering.

Table 5. Patterns of Business Model Engineering

Item	description	example
Create new services	Create new services from a scratch. Provide a new choice for consumers.	Create new intermediary marketplace like e-marketplace, price comparison, viral marketing or auction.
Financial engineering	Turning a revenue stream under a different payment mechanism.	Rental/leasing. Application service providers (ownership to pay-per-use).
Conversion of revenue flow	Turning a revenue flow into new patterns.	Sell a cheap machine and expensive supplies e.g. printer business.
Reengineering of value-chain	Inclusion or updates of value chain to perform reengineering of revenue flow patterns.	Turn handset-bundled applications to third-party application distribution in the application market.
Gate opening	Enabling a drastic landscape change that causes the facilitation of core competence in the long-term in the larger picture.	Provide new technology in order to make landslide change of business patterns.

6 Discussion

6.1 Advantages of the Enabler Analysis

The advances in computer and communication technology enable global scale changes in an efficient manner. In this emerging landscape of technology, it is more important to conduct business engineering of an enabler, in the context of the gate opening effect.

In the mobile services context, diffusion can require a complicated process including activation, use and adoption. There are many examples of mobile services where activation does not mean use. Underlying enablers which are required for activation are implemented, but not used. Even with wide use, there are many cases where services are deployed in almost all handsets, however, end users have almost no intention to use them. Bilateral video conferencing services have been widely equipped in many Japanese 3G phones since 2002, however, their use has been slim.

In many cases, micro-value-chain analysis is not effective in mobile business engineering. Much of mobile business engineering is dynamic and does not fit the static, micro-value-chain analysis. In many regions, mobile business continues to change the landscape, network infra-structure, user experience, and business models. Also, the existence of large-scale content and services presents a challenge to any closed business models because the conversion of existing services and content has a landslide impact on mobile business. This transitive nature presents a never-ending challenge to any static mobile value chain analysis.

In the past decade, i-mode was often referred to as a win-win example of ecosystem success with the mobile Internet in Japan. In retrospective, it is worth reconsidering this win-win ecosystem framework. I-mode services have brought significant network traffic revenue to NTTDOCOMO. Contrarily, many start-up companies that focused i-mode services have been just wiped off from the market, from either launching failure or failure during service evolution. The author believes that it is more appropriate to get a viewpoint of enabler business model engineering from i-mode service engineering.

6.2   Driving Factors of Gate Opening Effect

Device convergence has been eliminating the boundaries between different devices. The increased visibility of Internet players is another factor. A human being is an integrated existence, whether or not he/she uses any device. And, this integrated existence exercises the purchase decisions.

6.3   Implications from Gate Opening Effect

From the viewpoint of a business model, the gate opening effect need to be carefully considered. The major players play a strategic game to build a large-scale convergence to leverage their mainstream revenue. It is risky for many other players to capture this at the surface level to run the long-term business growth. When a gate opener works, there is a risk that the whole service landscape under the legacy constraints needs revisits. It is different from value-chain analysis because the enabler is not designed to create a revenue flow, but to act as the gate opener for a business model transition.

6.4   Limitations

This is a descriptive study of the stage-specific business model engineering of mobile data services. The identification of stages and quantitative analysis of stage-specific comparison of the gate opening strategy and other economically-justifiable strategies are beyond the scope of this paper.

This is an exploratory work, therefore, in-depth analysis of the gate opening effect remain for further research.

7   Conclusion

The mobile Internet requires complicated business model engineering. Since the PC Internet preceded the mobile Internet, it has been a continuous challenge to determine how to utilize the content and services from the PC Internet, in the mobile Internet context. Also, with its increasing rise worldwide, the mobile Internet has been an ambitious target for many major Internet business players. In past literature, the STOF model has been frequently used for ICT business model engineering that involves service development with technological, organizational and financial considerations. The author argues that past lessons show that service engineering needs to address a landslide transition in the development of mobile services.

With the availability of large-scale content on the PC Internet, the business model engineering on the mobile Internet has a tendency to have a landslide effect for major stakeholders. It is of vital interest for such players to facilitate enablers for this transition. From the analysis of i-mode and Android business models, the author proposes the concept of enabler analysis. It is different from value-chain analysis because the enabler is not designed to create a revenue flow, but to act as the gate opener for a business model transition.

The author describes the past examples involving i-mode and Android to identify the uniqueness of the enabler from the standpoint of a business model.

References

1. Barnes, S.J., Huff, S.L.: Rising Sun: iMode and the Wireless Internet. CACM 46(11), 78–84 (2003)
2. Bouwman, H., Carlsson, C., Molina-Castillo, F.J., Walden, P.: Barriers and drivers in the adoption of current and future mobile services in finland. Telematics and Informatics 24(2), 145–160 (2007)
3. Dhamdhere, A., Dovrolis, C.: Ten years in the evolution of the internet ecosystem. In: IMC 2008: Proceedings of the 8th ACM SIGCOMM Conference on Internet Measurement, pp. 183–196. ACM, New York (2008), http://doi.acm.org/10.1145/1452520.1452543
4. Kim, H., Lee, J.N., Han, J.: The role of it in business ecosystems. Commun. ACM 53(5), 151–156 (2010), DOI http://doi.acm.org/10.1145/1735223.1735260
5. Lu, Y., Dong, Y., Wang, B.: The mobile business value chain in china. In: ICMB 2008, p. 24. IEEE Computer Society Press, Los Alamitos (2008)
6. Natsuno, T.: The i-mode Wireless Ecosystem. John Wiley & Sons Inc., Chichester (2003)
7. Quaadgras, A.: Who joins the platform? the case of the rfid business ecosystem. In: HICSS 2005: Proceedings of the Proceedings of the 38th Annual Hawaii International Conference on System Sciences, p. 269.2. IEEE Computer Society Press, Washington, DC (2005), DOI http://dx.doi.org/10.1109/HICSS.2005.693
8. Raivio, Y., Luukkainen, S., Juntunen, A.: Open telco: a new business potential. In: Mobility 2009: Proceedings of the 6th International Conference on Mobile Technology, Application & Systems, pp. 1–6. ACM, New York (2009), DOI http://doi.acm.org/10.1145/1710035.1710037
9. Zhao, X., Chen, S.: Integration of mobile business and traditional business to acquire competitive advantages: A case study in china entertainment industry. In: ICMB 2008, p. 29. IEEE Computer Society Press, Los Alamitos (2008)

A Mobile Intelligent Blood Pressure Monitor Based on the Android Smartphone

Yuan-Hsiang Lin*, Zhe-Min Lin, Ya-Ting Hsu, and Hau-Ying Ku

Department of Electronic Engineering, National Taiwan University of Science and Technology,
Taipei, Taiwan
{linyh,M9902134,M9902113,M9902117}@mail.ntust.edu.tw

Abstract. Self blood pressure (BP) management, monitoring, and treatment are very important and helpful for the people with hypertension. In this paper, we proposed a new mobile intelligent BP monitor based on a smartphone. This monitor comprises a homemade wrist BP monitor and an Android smartphone. The wrist BP monitor and smartphone are with high mobility. Users can set the alarm timer according their requirement. When the time is up, the friendly speech sounds will remind user to measure BP. The measuring data will be updated to the MySQL database and user can query the BP data from smartphone. The proposed monitor can help user to periodic measuring BP and managing BP and achieve the goal of prevention and health care to improve the quality of life. Accuracy of our wrist BP monitor has been verified by a commercial BP monitor and shown the differences of systolic blood pressure is -1.7 ± 6.7 mmHg and the differences of diastolic blood pressure is 2.8 ± 4.6 mmHg.

Keywords: Blood pressure monitor, Android, smartphone, blood pressure management.

1 Introduction

According to statistics, the over 40 years-old people approach 20% suffers hypertension in Taiwan. There are more than 100 million hypertension patients in China [1]. Besides, nowadays hypertension not only occurred in high age groups, but also had medical cases of illness in the adolescent groups [2][3]. RJ McManus et al. found the self BP management, monitoring and treatment for six months to 1 year, the systolic BP had significantly reduced mean difference 4.3mmHg (95% confidence interval 0.8 mmHg to 7.9 mmHg). Moreover, the cost of self monitoring BP is cheaper than normal medical care. Hence, periodic BP monitoring and tracking with treatment continuously not only can reduce the hypertensive BP but also can reduce medical costs [4].

The general oscillation sphygmomanometer has been extensive use at home care. But there are still few sphygmomanometers has management function. Wun-Jin Li et

---

* Corresponding author, IEEE member.

R.-S. Chang, T.-h. Kim, and S.-L. Peng (Eds.): SUComS 2011, CCIS 223, pp. 178–187, 2011.
© Springer-Verlag Berlin Heidelberg 2011

al. proposed a wireless BP monitoring and management system, users can track their past BP variation and the measuring data can also be regarded the reference for medical staffs [5]. However, people often too busy to forget to care their health in nowadays society. Especially the periodic BP monitoring is very important for the people with hypertension. With the rapid progress of smartphone and wireless network, give ours a new experience. Not only in communications and entertainment, but also at office et al. [6]. People use the smartphone increasingly in global. The smartphone combination functions of PC, PDA and cell phone; we can install or remove applications arbitrarily. More and more apps are taking advantage of built-in smartphone features, such as motion sensors, pedometers and sleep monitors et al. [7], to meet the demand for People.

Therefore, in this study we proposed a new mobile intelligent BP monitor based on a smartphone. This monitor comprises a homemade wrist BP monitor and an Android smartphone. The wrist BP monitor and smartphone are with high mobility. Users can set the alarm timer according their requirement. When the time is up, the friendly speech sounds will remind user to measure BP. The measuring data will be updated to the MySQL database and user can query the BP data from smartphone. The proposed monitor can help user to periodic measuring BP and managing BP and to achieve the goal of prevention and health care to improve the quality of life.

2   Methods

2.1   System Architecture

The system architecture of mobile intelligent BP monitor is shown in Fig. 1. The system includes a homemade wrist BP monitor and an Android smartphone. The wrist BP monitor is based on an ARM-based platform, which integrates with the G-sensor, pressure sensor and analog circuits including amplifiers and filters, pump and valve, and the Bluetooth module. The G-sensor can be used as position sensor, which reduces measuring error by the inappropriate measurement position. The measuring results can be transmitted to smartphone via the Bluetooth module. On the Android smartphone, BP values and heart rate (HR) value, measuring time and date information are recorded in the MySQL database. User can easy to see their past measuring data and BP variation curves through the developed graphic user interface (GUI) on Android smartphone.

Analog Circuits. The pressure sensor receives the cuff pressure from the wrist. The signal is amplified by a gain of 37.5 differential amplifier, and then the pre-amplified signal goes through a 2-order high-pass filter and a 2-order low-pass filter. Finally, the signal goes through a gain of 83.3 non-inverting amplifier. The finally AC signal (bloodstream oscillate signal) is obtained from the output of non-inverting amplifier and the DC signal (pressure value signal) is obtained from the output of differential amplifier. Both of AC and DC signal are transformed into digital signal by the built-in ADC of STM32F101C6, sample rate is 200Hz. The cut-off frequency of high-pass filter is 0.48Hz, and the cut-off frequency of low-pass filter is 40.81Hz.

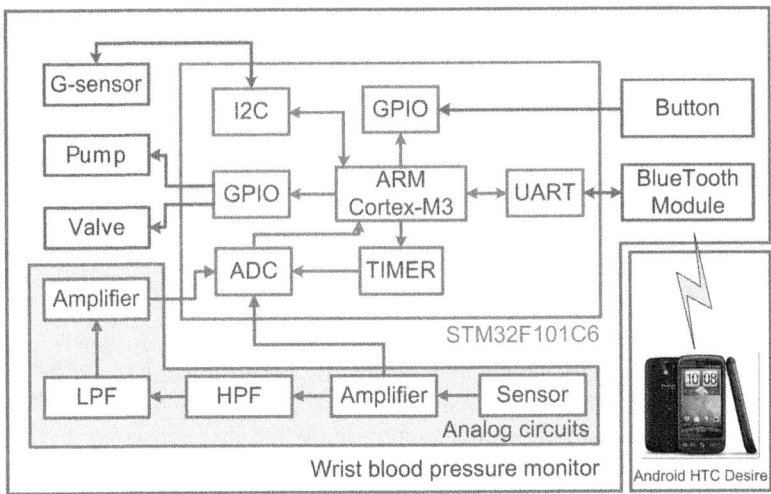

Fig. 1. System architecture of mobile intelligent BP monitor

ARM-based Platform. We used the ARM-based platform, which is made by STMicroelectronics Company. The STM32F101C6 is a high density ARM 32-bit microcontroller based on the Cortex-M3 core. There have 32Kbytes of embedded Flash memory, 6Kbytes of embedded SRAM, including 12-bit ADCs and I^2C, GPIOs and UARTs et al. The I^2C (inter-integrated circuit) bus interface serves as an interface between the microcontroller and the serial I^2C bus, it receive G-Sensor 3-axis values including x, y and z. The G-Sensor is a 3-D digital acceleration sensor. We chose the ADXL345 chip, it is small, thin and low power. The G-sensor can be used as position sensor to detect the wrist position for reducing the error caused by the inappropriate measurement position.

Android Smartphone. The Android smartphone we choose the HTC touch Desire A8181. The specification is shown in the Table 1. The Android operating system runs atop the Linux kernel from Google. They offer open source and SDK for all suppliers, which is conducive to develop applications easily. In general, application components are the essential building blocks of an Android application, and each component is a different point for system to access your application. There are four different types of application components: Activities, Services, Content providers and Broadcast receivers [8]. Besides, every Android application must have an automatically generated description file --- AndroidManifest.xml in its project root directory, it has essential information about all of these components must be declared [9]. In this paper, we implement a BP measurement and management application program on smartphone with Android operation system. We use the Eclipse IDE to develop the user interface and use java language to programming.

Table 1. HTC Touch Desire A8181 Specification

NAME	Specification
Android smartphone model	HTC Desire A8181
CPU Speed	1GHz
Memory	512 MB ROM and 576 MB RAM
Display screen	3.7-inch
Bluetooth	Bluetooth 2.1 with A2DP
Wi-Fi	Wi-Fi based on IEEE 802.11b/g standard

2.2   Software Implement and Operation Flow

This part will describe the design flow of Android GUI in details; the flow chart of software operation is shown in Fig. 2. In the beginning of executing the program, user needs to enter their ID and password. If user login successfully, there will enter the main menu which has four buttons on the menu. It includes Time Setting, BP Measurement, Emergency Contact Person Setting and Database Inspection.

First, the Time Setting interface shows a digit clock display current time and two alarm mode setting buttons, including once alarm mode and daily alarm mode. This design makes user more convenient to set alarm time to remind user to measure BP on time. Second, the BP Measurement interface. When user wants to measure BP by homemade wrist BP monitor, user need to connect to this BP monitor via Bluetooth. If connecting successfully, then user can press a start button to initialize measure procedure. On the contrary, if connecting unsuccessfully, system will turn back to main menu or trying connecting again. As measuring BP, user needs to place his/her arm as high as heart is. While arm's position is not correct, system will give a warning voice to remind user to adjust his/her arm's posture. Supposing his/her arm's position is correct, our homemade wrist BP monitor will begin to inflate; at the same time, the Android smartphone will also display current pressure value and accompanies a voice to express that Android smartphone have got values. At once finishing measurement, BP monitor will send the systolic BP (SBP), diastolic BP (DBP) and heart rate (HR) to Android smartphone to show on the screen and update MySQL database by Wi-Fi or 3G networking. Besides, if user's SBP, DBP, or HR over the default normal BP (SBP $\geq$ 140mmHg, DBP $\geq$ 90mmHg), the system will sent text message and notify user's emergency contact person automatically.

Third, the Emergency Contact Person Setting interface. User can set the phone number of emergency contact person, whom the system will contact with while physiological parameters get abnormal. With this automatic mechanism, user's families need not to examine the BP in every time. Fourth, the Database Inspection interface. As long as login successfully through the network, both user and user's family can easily observe past measuring data record and variation curve by computer or smartphone. It is really convenient and helpful for user and his family.

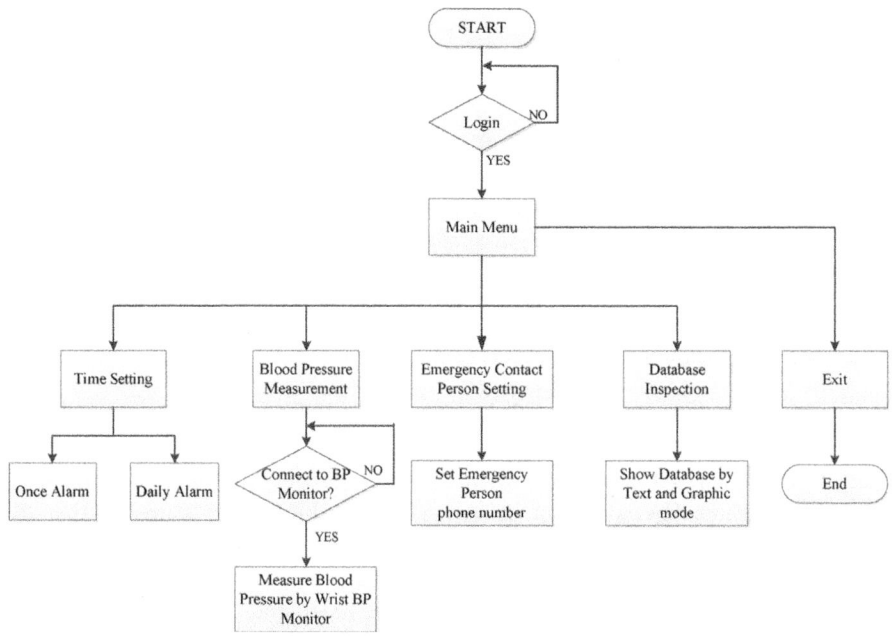

Fig. 2. Flow chart of software operation on Android smartphone

2.3   BP Calibration

The AC and DC signals of cuff pressure are transformed to the digital data, and through the ARM platform to calculate BP and HR values. In this paper, we developed a simple threshold-comparing method to perform peak detection. According to the oscillometric method, The DC cuff pressure value on the position that has maximum peak-to-peak (Pmax) AC pulse is defined as the mean BP (MBP). The automatic monitor A&D UA-767 (A&D Company, Ltd, Tokyo, Japan) is well known and widely used [10]. The validation of UA-767 device for the self-measurement devices has been recommended, so that we use it to verify and calibrate our homemade wrist BP measuring results. According to our test results, we got the SBP value is corresponding to the position that the peak-to-peak value of AC pulse is around 0.353 Pmax, and the DBP value is corresponding to the position that the peak-to-peak value of AC pulse is around 0.802 Pmax.

2.4   Subjects and Instruments

The study was carried out on 10 people. Two of these people were female and eight were male. The test was located in a quiet room with an appropriate temperature. In order to ensure the tester is in the rest state. Before start to measure BP, the tester is asked to rest for 5 min. All testers are lying on a bed and put his/her hands on both sides of their body. There are two BP monitors were used in this test. One is A&D UA-767 arm BP monitor used to measure left arm and another is our homemade wrist BP monitor used to measure left wrist. First, measurement with A&D UA-767 BP monitor and then taken at 1 min interval rest. Second, measurement with our homemade wrist BP monitor and then taken at 1 min interval rest. Repeat above two steps for three times and record these data.

3   Results

Fig.3 shows the Android smartphone and our homemade wrist BP monitor.

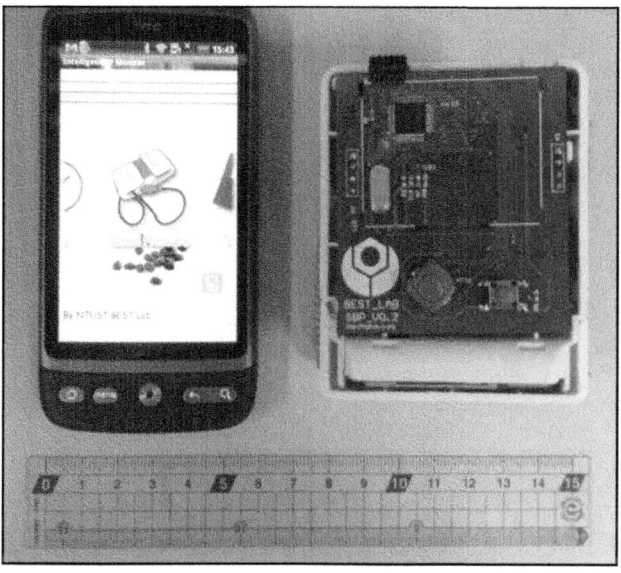

Fig. 3. Android smartphone and our homemade wrist BP monitor

3.1   Wrist BP Measuring Results

Statistical values are given as mean±SD, and using Bland-Altman limits of agreement were calculated. The study began with 10 people, the average age of the people was 24.3 ± 4.2 years old. Each person has been measured three times. According to the BP measurement results, the mean SBP was 111.6 ± 11.5 mmHg and the DBP was 68.3 ± 7.1 mmHg. The differences for the SBP between the UA-767 BP monitor and our wrist BP monitor was -1.7 ± 6.7 mmHg (shown in Fig. 4(A)), and the differences for the DBP between the UA-767 BP monitor and our wrist BP monitor was 2.8 ± 4.6 mmHg (shown in Fig. 4(B)). Both of the results are within the AAMI standard limits of 5 ± 8 mmHg.

3.2   GUI on the Android Smartphone

In this part, we will show the operation results on Android smartphone. In Fig. 5(A), there have two dialog boxes for user to input their personal ID and password. After succeed in login in system, the main menu shows four icons in Fig. 5(B) which includes Time Setting, BP Measurement, Emergency Contact Person Setting and Database Inspection. User can touch the icon into any function.

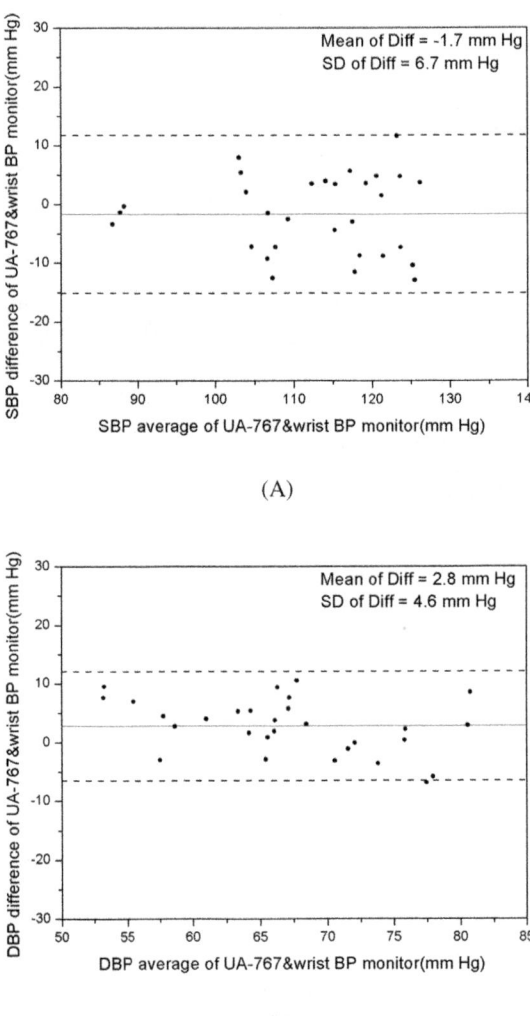

(A)

(B)

Fig. 4. (A) Plot of the differences for SBP against the mean values of the UA-767 and our wrist BP monitor and (B) Plot of the differences for DBP against the mean values of the UA-767 and our wrist BP monitor

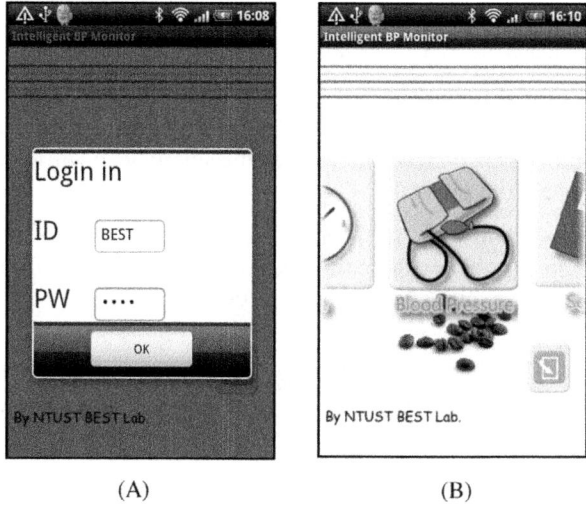

Fig. 5. (A) User login in interface and (B) main menu

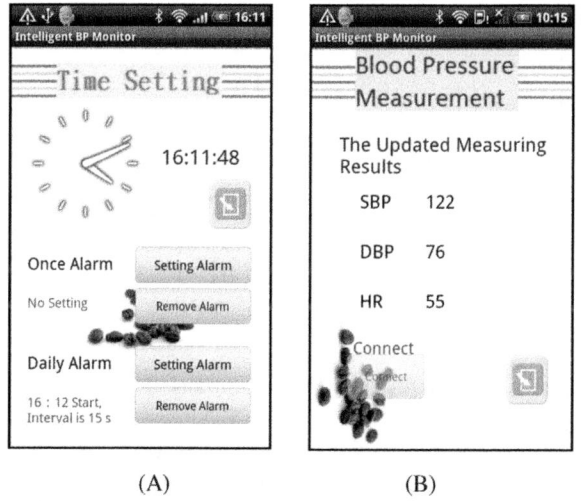

Fig. 6. (A) Time setting interface and (B) BP measurement

Time Setting. In Fig. 6(A), there show a current time and four buttons, including two alarm mode setting that are once and daily alarm mode. The once alarm setting means it just to remind BP measurement at that time once. Similarly, the daily alarm setting means it can remind BP measurement at that time every day. On the other hand, user can remove this alarm.

BP Measurement. When the alarm time is up, the speech sounds will remind user to measure BP. User need to connect smartphone to the wrist blood pressure monitor via

Bluetooth. After BP measurement, the measuring data will be updated to the MySQL database and user can query the BP data from smartphone. Fig. 6(B) shows measuring BP values, includes the SBP, DBP and HR.

Emergency Contact Person Setting. In Fig. 7(A), user can set the emergency contact person's telephone number. If the BP is larger than the default normal BP (SBP $\geq$ 140mmHg, DBP $\geq$ 90mmHg), then the smartphone will sent a message/call to the emergency contact person.

Database Inspection. Fig. 7(B) shows two curve figures, including HR and BP curve. User can easy to see the past measuring data and BP variation. Fig. 7(B) also shows the MySQL database below the two curve figures.

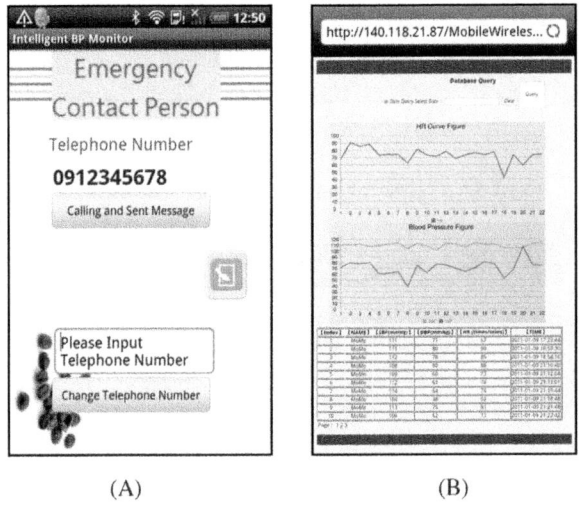

(A)   (B)

Fig. 7. (A) Emergence contact person setting and (B) MySQL database inspection

4   Discussion and Conclusion

In this paper, we proposed a new mobile intelligent BP monitor based on a smartphone. This monitor comprises a homemade wrist BP monitor and an Android smartphone. Accuracy of our wrist BP monitor has been verified by a commercial BP monitor. The differences for the SBP between the UA-767 BP monitor and our wrist BP monitor was -1.7 $\pm$ 6.7 mmHg, and the differences for the DBP was 2.8 $\pm$ 4.6 mmHg. Both of the results are within the AAMI standard limits of 5 $\pm$ 8 mmHg. However, the data set are only 10 people. It is not enough, so that we can increase the data set in the future.

On the other hand, because of the wrist BP monitor and smartphone are with high mobility. It is suitable for user to carry-on to achieve ubiquitous health care. One of the important features of our BP monitor is combining with smartphone and using speech sound to interact with people. Through our developed application program, user can set the alarm timer to remind them to measure BP at a periodic time. When the time is up, the friendly speech sounds will remind user to measure BP. User can also change the speech sound to use the voice of their family. This is more comfortable for the elder. Besides, the measuring data will be updated to the MySQL database and user or user's family can query the BP data from their smartphone. The proposed monitor can help user to periodic measuring BP and managing BP and to achieve the goal of prevention and health care to improve the quality of life.

References

1. Jiang, J., Yan, Z., Shi, J., Prabhu, K., Adinda, F.: A Mobile Monitoring System of Blood Pressure for Underserved in China by Information and Communication Technology Service. IEEE Transactions on Information Technology in Biomedicine 14(3), 748–757 (2010)
2. Lurbe, E., Cifkova, R., Cruickshank, J.K., Dillon, M.J., Ferreira, I., Invitti, C., Kuznetsova, T., Laurent, S., Mancia, G., Morales-Olivas, F., Rascher, W., Redon, J., Schaefer, F., Seeman, T., Stergiou, G., Wühl, E., Zanchetti, A.: Management of high blood pressure in children and adolescents: recommendations of the European Society of Hypertension. Journal of Hypertension 27(9), 1719–1742 (2009)
3. Obarzanek, E., Wu, C.O., Cutler, J.A., Kavey, R.E.W., Pearson, G.D., Daniels, S.R.: Prevalence and Incidence of Hypertension in Adolescent Girls. The Journal of pediatrics 157(3), 461–467 (2010)
4. McManus, R.J., Mant, J., Roalfe, A., Oakes, R.A., Bryan, S., Pattison, H.M., Hobbs, F.D.R.: Targets and self monitoring in hypertension: randomised controlled trial and cost effectiveness analysis. BMJ 331(7515), 493–498 (2005)
5. Li, W.J., Luo, Y.L., Chang, Y.S., Lin, Y.H.: A wireless blood pressure monitoring system for personal health management. In: Proceedings of 32nd Annual Conference-IEEE/EMBS, pp. 2196–2199. IEEE Press, Buenos Aires (2010)
6. Hu, W., Chen, T., Shi, Q., Lou, X.: Smartphone Software Development Course Design Based on Android. In: 10th IEEE International Conference on Computer and Information Technology, pp. 2180–2184. IEEE Press, Los Alamitos (2010)
7. How to put your smartphone "on call." Applications that run on your cell phone put health and wellness aids just a touch away. Harvard Women's Health Watch 18(4), 2–4 (2010)
8. http://developer.android.com/guide/topics/fundamentals.html
9. http://developer.android.com/guide/topics/manifest/manifest-intro.html
10. Rogoza, A.N., Pavlova, T.S., Sergeeva, M.V.: Validation of A&D UA-767 device for the self-measurement of blood pressure. Devices and Technology 5(4), 227–231 (2000)

AdTouch: A 2D-Barcode Mobile Advertising Service System

Siriphat Oumtrakul, Natharin Chanuntawaree, and Jerry Gao*

San Jose State University, San Jose, USA
Hsing Mei, Fu Jen Catholic University, Taiwan
Frank Zhang, Putara Inc., Fremont, USA
jerrygao@email.sjsu.edu

Abstract. The rapid increase of the number of mobile device users and the fast advance in mobile technologies and wireless networks created new opportunities in mobile advertising and marketing. Although barcodes have been used to support conventional electronic commerce and mobile commerce, there is a lack of research work on building 2D barcode based advertising systems and solutions to support full-cycle advertising services for mobile users, advertisers, and publishers. This paper reports a recent development of one advertising system (known as AdTouch) based on QR barcodes. Unlike the existing research in mobile advertising, this paper offers a set of comprehensive services for advertisers and publishers to market their printable 2D-barcode ads in different media, including barcode-based ad posting, distributing, detecting, and capturing using Android mobile devices. In addition, this paper presents the underlying business workflows, system architecture design, and technical solutions. Moreover, some application examples and case study results are presented.

Keywords: wireless advertising, mobile advertising, mobile commerce, mobile computing, 2D barcode based application.

1   Introduction

With the advance in wireless networking and mobile technology, the number of mobile device users is increasing rapidly. For example, in the United States, the number of mobile phones has increased from 169 million in 2004 (57% of population) to 276 million in 2009 (89% of population)[1]. This brings many opportunities and strong demands in mobile commerce and mobile advertising.

Barcode technology was developed to support electronic commerce and conventional supply chain. People started applying barcodes in mobile commerce applications as today's mobile devices have built-in quality camera with increasing memory capacity.

There are several types of mobile barcode applications. Based on our recent literature survey and product search, a popular 2D barcode application in Japan is to

---

[1] "Mobile Barcodes in Japan", retrieved from,
http://www.i-nigma.com/SuccessStories.html

R.-S. Chang, T.-h. Kim, and S.-L. Peng (Eds.): SUComS 2011, CCIS 223, pp. 188–202, 2011.
© Springer-Verlag Berlin Heidelberg 2011

store web address in product ad to assist the tracking and discovery of the product information by accessing barcode-embedded URL in advertisements. As of 2007, 2D barcodes are recognized by over 90% of Japanese mobile users, and over 50% of them use QR code. 2D barcode usage is becoming popular in European countries as well because barcodes frequently appear in diverse print media, such as poster, billboard, magazine, newspaper, promotional materials, product packaging, etc.

Although we begin to see more usage of 2D barcode in mobile commerce applications, there is a lack of published technical papers discussing its technical design, business workflows, and underlying architectures. The major technical contribution of this paper is the focus on how to build 2D barcode-based mobile advertising system. The paper presents different types of business workflows for barcode-based advertising to offer services to different user groups, including advertisers, publishers, and mobile users. Meanwhile, a new 2D barcode-based mobile advertising system, known as AdTouch, is presented, including its system architecture, functional components, as well as detailed techniques and implementations. Unlike other existing mobile advertising systems, AdTouch provides a comprehensive set of service functions for mobile advertising using 2D barcodes, with focus on services to publishers and advertisers.

The AdTouch system offers online advertising services for both advertisers and publishers to manage, schedule, publish, and deliver their 2D barcode-based advertisements. It also supports mobile device users on Android platform to access posted 2D barcode ads in diverse media, capture the barcodes, connect to the websites following the embedded URL, retrieve product details, and hence, potentially enable further mobile commerce transactions.

This paper is structured into the following sections. Section 2 provides some basic background, reviews the related research work in mobile advertising and m-commerce applications with 2D barcode. Section 3 presents the AdTouch system, including its business workflows, system architecture and components, as well as technical solutions. Section 4 presents some application examples, and Section 5 reports some case study results. Conclusion and potential future work are given in Section 6.

2   Background and Related Work

2.1   Background on 2D Barcode Technology

For decades, barcodes have been successfully used in commercial applications in many industries all around the world. The 2D barcode technology is used to contain (embed) thousands of characters. Unlike 1D barcodes (which contains a single number or serial code such as EAN, UPC, ISDN), 2D barcodes can store many types of information such as URL, product, vendor, sales, and promotional information. The embedded information in 2D barcodes can be decoded and displayed using barcode readers without internet connection.

With this capability, 2D barcode technology becomes one of the business solutions support e-commerce and business supply chains. Today, in the advertising industry, many companies use a 2D barcode in their ads to contain a URL of a merchant's website for mobile-commerce. Unlike traditional advertisements (that is not easy to support mobile accesses and M-Commerce), using 2D barcode technology in advertisements brings a new effective way to enable M-Commerce by providing a direct channel between merchants and mobile users.

QR Code Standard

QR code is one 2D barcode standard, which is widely used in different applications including advertising. Recently, it appears frequently in posted ads in magazines, newspapers, and posters. Based on its published specification (www.qrcode.com), a QR code is comprised of five patterns: finder pattern, timing pattern, formatting information, alignment pattern, and data cell. These patterns defined the structure of QR codes. To decode and retrieve information from 2D barcodes, image processing algorithms are needed. Its decoding process has five steps in [2]:

- *Pre-processing:* The step is to adopt the gray level histogram calculation.
- *Corner marks detection:* The marks on the three corners are detected using the finder pattern.
- *Fourth corner estimation:* The special algorithm is used to detect the fourth corner.
- *Inverse perspective transformation:* Bi-level code image is used to normalize size and shape of the barcode.
- *Scanning of code:* data cell inside the code is read.

QR Code (QR stands for Quick Response) was originally developed by Denso Wave (a division of Denso Corporation in Japan).

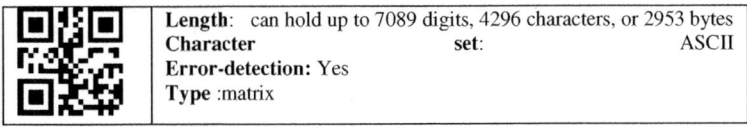

Length: can hold up to 7089 digits, 4296 characters, or 2953 bytes	
Character set: ASCII	
Error-detection: Yes	
Type :matrix	

Fig. 1. QR Code (http://www.denso-wave.com/qrcode/index-e.html)

QR Code is represented by a square area that consists of black and white square dots with a finder pattern located on three corners of the area. By 2007, QR codes are extensively used by over 50% of Japanese mobile users. It is also becoming popular in European countries. There, QR codes are mostly used in print media such as poster, billboard, magazine, newspaper, promotional materials, product packaging, and etc.

Table 1. QR Code Advantages

Advantages	Description
High Capacity Encoding of Data	QR Code is capable of handling all types of data, such as numeric and alphabetic characters, symbols, binary, and control codes. Numeric only has a maximum capacity of 7,089 characters. Alphanumeric only has a maximum capacity of 4,296 characters. Binary (8 bits) only has a maximum capacity of 2,953 bytes.
Small Footprint Size	QR Code carries information both horizontally and vertically and is capable of encoding the same amount of data in approximately one-tenth the space of a traditional 1D barcode.
Readable from any direction	QR Code accomplishes this task through position detection patterns located at the three corners of the symbol. These *position detection pattern* guarantees table high-speed reading, circumventing the negative effects of background interference.

2.2   Related Work in Mobile Commerce

With the significant increase of the mobile network, mobile users have become a focusing target by the advertising and marketing industry due to the major advantages of wireless advertising in mobile accessibility, personalization, and location awareness. These advantages critically increase the effectiveness of wireless advertising [3]. In fact, mobile advertising can deliver text message as well as rich content, such as pictures, audio, or video, to individual subscribers. According to Houston and Gassenheimer [6], mobile advertising enhances long-term relationship between end users and merchants/manufacturers. Experts believe that mobile advertising will play an important role in the advertising industry in the future [7].

There are several types of mobile advertisements. They include mobile web banners, mobile SMS, MMS, mobile web posters. Once a mobile ad has been delivered to viewers, on-going mobile user reactions and responses can be collected and provided back to merchants and manufacturers with ad tracking techniques. These tracked data can be used by the advertisers to analyze the performance of the posted ad. Some pioneering researches on mobile advertising have been reported in [1][3].

According to [1][3], there are two primary ad delivery methods in mobile advertising. They are known as push and pull methods. In the push approach, advertisers push and deliver mobile ads using systematic solutions to mobile devices directly with user permissions. In the pull approach, mobile users pull in mobile ads through clicking event or subscribed ad channels. In [5], Zoller, Housen, and Matthews classify mobile advertising into three types: a) permission-based advertising, b) incentive-based advertising, and c) location-based advertising. In the permission-based advertising, mobile users only receive the subscribed ads. In the incentive-based advertising, mobile users will be rewarded for receiving more promotions and providing their ad responses. In the location-based advertising, mobile ads are sent to mobile devices based on their location.

According to [4], the business workflow of mobile advertising process consists of three parties: a) publishers who manage and deliver an advertisement, b) advertisers who need to communicate advertisement to audience, and c) public mobile users who view the ads and may take responses to enable purchasing products from the posted ads. As discussed in [4], the process of mobile advertising includes six phases:

- *Ad space catalog*: The catalog, which is created and maintained by advertising publisher, contains the ad space basic information such as location, schedule, payment method, and current status.
- *Ad space trading*: The advertisers and publishers follow certain business steps and rules in order to initiate a business transaction.
- *Ad space schedule*: The advertisers and publishers make an agreement on when advertisement will be delivered.
- *Ad space fulfillment*: The publishers deliver the advertisement as committed.
- *Ad space measurement*: The publishers track and monitor the performance of the delivered advertisement.
- *Ad space payment*: After advertisement is delivered, the publishers collect payment from the advertisers based on the committed contract agreement.

Two other mobile advertising processes for publishers and ad service agencies are discussed in [1].

Personalization and mobility of mobile devices bring lots of business opportunities to mobile marketing and advertising. In the past years, lots of existing research work in different countries (Austria, Japan, Taiwan, and China) have shown the patterns of positive and negative attitudes (responses) of mobile consumers towards mobile advertising[11][12]. Informative and entertainment are the major factors that drive the mobile users to have positive attitudes (responses) and accept mobile advertising. In contrast, irritating is the most common negative attitudes (responses) of the mobile users thinking about mobile advertising, especially the ones that are sent without prior consent. Hence, it implies that permission-based mobile advertising might be a common approach in the future.

In wireless advertising, user privacy is always a major concern. There are a number of research papers addressing user privacy issue. For example, the MoMa project in [9] distinguishes public and private context information by requiring some personal information from users, such as profile information [9]. Another approach is to filter the ad information to separate the spam-messages from the real ads which are matched to pre-configured user interests and ad services [15]. A third approach given in [16] provides some ad search tools to allow mobile users to find the interested ads.

Recently, there are a number of papers discussed mobile advertising systems. One such advertising system is location based. In [10], the authors presented AdNext, A Visit-Pattern-Aware Mobile Advertising System for Urban Commercial Complexes. This system tracks the visited places by the mobile users, and uses a probability-based algorithm to predict the next places the same mobile users likely will visit. Based on the prediction, the system is able to provide the relevant ads relating to the predicted locations. According to [13], location-based context can be used in mobile advertising to increase the relevance of the advertisement delivered to the targeted consumers. Based on the research results given in [14], the closer to the physical location of promotional event where mobile consumers are, the more they respond to the received ad. Hence, location-based context can be effective for advertisers to create integrated mobile advertising strategies which suit the mobile users' interest at the right time and right place.

Unlike the research works addressed before, this paper presents a 2D barcode-based mobile advertising system, in which ads can be posted in diverse media (such as poster, newspaper, magazine, mobile page, and online page) with embedded 2D barcode. The barcode can be used to contain the related product information and shopping website URL address. As discussed in [8], 2D barcode-based advertising in mobile commerce offers three major benefits.

- An advertisement can be delivered in a small 2D barcode encoded with detailed product information for mobile users, including product supply-chain, product history information, and promotions and events associated.
- Capturing and decoding a 2D barcode in the posted ad, mobile users can easily discover the details about the product, and related information.
- Following URL in a 2D barcode, mobile users can easily browse to a merchant's website to conduct further m-commerce transactions, such as purchasing, payment, and delivery, as well as validation.

The authors in [8] presented our initial work in 2D barcode-based advertising. It focuses on how to develop 2D barcode-based advertising solution to support ad posting and delivery in mobile content pages. In [8], the 2D barcode standard used is Data Matrix. In this paper, the presented AdTouch system can be considered as a major extension of the research work in [8]. Unlike [8], the AdTouch system developed and implemented a comprehensive solution to support 2D barcode advertising in diverse media, including posters, newspapers, magazines, and mobile pages. The major focus here is to support three different business workflows and to facilitate publishers and advertisers to generate, manage, deliver, and post 2D barcode based mobile ads. In addition, at the mobile client side, we used Android platform and technology instead of J2ME-based platform and mobile technology. Furthermore, QR barcodes are used instead of Data Matrix.

3   AdTouch System

This section presents our developed 2B barcode based advertising system for mobile commerce. It includes three parts: a) business workflows, b) system architecture and functional components, and c) used technology and implementation.

Business Workflows

Since the system supports different types of services to three types of users, three corresponding business workflows are designed and implemented.

- **Advertisement Business Workflow** - Figure 2 shows the business workflow for advertisers. Firstly, advertisers browse the advertisement catalog and book for advertisement spaces posted by publishers. Then, they provide a preferred advertising schedule and send a request to publishers for approval. Later, the advertisers provide the information for advertising payment contracts. Once an advertisement request has been approved by a selected publisher, the advertiser provides the detailed advertisement content and generates 2D barcode advertisement with a provided barcode generation function. Later, the advertisement will be sent to the publishers for printing and posting. After ad is posted, both advertisers and publishers are able to access ad performance information and reporting functions to track and evaluate the effectiveness of the posted ads.

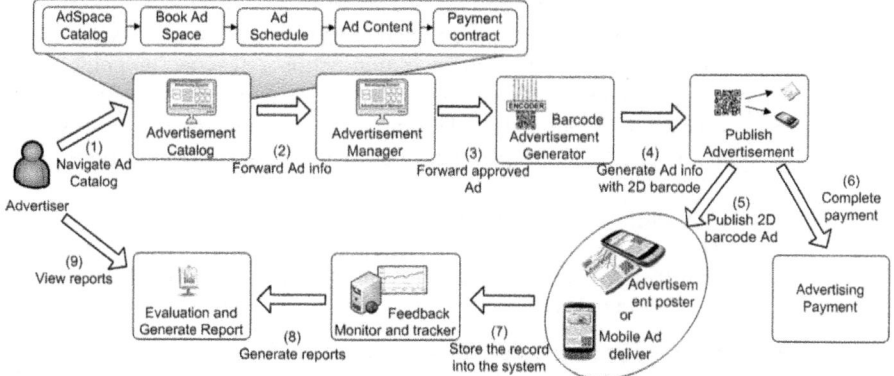

Fig. 2. The Advertisement Business Workflow

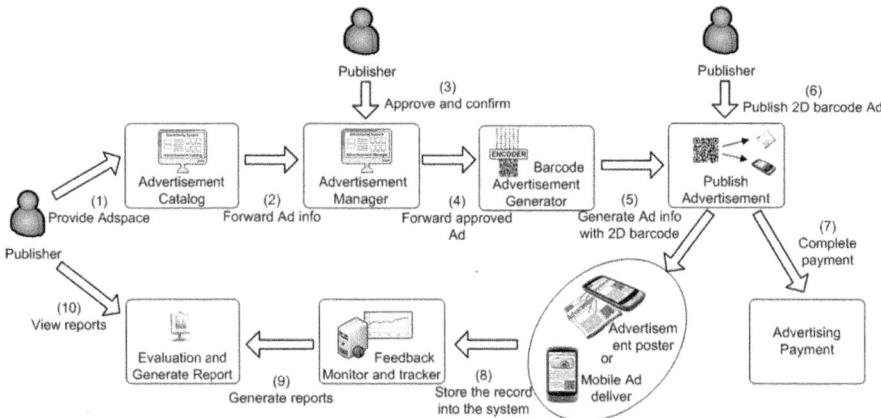

Fig. 3. The Publishing Workflow

- **Publishing Business Workflow** - Figure 3 shows the publishing workflow in which a publisher is able to access the provided online Ad Space Catalog to create, update, and delete their advertisement spaces. After advertisers check the advertisement space catalog and select ad spaces with their desired posting schedule using Ad Manager, they will need to send the request to publishers for approval. When publishers approve and confirm the posting schedule of an advertisement from the advertisers, publishers need to get the required ad information, generate and publish the corresponding 2D barcode with each confirmed advertisement. Then, publishers will post ads on publication media (such as magazines or posters), online or mobile advertisement spaces. Finally, when the ad is posted, publishers are able to access the advertisement performance report.

Mobile User Workflow to Access Mobile Ads

Figure 4 shows a workflow (or operation workflow) for mobile users. Mobile users can capture the posted 2D barcode in advertisement using the camera on their mobile devices. Then, they can view the decoded ad information from the captured 2D barcode, track the related product details, and connect to a mobile/online website from a merchant to conduct further M-Commerce transaction (such as shopping). The selected ad content and related merchant's URL can be stored for further retrievals for m-commerce. As shown in Figure 5, the AdTouch System supports four types of system users, including mobile users, advertisers, publishers, and system administrators.

AdTouch System Architecture and Components

As shown in Figure 6, the AdTouch system is structured as a three-tiered wireless internet application system below.

- *The Client Tier* - The client-tier is a presentation layer which supports the interactions between end users and different application servers in AdTouch. The online clients are developed to support publishers and advertisers to access different

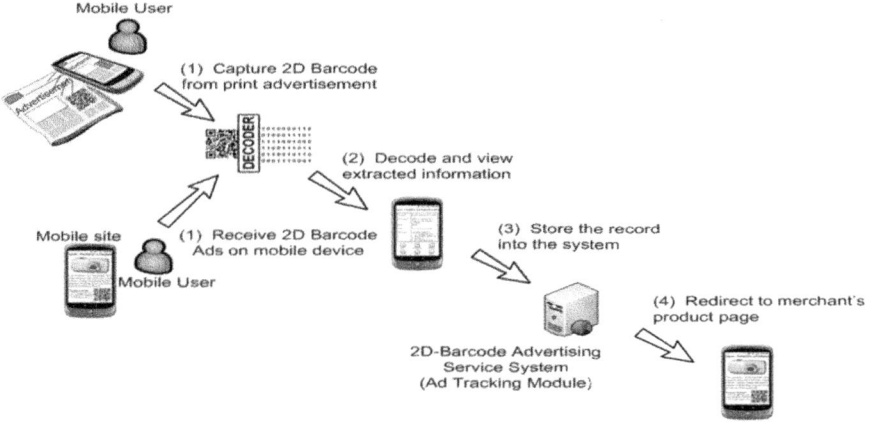

Fig. 4. Mobile User Workflow for Mobile Ads

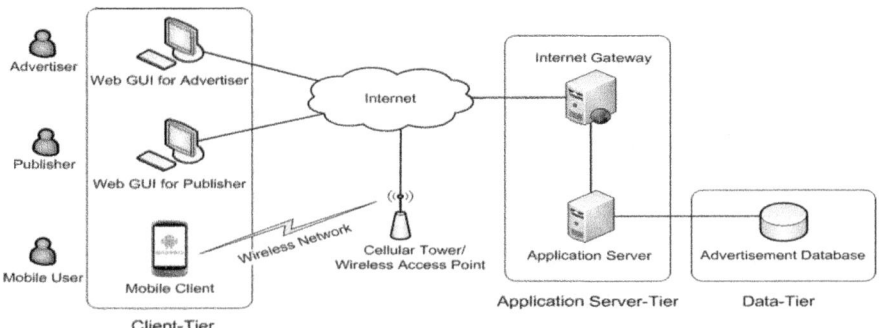

Fig. 5. The AdTouch System Architecture

types of service functions in the AdTouch system. Mobile client is implemented using Android platform, while online clients are developed as web applications.

- *The Server Tier* – The AdTouch server includes most of functional components. The application server is supported with middleware, such as web server and wireless server to interact with client software supporting mobile users at anytime and anywhere, as well as publishers and advertisers online.
- *The Data Store Tier* – This tier includes a database server (MySQL) and the database access program which manages the application database for mobile advertising, including ad-space catalog, advertisements and their posting schedule, as well as related barcodes and performance evaluation metrics.

AdTouch Application Server Architecture

Figure 6 shows the major functional components in the AdTouch application server. It is a web-based application server, which is developed based on Oracle's GlassFish application server (it is originally developed by Sun Micro System). The application server consists of the following major components:

- **Advertisement Catalog** – it offers an online accessible ad catalog for publishers and advertisers to list, select, search, and sort ad templates for ad spaces.
- **Advertisement Manager** – it controls and manages all of ads in the system to support advertisement posting, editing, deleting and retrieving. Moreover, advertisers can pick up an existing ad and preview it in a selected ad space.
- **Advertisement Scheduler** – it allows advertisers to schedule and manage ad posting schedule for their ads in each contracted ad space.
- **Advertisement Space Manager** – it controls the ad spaces in the system, such as adding, listing, editing, deleting, and retrieving ad spaces.
- **Payment Contractor** – it supports ad payment contracting and links to payment system to handle the payment process for advertising.
- **User Profile Manager** – it manages and controls the user profiles for all of existing users in the system, including advertisers, publishers, and mobile device users.
- **2D Barcode Framework** – It supports 2D barcode processing, such as: encoding, decoding, and displaying.
- **AD Tracking Manager** – It controls the tracking process so that the detailed steps of advertising process for each ad are tracked and monitored. In addition, all types of mobile users' reactions, behaviors, and responses can be tracked and stored in the AdTouch Server for ad performance evaluation later.
- **AD Performance Evaluation** - It provides different types of ad performance evaluation reports based on the stored tracking records about each ad space and its posted ads. This service function is very useful for both publishers and advertisers to understand the effectiveness of each ad space

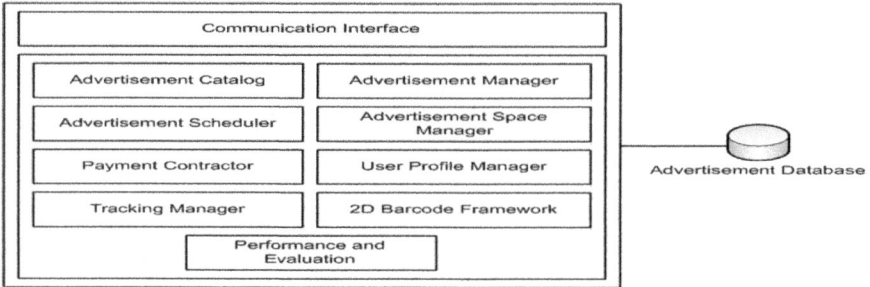

Fig. 6. The System Application Server Components

Mobile Client Architecture

AdTouch provides two kinds of user interfaces, a) online html-based user interfaces, this are particularly needed for the advertiser and the publisher, and b) android-based mobile user interface, which is primarily intended for the mobile users. Figure 7 shows the functional components in a mobile client. The following is a brief discussion of these components.

- **Ads Web Viewer** - This web viewer allows a user to view the ad contents.
- **2D Barcode Framework (Detector/Decoder/Viewer)** - This handles barcode decoding and content displaying.

- *Ads Viewed Barcode Manager* - This manages the viewed barcodes in a history file, so that mobile users can manage (retrieve and delete) stored barcodes in the history file as needed.
- *Ads Detail viewer* - This web viewer for detailed ad contents by retrieving 2D barcode data and provide means for following the embedded URL to merchant website.
- *Print 2D Barcode Ads Retriever* – This retrieves captured barcode information to mobile client user.
- *Ads Tracker* - This supports the ad tracking and performance reporting as a part of the application server.

In addition, it also includes some security functions, such as authentication and session management. To support 2D barcode capture function, we developed an abstract camera API stacked on top of the existing camera API given in the Android platform to increase the portability of the mobile client. Besides, the mobile client has a location-based service interface which connects to another location-based mobile ad system. Furthermore, a temporary storage is used on the mobile client side to keep certain ad tracking data and the storage of the temporary barcodes to support the viewer component. The mobile client architecture is shown in Figure 8.

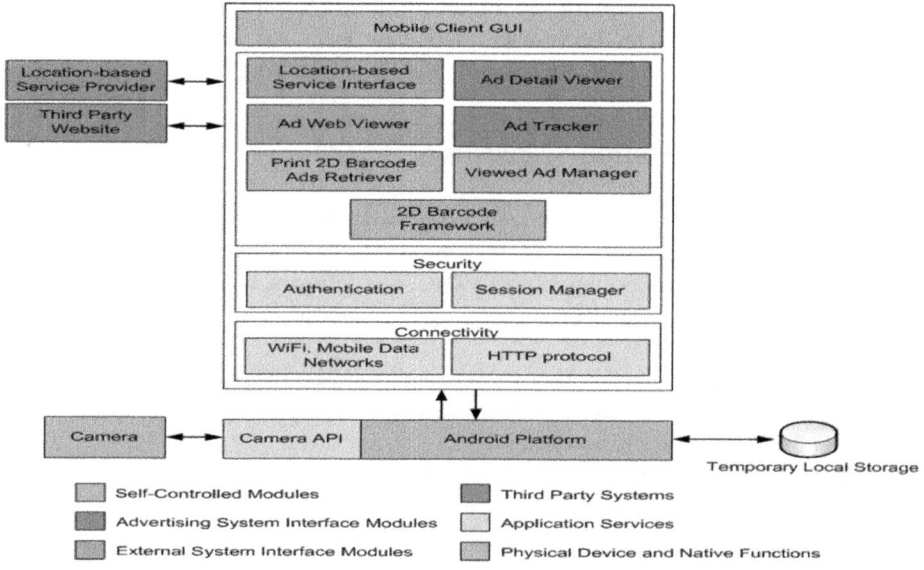

Fig. 7. Mobile Client Architecture in AdTouch

Implementation Solutions and Technology:

- *Ad space formats and types:* For publishers, AdTouch provides four types of ad spaces for different media, including poster, billboard, online page, and magazine. Meanwhile, certain types of ad space templates are provided for users to choose.

- *Advertisement types:* AdTouch currently supports different types of advertisements, including coupons, promotion ads, and product ads. Each advertisement includes 2 parts: a) a 2D barcode of the ad, and b) the detailed ad information. Whenever an ad is created or uploaded to the system, its corresponding barcode can be generated.
- *Communication support:* The communication between clients and the AdTouch server is supported by the RESTful protocol. The Spring Framework provides an easy way to connect third-party applications using the RESTful protocol. Moreover, it supports many data formats, such as JSON and XML, which allows the server to read/write and convert XML easily.
- *Mobile client implementation:* On the mobile client side, Java-based Spring Framework is used to build the mobile client using the Android device platform. Its advantage is to separate mobile client software into three parts: model, viewer and controller. In addition, a set of Android APIs are used, including Camera APIs, SQLite, GPS APIs, Zxing Barcode APIs. In order to avoid the dependency of Android-specific camera API, an abstract layer of the camera API was developed.
- *Server implementation:* The AdTouch server is developed using the MVC Spring Framework technology based on a Glassfish Application Server. JSP technology is used to present dynamic HTML pages, and Servlets are used to handle web users' requests. In addition, a MySQL database server is used to support data storage, persistence, and data access in the mobile advertising database.

4   System Application Scenarios

This section provides a scenario going through a completed scenario that accesses the primary functional operations in the system. The scenario starts with ad and ad-space creation until the ad has been published. Then, it is followed by mobile usage scenario in which a mobile user captures and accesses the published advertisement.

Step 1: A publisher creates user account and the related login access information.

Step 2: A publisher creates any ad space for advertiser to pick this ad space.

Step 3: An advertiser logins as a user.

Step 4: Advertiser enters a product's information and its ad.

Step 5: Advertiser picks an advertisement space.

Step 6: Once the ad space selected, publishers have to review and approve or decline it.

Step 7: After advertisement has been approved, contract is created.

Step 8: Advertisement is posted.

Due to paper size limitation, screen captures from some of the web client operations are provided in attached figures. Figure 8 shows the web client start screen. Figure 9 presents the ad space catalog screen. Figure 10 shows an ad with a QR barcode.

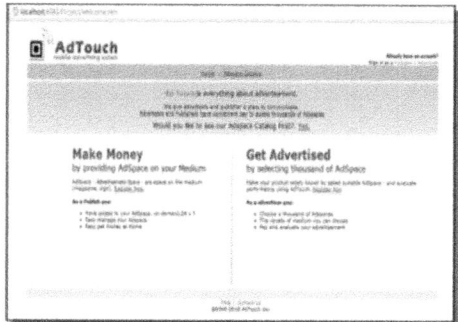

Fig. 8. Web Client Start Screen

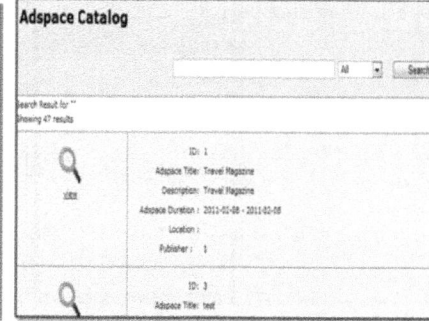

Fig. 9. Ad Space Catalog Screen

Fig. 10. Advertisement with a QR Code

The mobile user scenario is given below:

Step 1: A mobile user starts a mobile client.
Step 2: A mobile user captures the barcode in a posted advertisement.
Step 3: A mobile user views the ad contents by decoding the captured barcode in ads.
Step 4: Advertisers/publishers can track the responses of the ads in ad spaces.
Step 5: Advertisers/publishers are able to access and check ad tracking states.
Step 6: Advertisers/publishers access the different summary reports.

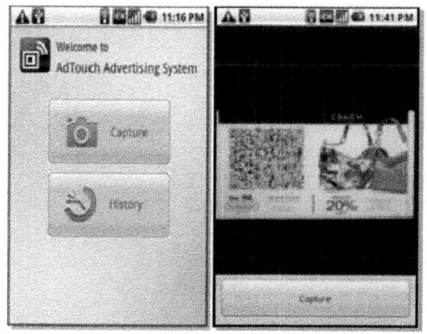

Fig. 11. Mobile Client Barcode Capturing Screens

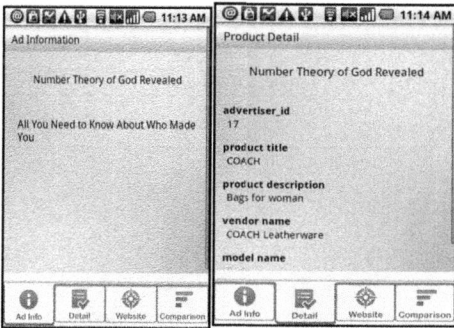

Fig. 13. Mobile Ad Detailed Screens

Due to the paper size limitation, only a few of the mobile client screens are presented here. Figure 11 presents the mobile client screens where a user is able to capture 2D barcodes in any posted ad and views it on a mobile device. Figure 12 shows the mobile screens that allows a mobile user to access the decoded ad contents. Figure 13 displays mobile tracking screens for advertisers, and Figure 14 shows the online tracking support.

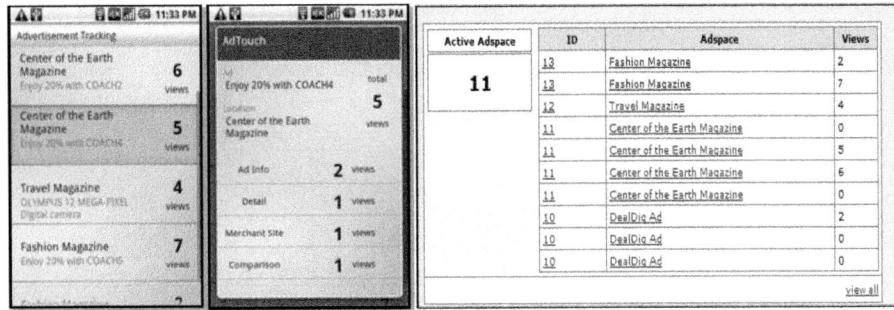

Fig. 13. Mobile Ad Tracker Screens   **Fig. 14.** Web Ad Tracker Screen

5   Performance and Benchmarks

Certain performance tests are conducted to measure the speed and response time of the AdTouch System from the mobile client side. We selected three scenarios from a mobile client to measure: (a) page querying, (b) ad status tracking and update, and (c) QR barcode decoding time. We performed the tests by collecting and tracking operation time for each task. For each scenario, we performed multiple tests and find the associated performance, such as the average user-oriented response time. For system validation, mobile clients are used to connect to the application database server in AdTouch over a wireless internet.

Page Loading Performance
In this test set, we measured the page loading time for mobile clients, including the pages in Ad Information, Product Detail, Merchant Site, and Location-Based Price Comparison. The detailed test results are given in Table 2.

Table 2. Page Loading Performance

Processing Time (msecs)	Test 1	Test 2	Test 3	Average
Ad Information Page	30	28	47	35
Product Detail Page	3630	1711	1292	2211
Merchant Site Page	30	24	31	28.3
Location-Based Price Comparison Page	2737	3124	3598	3153

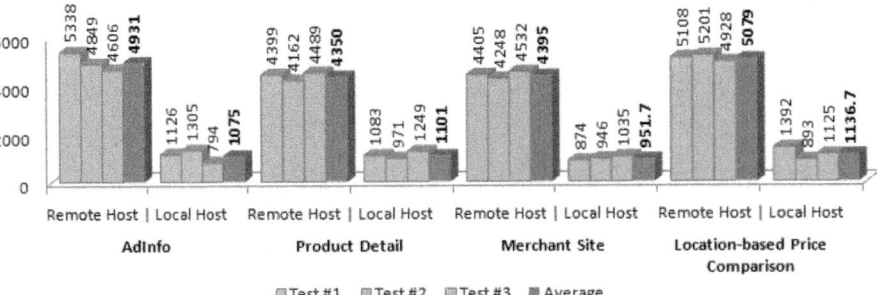

Fig. 15. User Response Performance

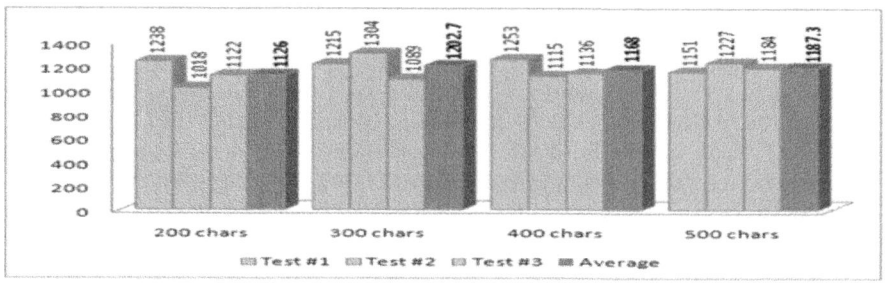

Fig. 16. QR Code Decoding Performance

Performance of Tracking Status Updating
When mobile users open a page in the mobile client, the system updates the advertisement status to the server. In this test set, we measured the performance of ad updating and tracking for a mobile client. This test set includes different mobile client pages, including Ad Info, Product Detail, Merchant Site, and Location-based Price Comparison. The detailed results are shown in Figure 15.

QR Barcode Decoding Performance
We also conducted some performance tests on QR code decoding feature. QR barcodes with different lengths of characters are tested. Figure 16 shows the detailed decoding performance data for QR barcodes. The average decoding time was approximately one second for each QR barcode. However, the current prototype has a limitation to support QR barcodes with more than 600 chars due to the limited memory sixe on the mobile device (T-Mobile G1).

6   Conclusion and Future Work

This paper presented a 2D-barcode based mobile advertising service system, known as AdTouch, which provides a direct channel among publishers, advertisers, mobile users, and merchants. All advertisements are created with accessible QR-based 2D barcodes for advertisers to allow mobile users to connect to merchants' websites anywhere and anytime.

This paper reports the developed business processes, system architecture, and design, as well as its implementation. For future research, we are working on the integration of other mobile-based advertising techniques and solutions, such as location-based and context-based methods. Meanwhile, we are developing mobile targeting techniques to enhance and improve the effectiveness of mobile advertising. Finally, we are building a new service-oriented advertising system in clouds.

References

1. Gao, J.Z., Shim, S., Su, X., Mei, H.: Engineering Wireless-Based Software Systems and Applications. Artech House Publishing, Boston (2006)
2. Ohbuchi, E., Hanaizumi, H., Hock, L.A.: Barcode Readers using the Camera Device in Mobile Phones. In: Proceedings of the International Conference on Cyberworlds, Washington D.C. (2004)

3. Yunos, H.M., Gao, J.Z., Shim, S.: Wireless Advertising's Challenges and Opportunities. IEEE Computer 36 (2003)
4. Gao, J.Z., Ji, A.: Smart Mobile AD: An Intelligent Mobile Advertising System. In: 3rd International Conference on Grid and Pervasive Computing (2008)
5. Chen, P.-T., et al.: Broadband Mobile Advertisement: What are the Right Ingredient and Attributes for Mobile 14 Subscribers. Management of Engineering &Technology (2009)
6. Houston, F.S., Gassenheimer, J.B.: Marketing and Exchange. Journal of Current Issues and Research in Advertising 51 (1987)
7. Dezoysa, S.: Mobile Advertising Needs to Get Persona. Telecommunications International (2002)
8. Gao, J.Z., et al.: A 2D-Barcode Based Mobile Advertising Solution. In: 21st International Conference on Software Engineering & Knowledge Engineering (SEKE), Boston, Massachusetts (2009)
9. Bulander, R., et al.: Advertising Via Mobile Terminals–Delivering Context Sensitive and Personalized Advertising While Guaranteeing Privacy. In: E-business and Telecommunication Networks. CCIS, vol. 3. Springer, Heidelberg (2007)
10. Kim, B., et al.: AdNext, A Visit-Pattern-Aware Mobile Advertising System for Urban Commercial Complexes. ACM HotMobile (2011)
11. Haghirian, P., et al.: Mobile Advertising in Different Stages of Development: A Cross-Country Comparison of Consumer Attitudes. In: Proceedings of the 41sth Hawaii International Conference on System Sciences (2008)
12. Tsang, M.M., et al.: Consumer Attitudes Toward Mobile Advertising: An Empirical Study. International Journal of Electronic Commerce 8(3) (2004)
13. Goh, K.Y., Chu, H., Soh, W.: Mobile Advertising: An Empirical Study of Advertising Response and Search Behavior. In: Proceedings of ICIS (2009)
14. Bruner II, G.C., Kumar, A.: Attitude Toward Location-based Advertising. Journal of Interactive Advertising (2007) retrieved from, http://jiad.org/article89
15. Kim, Y.S., et al.: Mobile Advertisement System using Data Push Scheduling based on User Preference. In: Wireless Telecommunications Symposium (2009)
16. Lovitskii, V., et al.: Mobile Search and Advertising. In: Second International Conference on Intelligent Information and Engineering Systems (2009)

MIMO Relay Selection with Suboptimal Power Allocation Transmission over Cooperative Communication Networks

Yi-Sian Wu[1], Chia-Hung Yeh[1,2], Wen-Yu Tseng[1],
Wan-Jen Huang[1,2], Min-Kuan Chang[3]
Ruey-Nan Yeh[4], Chiu-Lan Chu[4], and Po-Yi Sung[4]

[1] Department of Electrical Engineering
[2] Institute of Communication Engineering,
National Sun Yat-sen University,
No. 70, Lienhai Rd., 80424 Kaohsiung, Taiwan
[3] Department of Electrical Engineering,
National Chung Hsing University
No. 250, Kuo Kuang Rd., 402 Taichung, Taiwan
[4] Chung-Shan Institute of Science and Technology
No. 481, Sec. chia an, Zhongzheng Rd., 325 Taoyuan County, Taiwan
yeh@mail.ee.nsysu.edu.tw,
wjhuang@faculty.nsysu.edu.tw

Abstract. In order to enhance the relay's performance, and use the resource efficiently, a multiple input multiple output (MIMO) relay selection scheme based on amplify-and-forward (AF) cooperative system is proposed. In this paper, we consider the diversity combining at MIMO relays, and provide a condition to maximize the overall output signal-to-noise ratio (SNR). In this condition, the ineffective relays will be excluded in sequence from the cooperation; therefore the unused relays can be reallocated to other users. In the proposed system model, we use the maximal ratio combining (MRC) at MIMO relay, and employ the best channels from each relay to the destination. Each relay transmits the signal with identical power; meanwhile, the total power allocated to the source and the selected relays is set by suboptimal distribution. Simulation results indicate that the effect of bit error rate (BER) through the relay selection is similar to the scheme which applies all relays, but the amounts of used relay decreased. And the proposed MIMO relay scheme is superior to the single input single output (SISO) one about 7dB. Therefore, the relay resource could be used more efficiently than we employ all relay. In addition, the MIMO relay scheme can enhance the relay's performance.

Keywords: MIMO relay, amplify-and-forward (AF), relay selection, power allocation, cooperative relay networks.

R.-S. Chang, T.-h. Kim, and S.-L. Peng (Eds.): SUComS 2011, CCIS 223, pp. 203–211, 2011.
© Springer-Verlag Berlin Heidelberg 2011

1   Introduction

The relay has become a significant role in the wireless cooperative communication. In general, the relaying techniques contain amplify-and-forward (AF) and decode-and-forward (DF). In this paper, we consider cooperative system using AF scheme.

The signal intensity at relay may be weak to cause the relays ineffective, although the relay set also can provide the spatial diversity for destination. In order to endure the bad channel state from source to relays and the channel form relays to destination, the MIMO relay is used for our system model. The MIMO relay system can provide the spatial diversity for relays, so the relay performance will be enhance. The performance analysis of AF based MIMO relay is discussed in [1]. We consider an AF based cooperative system with multiple relays and the channel state information (CSI) [2]. The source and the destination have single antenna, and each relay supports multiple antennas.

The power allocation strategies have become a promising technique to increase the transmission efficacy. The three-node models and the multi-hop relay system are discussed in [3]-[10]. In [6], the transmission power allocation is explored between the source and relay set to maximize the output signal to noise ratio (SNR) at destination.

However employing all relays is not effective, when some of those relays in deep channel fading are no helpful in the cooperation. In this paper, a condition is introduced to find the minimum relay numbers, which can provide the maximum output SNR. In this condition, the effective relays are excluded in sequence from the cooperation, so that the unused relays can be reallocated to other users.

The simulation results show that the MIMO relay scheme is superior to the SISO one [11] about 7dB. And the relay selection scheme with suboptimal power allocation can achieve similar BER performance with the scheme which uses all relays.

In Section 2, the system model is presented. In Section 3, the overall output SNR with MIMO relay is analyzed, and the relay selection is introduced. The simulation results are showed in Section 4. Section 5 concludes the paper.

2   System Model

We consider an AF based cooperative system with MIMO relay, as show in Fig. 1, the source (S) and the destination (D) have single antenna, and the relays (R) support multiple antennas. There are one source, N relays and one destination in the system. The i-th relay has M_r antennas that are used for reception from source to relay link, and transmitting on the best channel from relay to destination. All transmissions using binary phase shift keying (BPSK) over orthogonal channels. Let x denotes the symbol transmitted at the source with power P_s. The received signals at the j-th antenna of the i-th relay is represented by y_i^j. The fading channel coefficients on the S-D, S-R and R-D links are $h_{s,d}$, h_{s,r_i^j} and $h_{r_i,d}$ respectively. We suppose the fading channels are independent and constant with one transmission block which change independently from one block to another. The corresponding additive white Gaussian noise (AWGN) are denoted by $n_{s,d}$, n_{s,r_i^j} and $n_{r_i,d}$ respectively.

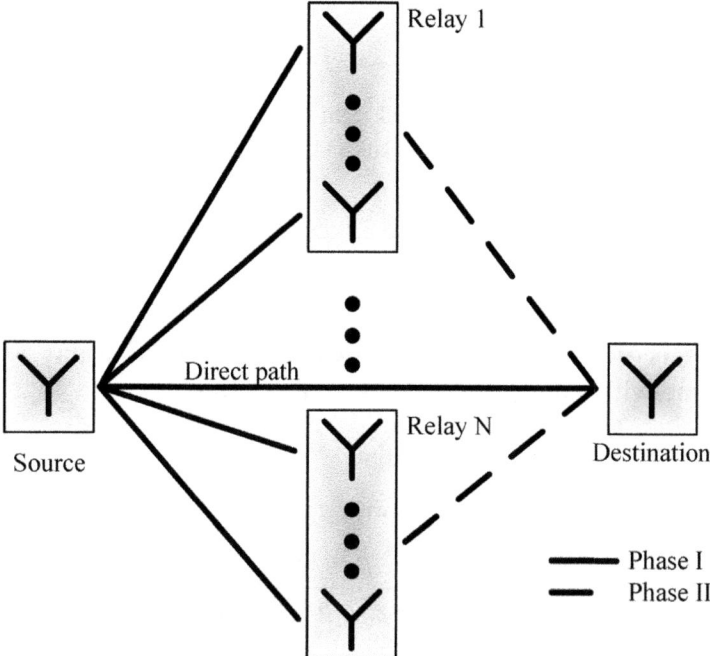

Fig. 1. MIMO relay based model for cooperative system

In the first phase, the source broadcasts the signal to both the relays and the destination. The received signal on the S-D and S-R links are respectively expressed as

$$y_{s,d} = \sqrt{P_s} h_{s,d} x + n_{s,d}. \tag{1}$$

$$y_{s,r_i^j} = \sqrt{P_s} h_{s,r_i^j} x + n_{s,r_i^j}, \qquad i = 1, \dots, N, \qquad j = 1, \dots, M_r. \tag{2}$$

The channel coefficients are assumed to be Rayleigh fading. Hence $a_{s,d} \sim \mathcal{CN}(0, \sigma_{s,d})$, $a_{s,r_i^j} \sim \mathcal{CN}(0, \sigma_{s,r_i^j})$ and $a_{r_i,d} \sim \mathcal{CN}(0, \sigma_{r_i,d})$ are complex Gaussian random variables with zero mean and variances $\sigma_{...}$. $n_{s,d}$, n_{s,r_i^j} and $n_{r_i,d}$ are zero mean complex Gaussian random variables with variance of N_0. The AF mechanism is used at the relays using combination of MRC to achieve cooperative diversity. Applying MRC [12] at i-th relay, we have

$$x_i = \sum_{j=1}^{M_r} a_{s,r_i^j}^* y_{s,r_i^j}, \qquad i = 1, \dots, N. \tag{3}$$

In the second phase, the signal x_i is transmitted by the i-th relay using a single antenna which has best channel state. The i-th relay transmission power P_i used for this transmission, obtained as a amplification factor of [13], is given by

$$\beta_i = \sqrt{\frac{1}{P_s C_i + N_0}}, \qquad C_i = \sum_{j=1}^{M_r} \left| a_{s,r_i^j} \right|^2, \qquad i = 1, \dots, N. \tag{4}$$

The received at the destination through the i-th relay can be written as

$$y_{r_i,d} = \sqrt{P_i} a_{r_i,d} x + n_{r_i,d}, \qquad i = 1, \ldots, N. \tag{5}$$

At the destination, the signal received from the relays and the signal received from the source are combined using MRC. The output of MRC, as shown in [13] can be expressed as

$$y = \frac{\sqrt{P_s}}{N_0} a_{s,d}^* y_{s,d} + \sum_{i=1}^{N} \frac{\beta_i C_i \sqrt{P_s} \sqrt{P_i}}{\left(\beta_i^2 C_i P_i |h_{r_i,d}|^2 + 1\right) N_0} a_{r_i,d}^* y_{r_i,d}. \tag{6}$$

3   Analysis of Overall Output SNR and the MIMO Relay Selection Scheme with Suboptimal Power Allocation

3.1   The Analysis of the Overall Output SNR

In order to analyze the output SNR, we write y in terms of x as

$$
\begin{aligned}
y = {} & \frac{P_s}{N_0}\left(|a_{s,d}|^2 + \sum_{i=1}^{N} \frac{\beta_i^2 C_i^2 P_i |a_{r_i,d}|^2}{\beta_i^2 C_i P_i |a_{r_i,d}|^2 + 1}\right)x + \frac{\sqrt{P_s}}{N_0} a_{s,d}^* n_{s,d} \\
& + \sum_{i=1}^{N} \frac{\beta_i C_i \sqrt{P_s}\sqrt{P_i} a_{r_i,d}^*}{\left(\beta_i^2 C_i P_i |a_{r_i,d}|^2 + 1\right) N_0}\left(n_{r_i,d} + \sum_{j=1}^{M_r} \beta_i a_{s,r_i^j}^* n_{s,r_i^j}\right).
\end{aligned}
\tag{7}
$$

When N relays are used, the output SNR is denoted by $\gamma(N)$, and it can be expressed as

$$\gamma(N) = \frac{P_s}{N_0}\left(|a_{s,d}|^2 + \sum_{i=1}^{N} \frac{\beta_i^2 C_i^2 P_i |a_{r_i,d}|^2}{\beta_i^2 C_i P_i |a_{r_i,d}|^2 + 1}\right). \tag{8}$$

From (4) and (8), we obtain

$$\gamma(N) = \frac{P_s}{N_0}\left(|a_{s,d}|^2 + \sum_{i=1}^{N} \frac{C_i^2 P_i |a_{r_i,d}|^2}{C_i P_i |a_{r_i,d}|^2 + C_i P_s + N_0}\right). \tag{9}$$

In order to simplify theo equation, we approximate the output SNR at high SNR, and using the inequality of arithmetic and geometric means $(\alpha^{-1} + \beta^{-1})^{-1} \leq \frac{1}{2}\sqrt{\alpha\beta}$ for $x, y \geq 0$. It gives a very close expression as following:

$$
\begin{aligned}
\gamma(N) &= \frac{P_s}{N_0}\left(|a_{s,d}|^2 + \sum_{i=1}^{N} \frac{C_i^2 P_i |a_{r_i,d}|^2}{C_i P_i |a_{r_i,d}|^2 + C_i P_s}\right) \\
&= \frac{1}{N_0}\left\{P_s |a_{s,d}|^2 + \sum_{i=1}^{N}\left[(P_s)^{-1} + \left(P_i |a_{r_i,d}|^2\right)^{-1}\right]^{-1} C_i\right\} \\
&\leq \frac{1}{N_0}\left(P_s |a_{s,d}|^2 + \frac{1}{2}\sum_{i=1}^{N} \sqrt{P_s P_i} |a_{r_i,d}| C_i\right).
\end{aligned}
\tag{10}
$$

After above approximation, we obtain the optimization problem which can be written as

$$\max_{P_s, P_i} \frac{1}{N_0} \left(P_s |a_{s,d}|^2 + \frac{1}{2} \sum_{i=1}^{N} \sqrt{P_s P_i} |a_{r_i,d}| C_i \right)$$

$$s.t \quad P_s + \sum_{i=1}^{N} P_i = P. \tag{11}$$

where P denotes the total transmission power.

3.2   The MIMO Relay Selection Scheme with Suboptimal Power Allocation

As the number of the relays N increases, the closed form expression of the optimal solution become quite complicated. In order to reduce the complexity of the optimization problem in (11), we use the relay selection scheme with simplified power allocation [11], and the scheme is as following:

Each relay transmits the signal with identical power, and the total transmission power of the second phase is donated as P_r. For relay selection, let Z denote the number of the selected relays, and the output SNR is represented as

$$\gamma(Z) \le \frac{1}{N_0} \left(P_s |a_{s,d}|^2 + \frac{1}{2} \sqrt{P_s P_r} \sum_{i=1}^{Z} |a_{r_i,d}| C_i \right), \quad i = 1, ..., Z, \quad Z \le N. \tag{12}$$

The output SNR apply all $Z \le N$. Then, we can find the optimal relay selection set overall relay selection set of Z:

$$\gamma(Z) = \max_Z \gamma(Z). \tag{13}$$

In order to find the minimum K which has the maximum output SNR, let the index set of all relays be sorted by the following rule:

$$|a_{r_i,d}| C_i \ge |a_{r_{i+1},d}| C_{i+1}. \tag{14}$$

Therefore, the relays which have bad channel state of the S-D and D-R links will be excluded initially. The simplified optimization problem can be expressed as

$$\max_{P_s, P_r} \frac{1}{N_0} \left(P_s |a_{s,d}|^2 + \frac{1}{2} \sqrt{P_s P_r} \sum_{i=1}^{Z} |a_{r_i,d}| C_i \right)$$

$$s.t \quad P_s + P_r = P. \tag{15}$$

By introducing Lagrangian multiplier, the suboptimal power allocation is

$$P_s^* = \frac{P}{2} \left(1 + \frac{\mu}{\sqrt{4 + \mu^2}} \right), \quad P_r^* = \frac{P}{2} \left(1 - \frac{\mu}{\sqrt{4 + \mu^2}} \right). \tag{16}$$

where $\mu = \frac{4\sqrt{Z} |a_{s,d}|^2}{\sum_{i=1}^{Z} |a_{r_i,d}| C_i}$.

After the relay selection set and the suboptimal power allocation, we want to find the optimum K of the relay selection set. So we defined ψ as the set of the selected relays, and the set ψ contains N relays intially. In order to eliminate the ineffective relay from ψ, the $\gamma(Z)$ should satisfy:

$$\gamma(Z) < \gamma(Z-1). \tag{17}$$

On account of above analysis, we outline the relay selection scheme as following:

(1) We assume that N relays contribute to the cooperative system. Let the set ψ contains N relays initially.
(2) Let the index set of all relays be sorted by the following rule in (14). Obviously, the worse channel state of the relay is, the smaller the value of $\left|a_{r_{i},d}\right|C_i$ is.
(3) To allocate the power between the Z relays and source using the suboptimum power allocation in (16).
(4) If $\gamma(Z) < \gamma(Z-1)$, then exclude relay Z from ψ. Otherwise, go to step (6).
(5) Let $Z = Z - 1$, if $Z = 1$, go to step (3). Otherwise, go to step (6).
(6) End.

Based on above mother, the ineffective relays will be excluded in sequence from the cooperation; therefore the unused relays can be reallocated to other users.

4   Simulation Results

In this section, we provide the simulation results for SISO and MIMO relay scheme. The relay selection scheme with optimal power allocation is used for both two kinds of relay scheme. And the total power P is allocated to the source and the relay set by suboptimal distribution. Further, the total relays power P_r is shared equally among the used relays. We assume the channel fading coefficients from source to relay, relay to destination and source to destination are independent and identically distributed (i.i.d.) complex Gaussian distribution with zero mean and variance $\sigma^2 = 1$. The noise variance N_0 is assumed to Gaussian distribution. The MIMO relay system is assumed with $M_r = 2$, $N = 4$.

Due to the bit error rate can be represented as the target of the system performance [14], the maximization of the output SNR is equivalent to the minimization of the BER. Fig. 2 shows the BER performance of SISO relay selection scheme in [11], the proposed MIMO relays scheme which employs all relay and the MIMO relay selection scheme. It can be observe that the MIMO relay scheme is superior to the SISO relay scheme about 7dB at the BER of 10^{-3}.

As shown in Fig. 3, the average number of selected relays with MIMO relay selection is similar to the SISO relay selection scheme. When the P/N_0 increasing, the average number is about 2.5 which is less than the scheme by using all relay. It also indicates that the MIMO relay selection scheme can achieve similar performance to the SISO relay scheme, but the relay amount used are few.

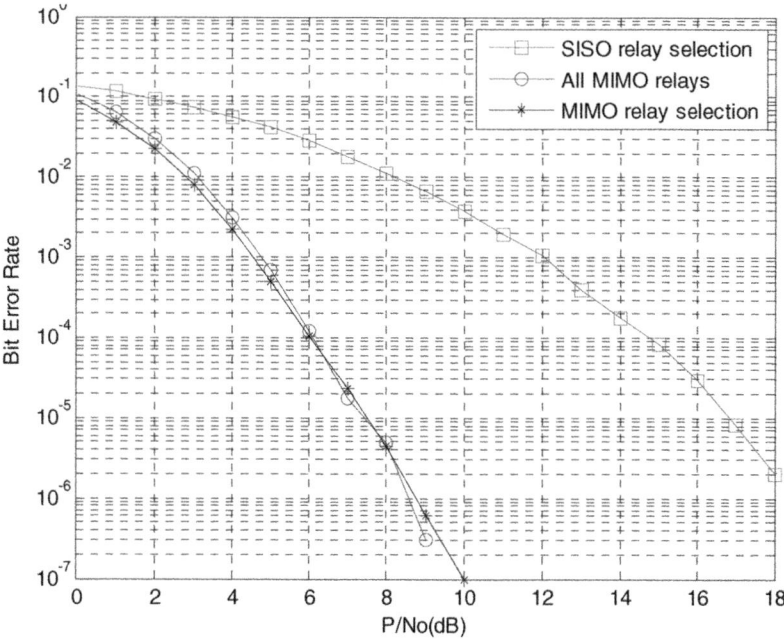

Fig. 2. Comparison of the BER for the MIMO relay scheme of using all relays, the MIMO relay selection scheme and the SISO relay selection scheme

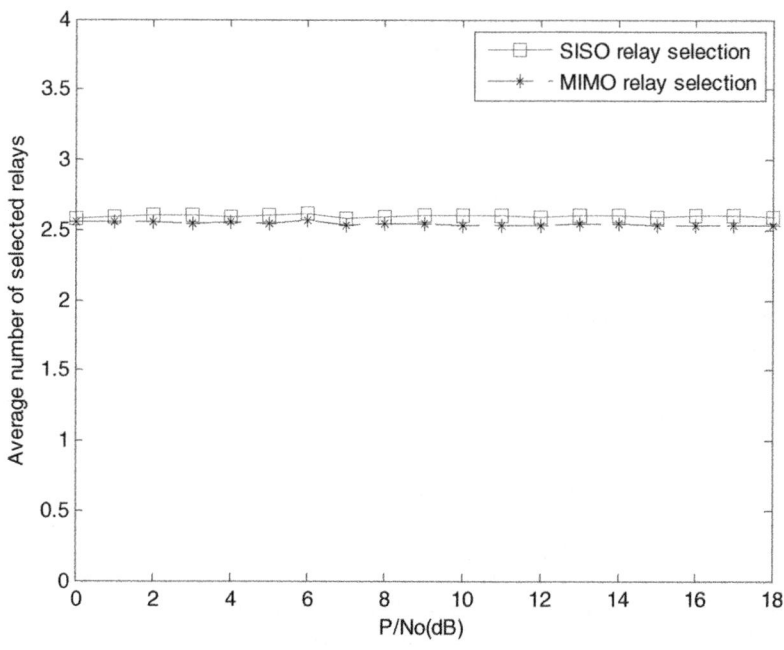

Fig. 3. The average number of selected relays among N=4 relays

5 Conclusions

In this paper, we propose the MIMO relay selection scheme based on AF cooperative system. We use the maximal ratio combining (MRC) at MIMO relay, and then we employ the best channels from each relay to the destination. After that, we provide a circumstance to maximize the overall output SNR. The simulation results indicate that the effect of BER through the relay selection is similar to the scheme which applies all relays, but the amounts of used relay decreased. And the proposed MIMO relay selection scheme appears better BER performance about 7dB than the SISO one. Therefore, the relay resource could be used more efficiently than we employ all relay. In addition, the MIMO relay scheme can enhance the relay's performance.

Acknowledgments. This work was supported by the National Science Council, R. O. C., under the Grant NSC-99-2628-E-110-008-MY3.

References

1. Ganwani, V., Dey, B.K., Sharma, G.V.V., Merchant, S.N., Desai, U.B.: Performance Analysis of Amplify and Forward Based Cooperative Diversity in MIMO Relay Channels. In: 69th IEEE Conference on Vehicular Technology, pp. 1–5 (2009)
2. Tsiftsis, T.A., Karagiannidis, G.K., Kotsopoulos, S.A., Pavlidou, F.N.: Ber Analysis of Collaborative Dual-hop Wireless Transmissions. IEE Electronic Letters 40(11) (2004)
3. Host-Madsen, A., Zhang, J.: Capacity Bounds and Power Allocation for Wireless Relay Channels. IEEE Transactions on Information Theory 51(6), 2020–2040 (2005)
4. Brown, I.D.R.: Resource Allocation for Cooperative Transmission in Wireless Networks. In: 38th Asilomar Conference on Signals, Systems and Computers, pp. 1473–1477 (November 2004)
5. Seddik, K.G., Ray Liu, K.J.: Outage Analysis and Optimal Power Allocation for Multinode Relay Networks. IEEE Signal Processing Letters 14(6), 377–380 (2007)
6. Li, Y., Vucetic, B., Zhou, Z., Dohler, M.: Distributed Adaptive Power Allocation for Wireless Relay Networks. IEEE Transactions on Wireless Communication 6(3), 948–958 (2007)
7. Hasna, M.O., Alouini, M.-S.: Optimal Power Allocation for Relayed Transmissions over Rayleigh-fading Channels. IEEE Transactions on Wireless Communication 3(6), 1999–2004 (2004)
8. Dohler, M., Gkelias, A., Aghvami, H.: Resource Allocation for FDMA-based Regenerative Multihop Links. IEEE Transactions on Wireless Communication 3(6), 1989–1993 (2004)
9. Annavajjala, R., Cosman, P.C., Milstein, L.B.: Statistical Channel Knowledge-based Optimum Power Allocation for Relaying Protocols in the High SNR Regime. IEEE Journal on Selected Areas in Communications 25(2), 292–305 (2007)
10. Hammerstrom, I., Kuhn, M., Wittneben, A.: Impact of Relay Gain Allocation on the Performance of Cooperative Diversity Networks. In: IEEE Conference on Vehicular Technology, Los Angeles, USA, pp. 1815–1819 (2004)

11. Wu, H., Wang, Y., Xiong, C., Yang, D.: A Novel Relay Selection Scheme with Simplified Power Allocation for Wireless Relay Networks. In: IEEE Conference on Global Telecommunications, pp. 1–5 (2009)
12. Brennan, D.G.: Linear Diversity Combining Techniques. IEEE 91(2), 331–356 (2003)
13. Laneman, J.N., Wornell, G.W.: Energy-efficient Antenna Sharing and Relaying for Wireless Networks. IEEE Conference on Wireless Communications and Networking 1, 7–12 (2000)
14. Proakis, J.G.: Digital Communications, 3rd edn. McGrow-Hill, Inc., New York (1995)

Agent Based Approach in Accessing Distributed Health Care Services

Srividya Bhat[1], Nandini S. Sidnal[2], and Sunilkumar S. Manvi[3]

[1] Dept. of PG Studies, VTU, Belgaum, Karnataka, India
bhatsrividya.127@gmail.com
[2] Dept. of CSE, K.L.E.S.C.E.T, Belgaum, Karnataka, India
sidnal.nandini@gmail.com
[3] Dept. of ECE, REVA ITM, Bangalore, Karnataka, India
sunil.manvi@revainstitution.org

Abstract. Healthcare organizations are facing the challenge of delivering high-quality services through effective process management at all levels- locally, regionally, nationally, and internationally. There have been frequent changes of clinical processes and increased interactions between different functional units. Software agents were adopted to provide the means to accomplish real-time application, due to their autonomous, reactive and/or proactive nature, and their effectiveness in dynamic environments by incorporating coordination strategies. Multi Agent Systems (MAS) will helps in minimizing the waiting time of patient and cost of the care also it can be used to represent the real conditions, courses, and the human decision behavior. This paper presents an overview of health care system, intelligent software agents and integration of both to achieve better Quality of service.

Keywords: Mobile users, Software agents, Multiagent systems, medical ontology, FIPA-ACL.

1 Introduction

In the last few years there has been a shift in healthcare practice towards healthcare promotion, shared patient provider decision-making and managed care, creating an increased demand for information and online services. The shared decisions and actions of all concerned need to be coordinated to make sure that the care is efficient and effective. To facilitate this, software systems are needed to reduce error in diagnosis and treatments, deliver healthcare to remote locations, improve medical training and education, and make healthcare information more accessible to patients. In this concern we intend to develop ontology for patient medical record in healthcare organizations and share information through the web to be used in different departments, healthcares, clinics or hospitals of a city, town or a remote area abroad and help to have a better treatment and efficient care system. An increase in specialization and technology, especially in the health care department requires efficient management of the resources and more timely treatment of the patients. Agents are used to solve the patient scheduling problem in the hospitals because they

R.-S. Chang, T.-h. Kim, and S.-L. Peng (Eds.): SUComS 2011, CCIS 223, pp. 212–221, 2011.
© Springer-Verlag Berlin Heidelberg 2011

work well in a distributed, decentralized and dynamic environment. An agent is a software program that acts on behalf of a user, typically used to retrieve and process information. An agent is used to represent each patient and resource in the hospitals. Interaction protocols are used to reduce the search space of possible responses to an agent messages. A medical centre contains a lot of professionals such as nurses, doctors, administrators, etc., and resources such as x-ray, gym, rehabilitation unit, etc. All of them play a specific role within the medical centre, and they must coordinate their activities to provide the best possible care to patients. Agents are often described as intelligent. That indicates that the agent takes actions on its own, and pursues the goals in the best way possible. They are not perfect, but they can operate flexibly and rationally in a variety of environmental circumstances, given the information they have and their perceptual and effectual capabilities.

The challenges in Health care services includes, Communication between services-sharing ontologies and semantics which could be heterogeneous even within the health care domain. Second challenge is Security/Authorization- accessing/editing sensitive medical data, such as the medical records of the patients. Third challenge is that creating an environment where agents can discover one another and access one another's services. Fourth challenge is the Communication between users and agents-graphical user interfaces to communicate with personal assistants. The last challenge is the Coordination between distributed services. Thus it is necessary to develop a model or a framework which overcomes the above mentioned challenges that may emerge as one of the efficient way for accessing distributed health care services.

In this paper we describe the design of Multi Agent System (MAS) which contains agents that allow the user to search for medical centers satisfying a given set of requirements, to access his/her medical record or to make a booking to be visited by a particular kind of doctor. Some of the agents in the system can provide information about the medical centers that are available in a given city. The MAS also contains an agent for each medical center in town, these agent may be asked about the doctors working in that hospital, or may be requested to perform a booking in the schedule of a specific doctor and also can access a database.

2   Related Works

Here we present accessing of health-care related services by deploying intelligent agents. The software-agent paradigm [2] [3] [4] was adopted due to its autonomous, reactive and/or proactive nature, which comprises of important features in real-time application deployment for dynamic systems like the one under consideration. Furthermore, software agents can incorporate coordination strategies, thus enabling them to operate in distributed environments and perform complex tasks. Software-agent technology is considered an ideal platform for providing data sharing, personalized services, and pooled knowledge. The work in [7] presents the Foundation for Intelligent Physical Agents (FIPA) that defines standards for agent interoperation. The aim in the Agent Cities is the construction of a worldwide publicly accessible network of FIPA based agent platforms. Each platform will support agents that offer services similar to those that can be found in a real city. Once the initial services have been deployed, it will be possible to implement intelligent complex compound services. In the research literature, there are several agent-based applications reported in the healthcare domain. In particular, one of the earliest examples of work examining the role of multi-agent systems in healthcare is offered by [6]. The focus of the work presented there, and of the broader context, in which it was conducted, is upon appropriate theorem proving in decision support systems that have to deal with complex, incomplete, inconsistent and potentially conflicting data. The agent component is designed to support of tasks amongst players in the system. Heine et al [17] simulate an agent oriented environment for German hospitals with the objective to improve or optimize the appointment scheduling system, resource allocation and cost benefit of clinical trials. Nealon and Moreno [12] have discussed the potential and application of agents to assist in a wide range of activities in health care environments. Mabry et al [18] employ the Multi agent system for providing diagnosis and advice to health care personnel dealing with traumatized patients. Nealon and Moreno [19] have discussed various applications of MAS in health care e.g., coordination of organ transplants among Spanish hospitals, patient scheduling, senior citizen care etc. A research project, called PalliaSys is offered by [20]. It incorporates information technology and multi-agent systems to improve the care given to palliative patients. An Intelligent Healthcare Knowledge Assistant [21] was developed which uses multi agent system for dynamic knowledge gathering, filtering, adaptation and acquisition from Health care Enterprise Memory unit.

The decision of using a Multi-Agent System in this medical setting and not other more traditional AI techniques such as an expert system or a decision support system is motivated by the following reasons:

- The information that must be dealt with is geographically distributed, because each hospital or medical centre will keep its own data, each doctor will have his/her personal information an up-to-date daily schedule in a personal computer, the medical records of the potential users of the system may be located in different databases, etc. Therefore, a distributed AI approaches such as the one offered by multi-agent systems seems suitable in this case.

- There must be a fluent communication between the user and the medical centers. For instance, the user's personal assistant should be able to ask for a booking with a certain doctor, and be able to react quickly if the doctor's schedule is full (so another doctor has to be chosen). Agents are not only reactive but also endowed with social abilities, so they are able to communicate with other agents in order to negotiate and co-ordinate their activities.

- Existing systems such as databases containing medical records may be easily included in a multi agent system. The standard way of agentifying a database is to put a wrapper around it. A wrapper is an agent that receives the queries to be made to the database in a standard agent communication language such as FIPA-ACL or KQML and is able to translate these requests into queries in SQL to the database; the wrapper may translate the answer to the common agent communication language and send it to the requesting agent.

- The most important reason for capturing services as agents in this way is to enable the individual medical services to interact with each other at a high enough level to ensure that they can all interoperate. Agent communication languages such as FIPA – ACL [8], content languages such as SL [9], and formal ontologies are very useful in describing communication between different services at the application level- i.e. in a way which relates to the domain of discourse rather than to any single implementation.

However, it is observed from literature survey that when the Agent Cities initiative was made public, the potential development of agents that could offer not the usual leisure-oriented services but health-care related services. The work here describes automation of a multi-agent system that caters to special types of patients or providing assistance to patients for appointments. So, the concept of intelligent agent and mobile technology is used to achieve automation, efficiency, reliability and scalability in devising Health care domain for distributed, decentralized and dynamic environment to treat the patients efficiently by cutting down the time and cost.

3   Proposed Work

This section describes the Multi-Agent System which has been developed. The primary design objectives of the work were the following:

- To provide a decomposition of the problem that matched agents to entities which could be realistic players in such a domain (e.g. medical centers, personal agents, etc).and to take care in who had access to which information.
- To provide ontology for the domain.
- To make the developed agent services as reusable as possible by using standard languages and providing detailed service models to describe the individual functioning and objective of each agent including descriptions of actions, protocols used.

The aim of the multi-agent system is to provide access to the basic health-care services in a given city to the users. This system supports routine activities of physicians at the hospitals by maintaining information such as appointments for a specific day or week, the patients that the physician has examined, and notes related to patients. Although this distributed healthcare system provides user-friendly interfaces for busy healthcare professionals and patients. The system authenticates users and logs session information for security and privacy, so that only privileged users can view or modify the data.

The basic architecture of the MAS is shown bellow. The architecture shows interactions among agents, and also the interactions between humans/resources and agents. Here the Patient interacts with the system through a Patient Agent, provided a GUI through which patients could make queries and receives answers. This agent stores static data related to the user such as the national healthcare number, name, address, phone number, and information for allowing secure access to the system.

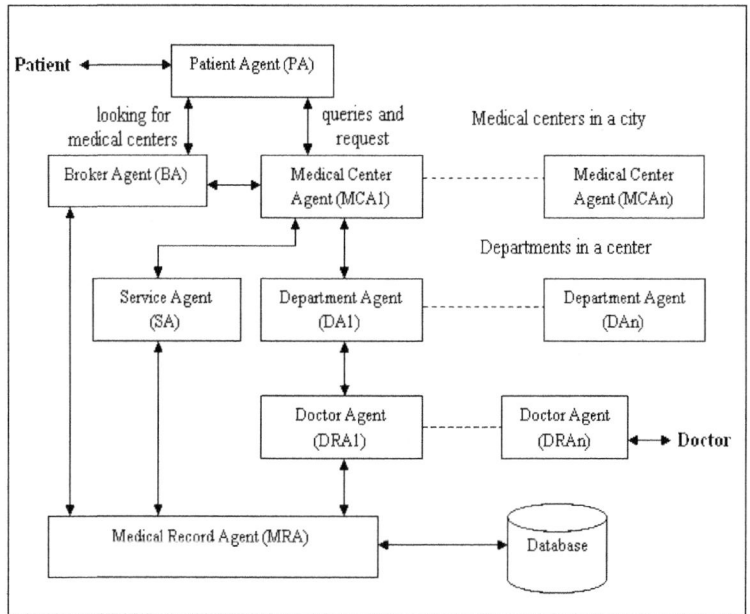

Fig. 1. MAS Architecture

It also stores dynamic data such as the agenda of the patient. The static data will be used to identify the patient in the system (authentication and ciphering). The agents of the system will exchange required data automatically in each step, *e.g.* a doctor needs to know personal details of a patient before the medical visit, in order to retrieve his/her medical record from a database. The dynamic data is very useful to guide negotiations between any Patient Agent (PA) and other agents, because PA can avoid coincidences in those negotiations, *e.g.* if the patient works from 9:00AM to 14:00PM, his agent would arrange meetings during the afternoon and night.

All PAs can talk with a Broker Agent (BA) provided an interface between all the agents internal to the system and the user agents. The BA is the bridge between patients and the medical centers, and it is used to discover information about the system. All PAs can ask this agent in order to find medical centers satisfying certain criteria. The BA covers all the medical centers located in a city or nearby area.

Any patient can access the system through the Medical Centre Agent (MCA) that centralizes and monitors the outsider's accesses. Each medical center is represented by Medical center Agent which contains all the information related to the medical center such as address, phone number, opening times, location, and so on. A MCA monitors all of its departments, represented by Department Agents (DAs), and a set of general services represented by Service Agents (SAs), such as a blood test service, etc. Each department is formed by several doctors represented by Doctor Agents (DRA) and more specific services known as Service Agents (SA).Database is used to store all users' medical records which can be accessed through Medical Record Agent (MRA). This agent provides a secure access to the data using authentication and ciphering through a Public Key Infrastructure (PKI).

When a patient wants to arrange an appointment with a doctor, or a doctor must arrange a visit of a patient with a service, it is required to schedule a meeting according to different constraints such as timetable of services or doctors, and agenda of the patient. Here the patient will search nearby hospitals by selecting city or area and category of hospitals also the available services in the hospitals, patient will then request for the appointment dates with the doctor online. The contacted doctors can see the request of appointments online and can accept, schedule or reschedule the meetings and can also confirm the same to the respective user.

4   Algorithm

The complete life cycle of the multiagent system to access the distributed health care services is given bellow in steps.

Step 1: Maintain central databases containing a list of hospitals in a city, with each hospital containing different departments with associated services and list of doctors with different specialization and free time and day of doctors.

Step 2: Here any number of patients can access the system by filling all the details such as nature of disease, preferable time and date provided in the meeting request form to fix the appointments with appropriate doctor by searching the nearby hospital in the city.

Step 3: The patient has to first open the login page. If he/she is a new patient then he/she has to click new patient and Register. The window will be the registration page of the patient. Once the patient registers he will be activated by the broker and can easily login.

Step 4: The patient may request information about all the medical centers available in a particular city. If the patient is aware of a specific medical centre in the area, he/she may request information about the medical services, departments and doctors in that centre also it is possible to book a visit to a doctor. In this kind of request the patient has to select the Broker Agent (BA) as the recipient of the message. As BA is aware of all Medical Center Agents (MCAs) in town, it will find out which of them satisfy the patient's constraints.

Step 5: Broker Agent (BA) must have a predefined Broker name and password through which he can do various operations and can insert, update any data from the database based on complaints received from patient. Broker can deactivate any member at any time. Broker can add new area, category of hospital, specialty of hospital and new hospital.

Step 6: The Patient Agents (PA) sends a request (REQ) to the MCA through BA. This REQ is forwarded to the department selected by the patient. The Department Agents (DA) will send the REQ to all the doctors of the department. Each Doctor Agent (DRA) replies to the request, in which it displays the earliest time in which the doctor has a free slot for making a visit. The patient can view all Meeting status such as postponed, completed, and in completed meetings.

Step 7: The Doctor can login at any time and can view the List of recent appointment request, List of forthcoming appointments and the calendar showing the available dates and time for meeting.

Step 8: Upon receiving the patient request, doctor will accordingly schedule, or postpone the appointment meetings by viewing the available date in the appointment calendar. If the patient arrival occurs at emergency case, the doctor will give first preference to emergency case and reschedule the appointment of already scheduled meetings and convey the same to the concerned patient. Finally, DRA confirms that the schedule of the doctor has been modified, and this confirmation is sent to the patient through DA and MCA.

Step 9: The medical records of the patients are stored in a database called Medical Record Agent (MRA), the access to which is controlled by Database Wrapper (DW). There are two services that this agent provides: accessing a medical record and updating it.

5   Performance Analysis

In this section, the simulated results obtained with the proposed work are discussed.

Doctor Availability

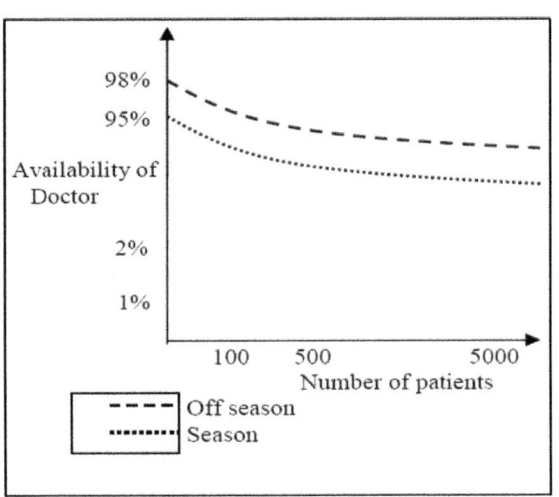

Fig. 2. Doctor Availability

The fig2 depicts the success rate of getting an appointment. The X axis represents the number of patients and Y axis represents the availability of doctor in terms of percentage during off season and season. During off season, the number of diseases will be less (summer) and the availability of doctor will be more (98%) when compared to season (winter). During season, the number of diseases will be more, hence the requests will be more and also the availability of doctor will be less (95%).

Response Time

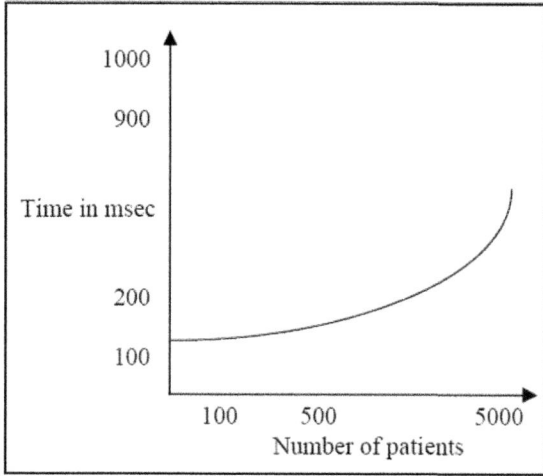

Fig. 3. Response Time

The fig3 depicts the response time. i.e. the time required to process the patient request. Here the X axis represents the number of patients and Y axis represents the time in terms of mili seconds. As the number of patients increases it takes more time to process the requests.

Availability of patients

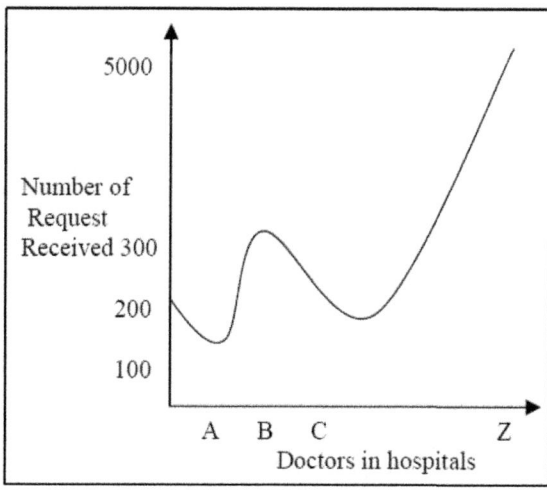

Fig. 4. Availability of patients

The fig4 depicts the Availability of patients. Here the X axis represents the doctors in the hospitals and Y axis represents the Number of request received from the patients. Doctor will get more patients as the number of requests is more.

Reliability

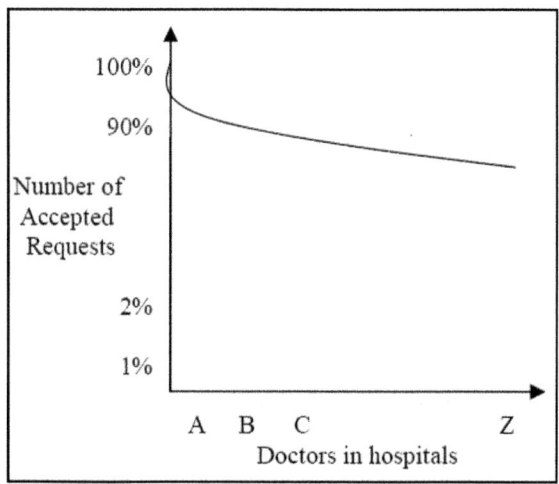

Fig. 5. Reliability

The fig 5 depicts the reliability of the system. The X axis represents the Doctors in the hospitals and Y axis represents the number of accepted requests (processed or confirmed request) in terms of percentage. As the number of requests increases, the numbers of requests accepted by the doctor will decreases.

6   Conclusion

The use of agents in health care has experimented an important growth. One of the main benefits of this paradigm is to allow the interoperability of preexisting systems for improving its general performance. We have designed an agent-based architecture respecting the health care national organization, but it could be adapted to other situations. The architecture defines the interaction between agents, also between humans and agents. The interaction human-agent is made through personal agents that could be located in computers or mobile devices.

Intelligent agents have a set of properties (sociability, proactivity, autonomy) that make them suitable to be used to solve many problems that appear in the health care domain. One such problem we discussed here is access to medical information of a city. The MAS described in this paper can be implemented using JADE (Java Agent Development Framework). JADE is a library of Java classes that eases the implementation of FIPA- compliant multi agent systems. The content of all messages must be in FIPA-SL and the medical record databases in MySql.

This paper explains the combination of agents with health care services in order to provide coordination among different types of agents. If a patient arrives at the emergency case, then agents negotiate the best alternative according to the preferences/constraints of the patient, the doctor and the services. The system implements services as reusable as possible by using standard languages for communicating and for the content and the representation of ontologies. It could easily allow the addition of new agents or features to further improve the time efficiency.

References

1. Zgaya, H.: Design and Distributed Optimization of an Information System to Aid Urban Mobility: A Multiagent Approach to Research and Composition of Services Related to Transportation. Doctoral Thesis, Ecole Centrale of Lille (2007)
2. Nealon, J., Moreno, A.: The Application of Agent Technology to Health Care. In: Proceedings of the Workshop AgentCities: Research in Large-scale Open Agent Environments, in the 1st International Joint Conference on Autonomous Agents and Multi- Agent Systems (AAMAS), Bologna, Italy, pp. 169–173 (2002)
3. Weiss, G.: Multiagent Systems: A Modern Approach to Distributed Artificial Intelligence. M.I.T. Press, Redmond (1999)
4. Becker, M., Heine, C., Herrler, R., Krempels, K.-H.: OntHoS – an Ontology for Hospital Scenarios. In: Nealon, J.L., Moreno, A. (eds.) Applications of Software Agent Technology in the Health Care Domain. Whitestein Series in Software Agent Technologies, pp. 87–104. Birkhäuser Verlag, Basel (2003)
5. Haux, R., Ammenwerth, E., Herzog, W., Knaup, P.: Health Care in the Information Society: A Prognosis for the year 2013. International Journal of Medical Informatics 66, 3–21 (2002)
6. Shankararaman, V., Ambrosiadou, V., Panchal, T., Robinson, B.: Agents in Health Care. In: Shankararaman, V. (ed.) Workshop on Autonomous Agents in Health Care, pp. 1–11 (2000)
7. Heine, C., Herrler, R., Stefan, K.: Agentbased Optimisation and Management of Clinical Processes. In: Proceedings of the 16th European Conference on Artificial Intelligence (ECAI)-The 2nd Workshop on Agents Applied in Health Care (2004)
8. Mabry, S.L., Hug, C.R., Roundy, R.C.: Clinical Decision Support with IM-Agents and ERMA Multi-agents. In: 17th IEEE Symposium on Computer-Based Medical Systems (CBMS 2004), pp. 242–247 (2004)
9. Nealon, J., Moreno, A.: Agent-Based Applications in Health Care. In: Applications of Software Agent Technology in the Health Care Domain. Whitestein Series in Software Agent Technologies. Birkhauser Verlag, Basel (2003)
10. Riano, D., Prado, S., Pascual, A., Martin, S.: A Multi-Agent System to Support Palliative Care Units. In: Proceedings of the 15th IEEE Symposium on Computer-Based Medical Systems, CBMS 2002 (2002)
11. Hashmi, Z.I., Abidi, S.S.R., Cheah, Y.N.: An Intelligent Agent-Based Knowledge Broker for Enterprise Wide Healthcare Knowledge Procurement. In: Proceedings of the 15th IEEE Symposium on Computer-Based Medical Systems, CBMS 2002 (2002)
12. Petrie, C.: Agent-Based Software Engineering. In: Ciancarini, P., Wooldridge, M.J. (eds.) AOSE 2000. LNCS, vol. 1957, pp. 59–75. Springer, Heidelberg (2001)
13. Jennings, N.: On Agent-based Software Engineering. Artificial Intelligence 117, 277–296 (2000)

Energy-Saving Information Multi-agent System with Web Services for Cloud Computing

Sheng-Yuan Yang[1], Dong-Liang Lee[2], Kune-Yao Chen[2], and Chun-Liang Hsu[3]

[1] Dept. of Computer and Communication Engineering, St. John's University, Taiwan
ysy@mail.sju.edu.tw
[2] Dept. of Information Management, St. John's University, Taiwan
{lianglee,kychen}@mail.sju.edu.tw
[3] Dept. of Electrical Engineering, St. John's University, Taiwan
liang@mail.sju.edu.tw

Abstract. This paper focuses on designing an information multi-agent system with Web service techniques for cloud computing and its interaction paradigms. It employs the concept of SQL IC to construct the operational interface of cloud database as a data warehouse. This approach not only can look after both sides of ubiquitous access advantages of cloud techniques, but also retain the consistent user interface of a data warehouse. It enables information users to conveniently use the Internet to quickly access the system information in clouds. This paper preliminarily proposes an energy-saving information multi-agent system architecture with Web services for cloud computing. Related presentations and comparisons of the system prototype also verify its feasibility.

Keywords: Web Services, Energy-saving Information Systems, Agent Systems, Cloud Computing.

1 Introduction

Computer popularization and network technology improvement are two great achievements of Internet applications. People can only rely on browsers to easily use various Web services, for example, on-line shopping, Web games, Web banks, etc. In view of the advantages brought by Internet technology, many conventional applications continuously shift their running models into the Internet. In regard to Web services development, however, most information WebPages are prepared by people, read by people, and judged by people. Lacking interactive communication mechanisms, it is fundamentally impossible to make application programs actively deal with related service information. Therefore, it is imperative to specially establish Web services for modern application programs. In addition, it is necessary to strengthen the communication requirements of application procedures. It is even more important to establish universal standards and agreements on communication information. Examples include: HP's information communication standard: e-Speak; Microsoft's .Net strategy; WSTK (Web Service Toolkit) and WSDE (Web Service Development Environment) published by IBM; Dynamic Services developed by Oracle; SUN also announced its network service framework and joined the standard into the operational

R.-S. Chang, T.-h. Kim, and S.-L. Peng (Eds.): SUComS 2011, CCIS 223, pp. 222–233, 2011.
© Springer-Verlag Berlin Heidelberg 2011

environment of J2EE; finally, W3C established and unified all of its Web service standards, resulting in a widely operational infrastructure and platform for Web services.

Web Services principally provide services for application programs on Web and enable the usage of programs in other machines, which are provided with powerful inter-communication and extendibility. It can easily integrate application programs and related programs on the Web and achieve some complicated information service processes through interactive programs. Related standards contain XML (Extensible Makeup Language), SOAP (Simple Object Access Protocol), WSDL (Web Services Description Language), and UDDI (Universal Description, Discovery and Integration) [2]. Cloud computing is a technique of Internet- ("cloud-") based development and use of computer technology. In other words, it will set up the necessary operating resources and related data in the Internet so that users can directly use them when they access the Internet. Furthermore, determining how to construct an interaction diagram of cloud computing for extensively and seamlessly entering related Web information agent systems through Web service techniques is also an investigation point of this study.

To sum up, this paper focuses on designing an information multi-agent system with Web service techniques for cloud computing and its interaction paradigms. It employs the concept of SQL IC to construct the operational interface of cloud database as a data warehouse. This approach can regard both sides of ubiquitous access advantages of cloud techniques, and also retain consistent user interface of the data warehouse. It enables information users to conveniently use the Internet to quickly access the system information in clouds. The paper preliminarily proposes an energy-saving information multi-agent system architecture with Web services for cloud computing. Related presentations and comparisons of the system prototype also verify its feasibilities.

2   Background and Technique

2.1   Introduction to Energy-Saving Information System

Due to the distribution of space and monitoring hosts, energy-saving information systems need a more flexible manner of program development. Replacing existent application interface with functions of network transmission and Web services can not

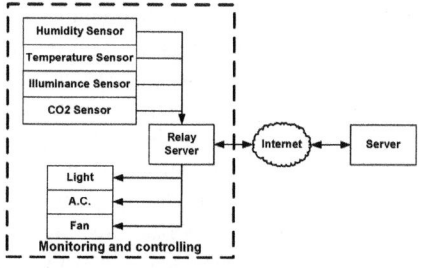

Fig. 1. Conceptual architecture of an energy-saving information system

only easily achieve on-line and real-time addition/modification services, but also immediately extend its powerful functions. Fig. 1 illustrates the conceptual architecture of an energy-saving information system. Monitoring and controlling were constructed with a wireless sensor network to detect and collect the running parameters of all electrical devices; then the related data would be sent to a server through embedded mid-way by wireless communication of ZigBee modules or Bluetooth. The embedded mid-way not only plays the role of data collector between the server and end-devices, but also receives the control commands delivered by the server to feedback control the facilities in the power consumption space [4]. The server system is a multi-agent system, including: Interface Agent, Data Mining Agent, Case-Based Reasoning Agent- CBR Agent, and Web-Service-Based Information Agent System- WIAS, as shown in Fig. 2. The Interface Agent is responsible for providing energy-saving monitoring of information access and intelligent decision making. The latter is aimed at providing corresponding control decisions to monitor information, including whether prediction solutions exist, as judged by the Data Mining Agent; whether CBR solutions exist, as judged by the CBR Agent; and whether predefined solutions exist, as judged by the Interface Agent in accordance with predefined rules within WIAS; this is called three-stage intelligent decision processing. WIAS employs the concept of SQL IC to be responsible for providing various Web services of energy-saving information from the abovementioned agent systems, which can achieve the investigation on fast accessing system information in clouds via the Internet.

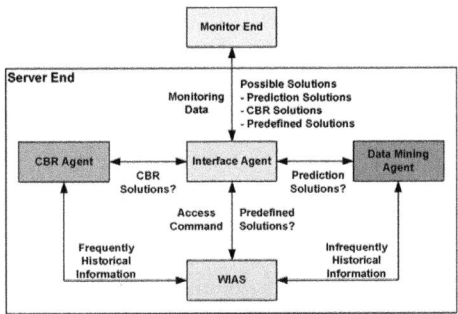

Fig. 2. System structure of backend multi-agent system

2.2 Cloud Computing

Cloud computing is an information technology that enables users to take advantage of information services whenever they can access the Internet, even with an incomplete understanding of the complex information service structure and without any professional knowledge. Back in the early 1990s, initial cloud computing was developed from the techniques of Grid Computing and Utility Computing. In the 21st century, the related network services have been developed vigorously, in tandem with improvements in network techniques. In 2007, Google proposed the concept of cloud computing that offered huge business opportunities, including Infrastructure as a Service (IaaS), Platform as a Service (PaaS), and Software as a Service (SaaS)., comprising the new 3C, i.e., Cloud Computing, Connecting and Client Devices [1]. This paper focuses on an information multi-agent system with Web service techniques for cloud computing and its interaction paradigms. That is to say, in cloud computing environments, the system prototype plays the SaaS role of cloud computing provider. Furthermore, it can explore how to construct an interaction diagram of cloud computing for extensively and seamlessly entering relevant Web information agent systems through Web service techniques.

2.3 Web Services

Traditional programs deal with all operations in individual processes, one by one, which greatly inhibits processing performance. This approach not only wastes time on meaningless processes, but also cannot effectively control processing efficiency. However, program development has gradually improved designing procedures, with more and stronger support of programs, along with science and technology advancements, such as object concept production that can not only increase convenience in programming but also decrease complexity in maintenance. In the middle stage, the development of API (Application Programming Interface) enabled programmers to develop various and universal functions as well as modularized interfaces to apply to each type of program. The convenience of this approach is greater than it was before. In the networking era, many Web services resulted from developing the interface of traditional program providers with cloud computing techniques. It is ready to go through networks, transmit necessary service interfaces to needed programs, and even proposes formats of communication standards. When program scales need addition or modification, they can immediately be achieved through Web services. In regard to cloud computing environments, this paper developed a backend information agent system on the basis of Web service techniques, which can easily achieve the application goal of ubiquitously accessing energy-saving information.

2.4 Developing Techniques

The system prototype adopted MS SQL Server and My-SQL Server as the sharing platform of backend databases; the information safety can be guaranteed by different servers with mutual backup information. The former has powerful analysis and optimization mechanisms, which mainly draws on websites of large-scale companies and international enterprises. Its cost is comparatively high, but it has excellent and stable operational efficiency for a large amount of continual information processing. The latter not only possesses the advantages of the MS SQL Server, but also is a freeware of relational database. SQL is a query language for obtaining data from the relational database. This paper employed the concept of SQL access templates to construct the usual SQL IC with C#. Their functions are like those of the IC's, which can bind different parameters to easily access corresponding query results. Not only can this approach expand the Web service functions of WIAS, but it can also provide various query services of energy-saving information to other agents within the system. The rest of the agents were developed by Java and collocated in the multi-threading building manner, easily leading to a double-win strategy for multi-tasking processes and enhancing system performance. In addition, Interface Agent also introduced JFree Chart to develop related statistical tables of energy-saving information. This approach can not only complete dynamic analyses of energy-saving information, but also finish display functions of the example energy-saving information system.

3 System Architecture of Clouding and Multi-agent Information System with Web Services

The system architecture realizes on-line interfaces of Web services with cloud computing and information transmission techniques on the Internet. It enables individual agents to access the common function library to immediately respond to the corresponding agent that uses this Web service. Not only can it easily achieve communication with the backend database, but it can also easily add and renew related functions for the research purpose of designing a Web-service-based information agent with clouding techniques.

3.1 Structure of Web-Service-Based Information Agent System

Fig. 3 is the structure of the Web-service-based Information Agent System, WIAS. If the query information is an access command, WIAS directly goes through Web-Service-Based Interface to employ the SQL IC Constructor to trigger the corresponding SQL access templates, part of them as shown in Table 1. After binding related access parameters, WIAS retrieves the corresponding access results from the Raw Data Base. Finally, it goes through the Web-Service-Based Interface to return those results to the Interface Agent. If the query information is whether predefined solutions exist, WIAS also goes through the Web-Service-Based Interface to ask the Predefined Rule Base to return the corresponding predefined solutions to the Interface Agent. Furthermore, Raw Data Base also provides all of the frequent historical information to the CBR Agent as information material for the production of cases, and supplies all infrequent historical information into the Data Mining Agent as information material to trigger the production of prediction solutions. Detailed function description and relationship with agents are shown in Table 2.

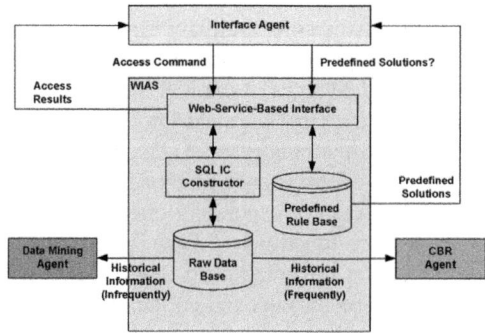

Fig. 3. Structure of WIAS

Table 1. Part of SQL Ics and their function description

SERVICE NAME	SERVICE DESCRIPTION	TO WHOM
CCMonitor_InsertTmpData	Case Cycle's Temporal Data	CBR Agent
CCMonitor_Main	Case Cycle's API	CBR Agent
CMonitor_Main	Transfer Case Information into Predication Rules	Data Mining Agent
CMonitor_ViewPredRule	Reviewing Predication Rules	Data Mining Agent
DMonitor_Main	Transfer Raw Data and Rules into Cases with semantics	CBR Agent
ESAS_InsertRawData	Insert Raw Data to DB	Interface Agent
ESAS_ViewMacType	Checking Sensor Types of MACs	Interface Agent
PMonitor_Main	Data Mining's API	Data Mining Agent
System_ViewDBSDT	Providing System Time Stamp	Sharing

Table 2. Detailed function description and relationship of WIAS

4 WIAS		
Function Description		
4.1 Information Query: Thread Processing, through **Web-Service-Based Interface** (Interrupted Processing)		
4.2 Frequent Information Providing: Thread Processing, through **Data Monitor** (Interrupted Processing)		
4.3 Infrequent Information Providing: Thread Processing, through **Data Monitor** (Interrupted Processing)		
4.4 Predefined Solutions Providing: Thread Processing, through **Web-Service-Based Interface** (Interrupted Processing)		
4.5 Predefined Rules Constructing: Thread Processing, through **Rule Maker** (Interrupted Processing)		
I/O Description		
Input	Function	Output
1 Interface Agent: User Interface	4.1 Information Query	4 WIAS: Web-Service-Based Interface
4 WIAS: Data Monitor	4.2 Frequent Information Providing	3 CBR Agent: Case Generator
4 WIAS: Data Monitor	4.3 Infrequent Information Providing	2 Data Mining Agent: Prediction Monitor
1 Interface Agent: Decision Maker	4.4 Predefined Solutions Providing	4 WIAS: Web-Service-Based Interface
Expert Interrupted	4.5 Predefined Rules Constructing	4 WIAS: Rule Maker

3.2   Structure of Interface Agent

The functions of Interface Agent are accessing energy-saving monitor information and intelligent decision making. Fig. 4 is the system block diagram, including Receiver/Transmitter, Decision Maker, and User Interface. All three are independent operational procedures and operate in the manner of multi-threading to achieve the function of parallel processing. First, the Receiver gets all of the sensor data from the Monitor end, carries out filtering and arrangement [4], and then goes through WIAS (ESAS_InsertRawData) to store the information into the system clouding databases. The User Interface periodically goes through WIAS (ESAS_ViewMacType) to real-time renew all of the monitoring information from the clouding database and also accepts user queries about various commands related to energy-saving information. The Decision Maker, responsible for intelligent decision making, proceeds with the three-stage intelligent decision processing for producing Possible Solutions through the help of the Data Mining Agent, CBR Agent and WIAS. Finally, the Transmitter returns Possible Solutions to the Monitor end to achieve the system goal of energy-saving feedback control. Detailed function description and relationship with agents are shown in Table 3.

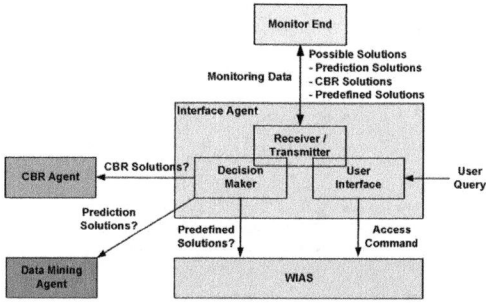

Fig. 4. Structure of interface agent

Table 3. Detailed function description and relationship of Interface Agent

1 Interface Agent		
Function Description		

1.1 Information Processing: Thread Processing, through **Receiver/Transmitter** (Real Time Processing)
    1.1.1 Information Receiving
    1.1.2 Information Transmitting		

1.2 Information Browsing: Thread Processing, through **User Interface** (Interrupted Processing)
    1.2.1 User Query
    1.2.2 Information Figures and Tables Displaying		

1.3 Three-stage Intelligent Decision Making: Thread Processing, through **Decision Maker** (Real Time Processing)
    1.3.1 If Prediction Solutions Exist?
    1.3.2 If CBR Solutions Exist?
    1.3.3 If Predefined Solutions Exist?		

I/O Description		
Input	Function	Output
0 Monitor End	1.1.1 Information Receiving	1 Interface Agent: Receiver
1 Interface Agent: Decision Maker	1.1.2 Information Transmitting	0 Monitor End
User Access Commands	1.2.1 User Query	4 WIAS
1 Interface Agent: User Interface	1.2.2 Information Figures and Tables Displaying	4 WIAS
1 Interface Agent: Decision Maker	1.3.1 If Prediction Solutions Exist?	2 Data Mining Agent
1 Interface Agent: Decision Maker	1.3.2 If CBR Solutions Exist?	3 CBR Agent
1 Interface Agent: Decision Maker	1.3.3 If Predefined Solutions Exist?	4 WIAS

3.3   Structure of Data Mining Agent

Fig. 5 illustrates the structure of the Data Mining Agent [3]. First, it goes through the Case Base constructed by the CBR Agent to get Case Information. Then the Rule Maker employs algorithms of Information Entropy (such as ID3, C4.5, and C5.0) in accordance with the information to calculate and obtain related Object-Action Pairs (for instance, what are their corresponding energy-saving actions to the range from maximum to minimum of some monitoring data) for constructing suitable Prediction Rules. If the query information is whether prediction solutions exist, it is usually abnormal energy-saving information, i.e., Infrequent Historical Information from WIAS (CMonitor_Main). The Data Mining Agent produces corresponding prediction solutions into the Solutions Pool in accordance with the Prediction Rules (CMonitor_ViewPredRule). The system then sends suitable prediction solutions back to the Interface Agent in accordance with the system threshold. When the prediction solution is successful, it will become learning material of the CBR Agent. Its learning efficiency is gradually incorporated into the Case Base within CBR Agent, and then the CBR Agent provides corresponding Case Information into Data Mining Agent, the Rule Maker revises Prediction Rules and correspondingly enhances its prediction robustness. Detailed function description and relationship with agents are shown in Table 4.

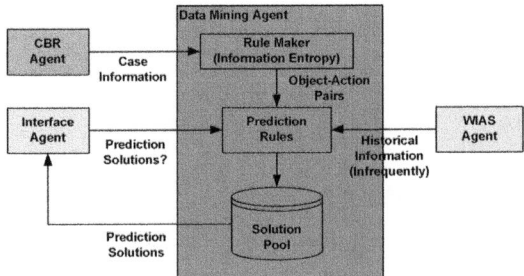

Fig. 5. Structure of Data Mining Agent

Table 4. Detailed function description and relationship of Data Mining Agent

2 Data Mining Agent		
Function Description		
2.1 Prediction Rules Constructing: Thread Processing, through **Rule Maker** (Periodical Processing)		
2.2 Prediction Solution Producing: Thread Processing, through **Prediction Monitor** (Interrupted Processing)		
2.3 Prediction Solution Providing: Thread Processing, through **Prediction Monitor** (Interrupted Processing)		
I/O Description		
Input	Function	Output
3 CBR Agent: Case Information	2.1 Prediction Rules Constructing	2 Data Mining Agent: Rule Maker
4 WIAS: Infrequently Historical Information	2.2 Prediction Solution Producing	2 Data Mining Agent: Solutions Pool
1 Interface Agent: Decision Maker	2.3 Prediction Solution Providing	2 Data Mining Agent: Prediction Monitor

3.4 Structure of CBR Agent

Case-based reasoning (CBR) is a problem-solving technique employing previous experiences and past success cases for solving current problems. For this reason, the system gives a Case a definition: the most usual occurrence situation (that is most frequent happening) and its corresponding energy-saving operational mode at a specific time slot. Its 'meaning' is the most stable energy-saving operational plan in the specific monitor space. Fig. 6 is the production concept of cases. However, the original cases storage in Fig. 6 cannot directly apply to various energy-saving operational modes. They have to be transformed into suitable semantic cases in accordance with the corresponding MAC Tables; then they can be applied to the mechanism for the reasoning of the majority of energy-saving cases. Fig. 7 is the transformation concept of semantic cases.

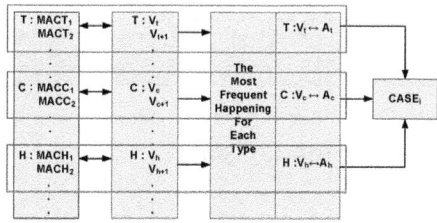

Fig. 6. Production concept of Case (T: Temperature, C: CO_2, and H: Humidity)

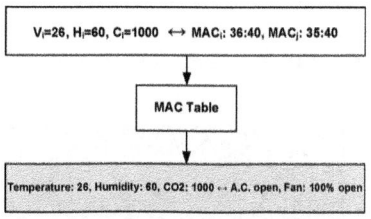

Fig. 7. Transformation concept of semantic case

Fig. 8 is the structure of the CBR Agent. The Case Generator is responsible for constructing case resources and storage in Case Base, which is based on Historical Information provided by WIAS (DMonitor_Main). If the query information is whether CBR solutions exist, the CBR Agent starts the cycle of case-based reasoning through help of WIAS (CCMonitor_Main), as detailed in [3]. The Case Base also provides Case Information to become information material for constructing Prediction Rules within the Data Mining Agent. Detailed function description and relationship with agents are shown in Table 5.

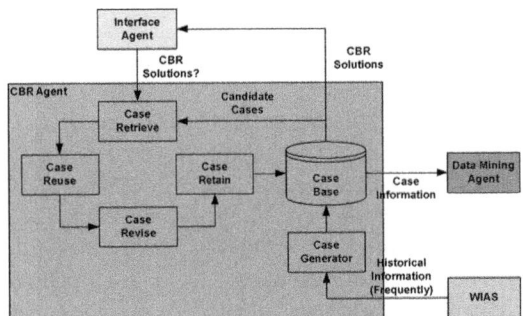

Fig. 8. Structure of CBR Agent

Table 5. Detailed function description and relationship of CBR Agent

3 CBR Agent		
Function Description		
3.1 Case Base Constructing: Thread Processing, through **Case Generator** (Periodical Processing)		
3.2 Case Information Providing: Thread Processing, through **Case Monitor** (Periodical Processing)		
3.3 CBR Solutions Providing: Thread Processing, through **CBR** (Interrupted Processing)		
I/O Description		
Input	Function	Output
4 WIAS: Frequently Historical Information	3.1 Case Base Constructing	3 CBR Agent: Case Generator
3 CBR Agent: Case Monitor	3.2 Case Information Providing	2 Data Mining Agent: Rule Maker
1 Interface Agent: Decision Maker	3.3 CBR Solutions Providing	3 CBR Agent: CBR

4   System Display and Comparisons

Fig. 9 is the interface of the system prototype. For the moment, the browsing functions of energy-saving information to users contain real-time browsing and historical query. The interface display is divided into three parts. One is the page tags of all sensor data on the top of the interface. Those tags are constructed in the tree structure,

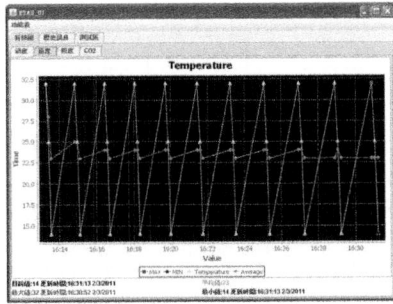

Fig. 9. Interface of system prototype

which orderly subdivide from big to small data type and end in a single sensor data. The system establishes the page tags structure of the interface with the data structure of the page tags from clouding database through WIAS, and then the structure can bind corresponding browsing data. The other is the dynamic curve diagram corresponding to the browsing data on the middle part of the interface. The diagram can real-time and dynamically extend its time axle from left to right and provide four types of information: real time data curve (yellow color), average data curve (green color), mark of the maximum value (red color), and mark of the minimum value (blue color). The last one is data script on the bottom of the interface. It immediately provides all of the newest data of the system operation, including current value, average value, maximum value, minimum value, and the corresponding times of the last updating. On the page of historical query, its interface is similar to the page of real-time browsing. Its interface only additionally provides a series of list menus which enables users to select corresponding query conditions. The list menu contains all of the conditions that are orderly permutations from coarse to fine items, including year, season, month, day, hour, and sensor type. The system provides the necessary query solutions and shows the corresponding data curve diagrams in accordance with the selected query conditions through the help of WIAS.

Fig. 10 is the monitor system interface of energy-saving information of the Industrial Technology Research Institute, ITRI, in Taiwan. It can provide tables, figures, and corresponding data displays of all monitoring data; the red color means the overtaking prompt value is greater than the corresponding threshold. Up to now, the system prototype can present all of the functions rather than ITRI's and display current value, average value, maximum value, minimum value, their corresponding times of the last updating, and their corresponding colors of value representation. Fig. 11 is the energy-saving website display of Providence University in Taiwan. Its display function of the maximum contract electrical capacity will become the focus of one of our future investigations. The most important point is that the two systems mentioned above do not have the true control function of energy-saving feedback, as shown in Fig. 12. The left part of the interface is real-time monitoring data, while the right part of the interface is corresponding electrical equipments of feedback control and their operational modes. That is a unique advantage of the system prototype.

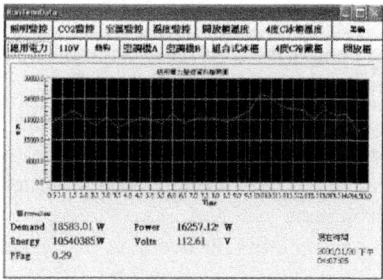

Fig. 10. Monitor system interface of energy-saving information of ITRI

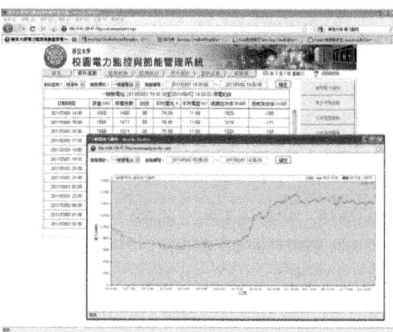

Fig. 11. Energy-saving website display of Providence University

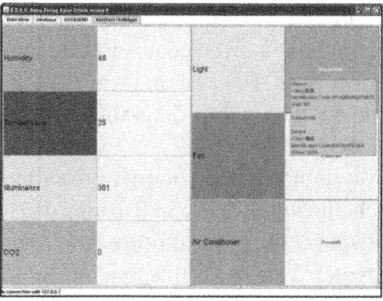

Fig. 12. Clouding user interface of the system prototype

5   Conclusion and Discussion

The paper has developed an information multi-agent system with Web service techniques for cloud computing and its interaction paradigms. It employed the concept of SQL IC to construct the operational interface of cloud database as a data warehouse. This approach can not only look after both sides of ubiquitous access advantages of cloud techniques, but also retains the consistent user interface of a data warehouse. It enables information users to conveniently use the Internet to quickly access the system information in clouds. The paper preliminarily proposes an energy-saving information multi-agent system architecture with Web services for cloud computing. Related presentations and comparisons of the system prototype also verify its feasibility and provide some interesting points:

(1) It is the first energy-saving information monitor and management information system with Web service technique in clouding environment.
(2) The proposed architecture is the first multi-agent structure of energy-saving system in practical environment.
(3) The presented three-stage intelligent decision processing strategy is the first appearance in intelligently energy-saving systems.

Truly completing the display functions of the maximum contract electrical capacity and three-stage intelligent decision processing will be the focus of our future investigation.

Acknowledgement. The authors would like to thank Hung-Chun Chiang, Ming-Yu Tsai, and Guo-Jui Wu for their assistance in system implementation and experiments. This partial work was supported by the National Science Council, ROC, under Grant NSC-99-2221-E-129-012 and the Ministry of Education, Taiwan, R.O.C., under Grant Skill of Taiwan (1) Word No. 1000041444t.

References

1. Gu, S.R.: Cloud Computing Robs Their Turfs, A New Warring Age of IT Industry. Common Wealth Magazine 423, 178–181 (2009)
2. Wu, H.H.: Introduction to Web Service Techniques,
   http://www.ascc.sinica.edu.tw/nl/93/2023/02.txt
   (visited on March 9, 2011)
3. Yang, S.Y., Hsu, C.L.: An Ontological Proxy Agent with Prediction, CBR, and RBR Techniques for Fast Query Processing. Expert Systems with Applications 36(5), 9358–9370 (2009)
4. Yang, S.Y., Chiang, H.C., Wu, K.J.: Developing an Intelligent Energy-saving Information Processing and Decision Supporting System. In: Proc. of 2010 Symposium on Constructing Industrial and Academic Park of Green Energy Science and Technology and Intelligent Energy-saving Techniques and Project Achievement Lunching Ceremony, Taipei, Taiwan, pp. 41–47 (2010)

Role-Based Mobile Agent for Group Task Collaboration in Pervasive Environment

Chih-Hao Liu and Jason Jen-Yen Chen

Department of Computer Science and Information Engineering
National Central University
945402024@cc.ncu.edu.tw

Abstract. The agent paradigm truly enhances the power of network software in pervasive environment. Agents with features such as autonomy and social ability form an agent community called agent group. Moreover, mobile agent technology that integrates mobile device with application server enables mobile users to obtain information or services over the Web anytime anyplace. However, one problem with agent community is that there seems no definition or knowledge representation for role-based agent to form an agent group that resembles a human group with roles. In this work, we propose the role-based mobile agent architecture, in which agents will be grouped into a specific group according to their roles. Further, through agent communication, mobile agents of an agent group can collaborate with each other to contribute to group tasks. A hospital example based on the Java agent development environment (JADE) platform is included for illustration.

Keywords: Mobile Agent, Role-based, Group Task Collaboration.

1   Introduction

The current research on web service primarily concentrates on somewhat of "low-level" distributed techniques and standards such as web service description language (WSDL), simple object access protocol (SOAP) and universal definition and discovery integrated (UDDI). The main advantage of this is to provide consistent interface for software entity to access web services. However, these web services are neither reliable nor easy-to-use due to the fact that they are at remote sites where a user has no control at all. Additionally, the web services provide a static description, thereby making it extremely difficult to update in a real-time manner.

On the contrary, the research on agent focuses on problem solving mechanisms in pervasive environment. Multi-agent system (MAS), which is composed of multiple interacting agents to form an agent community, is a powerful paradigm in pervasive environment for collaborative systems. Notably, an agent is a program with such features as autonomy and social and reasoning abilities. Additionally, it autonomously manages its resources and proactively collaborates with other agents with the same purpose to execute complex tasks such as making appointments or scheduling [5, 7, 8]. For example, an agent is able to proactively request other agents for medical recommendation, and then the requested agents respond reactively with the name of

R.-S. Chang, T.-h. Kim, and S.-L. Peng (Eds.): SUComS 2011, CCIS 223, pp. 234–240, 2011.
© Springer-Verlag Berlin Heidelberg 2011

some recommended medicine through agent communication. Further, the Foundation for Intelligent Physical Agent (FIPA) standard that includes 22 communicative acts and some interaction protocols is widely used by agent developers to coordinate interoperation among agents [6]. However, one problem with agent community is that there seems no definition or knowledge representation for role-based agent to form an agent group that resembles a human group with roles.

In addition, a mobile agent is an agent with mobility, meaning it can suspend its execution, store its state, migrate to another web site, and resume its execution. Thus mobile agent is a promising technology for mobile applications [11], in which a mobile agent migrates to a remote web site to gather information or execute tasks. This technology is therefore suitable for pervasive environment.

Incidentally, the Semantic Web technology is highly-anticipated in developing an infrastructure for agents to perform complex tasks for their users [1, 2, 4]. The web ontology language (OWL) is a popular language to describe domain knowledge called domain ontology, and it allows people to utilize the uniform referential identifier (URI) to give each and every concept a formal term to be used in agent communication. It also defines semantics of the terms, and organizes all kinds of terms by using relations among them. Further, using OWL to annotate web services forms the semantic web service called web ontology language for service (OWL-S) with three OWL documents: 1) service profile, 2) service process, and 3) service grounding. Those documents can be viewed as the resources that an agent can autonomously manage.

Much recent research attention of multi-agent system has been upon agent group. Veiel, et al. propose agent-based approach to facilitate context-based adaptations using context information of a group of users [9]. Jiang, et al. simulate group behavior in E-Government to help making policy decisions [10]. However, these seem to lack knowledge representation about specific role of agent and agent group task. We thus proposed a role-based mobile agent architecture, in which agents will be grouped according to their role. Further, each agent in the group will contribute to the group task according to its role and personal knowledge.

To summarize the above, we propose a role-based mobile agent architecture in which an agent manages or updates its knowledge and resources and will be grouped according to their role and relationship. Through the communication mechanism, the role-based agents can collaborate with each other to perform their group tasks that will generate various actions that the agents will execute. In this work, the actions are implemented as semantic web services that are annotated web services.

2   Role-Based Mobile Agent Architecture

In this section, we will explain the role-based mobile agent architecture as shown in fig. 1. Our architecture contains Location Server, which provide web services to user. The server includes five parts: 1) provider service, 2) user service, 3) role-based agent model, 4) role-based agent ontology, and 5) multi-agent system. Firstly, the provider service is a web service, which is responsible for registering a service provided by service provider. Secondly, the user service is a web service running on the server and it is responsible for receiving user's request. Thirdly, the role-based mobile agent model is responsible for dynamically creating role-based agent according to role information, which is described in role-based agent ontology.

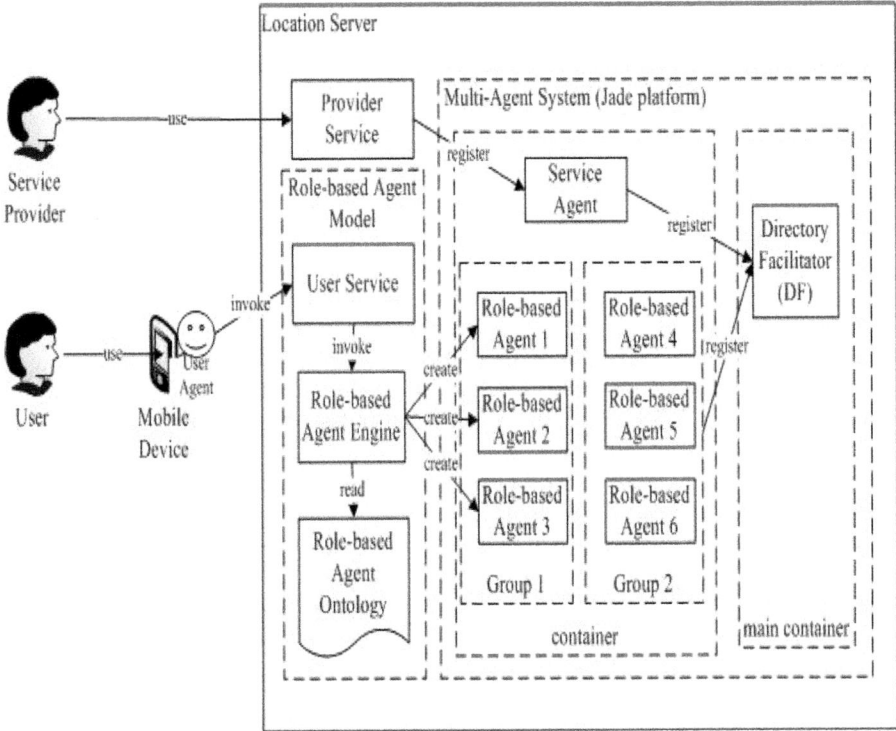

Fig. 1. Role-based Mobile Agent Architecture

The role-based agents could compose a group according to their role and relationships to share information or to achieve tasks through collaboration. In the Fig. 1, the role-based agent 1, the role-based agent 2 and the role-based agent 3 are in the group 1, because the friendship exists among them. Fourthly, the role-based agent ontology will be described shortly. Fifthly, the multi-agent system is based on the Java agent development framework (JADE) platform [3], which is a widely-used agent development tool that supports efficient deployment of mobile agents. And, it contains main container and the container. The main container includes directory facilitator (DF) agent, to which an agent can register. And the container includes service agent and role-based agent, which are created by the service provider and the user, respectively. Next, the role-based agent ontology is shown in Fig. 2.

In Fig. 2, an agent in "Agent" class has roles defined in "Role" class. Agents are of a group if their roles have relationships in a specific domain, which is defined in "Domain" class. For example, a patient named John and his doctor has medical relationship in the medicine domain, thus they belong to the same group. A group is defined in "Group" class that has tasks, which group members will collaborate to achieve. The task is defined in "Task" class and it belongs to the domain. When an agent executes a task, it will trigger an event. And then, the event will generate an action, which an agent will execute, to satisfy the task.

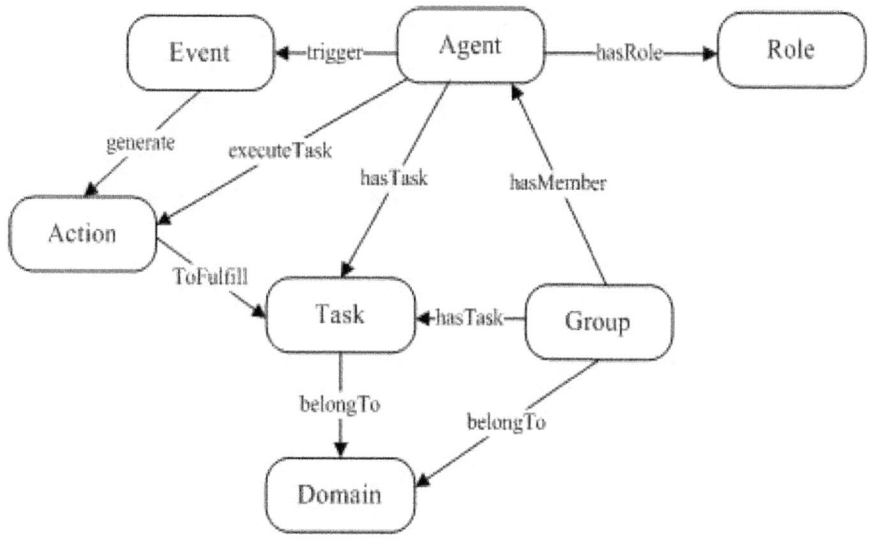

Fig. 2. Role-based Agent Ontology

When composing a group, agents refer to some rules. There is a rule definition about simple medical relationship of the medicine domain as shown below:

$(Role_{Doctor} \wedge Role_{Nurse} \wedge Role_{Patinent} \wedge$ Treat (doctor, patient) $\wedge$ Nursing (nurse, patient) | Domain$_{Medicine}$) $\rightarrow$ trigger (ComposeGroup)

where RoleDoctor stands for a doctor; RoleNurse for a nurse; RolePatinent for a patient. And, there exists a "Treate" relationship between the doctor and the patient in the medicine domain. Note "|" specifies the domain. Similarly, there exists a "Nursing" relationship between the nurse and the patient. Thereby, they will be grouped into the same group.

3 An Example

This section illustrates a hospital example based on our architecture as shown in Fig. 3. The JADE platform runs on a hospital server that includes main container and container. A DF agent runs on main container. Agents in container will be registered into the DF agent.

In the container, the service agent provides all web services of the hospital server. Each and every person will use a mobile device, on which a personal agent runs. For example, a patient, called John, uses a mobile device on which his personal agent, John agent, runs. And, John's doctor and nurse also have their personal agents "Doctor 1" agent and "Nurse 1" agent, respectively. When those personal agents migrate to the hospital server, they will be grouped into "Group 1" according to their role and relationships. Because John is a patient, we know that John has medical relationship with his doctor and his nurse. Similarly, when Mary agent migrates to the hospital server, it will be grouped into "Group 2" along with her doctor and her nurse.

Assume that John measures his temperature, pulse, respiration (TPR) values. If he gets an unusual temperature of 38.5℃. The John agent will trigger a TPR unusual event with an event description, which will be written into a task document as the group task. The John agent will also notify doctor 1 agent and nurse 1 agent about the event. After that, doctor 1 agent gets the unusual temperature value and requests nurse 1 agent for TPR curve. When nurse 1 agent receives the request, it will reply to doctor 1 agent with the TPR curve. Next, doctor 1 agent determines to prescribe an antipyretic named "Ibuprofen Suspension" and to send a call-for-proposal communicative act with unusual temperature to nurse 1 agent.

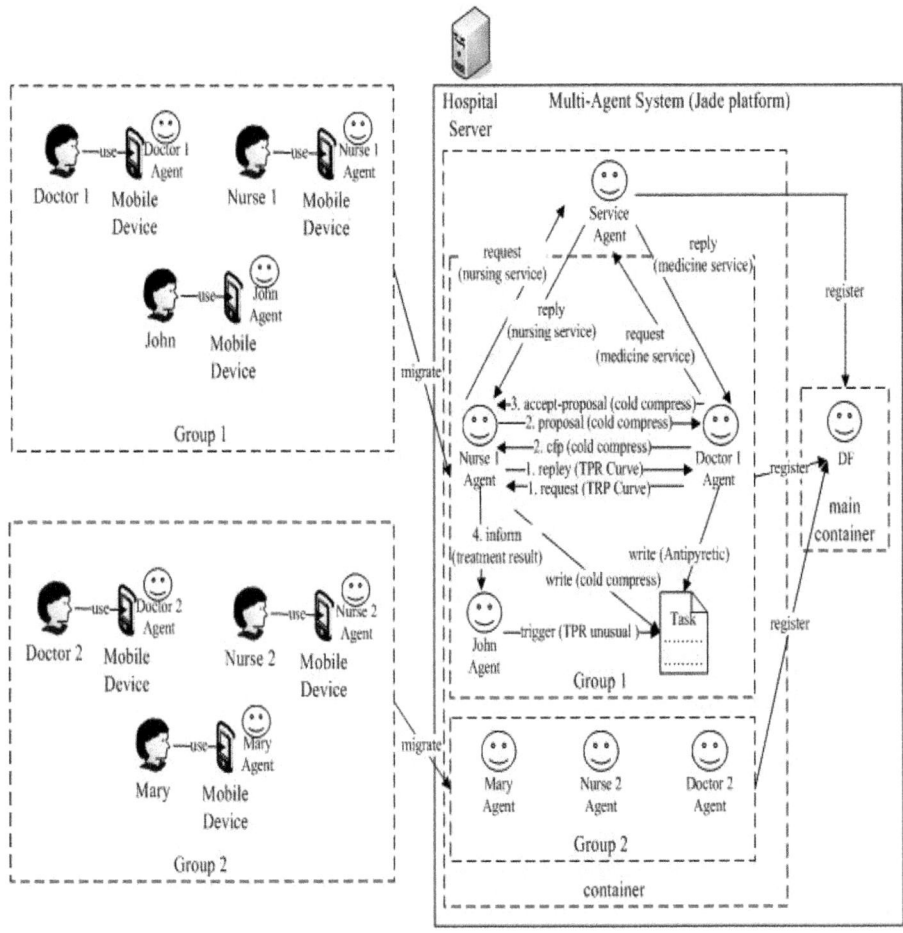

Fig. 3. Hospital Example

For the prescription, it requests service agent for medicine service. Notice that the medical service here is assumed to be a unique service in the hospital service agent, making it unnecessary to annotate the web service to turn it to a semantic web service. Now, the service agent replies to doctor 1 agent with the URI of the medicine service.

After that, doctor 1 agent will write the antipyretic named "Ibuprofen Suspension" into the task document. As for the call for proposal, nurse 1 agent proposes cold compress to doctor 1 agent. Doctor 1 agent decided to accept this proposal. After that, nurse 1 agent requests the service agent for nursing service. Next, the service agent will reply to nurse 1 agent with the URI of the nursing service. Nurse 1 agent will then write the cold compress procedure into the task document. Finally, it will inform John agent about the results of the treatment. A segment of the results is shown in Fig. 4.

```
...
<A0:Task rdf:ID="TPRUnusual">
   <A0:BelongTo>
      <A0:Domain rdf:ID=medicine/>
   </A0:BelongTo>
</A0:Task>
...
<A0:Action rdf:ID="MedicineService">
   <A0:ToFulfill>
      <A0:Task rdf:resource="#TPRUnusual"/>
   </A0:ToFulfull>
   <A0:hasContent> Perscribe antipyretic "Ibuprofen
                   Suspension"
   </A0:hasContent>
</A0:Action>
...
<A0:Action rdf:ID="NursingService">
   <A0:ToFulfill>
      <A0:Task rdf:resource="#TPRUnusual"/>
   </A0:ToFulfull>
   <A0:hasContent>
      Cold Compress Procedure
      ...
   </A0:hasContent>
</A0:Action>
...
```

Fig. 4. Group Task Document

4   Conclusions

This work proposes the role-based mobile agent architecture. The expected advantages of it are:

1. The role-based mobile agent will be grouped into a specific group according to their roles and relationships. Through agent communication, all of the mobile agents in the group collaborate with each other to contribute the group task according to their role and knowledge.
2. The definition of role and group is defined in the role-based agent ontology that provides knowledge representation for the role-based mobile agent to facilitate collaboration among agents.

References

1. Tim, B.L., Hendler, J., OLassila, O.: The Semantic Web. In: Scientific American (May 2001)
2. Palmer, S.B.: The Semantic Web An Introduction (2001),
   http://infomesh.net/2001/swintro/
3. JADE Java Agent DEvelopment Framework (May 2003),
   http://jade.tilab.com/
4. Hendler, J.: Agents and the Semantic Web. Intelligent Systems 16(2), 30–37 (2001)
5. Yen, J., Fan, X., Sun, S., Hanratty, T., Dumer, J.: Agents with shared mental models for enhancing team decision makings. Decision Support Systems 41, 634–653 (2006)
6. Foundation for Intelligent Physical Agents, FIPA (2002), http://www.fipa.org
7. Liu, C.H., Lin, Y.F., Chen, J.Y.: Using Agent to Coordinate Web Service. The International Journal of Computer Science and Information Security (IJCSIS) 2(1), 18–25 (2009)
8. Francisco, G.S., Rafael, V.G., Rodrigo, M.B., Leonardo, C., Jesualdo, T.F.B.: An ontology intelligent agent-based framework for the provision of semantic web ser-vices. Expert Systems with Applications 36(2), 3167–3187 (2009)
9. Dirk, V., Stephan, L., Martijn, W., Michel, A.O., Jorg, M.H.: Facilitating Group-based Adaptation of Shared Workspaces using a Multi-Agent System. In: The Proceedings of the Context-Adaptive Interaction for Collaborative Work (CAICOLL 2010) Workshop (2010)
10. Wu, J., Hu, B., Zhang, J., Fang, D.: Multi-agent Simulation of Group Behavior in E-Government Policy Decision. Simulation Modeling Practice and Theory 16(10), 1571–1587 (2008)
11. Zhiyong, W., Thomas, T.: A Mobile, Intelligent Agent-based Architecture for E-Business. International Journal of Information Technology and Web Engineering 2(4), 63–80 (2007)

A Cloud Based Information Integration Platform for Smart Cars

Yi Xu and Jun Yan

School of Information Systems and Technology (SISAT),
University of Wollongong
Wollongong, NSW, Australia 2522
yx661@uowmail.edu.au, jyan@uow.edu.au

Abstract. Current in-car computers have limited processing capabilities, and the content in smart car applications is poor extension. Even more, tradition software install approach which was used in smart cars lacks neither economy nor convenience. To solve these issues, we introduced a Cloud based Information Integration Platform for Smart Cars that has the ability to encourage flexibility in smart cars and enhance the value of them. To achieve the smart control and information sharing in smart cars, the platform collects data on the CAN bus automatically, with the ability to process CAN bus messages in Clouds. The Smart Car Information Service as the user interface was used to implement smart cars applications through customized business process. This fill up the information processing gap between the smart cars and cloud computing. Furthermore, we can use this platform for different purposes in smart cars.

Keywords: Web Services; CAN bus; Cloud Computing; Smart Cars.

1 Introduction

The smart car is the future trend in automotive improvement. With the development of automotive electronic technology, the smart car technology is evolving rapidly. Currently, the traditional in-car computers in smarts cars have limited processing capabilities to run many functions, such as navigation and display real time information. It is not smart enough without the information sharing among the real world and the computer. Thus, the smart car technology has the potentials to make the car easier to control, more dynamic and economical, and safer to drive. To achieve these benefits, in-car information systems need to be seamlessly integrated with the external information services, supporting the transfer, exchange, and sharing of information among them. Our motivation is to design a new information integration platform for smart cars to enhance the ability of processing the real time information from the smart cars and reduce the delay of smart car applications development. The mission is comprehensive applications of smart cars electronic control technology, car network technologies and intelligent control technologies.

Currently, a smart car mainly uses Controller Area Network (CAN) bus as the network connection. In this paper, we focus on the novel use of CAN bus applications and cloud computing technologies. Our primary contribution is the synthesis of ideas,

R.-S. Chang, T.-h. Kim, and S.-L. Peng (Eds.): SUComS 2011, CCIS 223, pp. 241–250, 2011.
© Springer-Verlag Berlin Heidelberg 2011

some of them are novel in their respective areas. The proposed platform seamlessly integrates the in-car information system with the external cloud information services, allowing smart car applications to be developed. A data conversion approach is developed which is able to convert the data from binary code in CAN bus to the XML format so that they can be processed by CAN message service in Clouds. As the participant to the smart cars information integration platform, the designed smart car information service can be easily extended by integrating various services to support new use case scenarios.

The rest of the paper is organized as follows. The second section reviews major technologies that are related to this research. In Section 3, we describe the architecture of the proposed platform in details. Then we present a use case scenario as a sample application to active our designed platform in Section 4. Finally, Section 5 concludes this paper and outlines our future work.

2   Related Technologies

The proposed Cloud based information integration platform for smart cars provides a novel approach to connecting the in-car system with external systems. This can lead to the development of new smart car applications. The platform is developed based on the technologies and components as follows.

- The in-car computer is a core of our platform. Traditionally, it is a mini PC or a SCM (Single-Chip Microcomputer). For example, the CarTel [1] node was described as a kind of in-car computer which runs on the Linux 2.4.31 kernel. An in-car computer can connect to the Internet via 3G or 3.5G networks, such as CDMA 1x EVolution Data-Only (EVDO), High-Speed Downlink Packet Access (HSDPA), and mobile WiMax [2].
- The Global Positioning System (GPS) navigation system in a car provides route planning, and even voice guidance [3-5].
- Controller Area Network (CAN) is a serial communication bus designed to provide simple, efficient and robust communications for in-car networks[6]. The car's electronic equipments were connected by this control network. One subset of a modern vehicle's network architecture [7], shows the trend towards incorporating ever more extensive electronics
- With Software as a service (SaaS), Cloud computing can provides the applications to users for use as a service on demand, either through a time subscription or a "pay-as-you-go" model. Cloud Computing refers to both the applications delivered as services over the Internet and the hardware and systems software in the datacenters that provide those services [8] .

3   Architecture

3.1   Components and Design

The Cloud based Information Integration Platform for Smart Cars has two different layers, namely the hardware layer and the services & software layer.

The hardware layer in this architecture acts as the basis of the Cloud based Information Integration Platform for Smart Cars. This layer includes the CAN bus subsystem and an in-car computer. The CAN bus subsystem has frequent internal communication, thus requiring high demanding real-time control. Most of the car electronics belong to the CAN bus subsystem. In a smart car, an in-car computer will collect messages from sensors via CAN bus. The gateway controller which is between CAN bus and in-car computer can converts CAN bus messages allowing the in-car computer process the CAN bus messages in the IT data bus.

In our designed platform, the gateway controller provides one procedure to deal with standard CAN bus messages. With the gateway controller, messages from each node in the CAN bus can be read or written by the in-car computer. This process is a two-way transmission in CAN bus which provides an information sharing platform for all kinds of electronic control systems to share information [9]. Currently, most cars use two different CAN buses in network connection, a high-speed CAN bus and a low-speed CAN bus.

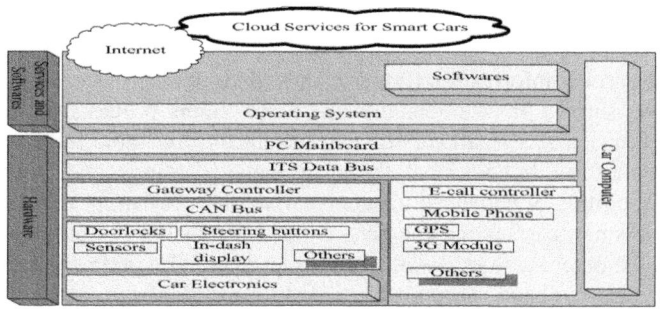

Fig. 1. Architecture of Cloud based Car Information Integration Platform

The main mission of the high-speed CAN bus is to connect the engine controller (ECU), ASR and ABS controllers, airbag controllers, and those instrument clusters have same basic features. The high-speed CAN bus in a car could run more real-time-critical functions to enhance the safety, comfort, and added-value of passenger car and improve its service quality and performance [7, 9]. For less speed demands, the low-speed CAN bus is used to run a few small wirings that are connected together to form several subsystems. These subsystems use the gateway to share information and coordinate ECUs. The low speed CAN system deals with the connection with central locking, power windows, mirrors and lighting, etc. [10]. The speed of a high-speed CAN bus in a drive system can reach 500kbps, while the speed of the low-speed CAN bus in an electronics system is 100 kpbs [9, 11].

For processing the information in smart cars, the in-car computer will collect information from the gateway controller and delivers those CAN bus messages to the smart car information service in Clouds. It is a bridge between a smart car platform and the Cloud based information services.

Global Positioning System (GPS) and wireless communication technology were used in the in-car computer as important roles. We need GPS sensor to provide the information of smart car's location to the smart car information service in Clouds.

The bandwidth of the current wireless network is sufficient for the communication between the smart car and the Cloud based services. The communication device also provides mobile networking access of several Mbit/s to laptop computers and smart phones.

The Cloud based Information Integration Platform allows smart car users to use smart car applications as services in Clouds. It provides intelligent processing, cloud computing capability and infrastructure to users and various smart car services. In addition, the design of the Cloud based Information Integration Platform uses the master-slave structure. The overall distribution of the network structure is a tree. From the perspective of the network topology, the entire communication system is organized by the in-car computer. GPS, wireless, gateway controller, CAN bus and automotive electrical components were controlled by in-car computer in a smart car.

3.2   Workflow and Messages

We present a smart car information service to execute a custom developed smart car applications in Clouds. Each service feature of smart car information service has its backed smart car application with different well-defined business process for smart cars. Each smart car information further makes use of core services that include CAN bus message service in the Clouds. To adopt cloud processing, the smart car information service as a smart car services interface is available for cloud computing in designed platform. In additional, there are many existing technologies in the cloud that can be modified or enhanced to support new smart car applications. As shown in figure 2, one smart car service can acts as service consumer to use the functionality exposed by the other services. In other words, each cloud based service for smart cars can invoke other designed in-car applications by defined business process in Clouds.

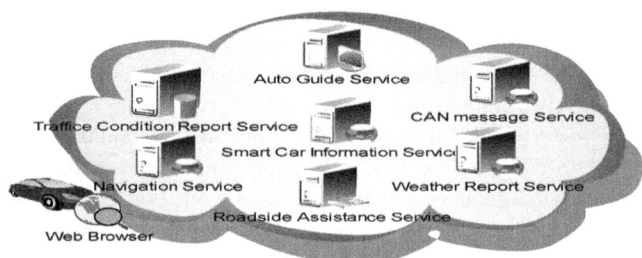

Fig. 2. Cloud Services for Smart Cars

To achieve the smart car control, we connect the IT data bus and the CAN bus via a gateway controller in designed platform, the principle as shown in Figure 3 below. Currently, the in-car computer uses the IT data bus to exchange messages among GPS, 3G module, Bluetooth and so on. The IT data bus requires high data transfer rate of modules connected together. The gateway controller exchanges messages between IT data bus and CAN bus on mission. In our designed platform, the CAN bus uses the standard protocol with the high data transmission rate to control the smart car electric system, such as the door lockers, LED displays and steering buttons.

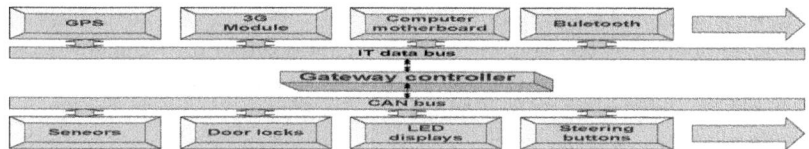

Fig. 3. CAN and IT data bus

To explore what and how to collect context information from a smart car, we present a CAN message service as the core smart car service in clouds to process CAN messages which are from smart cars. This service is used in data exchange, applications integration and XML data management. The CAN message service saves its content data from CAN bus in XML format in thr Clouds. Access is available through the designed smart car information service as the interface. The process is shown in Figure 4.

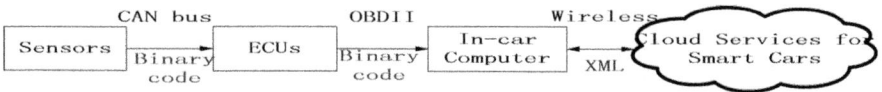

Fig. 4. Data conversion process

Some smart car services in Clouds are the periodic context data updates. For example, a traffic condition report service could similarly send to the navigation service periodic updates of local traffic conditions so that affected users could adapt their travel plans correspondingly.

3.3 Discussion of Designed Architecture

The designed Cloud based Information Integration Platform for Smart Cars is economical and practical for both car users and smart car service providers.

The new platform does not require high cost hardware as the smart equipment for users. Our platform can be built with current in-car devices with low cost, cause the in-car computer in designed platform just provides a terminal of those smart car applications. Cloud processing for smart cars allows car users to start small and increase budget only when there is an increase in their smart car services or applications needs. In Clouds, the appearance of infinite service resources available on demand, quickly enough for provisioning applications which come from smart car service providers or car companies. In addition, the cloud based services for smart cars are dependable and secure. Users do not need to worry about the problems like safety and privacy while using smart car services in Clouds.

For information and entertainment providers, using SOA and SaaS in Cloud based Information Integration Platform can help smart car service providers to reduce the cost of smart car applications design, development, deployment and services support. By adopting the platform, smart car application developers can design different products in application layer, while using common hardware standards to achieve flexibility, functionality, low cost and success.

Furthermore, Cloud based Information Integration Platform for Smart Cars possibly can help automotive manufacturers and their suppliers follow the rapid development of consumer product technology. By selecting our platform, car manufacturers can reduce the overall investment, but also shorten the learning cycle, improve function and reduce the costs.

4   Scenario

4.1   Scenario Process

Now, we show how we can apply smart car information service and CAN message service in the cloud based information integration platform for illustration. We choose the smart car repair scenario as the primary example. A sample is presented in this section to demonstrate the functions of the J1939 TestFeatureSet. An ECU will be tested for tire pressure control, which is simulated in CANoe [12]. The process of this scenario is described as follows.

1. The sensor that monitors the tire pressure will submit an error message to CAN bus once an abnormal tyre pressure is identified (yellow tyre as in Figure 5). The error message will be sent to the smart car information service, and then the smart car information service can find all the details of the abnormal tyre, such the maker, model and so on. Meanwhile, the screen in the smart car displays the error message to driver for warning. It will prompt driver to go to the car repair station.

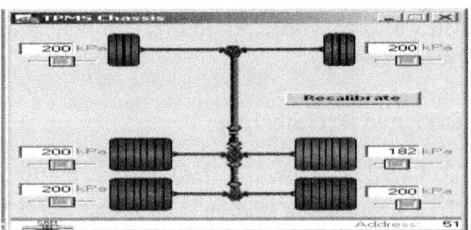

Fig. 5. CANoe simulation

2. We call the Geocoder service[13] and stored repair stations information in the station database service as static context before the next step. Those static and dynamic context elements were collected in different steps as shown in Figure 6. The static context in the station database service includes station locations, categories, station names and reviews of products and services.
3. The in-car computer collects the dynamic information from CAN bus and GPS receiver, then submits them to the smart car information service via wireless network. The dynamic context comes from CAN bus messages provides some information about travel range, time, broken car part and car location to user. Some other dynamic context likely time, day, data and weather condition will be collected from other source.

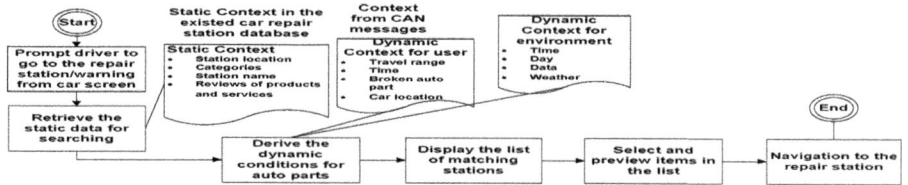

Fig. 6. Application activity diagram with example context elements

4. The smart car information service in this example presents a list of available repair stations. We use the Google Maps Service to overlay available car repair stations data which from the smart car information service.

5. The smart car information service finds addresses of repair stations based on the existing database. It then returns a point location that contains the latitude-longitude coordinates of those stations.

The smart car information service will give you a handy navigation at the fine step in the scenario.

4.2 Smart Car Information Service

We designed a smart car information service to apply the proposed Information Integration Platform for Smart Cars. Our platform allows the smart car services to run in the cloud computing environment by using Business Process Execution Language (BPEL) which is used in a business-process level contract for aggregating multiple services.

By using Web Services in Clouds, smart car applications lend themselves very nicely to the designed smart car environment. They are easy to invoke, produce a discretely formatted response, and are usually parsed easily using event-driven XML parsing which is less memory intensive than tree based parsing.

CAN bus message is one of the inputs of the smart car information service. The smart car information service currently collects CAN messages and other data from IT data bus, monitors the location information and gathers a variety of data from the On-Board Diagnostic (OBD II) interface on smart cars.

The smart car information service allows different combinations to be selected for demonstration to highlight service interoperability. The composition structures can be specified using composition approach in Clouds, e.g., SwinDeW-S [14]. As we described above, a variety of smart car services can call each other to set the new smart car service with different business process in Clouds. Thus, it is possible to provide a smart car application store for end user to select the services they need.

4.3 Data Conversion and CAN Bus Message Service

The CAN message XML file needs to be changed before the data is stored into the database. By adopting XML technology, those CAN message elements were stored in a XML file as the figure 7 below:

```
<?xml version="1.0" encoding="iso-8859-1" standalone="yes" ?>
<!-- Version -->
<!DOCTYPE LoggingExport (View Source for full doctype...)>
<LoggingExport>
  <header hexdec="hexadecimal" symnum="symbolic" timemode="absolute">
    <columntitle>Time</columntitle>
    <columntitle>Chn</columntitle>
    <columntitle>PGN</columntitle>
    <columntitle>Name</columntitle>
    <columntitle>Send node</columntitle>
    <columntitle>Src</columntitle>
    <columntitle>Dest</columntitle>
    <columntitle>Prio</columntitle>
    <columntitle>Dir</columntitle>
    <columntitle>DLC</columntitle>
    <columntitle>Data</columntitle>
  </header>
  <event timestamp="0.000556" bustype="CAN" channel="1" fgColor="#008000" bgColor="#ffffff">
    <col name="Time" />
    <col name="Chn">1</col>
    <col name="---">FE00p</col>
    <col name="Name">ACL</col>
    <col name="Send node">TPMS</col>
    <col name="---">51</col>
    <col name="---">all</col>
    <col name="---">6</col>
    <col name="Dir">Tx</col>
    <col name="DLC">8</col>
    <col name="Data">4F 34 A9 E8 00 26 00 00</col>
  </event>
  <event timestamp="0.260576" bustype="CAN" channel="1" fgColor="#000000" bgColor="#ffffff">
```

Fig. 7. A message episode from CAN bus under XML format

The "Data" field in the CAN bus message was augmented with some attributes. In our scenario, the second bit represents the pressure of tyre. For example, we got a data string from a normal status:

Data 10 C8 60 24 FF FF FF FF

The highlighted value C8 indicates that the type pressure of 800kPa is at the normal level. Figure 8 shows the data collected from the CAN bus in the simulation platform. In that time point (second 70.261140), the tyre pressure is below the normal. B6 means only 728kPa in the tyre. According to the CAN bus simulation, we can get the status of the tyre which was broken. The warning message from the CAN message service will let the driver knows that there is a tyre should be replaced soon.

Time	Chn	PGN	Name	Send node	Src	Dest	Prio	Dir	DLC	Data
70.261140	1	FEF4p	TIRE_TPMS	TPMS	51	--	6	Tx	8	01 B6 60 24 FF FF FF FF
∿ Priority: 6 Data page: 0 Source : 51 Destination: --				CAN-Id 18FEF451x						
∿ TirePressThresholdDetection				NotAvailable	[				7]	
∿ TireAirLeakageRate				<Not avail.>	[				FFFF]	

Fig. 8. Data example in simulation

In this work, we designed the CAN bus message service to collect the data from in a smart car. In the scenario, CAN bus message service was invoked by the smart car information service to apply the car repair process.

The CAN bus message service WSDL provides all the information about the CAN bus message service that can be read by a service client. The WSDL defines an interface of the CAN message service in Clouds. The CAN bus message service get a request to deal with a CAN message file which can be uploaded to the Cloud. There is one port in the CAN message service which is used to process specified SOAP messages for upload CAN message file.

4.4 Message Flow

An open and simple protocol was designed to use smart car information service over the Internet for smart cars. The message flow in our scenario is shown in figure 10. The in-car computer will collect messages (CAN and GPS) periodically.

In the scenario, the information service starts by issuing a diagnosis service request. Then the information service forwards the CAN diagnosis request periodically to the

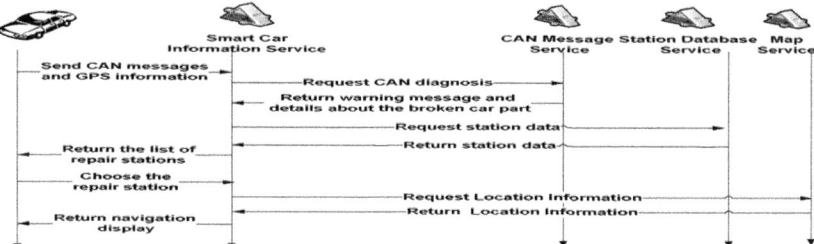

Fig. 9. Message flow in Scenario

CAN message service in which the CAN bus information from the smart car is stored. After that, the car information service finds an appropriate stations list by querying a station database service. The selection of stations could be based on the location, user pre-specified preferences and feasibility of the travel range. After the user chooses the station, the smart car information service sends the location information request to the map service. Finally, the location information is returned to the smart car information service and then to the smart car for information display and navigation. The figure 11 below shows the search result page which was displayed by the smart car information service.

Fig. 10. Search Result of Designed Service

5   Conclusion

This study presented the architecture of cloud based information integration platform for smart cars. Experimental investigations showed that the platform is a feasible scheme. Our results confirm that we can use current technologies to build the platform in smart cars. The designed platform can use the CAN bus messages that make applications context aware. The designed system provides the information from the in-car devices to the car terminal, network, Clouds and smart car application services at all levels. An open and simple protocol was designed to share the data over the Web Services. Cloud computing services can be enhanced with SOA based services to create new smart car services that exceed the capabilities of traditional in-car computer. Combining these creates the opportunity to develop a completely new paradigm of consumer services.

Further work is underway to further explore the software layer in the platform. Different cloud service deployment models will be considered in details as well. The methods used in this paper appear to be rather case-specific and possible extensions and applications of these methods to generic design cases require further study.

References

1. Bret, H., et al.: CarTel: a distributed mobile sensor computing system. In: Proceedings of the 4th International Conference on Embedded Networked Sensor Systems. ACM, Boulder (2006)
2. Keon, J., et al.: 3G and 3.5G wireless network performance measured from moving cars and high-speed trains. In: Proceedings of the 1st ACM Workshop on Mobile Internet Through Cellular Networks. ACM, Beijing (2009)
3. Shinder, D.L.: Smartphone location and navigation services (2010)
4. Peter, H.D.: Global Positioning System (GPS) Time Dissemination for Real-Time Applications. Real-Time Syst. 12(1), 9–40 (1997)
5. Gupta, C.D.: Application of GPS and Infrared for Car Navigation in Foggy Condition to Avoid Accident. In: 2010 Second International Conference on Computer Engineering and Applications (ICCEA) (2010)
6. Davis, R., et al.: Controller Area Network (CAN) schedulability analysis: Refuted, revisited and revised. Real-Time Systems 35(3), 239–272 (2007)
7. Leen, G., Heffernan, D.: Expanding automotive electronic systems. Computer 35(1), 88–93 (2002)
8. Above the Clouds: A Berkeley View of Cloud Computing, in Technical Report. In: Armbrust, M. et al., (eds).,Berkeley (2009)
9. Jian, H., Gangyan, L.: CAN-based passenger car starter information integrated control method and its implementation. In: IEEE International Symposium on Industrial Electronics, ISIE 2009 (2009)
10. Paret, D.: Multiplexed networks for embedded systems: CAN, LIN, flexray, safe-by-wire... John Wiley & Sons, Ltd., Chichester (2007)
11. Murphy, N.: A Short trip on the CAN bus. Embedded Systems Programming 16(9), 9+- (2003)
12. http://www.vector.com/vi_index_en.html Vector
13. Gilmore, J.: Introducing Google's Geocoding Service (2006), http://www.developer.com/lang/jscript/article.php/3615681
14. Jun, S., Jun, Y., Yun, Y.: SwinDeW-S: extending P2P workflow systems for adaptive composite Web services. In: Software Engineering Conference, Australian (2006)

Paradigm Shift and the State of the Art of LBS in the Advent of Smartphone

Gu-Min Jeong[1], Wan-Sik Choi[2], Gyu Young Han[3],
Dong-Kwon Suh[4], and Jong-Yun Yeo[1]

[1] School of Electrical Engineering, Kookmin University, Korea
gm1004@kookmin.ac.kr
[2] ETRI, Daejeon, Korea
choiws@etri.re.kr
[3] SK Telecom, Seoul, Korea
han03@sk.com
[4] HYUNDAI MNSOFT, Seoul, Korea
sdkara@hyundai-mnsoft.com

Abstract. This paper presents the paradigm shift and the state of the art of LBS(Location Based Service) in the recent mobile environment. The advent of smartphone, especially, HW(Hardware) for localization, the middleware for LBS and map DB(Database), leads a big step towards LBS as a killer application. The LBS grows very fast with various smartphone applications. In feature phone, the service area of LBS was limited and the main usage was finding buddy. However, in smartphone, LBS merges other killer applications such as SNS(Social Network Service), AR(Augmented Reality), game, mobile commerce and so on. The abrupt evolution of technology and service requires appropriate laws and systems for the future development.

Keywords: LBS, Smartphone, Platform, Applications.

1 Introduction

With the advance of smartphone technologies, various LBS applications are being provided to the user. The main characteristics of cell phone, portability and mobility, make the device optimized for LBS[1,3].

In feature phone environment, however, the platform and technologies are not open to the developers. It was a severe drawback for the services and applications. Hence, LBS was just a possible candidate for the killer applications during the feature phone era.

The open platform in smartphone causes a big change in LBS. The smartphone platform in iPhone and Android supports HW, SW(Software) and DB related to LBS. It becomes foundation for the open development of LBS applications.

For the platform aspect, smartphone platform provides location functions using GPS(Global Positioning System), WLAN(Wireless Local Area Network)and Cell-ID(Cell Identification), the function of orientation recognition using digital

R.-S. Chang, T.-h. Kim, and S.-L. Peng (Eds.): SUComS 2011, CCIS 223, pp. 251–258, 2011.
© Springer-Verlag Berlin Heidelberg 2011

compass, and the database for the map and the location. For the aspect of service, killer LBS applications such as Foursquare[4] appear merging other services such as SNS[4,5], AR[6,7], commerce[8], advertizement[8,9] and so on. However, the abrupt evolution of services causes problems of privacy preservation because anyone can be tracked easily.

In this paper, we analyze the paradigm shift of LBS in the advent of smartphone and describe the present and the future of LBS in smartphone, extending the previous work [10].

First, we analyze the main differences between conventional LBS based on feature phone and smartphone based LBS. Next, we summarize the LBS related technologies of smartphone and the state of the art of LBS applications. Finally, we present the future characteristics of smartphone LBS.

2   Paradigm Shift of LBS with Smartphone

The advent of smartphone causes a paradigm shift in LBS like other smartphone services. Table 1(a) and 1(b) show the characteristics of LBS in feature phone and smartphone, respectively.

Table 1. Characteristics of LBS according to the phone environment

(a) Characteristics of feature phone based LBS

Aspects	Characteristics
Technology and Industry	Telco. and manufacturer centric Not Open Platform Limited services
Law and System	Enable to control technology Only approved services Stable establishment
Monitoring	Monitoring of Telco. services

(b) Characteristics of smartphone based LBS

Aspects	Characteristics
Technology and Industry	User and developer centric Open LBS Platform Open services
Law and System	Impossible to control technology Difficult to approve services Difficult to establish laws Privacy protection is required
Monitoring	Difficult to monitor services

In feature phone environment, only telecommunication companies, cell phone manufacturers and approved companies can develop LBS applications. Thus, the

LBS platform is under control and service environment is restricted. In the aspect of law and system, government can control LBS related technologies according to the related regulations because only approved services can be provided to the user. Therefore, the whole services can be monitored with the help of telecommunication company.

Different from these, smartphone based LBS has different characteristics. The user and application developers are the main actors. Platform and service environment are open. Based on these facts, it is almost impossible to control technology. Also, the privacy protection becomes one of the main issues as anyone can be easily tracked.

As can be seen in Table 1(a) and 1(b), there is a difficulty in legislating laws and regulations appropriate to the smartphone environment. However, the establishment of law and systems will be very helpful to the evolution of smartphone based LBS.

3   LBS Related Technology in Smartphone

LBS related technologies in smartphone include the HW/SW technologies for the location, DBs for map and AP(Access Point) /Cell-ID and so on. Fig. 1(a) shows the components of LBS related technologies in smartphone. Several service DB's are important components as well as the platform in smartphone.

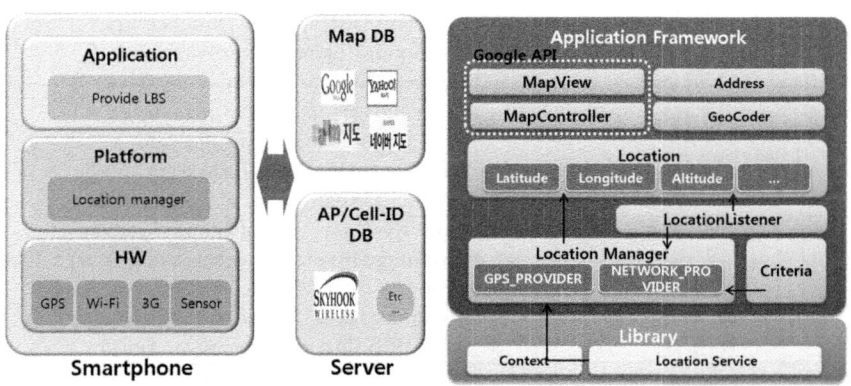

(a) Components of LBS for smartphone (b) LBS related components in Android

Fig. 1. Smartphone related LBS technology

The location is determined using GPS, WLAN and Cell-ID with the support of AP/Cell-ID DB. The digital compass measures 3-dimensional magnetic field and helps the determination of orientation. Map DB provides the geographic map to the smartphone. The application developer can make smartphone LBS

application using LBS related API(Application Programming Interface)s and
DBs. Fig. 1(b) shows LBS related components in Android platform.

There are other components, which are not related to LBS directly but utilized
for LBS. For example, AR services are widely provided based on LBS. In a certain
case, it may be very difficult to make a touch input when using LBS. In such a
case, voice search is very useful to LBS.

4   The State of the Art of Smartphone Based LBS

4.1   Service Types of LBS

In feature phone, the service types of LBS are limited such as tracking, finding
buddy, navigation, traffic information etc. However, in smartphone, LBS applications merge with other application types. As in Table 2, various services such
as AR, SNS, game etc. are combined with LBS and evolved to various applications. In fact, LBS smartphone applications have characteristics of many service
types. In Table 2, we describe just one specific service type for one application.

Table 2. Examples of LBS applications in smartphone

Service types	LBS examples
Finding buddy	Google Latitude (http://www.google.com/latitude)
Navigation	GINI (http://www.gini.co.kr) T-map (http://www.tmap.co.kr)
SNS	Foursquare(https://foursquare.com/) Playmap (http://www.playmap.co.kr/)
Restaurant and spot	Yelp(http://www.yelp.com/) Gowalla (http://gowalla.com/) WhereIs (http://www.whereis.co.kr/) WHERE (http://www.where.com)
AR	Bionic Eye(http://www.bionic-eye.com) WorkSnug (http://www.worksnug.com) Sekai camera (http://www.sekaicamera.com/) Scan search (http://www.scan-search.com/) OVJET (http://www.ovjet.com/)
Game	Foursquare(https://foursquare.com/) iButterfly (http://www.mobileart.jp/ibutterfly.html) T-map geocaching (http://www.tmap.co.kr)
Commerce & advertizement	SKT AdZone(http://www.sktelecom.com/) AliGo (http://www.aligo.co.kr/)
Car sharing	ZipCar(http://www.zipcar.com/)

Table 3 shows nominated LBS applications. As in Table 3, LBS applications
combining with other services become killer applications.

Table 3. Nominated LBS applications in smartphone

Application	Nomination
Yelp	App Store Essentials Hall of Fame
Golfscape GPS Rnagefinder	App Store Essentials Hall of Fame
Nike+GPS	App Store Essentials Hall of Fame
Yelp	Time 2009 Best Apps (Must Have Apps)
Trapster	Time 2009 Best Apps (10 Best iPhone Apps for Dad)
Fanfinder	Time 2009 Best Apps (10 Best iPhone Apps for Dad)
Kayak	Time 50 Best iPhone Apps 2011
Yelp	Time 50 Best iPhone Apps 2011
Weather Channel	Time 50 Best iPhone Apps 2011
Open Table	Time 50 Best iPhone Apps 2011
Hopstop	Time 50 Best iPhone Apps 2011
AroundMe	Time 50 Best iPhone Apps 2011
Google Earth	Time 50 Best iPhone Apps 2011
Zipcar	Time 50 Best iPhone Apps 2011
Foursqaure	Time 50 Best iPhone Apps 2011
Google Sky Map	Must Have Android App. Top 10 (NY Times)
CardioTrainer	Must Have Android App. Top 10 (NY Times)
UrbanSpoon	Must Have Android App. Top 10 (NY Times)
Playmap	Mobile Technology Awards 2009 (Korea)
OVJET	Korea Mobile App Awards 2010 (Korea)
Scan search	Korea Mobile App Awards 2010 (Korea)
I'm in	App Award Korea 2011 (Korea)
Seoul Bus	App Award Korea 2011 (Korea)

5   Toward Future LBS

Although many applications for LBS are provided in smartphone, there still remains lots of homework for the next generation LBS.

Most of all, in order to implement seamless LBS between outdoor and indoor LBS, the precision of location should be enhanced and indoor LBS should be fully developed. Hybrid location method can be applied to the smartphone with RFID(Radio Frequency Identification), ZigBee, VLC(Visible Light Communication), vision based LBS and so on. For map DB, 3D map should be provided for usability. With the user data for LBS, analysis of user experience can be very helpful to the LBS user. For the service aspects, the combination with mobile commerce and mobile advertizement can be profitable to LBS. Also, there are much problems for the privacy issues. Laws and systems should be established for the future LBS.

5.1   Technologies for the Evolution of LBS

Recently, indoor applications are commercialized based on WLAN or other technologies. Most of LBS applications are based on GPS and focus on outdoor LBS.

There should be the seamless LBS between outdoor and indoor LBS. Adequate technologies should be developed.

Also, the precision of location should be improved with various hybrid positioning scheme and for user's convenience, 3D map should be supported.

In ISO TC 211, the dynamic position identification scheme between indoor and outdoor environment has been discussed at ISO 19151. Also, in TC 204, the map format for indoor navigation and position DB have been under standardization.

For the aspects of technology, the following objectives are under consideration or being commercialized :

- Seamless LBS with indoor LBS [11]
- 3D map and 3D navigation [12][13]
- Precision enhancement of location determination
- Hybrid location identification
- Navigation for pedestrians
- Vision based LBS
- Convergence with navigation kit for automobile
- Unification of user interface between automobile and smartphone [14][15]

Fig. 2 shows examples of indoor LBS(SK Telecom) and 3D map(HYUNDAI MNSOFT).

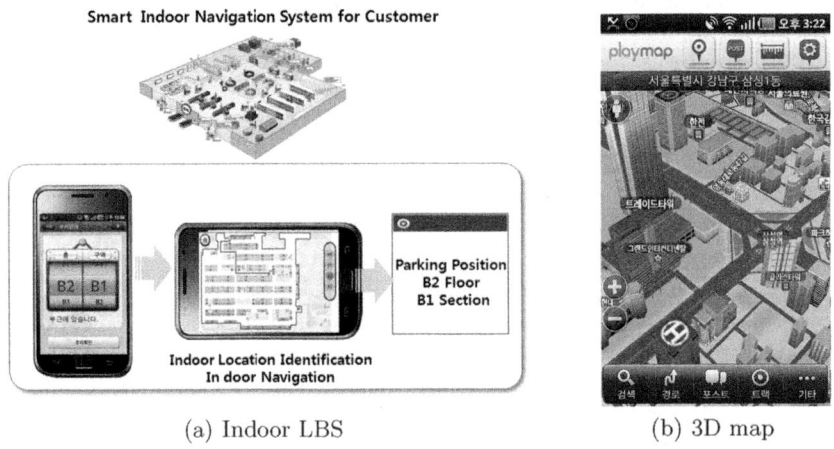

(a) Indoor LBS   (b) 3D map

Fig. 2. Examples of indoor LBS (SK Telecom) and 3D map (HYUNDAI MNSOFT)

5.2   Services and User Experience

Based on the accumulated user data, user experience can be analyzed and the result can be provided to the user. Also, the combination with mobile commerce and mobile advertizement can be profitable to LBS.

For the aspects of services, the following objectives are under consideration or being commercialized :

- Analysis of user's LBS data [16]
- Mobile commerce using LBS [8]
- Mobile advertizement based on the location [8,9]
- Event data recorder for automobile
- Convergence with SNS, AR, Game and so on
- Convergence with off-line services [17]

Fig. 3 shows an example of mobile commerce and advertisement using LBS.

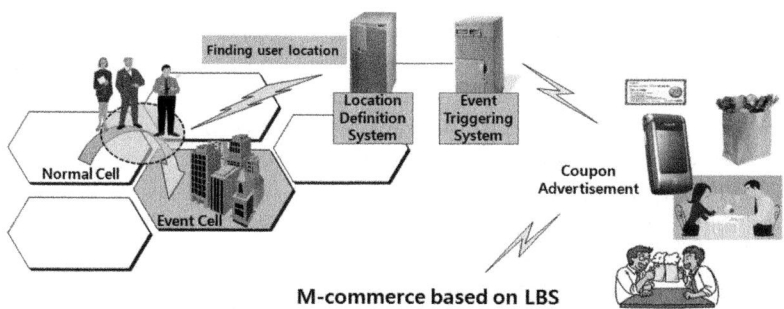

Fig. 3. Mobile commerce and advertisement using LBS of SK Telecom

5.3 Law and System for Smartphone LBS

Recently, the privacy problem for LBS service is being a critical problem. Location tracking issues for Google and Apple make critical issues for the location privacy and cause serious discussions for the safety of LBS.

In fact, the problem of LBS is more crucial than the general SNS. As in Table 4, in conventional SNS, only the data which the user has uploaded are reproduced. The data can be misused irrespective of user's intention, which can cause a problem.

In the LBS+SNS service like Foursquare, only the data which the user has uploaded are reproduced. Still, the location information can be misused irrespective of user's intention and it can cause a problem.

However, in LBS applications, there exist services which collect users location without any notice of user. Although there is a user's admission for the gathering location information at the fist stage of the service, it can cause a serious problem.

Table 4. Characteristics and problems of LBS and SNS

Application	Service type	Characteristics and problems
Google Latitude	LBS+SNS	Location information can be used without notice to user Cause serious problems for location privacy Essential information for LBS
Foursquare	LBS+SNS	Upload the location information by the user
General SNS	SNS	Upload information by the user

As in Table 4, there is a conflict that the location information is essential for the LBS applications but is dangerous for the user's privacy. Considering these facts, appropriate laws and systems should be established for stable LBS. Also, the user should protect user's own information by him/herself. For the popularity of LBS, we need more location information of users and we should establish concrete laws and systems, which will be the foundation of future LBS.

6   Conclusion

In this paper, we have presented the paradigm shift and the state of the art of LBS. With the open platform and the development of various applications, LBS becomes a killer application for the smartphone era.

Especially, LBS applications are now combined with other services like AR, SNS, game, commerce, advertizement, and even off-line services. The number of users grows fast in LBS applications such as Foursquare, Yelp, Playmap and so on over the world. Also, mobile commerce and mobile advertizement based on LBS will devote to the profit of LBS applications.

Although there are privacy problems for the location information, the establishment of laws and systems will be very helpful for the evolution of future LBS.

References

1. Kubber, A.: Location Based Services. Wiley and Sons, Chichester (2005)
2. Vaughan-Nichols, S.J.: Will Mobile Computing's Future Be Location, Location, Location? IEEE Computer 42, 14–17 (2009)
3. Bellavista, P., Küpper, A., Helal, S.: Location Based Services: Back to the Future. IEEE Pervasice Computing 7, 85–89 (2008)
4. Foursquare, http://www.foursquare.com
5. Playmap, http://www.playmap.co.kr
6. Bionic Eye, http://www.bionic-eye.com
7. WorkSnug, http://www.worksnug.com
8. AdZone, http://www.sktelecom.com
9. AliGo, http://www.aligo.co.kr
10. Jeong, G.-M., Choi, W.-S., Han, G.Y., Suh, D.-K., Yeo, J.-Y.: Smartphone based LBS: state of the art. Information and Communication Magazine 7 (2011) (in Korean)
11. Jan, S.-S., Hsu, L.-T., Tsai, W.-M.: Development of an Indoor Location Based Service Test Bed and Geographic Information System with a Wireless Sensor Network. Sensor 10, 2957–2974 (2010)
12. HYUNDAI MNSOFT 3D MAP, http://hyundai-mnsoft.com
13. TAT mobile user interface blog, http://mobileuserinterfaces.blogspot.com
14. Nokia Terminal mode, http://www.nokia.com/terminalmode
15. SKT MIV, http://www.sktelecom.com
16. Foursquare Merchant Platform, https://foursquare.com/business/venues
17. ZipCar, http://www.zipcar.com

A Mobile Homecare Application Combining with Alarm Clock and GPS Positioning Function

Rung-Shiang Cheng, Chun-Yu Ke, Chung-Ying Tsai, and Chien-Jen Wang[*]

Department of Computer and Communication, Kun Shan University,
Tainan, Taiwan (R.O.C)
{rscheng,cjw}@mail.ksu.edu.tw,
{sacitta,tsaitsaihonda}@gmail.com

Abstract. Along with the recent development of orange technology, there is a growing concern for homecare issue for the elderly. According to official statistics, it shows by the end of 2010, there have been 2,487,893 elderly people over 65 years old in Taiwan, occupying 10.74% of total population, and the number is growing continuously. According to the latest population projection conducted by Council for Economic Planning and Development (CEPD), it is estimated that in 2017, Taiwan will become an aged society, while in 2025 become a super aged society. In comparison with some European countries, such as Germany, France and United Kingdom, it demonstrates rapid population aging in Taiwan. Due to the coming of an aged society, homecare service becomes more and more important.

Smart phones have the characteristics of personalization, multi-function and portability, therefore, it is suitable to develop a mobile care system with high portability on the platform. This study utilizes Android open platform to develop a homecare system for the elderly combining with alarm clock, GPS global positioning system and call catcher. Alarm application reminds the patients to take the medicine regularly, while call catcher prevents the elderly from being fraud. And further, combining with GPS, it is also effective to prevent the elderly from getting lost.

Keywords: Android, Homecare, GPS, Clock.

1 Introduction

The coming of an aged society represents the ratio of chronic disease is increasing. Based on data prepared by Dept. of Population, Ministry of Interior, it shows chronic disease for the elderly in Taiwan occupies a ratio of more than 60 % of total. Chronic disease even occupies 7 causes of Taiwan Top 10 causes of death. However, taking medicine regularly is beneficial for controlling or improving the chronic illness. In consideration of the importance of regular medicine taking of chronic patients, we design simple alarm function combining with text message to

---

[*] Corresponding author.

R.-S. Chang, T.-h. Kim, and S.-L. Peng (Eds.): SUComS 2011, CCIS 223, pp. 259–268, 2011.
© Springer-Verlag Berlin Heidelberg 2011

remind the patient to take medicine on time. After users set their medicine taking time, when set time is up, the alarm will be triggered to remind the patient to take medicine. Meanwhile, the system will send text message to the family member's phone automatically, allowing family members to remind or express concern for medicine taking of the elderly.

Recently, there are many fraud organizations taking mainly the elderly or children as object worldwide. According to the statistics of Police Administration, money that people are swindled is up to 100 billion NT dollars, and there have been over 350 thousand people falling victim to fraud in Taiwan in recent years. This is an unignorable number. Hence, to provide better homecare service for the elderly and children, this study designs a homecare application combining with alarm clock, GPS and call catcher and hides GPS and call catcher under the alarm clock. The alarm application provides functions including: setting alarm, repeating alarm and sending text message when alarm rings. GPS receives text messages to trigger GPS application in mobile phones and reply text message to notify the present location. Call catcher utilizes text message to notify the number of incoming calls.

As to filter telephone number, when there are calls from unknown users, mobile applications will send text messages notifying the number of the incoming calls to the family members automatically. The family members are able to filter the number of the incoming calls after receiving the message. If the numbers are unfamiliar or suspicious, family members can call to express their concern timely, preventing the elderly from being fraud or loss of money.

Usually, along with the increase of age, memories of the elderly deteriorate and are possible to get lost. Due to the regulations, in Taiwan, the police only handle cases with people who have got lost for more than 24 hours, thus, police organizations usually fail to offer timely assistance. Under this circumstance, this system compensates this deficiency, utilizing message trigger Global Positioning System (GPS) to identify the location of the elderly. When family members find their elderly are lost, they can send text messages to the mobile phone held by the elderly. This mobile phone would identify the longitude and latitude of the location automatically and send text messages to the family member's mobile phone, allowing the family member to find their lost family member at the earliest time.

In addition, this application has theft-proof function. Because GPS and call catcher hide under the alarm clock, normal users would not be suspicious of the application. When mobile phones are lost, users can utilize message trigger GPS to obtain the present location of the mobile phone. Or when SIM cards in the mobile phones are replaced and unable to obtain number of this mobile phone (also unable to use message trigger GPS). When people call the one who takes the mobile phone, call catcher can get the phone number and further start GPS in the phone. This greatly enhances the possibility of finding the lost mobile phones.

The remainder of this paper is organized as follows. Section 2 introduces framework of Android development platform and basic components; Section 3 introduces the proposed implementation method; Section 4 introduces implementation layout of applications; Section 5 is conclusion of this study.

2   Background

According to the research reports, handset mobile phone has become one of the most commonly seen personal items of modern people. Meanwhile, built-in CPU of handset mobile phone is able to process great amount of computing data now and supports a variety of wireless access technology. In consideration of future development of mobile communication, thus, in 2007, Google initially established Open Handset Alliance (OHA), developing an open platform for mobile devices named Android.

To enable application developers to develop applications for more easily, Google provides full-function API, e.g. layout arrangement, layout conversion, data exchange between applications, etc. in Android SDK. It allows application designers can utilize services such as Google Map or Gmail to develop applications on open mobile development platform. To make application development of handheld device easier, Android also provide abundant support for mobile communication and various sensors, e.g. GPS, Video-Camera, compass, 3D Accelerometer and map/location function.

As shown in Fig 1, execution environment of Android contains the built-in core Libraries, thus, it can support most function of core Libraries of Java language. When executing program, every Android application would run the routine provided by the operation system separately and has individual Dalvik virtual machine (DVM). To make Android more applicable in mobile phones, Linux kernel of Android also enhances Interprocess Communication (IPC) and Power Management. Meanwhile, Linux Kernel (Version 2.6) also plays the role of abstract interface among all hardware and application, providing basic functions such as thread and memory management.

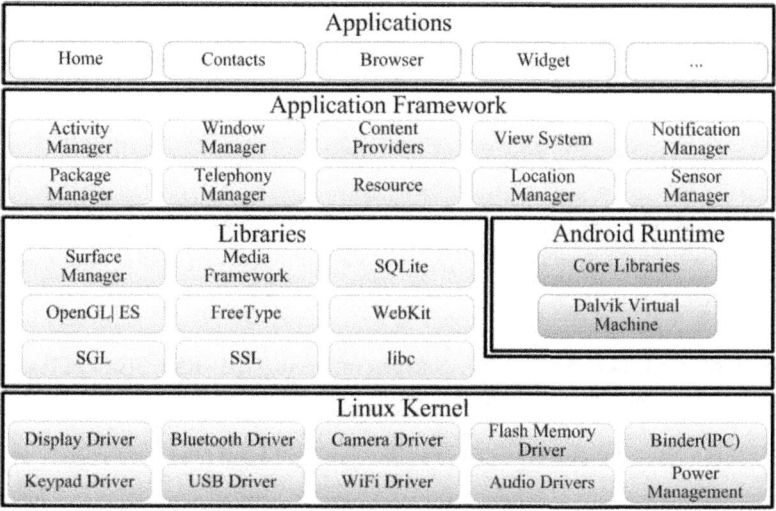

Fig. 1. Android system architecture

In general, most Android applications are comprised of four components: (1) Activity (2) Service (3) Broadcast Receiver and (4) Content Provider. In Android, users can make interaction through Activity. Activity displays View consisted of user interface and responds to events. When implementing in context for long time without interacting with users, it can utilizes Service component to provide service.

When the system is working, Android can start Activity, Service or Broadcast Receiver in the application through Intent messages. Intent is a Runtime binding mechanism which can build connection between two components. Intent has similar mechanism as Event, but there is still some difference from it. Traditional Event processing mechanism focuses on triggering Handler. When an Event occurs, the system would call Event Handler or directly transfer the Event to applications and then, applications decide the handling method. But in Event handling concept of Intent, Android attempts to explain the Event as Intent of applications or Intent of users and tries to explain the intention of the Intent through Intent. If Android can understand Intent of the application, it would process the work should be executed by the Intent. Every Intent message is followed by an Action and respond according to the Action.

Android is an open mobile platform, so it also supports call, SMS, data connection, SIM card and other phone services. The framework of phone service is consisted of four parts including Modem, RIL (Radio Interface Layer), phone service framework and applications. Because the 2G/3G module in mobile phones has been mature, there are a variety of consistent and simple software interface available for hardware service. Therefore, users only need to insert SIM card into the module and turn on the power to start working. Phone modules even finish the initialization such as searching the network and network registration. After initialization is done, phones can be used to make calls and send text messages.

On Android platform, positioning system plays a crucial role. Among the widely applied positioning systems, the most commonly seen is GPS and AGPS system which utilizes Cell signal to assist positioning.

3   System Implementation

The developed homecare application is consist of three components: (1) alarm clcok, (2) global positioning system and (3) call catcher. Following gives a brief discussion.

Alarm Clock

Usage of Alarm Clock Application getSystemService(ALARM_SERVICE)   obtains AlarmManager and utilizes setrepReperating to implement this alarm clock.

Step 1. Assign to implement CallAlarm.class in Set alarm time

```
Intent intent = new Intent(Clock.this,CallAlarm.class);
PendingIntent sender =
PendingIntent.getBroadcast(Clock.this,1, intent, 0);
```

Step 2. Implement the alarm repeatedly︰setRepeating()

```
AlarmManager am;
am=(AlarmManager)getSystemService(ALARM_SERVICE);
am.setRepeating(AlarmManager.RTC_WAKEUP,c.getTimeInMill
is(),times,sender);
```

Step 3. When implementing CallAlarm.class, Intent   would be created and it would call AlarmAlert.class and send reminding text messages

```
public class CallAlarm extends BroadcastReceiver
{  public void onReceive(Context context, Intent intent)
{Intent i = new Intent(context, AlarmAlert.class);
Bundle bundleRet = new Bundle();
bundleRet.putString("STR_CALLER", "");
i.putExtras(bundleRet);
i.addFlags(Intent.FLAG_ACTIVITY_NEW_TASK);
context.startActivity(i);

SMS ();} }
```

Where **SMS** () is a function of sending text message.

Step 4.   Call AlarmAlert.class and reminder window pops up

```
new AlertDialog.Builder(AlarmAlert.this)
.setIcon(R.drawable.clock)
.setTitle("TIME UP!!")
.setMessage("you have to take the medication!!!")
```

Furthermore,   to   add   code   android.permission.RECEIVE_SMS   to AndroidManifest.xml, it can be correctly executed only when applications obtain the user right for sending text message.

3.1   GPS Global Positioning System

Step 1.   GPS application utilizes its built-in GPS satellite positioning to identify the location of users. When receiving the text messages, it utilizes LocationManager component provided by Android system to obtain the coordinates of users. Usage of LocationManager is shown below:

```
Bundle bunde = this.getIntent().getExtras();
if (bunde != null)
{ localManager =
(LocationManager)getSystemService(GPS.LOCATION_SERVICE);
locationListener = new MyLocationListener();
localManager.requestLocationUpdates(LocationManager.GPS
_PROVIDER, 0, 0, locationListener);
} else{finish();}
```

Updates of GPS location to get coordinates address and identify the present location via sending text message:

```
if ( loc!= null){
strlatlon1 = "Lat" + String.valueOf(loc.getLatitude())
+ "Lon" + String.valueOf(loc.getLongitude());   }
```

When developing an application, it is applicable to adopt DDMS tool to detect faults and conduct test. Furthermore, to add code android.permission.ACCESS_FINE_LOCATION to AndroidManifest.xml, it can be correctly executed only when applications obtain the user right for positioning service.

3.2   Call Catcher

This application obtains TELEPHONY_SERVICE system service, obtaining call state and number of the incoming number. Then it sends text messages to notify number of the incoming number of the third party.

Step 1. Obtain TELEPHONY_SERVICE system service

```
mPhoneCallListener phoneListener=new
mPhoneCallListener();
TelephonyManager telMgr =
(TelephonyManager)getSystemService(TELEPHONY_SERVICE);
telMgr.listen(phoneListener,mPhoneCallListener.LISTEN_C
ALL_STATE); mTextView1 =
(TextView)findViewById(R.id.myTextView1);}
```

Step 2. Obtain call state and number of the incoming number, and then, it sends text messages to notify number of the incoming number of the third party.

```
public void onCallStateChanged(int state, String
incomingNumber ) { switch(state)   { case
TelephonyManager.CALL_STATE_RINGING:mTextView1.setText
( getResources().getText(R.string.str_CALL_STATE_RINGING)
+ incomingNumber );
SMS();
break;  default: break; }
super.onCallStateChanged(state, incomingNumber);}
```

4   Achievement Display

Firstly, enter the Initial Menu of Alarm (As shown in Fig 2). In this layout, users can set alarm. When there are setting errors or they want to cancel the alarm, they can click on delete button to cancel the setting.

Fig. 2. Initial Menu of Alarm

Then click on the alarm setting button to enter the layout of setting alarm and repeating alarm (As shown in Fig. 3).

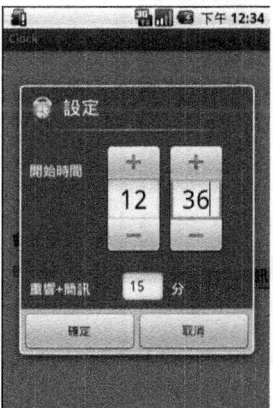

Fig. 3. Set Alarm Time and Repeating Alarm

After completing the setup, the menu would display the set time and repeating interval (As shown in Fig. 4).

Fig. 4. Setup Complete

When the alarm rings, reminder window pops up and send text message to family members. (As shown in Fig. 5).

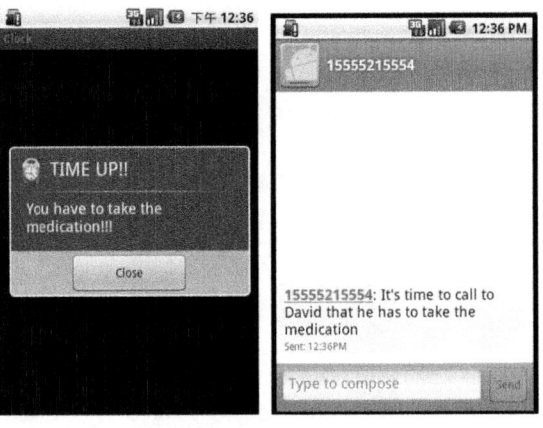

(a) Reminder Window   (b) Sending Text Message

Fig. 5. Alarm, Reminder Window and Sending Text Message

The target mobile phone uses message to trigger GPS function. After receiving the text message, the target phone will notify its present location (As illustrated in Fig. 6).

(a) Send Text Message   (b) Obtain GPS Location

Fig. 6. Mobile phone uses message to trigger the target GPS function

Finally, we show implementation of call catcher below. In the example below (See Fig. 7), while the unknown user calls the user being monitored (see Fig. 7(a)), owing to the user being monitored   starts using call catcher in the mobile phone and receives a call from unknown number (see Fig 7. (b)), call catcher will send the number of the user being monitored is calling to monitor via SMS (Illustrated in Fig. 7(c)).

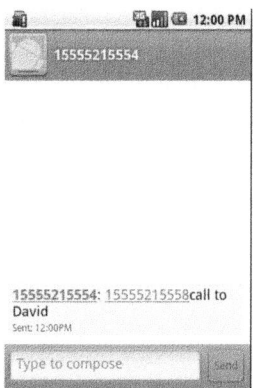

(a) A unknown user calls the   (b) The user being monitored   (c) Call catcher sends the
user being monitored   receives calling from unknown   obtained number to monitor
                                number   via SMS

Fig. 7. Illustrated of Call catcher

5   Conclusion

Smart phones have the characteristics of personalization, multi-function and portability, therefore, it is suitable to develop a mobile care system with high portability on the platform. This study utilizes Android open platform to develop a homecare system for the elderly combining with alarm clock, GPS global positioning system and call catcher. Alarm application reminds the patients to take the medicine regularly, while call catcher prevents the elderly from being fraud. And further, combining with GPS, it is also effective to prevent the elderly from getting lost.

6 Future Work

The future goal in this field will be using 3G network to solve this problem. Presently, GPS positioning has been widely applied in various fields. But the biggest limitation of GPS is it requires environments to have Line of Sight (LOS) with satellite system. Thus, if the place is located indoor or inside the building, owing to wireless signal is unable to be transmitted to user equipment, GPS fails to retain its accuracy under this situation. Furthermore, using GPS in smart phones consume much power, causing the standby hours shortened, failing to work for long time and finally, leading to service interruption.

Along with popularity of mobile device and WiFi technology, devices such as laptop, smart phones, etc can support services such as 2.5/3G, WiFi and so on. Using 3G network positioning can solve failure of satellite signal acquisition of GPS in indoor environments, and compared with using GPS, power consumption of using 3G network positioning is greatly decreased, extending the time for service.

References

1. Whipple, J., Arensman, W., Boler, M.S.: A Public Safety Application of GPS-Enabled. In: IEEE International Conference on Systems, San Antonio, TX, USA (2009)
2. Sukaphat, S.: An Implementation of Location-Based Service System with Cell Identifier for Detecting Lost Mobile. In: WCIT (2010)
3. Sposaro, F., Danielson, J., Tyson, G.: iWander: An Android Applicationfor Dementia Patients. In: 32nd Annual International Conference of the IEEE EMBS Buenos Aires, Argentina (2010)
4. Olufowobi, L.: Sms Based Android Asset Tracking System. Technology and Communication (2011)

On Adaptive Multi-channel MAC Protocol for MANETs

Chun-Cheng Lin[1], Yeong-Sheng Chen[2], and Der-Jiunn Deng[3,*]

[1] Department of Industrial Engineering and Management,
National Chiao Tung University, Hsinchu, Taiwan
[2] Department of Computer Science, National Taipei University of Education, Taipei, Taiwan
[3] Department of Computer Science and Information Engineering,
National Changhua University of Education, Changhua, Taiwan
djdeng@cc.ncue.edu.tw

Abstract. Carrier sense multiple access with collision avoidance (CSMA/CA) mechanism is a widely accepted medium access control (MAC) protocol for mobile ad hoc networks (MANETs). However, it does not function well in MANETs due to its several performance issues such as intensive collision and unfair channel access in congested scenario. The current wireless MAC protocol usually supports multiple channels, where mobile stations adapt their channels based on their channel selection strategies to transmit their own data packets. In this paper, we propose an adaptive channel allocation strategy for a multi-channel MAC protocol in MANETs. Simulations are conducted to evaluate the performance of the proposed scheme. The simulation results show a great performance improvement over the original single channel CSMA/CA MAC protocol.

Keywords: MANETs, fairness problem, hidden terminal problem, exposed terminal problem, multi-channel.

1 Introduction

MANET is a rapidly emerging field of activity in wireless networks and has received a lot of attention recently due to its dynamic topology, better targeting, and convenient usage. A MANET is a self-configuring infrastructure-less wireless network, and provides a cluster of mobile stations connectivity without being tethered off by wired links. MANETs can be deployed in many areas, such as battle fields and natural disasters. For MANETs, CSMA/CA mechanism [1-3] has been widely accepted and employed as the mandatory MAC protocol to share the channel. However, CSMA/CA does not function well in MANETs due to its several performance issues, such as intensive collision and unfair channel access in congested scenario. One approach to improving the MANET system performance is to utilize multiple channels. In the past, there were adequate discussions on the issues on multi-channel MAC protocols and their performance evaluation [4-10]. However, most of them are not designed for congested environments and are not able to alleviate the fairness problem effectively.

---

* Corresponding author.

R.-S. Chang, T.-h. Kim, and S.-L. Peng (Eds.): SUComS 2011, CCIS 223, pp. 269–276, 2011.
© Springer-Verlag Berlin Heidelberg 2011

Since the MANET system performance is greatly dependent on the adopted MAC protocol, in the paper, we propose a pragmatic adaptive channel allocation strategy for multi-channel MAC protocol in MANETs. In addition, we have carried out comprehensive simulations implemented by a customized C++ simulation program to evaluate the proposed scheme. The results show a great performance improvement over the original single channel CSMA/CA MAC protocol.

The rest of this paper is organized as follows. Our proposed algorithm is given in Section 2. Section 3 provides simulation results. Finally, in Section 4 we conclude this paper.

2 Proposed Algorithm

In order to solve hidden and exposed terminal problems, our algorithm utilizes multiple channels to increase the system throughput. Let ξ denote the total number of channels used. Consider a wireless network consisting of n nodes where each node has two network interface cards: one is always on channel 0 for controlling packets, while the other can change its channel number between 1 and $(\xi - 1)$ for transmitting data. The basic idea of our algorithm is that the neighbors of each node and the neighbors of those neighbors utilize a channel different from the node. Obviously, it can be achieved by setting the hop count of the transmitted packet to 2. By doing so, the nodes in a neighborhood transmit data on different channels, so that the hidden and exposed terminal problem can be alleviated and the system throughput can further be increased.

Based upon the above idea, our proposed algorithm is designed as follows. For each period of time, each node in the network is initialized to determine which channel to transmit data is used, according to the RTS/CTS communication with each other on the control channel (i.e., channel 0). In the beginning, each node determines its channel number randomly. Once the channel number of a node is determined, the node broadcasts a RTS with its channel number and a hop count 2 to its neighbors, i.e., the nodes in its transmission scale. Next, if the neighbor does not determine its channel number yet, then it tries to avoid from using the channel numbers that have been used in the received packets. That is, if there exists some free channel number (i.e., the channel numbers that are not used), then the neighbor uses the free channel number for transmitting data; otherwise, it uses a random channel number between 1 and $(\xi - 1)$. If the neighbor determines its channel number, it notifies its neighbors its channel number by a RTS with a hop count 2. In addition, in order to acknowledge each of other received RTSs and CTSs, the neighbor also sends the CTS reserving the channel number of the received packet with a decreased hop count not less than 0.

Note that the hop count of each packet is used for constraining the maximum hop number of transmitting the packet, and it is decremented by one every time when it hops a node. The hop count is set to 2 in our algorithm, because we require that the neighbors as well as the neighbors of the neighbors of each node use different channel numbers for transmitting data.

The initialization of our algorithm stops after the channel numbers used by all the nodes are determined. The pseudo code of the initialization of our algorithm is given in Algorithm 1. As for how to transmit data, after the initialization, if two nodes would like to transmit data, say node A transmits data packets to node B, node A stores its original channel number and then changes its channel number to the channel number used by node B to transmit data. After finishing the data transmission, node A changes the channel number back to its original one.

Algorithm 1. Choose-Channel

// Consider each node that has two network interface cards,
// in which one is always on channel 0 for controlling packets
// while the other can change its channel for transmitting data.

Initialization
hopCount := 2
channelNum := 0
isNotSetChannel := *true*
// If the node broadcasts its channel number, then isNotSetChannel would be false
repeat
   if the node receives a control frame (possibly from RTS or CTS) **then**
      // Let recvHopCount denote the hopCount of the received packet
      // Let recvChannelNum denote the channelNum of the received packet
      if *recvHopCount* > 0 **then**
         recvHopCount := *recvHopCount* – 1
         if *isNotSetChannel* is *true* or *channelNum* equals *recvChannelNum* **then**
            record the channel number of the received packet
            check whether there is any free channel
            if there exists some free channel **then**
               channelNum := the number of the free channel
            else
               channelNum := rand() % $(\xi - 1)$
            end
            broadcast a RTS with *hopCount* and *channelNum*
                  and a CTS with *recvHopCount* and *recvChannelNum*
         else
            broadcast a CTS with *recvHopCount* and *recvChannelNum*
         end
      else
         drop the received packet
      end
   end
until no more frame to transmit

For instance, consider a wireless ad hoc network with 6 nodes labeled by A-F in Figure 1. Each node starts to select a random channel number between 1 and $(\xi - 1)$, and immediately broadcasts to its neighbors a packet with a hop count 2. For example, node A selects channel 1 (see Figure 1) and immediately broadcasts a RTC to its neighbors in its transmission scale, i.e., nodes B, C, and D. If we consider that nodes B and C receive the RTC packets at the same time, then they check whether they use the same channel number as node A. If both nodes B and C select the same channel number, say 2, different from node A, they immediately broadcast RTSs to their respective neighbors. Once one node is late to receive the packet from the other node, it has to change its channel number and re-broadcast a RTS to its neighbors. As for node C, since its channel number is not equal to node A's, it broadcasts via channel 0 a RTS with a hop count 2 and a CTS with a decreased hop count, i.e., 1, at the same time.

Suppose that node D is included in the transmission scale of node C but not in the transmission scale of node A, as shown in Figure 1. Hence, node D would receive a CTS from A and a RTS from C, with channel numbers 1 and 2, respectively. After node D determines its channel number, say channel number 3, the hop count of the received CTS from node A is decreased to 0 and hence, the CTS does not hop to next node. Hence, node D broadcast a RTS with a hop count 2 reserving channel number 3 and a CTS (due to node C) with hop count 1 reserving channel number 2.

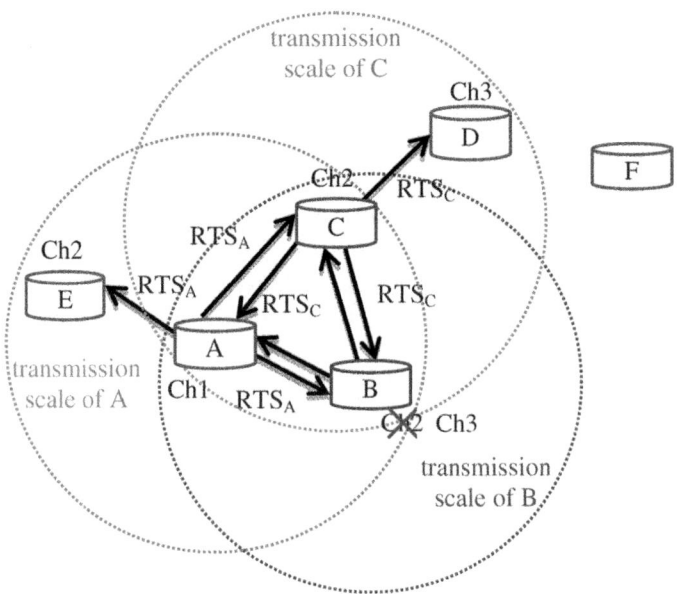

Fig. 1. Illustration of a wireless ad hoc network with 6 nodes labeled A-F

3   Simulation Results

3.1   Simulation Environment

Our simulation is in C++, and runs on a Toshiba A300 laptop, with Intel Core 2 Due CPU T9400 2.53GHz and memory size 4GB. The parameters used in our simulation are given in Table 1.

Table 1. Parameters in simulation

Attribute	Meaning	Value
β_{DATA}	Data channel bit rate	11 *Mbps*
β_{ACK}	Control channel bit rate	1 *Mbps*
$L_{MAC-header}$	Length of MAC header	192 *bits*
L_{PHY}	PHY header	160 *bits*
L_{ctr}	Length of control packet	112 *bits*
$L_{payload}$	MAC layer payload size	1000 *bytes*
W_0	Initial Contention window	32
W_m	Maximum Contention window	1024
m	Maximum backoff state	10
ξ	Total Channel Number	8
T_{slot}	Duration of time slot	20 μs
T_{DIFS}	DIFS time interval	50 μs
T_{SIFS}	SIFS time interval	10 μs
δ	Propagation delay	5 μs

3.2   Simulation Plots

Our simulation plots are given in Figures 2-5, in which the horizontal axis represents the device density. The experimental environment is a contested wireless ad hoc network consisting of at most 200 nodes in a 10m × 10m square.

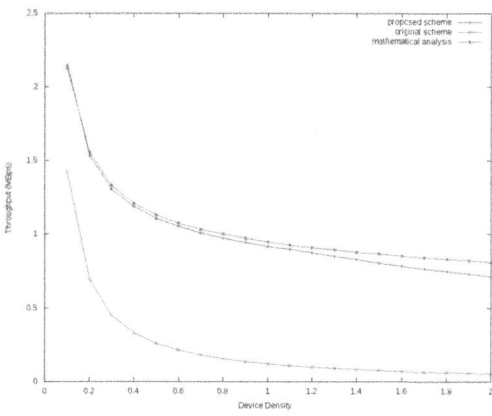

Fig. 2. Plot of throughput versus device density

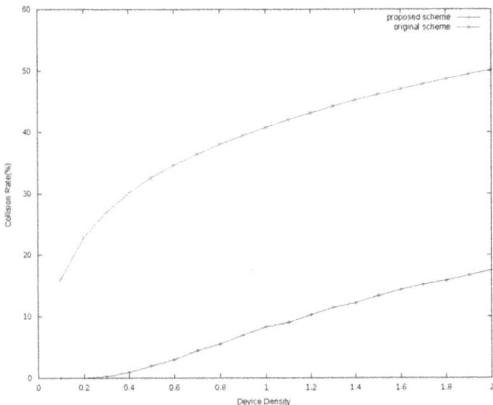

Fig. 3. Plot of collision rate versus device density

In each plot, our algorithm is compared with the method using a single channel. It can be found from Figure 2 that our algorithm outperforms the single channel method in term of throughput. In addition to throughput, we conducted a simulation on collision rate, as shown in Figure 3, from which we observe that our algorithm obviously decreases collision, in comparison to the single channel method. Our algorithm has high performance in the environments of high device density, which implies the reason why our algorithm improves the throughput.

We further analyze the blocking rate, which defines the ratio of the collision transmission over the total transmission. The simulation result is given in Figure 4, from which our algorithm also outperforms the original method.

We analyze the fairness problem in Figure 5, from which it can be found that the fairness using multiple channels is much better than that using a single channel. Note that the fairness index is defined in [11]. The fairness index represents the degree to which the throughputs of all the nodes are average. As a result, a high fairness index has a small denominator of the ratio, while the numerator of the ratio is always of the same value.

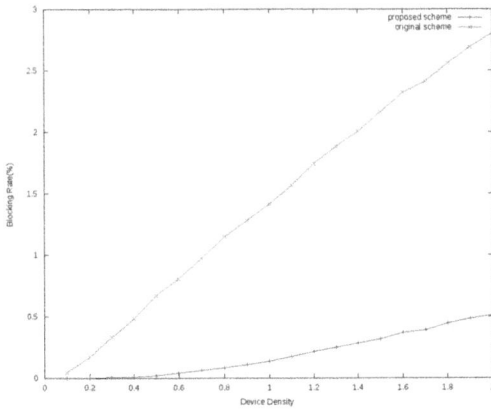

Fig. 4. Plot of blocking rate versus device density

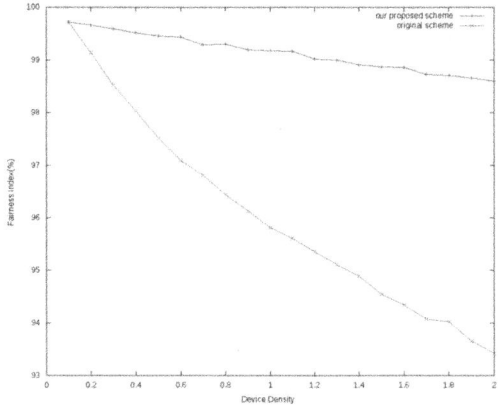

Fig. 5. Plot of fairness rate versus device density

4   Conclusion

In this paper, we have introduced an adaptive channel allocation strategy for multi-channel MAC protocol in MANETs which employs a distributed channel allocation algorithm to improve the system throughput and alleviate the fairness problem. Through extensive simulations, we have demonstrated that our proposed scheme is simple and effective. As perspective to this work, we will drive an accurate analytical model to study the saturated system throughput of the proposed scheme.

References

1. Bianchi, G.: Performance analysis of the IEEE 802. 11 distributed coordination function. IEEE Journal on Selected Area of Communications 18(3), 535–547 (2000)
2. Ni, Q., Li, T., Turletti, T., Xiao, Y.: Saturation throughput analysis of error-prone 802.11 wireless networks. Wireless Communications and Mobile Computing 5(8), 945–956 (2005)
3. Li, C.-S., Tsuei, T.-G., Chao, H.-C.: Evaluation of contention-based EDCA for IEEE 802.11e Wireless LAN. Journal of Internet Technology 35(4), 429–434 (2004)
4. Song, N.-O., Kwak, B.-J., Song, J., Miller, L.E.: Enhancement of IEEE 802.11 distributed coordination function with exponential increase exponential decrease backoff algorithm. In: Proc. of 57th IEEE Semiannual Spring VTC, vol. 4, pp. 2775–2778 (2003)
5. Bensaou, B., Wang, Y., Ko, C.C.: Fair medium access in 802.11 based wireless ad-hoc networks. In: Proc. of ACM International Symposium on Mobile and Ad Hoc Networking and Computing, pp. 99–106 (2000)
6. Sobrinho, J.L., de Haan, R., Brazio, J.M.: Why RTS-CTS is not your ideal wireless LAN multiple access protocol. In: Proc. of 2005 IEEE Wireless Communications and Networking Conference, vol. 1, pp. 81–87 (2005)
7. Choudhury, R.R., Yang, X., Ramanathan, R., Vaidya, N.H.: Using directional antennas for medium access control in ad hoc networks. In: Proc. of ACM MOBICOM 2002, pp. 59–70 (2002)

8. Wu, S.-L., Lin, C.-Y., Tseng, Y.-C., Sheu, J.-L.: A new multi-channel MAC protocol with on-demand channel assignment for multi-hop mobile ad hoc networks. In: Proc. of 2000 International Symposium on Parallel Architectures, Algorithms and Networks, pp. 232–237 (2000)
9. Tang, Z., Garcia-Lun-Aceves, J.J.: Hop-reservation multiple access (HRMA) for ad-hoc networks. In: Proc. of INFOCOM 1999, pp. 194–201 (1999)
10. So, J., Vaidya, N.H.: Multi-channel MAC for ad hoc networks: Handling multi-channel hidden terminals using a single transceiver. In: Prco. of 5th ACM International Symposium on Mobile Ad Hoc Networking and Computing, pp. 222–233 (2004)
11. Jain, R., Durresi, A., Babic, G.: Throughput fairness index: An explanation. ATM Forum/99-0045 (1999)

WiMAX DBA Algorithm Using a 2-Tier Max-Min Fair Sharing Policy

Pei-Chen Tseng[1], Jai-Yan Tsai[2], and Wen-Shyang Hwang[2,*]

[1] Department of Information Engineering and Informatics,
Tzu Chi College of Technology, Hualien, Taiwan
peichen@tccn.edu.tw
[2] Department of Electrical Engineering, National Kaohsiung,
University of Applied Sciences, Kaohsiung, Taiwan
1098304123@kuas.edu.tw, wshwang@mail.ee.kuas.edu.tw

Abstract. IEEE 802.16 leaves important issues like uplink bandwidth allocation to vendors. This paper proposes a WiMAX DBA algorithm using a 2-tier Max-Min Fair Sharing Policy (2tMMFS-DBA). In the first part of the algorithm, bandwidth reservations are set first for rtPS, then for nrtPS and BE applications. Next, the max-min fair sharing policy sets maximum connection demands for bandwidth requests and QoS provisioning. In the second part, the IEEE 802.16 MAC header is modified for piggybacking SS queue status messages to help base stations determine bandwidth allocation. 2tMMFS-DBA prioritizes bandwidth provisioning. An opportunity cost function bounds the cost of allocating bandwidth to different classes so as to maintain selected revenue levels to the service provider. Simulation shows the proposed dynamic provisioning scheme can satisfy the bandwidth requirements for different classes of traffic with overall improved system throughput.

Keywords: WiMax, IEEE 802.16e, QoS, DBA.

1   Introduction

The increasing popularity of cellular phones and similar devices is driving the development of wireless communication technology for voice, media and high capacity data rate services. Accordingly, IEEE 802.16e [1] is expected to support quality of service (QoS) for real time applications such as voice over IP (VoIP), video streaming and video conferencing with different QoS requirements and transmission guarantee. IEEE 802.16e's Mobile Broadband Wireless Access (BWA) is an extension providing for mobile subscriber stations (MSSs) and can even support MSSs moving at vehicular speeds. IEEE 802.16e also provides for combining fixed and mobile broadband wireless access. Compared to wired internet service providers, BWA systems are capable of faster deployment and lower deployment cost.

IEEE 802.16e is currently the most promising medium access control (MAC) protocol for high-speed wireless access in both the developed and developing world. At the MAC layer, each connection belongs to a single service flow type and is

---

* Corresponding author.

R.-S. Chang, T.-h. Kim, and S.-L. Peng (Eds.): SUComS 2011, CCIS 223, pp. 277–286, 2011.
© Springer-Verlag Berlin Heidelberg 2011

characterized by a set of QoS parameters. A number of uplink scheduling mechanisms are defined, including unsolicited bandwidth grants, polling and contention procedures. For uplink scheduling services, it supports five service flow types which identify specific sets of QoS parameters: UGS (unsolicited grant service), ertPS (extended real-time polling service), rtPS (real-time polling service), nrtPS (nonreal-time polling service), and BE (best effort). QoS in 802.16e is supported by allocating each connection between the SS and the BS (called a service flow) to a specific QoS class. Among them, UGS, ertPS, rtPS are suitable for real-time multimedia applications such as VoIP services.

Based on the IEEE 802.16 standard [2], WiMAX (Worldwide Interoperability for Microwave Access) provides high-speed data access for various transmission modes, e.g. point-to-multipoint links to portable and fully mobile Internet access. Two types of duplex methods separate uplink (UL) and downlink (DL) communication signals: Time Division Duplex (TDD) and Frequency Division Duplex (FDD). IEEE 802.16 defines two operation modes: the mesh mode and the point-to-multipoint (PMP) mode [3], [4]. In the mesh mode, direct communication between SSs without the need of a BS is supported. For the PMP mode (Fig. 1), multiple SSs and various public networks are connected by a BS.

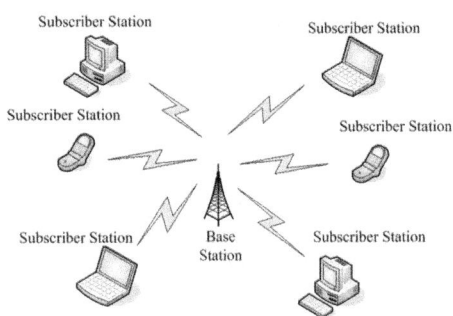

Fig. 1. Topology of WiMAX PMP networks

Implementation of the bandwidth allocation algorithm was not specified in the 802.16 standard [2]. A performance challenge in 802.16 TDD systems is the determination of the ratio of downlink to uplink capacities. TDD can handle flexibly both symmetric and asymmetric broadband traffic. Symmetric traffic using an equal split between uplink and downlink channels may lead to inefficient bandwidth utilization. Asymmetric traffic, such as ADSL, more demand for downloading and less for uploading, makes the bandwidth ratio determination problem even more complicated when the transport layer issue is taken into account. The last mile access for residential users tends to be asymmetric.

Chiang [5] proposed an Adaptive Bandwidth Allocation Scheme (ABAS) and Lei [6] proposed a CQQ scheme, dynamically adjust the Downlink/Uplink (DL/UL) bandwidth to match current DL/UL traffic in order to get better channel quality, but the method requires more complicated computing, resulting in reduced practical applicability. Chou [7] proposed the UBAR protocol (uplink bandwidth allocation and recovery), which employs a proportionally fair sharing scheme for efficient bandwidth utilization and further adopts a timeout-based UL-MAP retransmission scheme with uplink bandwidth reallocation algorithms to solve simultaneously bandwidth waste problems. But UBAR increases system complexity by modifying the TDD access mode. With regard to opportunity cost consideration, Bader [8] proposed what can be called the Rev scheme, which spans multiple time slots/frames and optimally allocates them to the different classes of traffic depending on their weights, the real-time bandwidth requirements of their connections, the channel quality conditions and the expected obtained revenues, but this scheme leads to least priority traffic BE starvation, therefore failing to achieve optimized fairness. Thus, Tsai [9] proposed the MMFS-DBA algorithm (a WiMAX DBA algorithm using a Max-Min Fair Sharing Policy). This system results in a real-time drop in calls due to insufficient real-time bandwidth reservation because no classification of real-time and non-real-time application traffic is included at the start.

The remainder of this study will focus on the issue of implementation of an efficient bandwidth allocation algorithm, such as is not specified in the IEEE 802.16 standard. This paper proposes a high performance WiMAX DBA (Dynamic Bandwidth Allocation) algorithm using a 2-tier Max-Min Fair Sharing Policy (2tMMFS-DBA). This algorithm adopts bandwidth reservations and the max-min fair sharing policy (MMFS) for efficient allocation of bandwidth. The rest of this paper is structured as follows: section 2 describes the proposed 2tMMFS-DBA algorithm. Simulation results are found in section 3. A final summary is presented in a concluding section.

2 2tMMFS-DBA Algorithm

The presented 2tMMFS-DBA algorithm is divided into two parts. In the first part of the algorithm, traffic classification, bandwidth reservation and QoS provisioning are performed, i.e. the different bandwidth reservations are set. The max-min fair sharing policy (MMFS) is used for the maximum connection demand for requested bandwidth, with QoS provisioning for rtPS applications. The requested bandwidth is allocated first to rtPS applications, then to nrtPS applications and finally to BE applications. BE applications have the least priority, i.e they have no QoS guarantee. To avoid starvation of BE applications, each applications has a weighting factor to make sure each achieves a relative QoS guarantee, with BE achieving at least a minimum available bandwidth to keep the BE alive in the WiMAX network. In the second part of the algorithm, the two reserved fields of the IEEE 802.16 generic MAC header are modified via monitoring of the SS queue status for urgent packets which need to be transmitted before other packets. It also monitors remaining packets in the SS queue. SSs are also allowed to ask for bandwidth via PiggyBack messages to the BS. Under the condition no requiring additional overhead, this allows the BS to make decisions for efficient allocation of bandwidth.

The 2tMMFS-DBA scheme especially considers QoS priority for optimal allocation of BS bandwidth to the SSs with regard to quality and system performance for real-time application services. The 2tMMFS-DBA method of BS allocation of bandwidth to the SSs improves the current IEEE 802.16 network, providing better QoS quality for multimedia services.

2.1   Bandwidth Reservation for rtPS Connection

This paper proposes a dynamic bandwidth provisioning scheme for future broadband wireless systems. The proposed scheme is designed to accommodate multi-class traffic with multiple connections having different bandwidth requirements and varying channel quality conditions. The main objective of our scheme is to optimally allocate bandwidth or the corresponding time frames for each class of traffic in order to satisfy the bandwidth requirements of their connections. In addition, the proposed scheme uniquely incorporates and bounds the cost (in terms of revenue loss) of bandwidth provisioning through an opportunity cost function. This provides greater flexibility to service providers for determining the levels of bandwidth provisioning to different traffic classes so as to guarantee a certain level of revenue.

To guarantee the real-time application services have higher QoS priority, this paper firstly considers the proportion, i.e. the number of rtPS connections occupying the number of total connections, thereby allowing determination of reserve rtPS connection bandwidth BW_{res_rtPS} as in equation (1). This ensures that rtPS connections have a higher QoS guarantee.

The notation in this paper is as follows:

N_{rtPS} : the number of rtPS connections

W_{rtPS} : the system weighting value for rtPS maximum connections

N_c : the total number of system connections

BW_{tot} : the total system bandwidth for the BS

BW_{res_rtPS} : the bandwidth reservation for rtPS

BW_{res_max} : the maximum bandwidth reservation for rtPS

$$BW_{res\_rtPS} = \begin{cases} BW_{res\_max}, & if \quad \dfrac{N_{rtPS}}{N_c} > W_{rtPS} \\ W_{rtPS} \times BW_{tot}, & if \quad \dfrac{N_{rtPS}}{N_c} \le W_{rtPS} \end{cases} \tag{1}$$

Max-Min Fair Bandwidth Sharing

In order to satisfy the maximum bandwidth request for the SS connection, this paper extends the Max-Min Fair Sharing Policy (MMFS), first using equations (2) and (3) to obtain the average bandwidth of the rtPS and (nrtPS +BE) connections, designated respectively BW_{avg_rtPS} and $BW_{avg\_nrtPS+BE}$. Then the Max-Min Fair Bandwidth Sharing policy is executed to satisfy the demands of the maximum bandwidth request of the rtPS and (nrtPS +BE) connections.

$$BW_{avg\_rtPS} = \frac{BW_{res\_rtPS}}{N_{rtPS}} \tag{2}$$

$$BW_{avg\_nrtPS+BE} = \frac{BW_{tot} - BW_{res\_rtPS}}{N_c - N_{rtPS}} \tag{3}$$

It is first determined whether the reserved rtPS bandwidth BW_{res_rtPS} for the rtPS connection is equal to or greater than the entire bandwidth request of the rtPS connection ($BW_{req,i}$). If YES, then there is enough bandwidth for the entire bandwidth request of the rtPS connection, so the reservation bandwidth is allocated to the rtPS connection as in equation (4), where i is the number of SS and δ_i is the bandwidth allocated to SS_i.

$$\delta_i = BW_{req,i} \tag{4}$$

Otherwise, when the reserved rtPS bandwidth BW_{res_rtPS} is less than the entire bandwidth request of the rtPS connection ($BW_{req,i}$), then the reserved bandwidth is insufficient for the entire bandwidth request of the rtPS connection. In this case, i.e. $BW_{req,i} > BW_{avg\_rtPS}$, so the MMFS scheme in equation (2) is executed to allocate the minimum necessary bandwidth R_{min} to the rtPS connection, otherwise allocating the necessary bandwidth request $BW_{req,i}$ to the rtPS connection, as in equation (5).

$$\delta_i = \begin{cases} BW_{req,i}, & if \quad BW_{req,i} \leq BW_{avg\_rtPS} \\ R_{min}, & if \quad BW_{req,i} > BW_{avg\_rtPS} \end{cases} \tag{5}$$

Similarly, bandwidth is allocated to the nrtPS, BE connection using the same way as in equations (1) to (5). After allocation, the information must be updated as in equation (6). BW_a is the remainder of the available bandwidth. The 2nd part will execute if $BW_a > 0$ in the 1st run of 2tMMFS-DBA scheme.

$$BW_a = BW_{tot} - \sum_{1}^{N_c} \delta_i \tag{6}$$

The first part of the 2tMMFS-DBA scheme is for rtPS application service with the greatest QoS guarantee. Thus, the rtPS service is handled first, calculating the average bandwidth BW_{avg} for each service flow, then executing the MMFS scheme for fair allocation of the bandwidth. After rtPS service traffic allocation is completed, a similar process is performed for non-real-time application service and finally for the BE service.

2.2   Evaluation of SS Queue Status

A request may be corrupted due to a collision when SSs perform bandwidth requests. Kim [10] proposed modifing the IEEE 802.16 generic MAC header in order to let an SS pass the message to the BS by transmitting data, so the BS allows the SS bandwidth request if no collision occurs. This idea is extended in the second part of the 2tMMFS-DBA algorithm, using two reserved bits in the IEEE 802.16 generic MAC header, one for the Critical Data bit (CD), the other for the Backlogged Data bit (BD) as shown in Fig. 2. As a result, with no additional SS overhead, the BS gets important information via an SS Piggyback message which monitors the packet status of the SS queue, including evaluation of critical data and/or backlogged data packets in the SS queue. The CD bit is for urgent packets that need to be transmitted in the SS queue. The BD bit is for packets not yet transmitted in the SS queue. The BS can use this information to allocate bandwidth more efficiently.

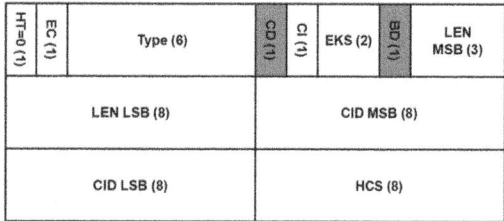

Fig. 2. IEEE 802.16 generic MAC header

Because of real-time service must take more better care of packet delay time, therefore rtPS need higher QoS priority to guarantee quality. Accordingly, the second part of the 2tMMFS-DBA system, with reference to [9], [11], calculates the rtPS packet delay expiry time $Deadline_k$ as in equation (7) and the expected Remain Time $RemainTime\, t_r$ for packet send-out as in equation (8). In equation (7), the rtPS packet delay expiry time $Deadline_k$ is the packet arriving time $ArrivalTime\, t_0$ plus $MaxLatency$. In equation (8), the expected Remain Time $RemainTime\, t_r$ for packet k to send out, is $Deadline_k$ minus the system current time $CurrentTime\, t_c$, where k is the transmitting packet number. The Critical Data CD bit is set to "1" if $RemainTime\, t_r$ is not more than one $Frame\, Duration$ time, as equation (9). This means that it is urgent that the packet be sent out.

$$Deadline_k = ArrivalTime\, t_0 + MaxLatency \tag{7}$$

$$RemainTime\, t_r = Deadline_k - CurrentTime\, t_c \tag{8}$$

$$If \quad t_r \leq Frame\, Duration \ then \ CD \ bit = \ "1" \tag{9}$$

After the full run (rtPS, nrtPS, BE) of the first part of the 2tMMFS-DBA algorithm, the rest of the bandwidth BW_a is assigned averagely to the critical rtPS service flow in the SS queue. In equation (10), $BW_{ins,i}$ indicates the insufficient bandwidth request for rtPS service connection i after running of the first part of 2tMMFS-DBA. In equation (11), α_i is the average proportion to the rest of the bandwidth BW_a for the insufficient request bandwidth for rtPS service connection. The goal of equation (12) is to limit the obtained bandwidth so that is not greater than the original request bandwidth for rtPS service connection. Then equation (13) is used to update the rest of the bandwidth BW_a'. Similar methodology is used to allocate bandwidth to the critical nrtPS and BE connections as in equations (10), (11) and (12).

$$BW_{ins,i} = BW_{req,i} - \delta_i \tag{10}$$

$$\alpha_i = BW_a \times \frac{BW_{ins,i}}{\sum_{SS_i \in rtPS \, \wedge \, CDbit="1"} BW_{ins,i}} \tag{11}$$

$$\delta_i' = \begin{cases} \delta_i + \alpha_i, & if \ (\delta_i + \alpha_i) < BW_{req,i} \\ BW_{req,i}, & if \ (\delta_i + \alpha_i) \geq BW_{req,i} \end{cases} \tag{12}$$

$$BW_a^{'} = BW_a - \sum_{1}^{N_{rtPS}} \delta_i^{'} \tag{13}$$

After the above process, the Backlogged Data BD bit in the IEEE 802.16 generic MAC header is changed to "1" if there is rtPS service still left in SS queue, as in equation (14). For BSs receiving this information (i.e. BD marked to "1"), the rest of the bandwidth $BW_a^{'}$ is assigned averagely to the rtPS service flow in the SS queue. $BW_{ins,i}$ is the insufficient request bandwidth for rtPS service connection i after full run of the first part of 2tMMFS-DBA. In equation (15), β_i is the average proportion to the rest of the bandwidth $BW_a^{'}$ for the $BW_{ins,i}$ for rtPS service connection. Equation (16) ensures the obtained bandwidth is not greater than the original request bandwidth for rtPS service connection. Then equation (17) is used to update the rest of the bandwidth $BW_a^{'}$. Similar methodology is used to allocate bandwidth to the critical nrtPS and BE connections as in equations (14), (15) and (16).

$$If \ \ sizeof(SS_i \in rtPS) > 0 \ \ then \ BD \ bit = \ "1" \tag{14}$$

$$\beta_i = BW_a^{'} \times \frac{BW_{ins,i}}{\sum_{BDbit="1"} BW_{ins,i}} \tag{15}$$

$$\delta_i^{"} = \begin{cases} \delta_i^{'} + \beta_i, & if \ (\delta_i^{'} + \beta_i) < BW_{req,i} \\ BW_{req,i}, & if \ (\delta_i^{'} + \beta_i) \geq BW_{req,i} \end{cases} \tag{16}$$

$$BW_a^{"} = BW_a^{'} - \sum_{1}^{N_{rtPS}} \delta_i^{"} \tag{17}$$

3   Simulation Results

This paper focuses on the IEEE 802.16 point-to-multipoint (PMP) mode, which is the primary operating mode of WiMAX for residential users. Under PMP, the IEEE 802.16e wireless network with a central BS serves several SSs and each SS communicates with the BS directly (Fig. 1).

To evaluate performance, 2tMMFS-DBA functionality is simulated by the SIMSCRIPT II.5 language for numerical analysis. The system weighting value is 0.3. The BS bandwidth is 20 Mbps. The entry possibility of UGS, rtPS, nrtPS, BS is 30%, 50%, 70%, 100%, respectively. This means for example, if the number of the connections =100, then UGS gets 30 (=100*30%), rtPS gets 35 (=(100-30)*50%), nrtPS gets 24.5(=(70-35)*70%) and BE gets 10.5(=(35-24.5)*100%). In order to obtain more detailed simulation values, the number of SSs is increased by 5.

Compared with Bader's Rev scheme [8], Fig. 3 shows that dropping rate of the proposed algorithm is 12.44% lower (better) for rtPS connections when the number of SSs is over 35. At the same time, it is 2% higher (worse) for nrtPS connections, 1.17% higher (worse) for BE connections. Fig. 5 shows that the throughput of the proposed algorithm is 1.2 Mbps higher (better) when the number of SSs over 10.

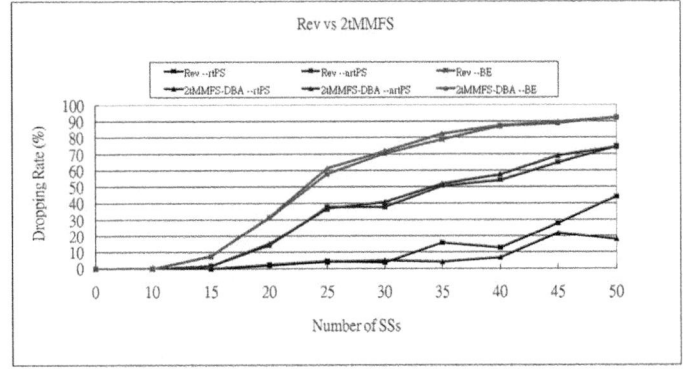

Fig. 3. Dropping rate for Rev vs 2tMMFS

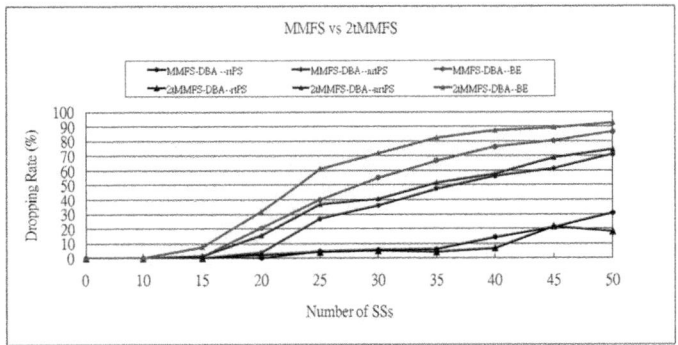

Fig. 4. Dropping rate for MMFS vs 2tMMFS

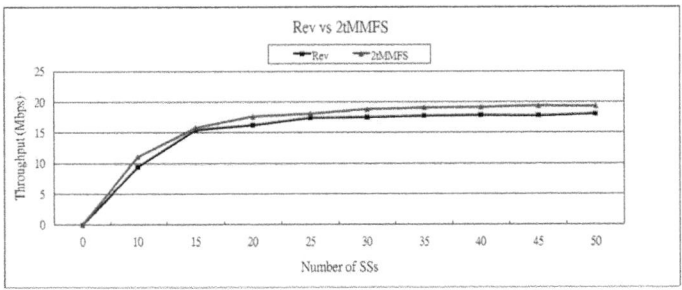

Fig. 5. Throughput for Rev vs 2tMMFS

Compared with Tsai's MMFS scheme [9], Fig. 4 shows that dropping rate of the proposed algorithm is 5.35% lower (better) for rtPS connections when the number of SSs over 35. At the same time, it is 4.15% higher (worse) for nrtPS connections and 10.57% higher (worse) in BE connections. Fig. 6 shows that the throughput of the proposed algorithm is 0.17 Mbps higher (better) when the number of SSs over 10. The results show that the proposed algorithm delivers better QoS for the prioritized rtPS users, with overall better system throughput.

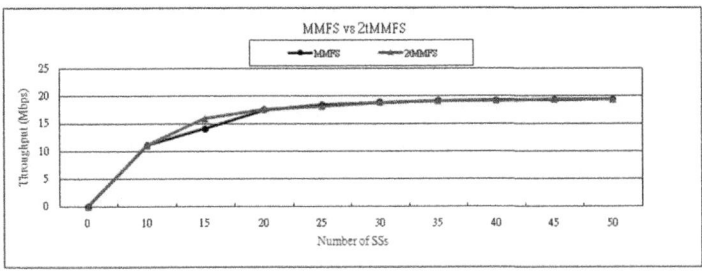

Fig. 6. Throughput for MMFS vs 2tMMFS

4 Conclusions

Future broadband wireless systems will support a wide range of multimedia applications for mobile users. However, to maximize user experience, bandwidth provisioning is critical. In this paper, a novel bandwidth provisioning scheme for broadband wireless network is proposed. The proposed scheme allows for prioritized bandwidth provisioning to different classes of traffic for support of multiple connections with different bandwidth requirements. It also incorporates a unique opportunity cost function to bound the cost of allocating bandwidth to different classes so as to maintain certain revenue levels to the service provider. Simulation results reveal the presented 2tMMFS-DBA algorithm efficiently allocates bandwidth for improved urgent multimedia requirements and provides higher QoS guarantees in IEEE 802.16e networks, with overall enhanced system throughput.

Fixed class weights, however, cannot achieve optimized fairness since the performance of each class is not fixed due to the varying bandwidth requirements and varying channel quality conditions. Thus, our future work will study a dynamic weight update scheme to compute dynamically the weights of different classes of traffic based on their performance history in order to maximize inter-class fairness. This way, the resulting fairness will be more adaptive to the performance of the classes since it is based on their performance history.

Acknowledgments. This research was supported by National Science Council of Taiwan under project number NSC 99-2218-E-277-001.

References

1. IEEE Std 802.16eTM -2005: IEEE Standard for Local and Metropolitan Area Networks – Part 16: Air Interface for Fixed and Mobile Broadband Wireless Access Systems - Amendment 2: Physical and Medium Access Control Layers for Combined Fixed and Mobile Operation in Licensed Bands (2006)
2. IEEE 802.16-2004: IEEE standard for Local and Metropolitan Area Networks -Part 16: Air Interface for Fixed Broadband Wireless Access Systems (2004)
3. Li, B., Qin, Y., Low, C.P., Gwee, C.L.: A Survey on Mobile WiMAX. IEEE Communications Magazine 45(12), 70–75 (2007)

4. Ni, Q., Vinel, A., Xiao, Y., Turlikov, A., Jiang, T.: Investigation of Bandwidth Request Mechanism under Point-to-Multipoint Mode of WiMAX Networks. IEEE Communications Magazine 45(5), 132–138 (2007)
5. Chiang, C.H., Liao, W.J., Liu, T.H.: Adaptive Downlink/Uplink Bandwidth Allocation in IEEE 802.16 (WiMAX) Wireless Networks: A Cross-Layer Approach. In: IEEE Global Telecommunications Conference, pp. 4775–4779 (2007)
6. Lai, Y.C., Chen, Y.H.: A Channel Quality and QoS Aware Bandwidth Allocation Algorithm for IEEE 802.16 Base Stations. In: 22nd International Conference on Advanced Information Networking and Applications, pp. 472–479 (2008)
7. Chou, Z.T., Lin, Y.H.: Bandwidth Allocation and Recovery for Uplink Access in IEEE 802.16 Broadband Wireless Networks. In: IEEE 66th Vehicular Technology Conference, pp. 1887–1891 (2007)
8. Bader, A.M., Abu, A.N., Nidal, N., Hossam, H.: Dynamic Bandwidth Provisioning with Fairness and Revenue Considerations for Broadband Wireless Communication. In: IEEE International Conference on Communications, pp. 4028–4032 (2008)
9. Tsai, M.Y., Hwang, W.S.: A High Performance WiMAX DBA Algorithm by Using Max-Min Fair Sharing Policy. In: 5th Workshop on Wireless, Ad Hoc and Sensor Networks, D1-2 (2009)
10. Kim, S.J., Kim, W.J., Suh, Y.J.: An Efficient Bandwidth Request Mechanism for Non-Real-Time Services in IEEE 802.16 Systems. In: 2nd International Conference on Communication Systems Software and Middleware, pp. 1–9 (2007)
11. Liang, C.C., Shao, S.K., Yu, J.C., Wu, J.S.: A Newly Proposed Bandwidth Allocation Algorithm for IEEE 802.16 Wireless Access Systems. In: International Symposium on Communications and Information Technologies, pp. 33–39 (2008)

High Security Authentication Mechanism for Mobile Networks

Ming-Huang Guo[1], Horng-Twu Liaw[1], Jui-Kheng Tang[1], and Chih-Ta Yen[2,*]

[1] Department of Computer Science and Information Engineering,
Shin-Hsin University, Taipei, Taiwan
{mhguo,htliaw}@cc.shu.edu.tw, fidodido0706@hotmail.com
[2] Department of Information Management, National Taiwan University of Science and
Technology, Taipei, Taiwan
D9709107@mail.ntust.edu.tw

Abstract. Because of the more and more services wireless communication technology can offer nowadays, the quality of wireless communication became an important key. In this research, 3G/UMTS and WLAN will be mentioned mainly. The former offers a wide-range, high-mobility, complete and safe record of accounting; the latter offers a narrow range, low mobility, high speed transmission access on the Internet. The complementary between these two techniques can not only enhance the quality of wireless communication but offer more services for customers to choose, and customers can use wireless application services regardless of any environmental limit. This research will focus on the problem of fast-handover when 3G/UMTS and WLAN is interworking, such as authentication and authorization. About the two formers, we will use W-SKE to accomplish authentication procedure, and achieve safer Mutual Full Authentication and Fast-Authentication.

Keywords: 3G/UMTS, WLAN, Mobile networks, Authentication.

1 Introduction

The mobile communication technologies have become more and more popular in recent years, and cell phone service is an important example among kinds of mobile communication. There is an idea to integrate 3G and WLAN networks to unify the advantages of the two systems as well as to minimize the disadvantages arise as a great market opportunity. They can't replace each other. When WLAN and 3G/UMTS coexist, the handoff mechanism should be created and provided. Many researches 000000000 have proposed about it actually, but it is insufficient to the security requirements. Therefore we will focus on the security of the communication sessions of 3G/UMTS and 802.11 WLAN when a handoff mechanism between them is trigged. However, some mechanisms are not secure or efficient. Hence, EAP-SIM 0 and EAP-AKA 0 have been proposed some authentication mechanism for 3G/UMTS and WLAN interworking. Both EAP-AKA and EAP-SIM provide user with anonymity

---

* Corresponding author.

R.-S. Chang, T.-h. Kim, and S.-L. Peng (Eds.): SUComS 2011, CCIS 223, pp. 287–296, 2011.
© Springer-Verlag Berlin Heidelberg 2011

through pseudonyms or temporary identities called Temporary Mobile Subscriber Identities (TMSI). However, the mobile subscriber called Mobile Node (MN) of real identity is exposed to the air when authenticating MN at the first time. This might cause the real identity of the user to be exposed and traced at some time periods. Moreover, EAP-AKA and EAP-SIM do not minimize the number of exchanges between the foreign domain and home domain. Such problems incur long latency and some packet loss when mobile nodes roam into foreign environment. Salgarelli proposed W-SKE to reduce the number of message exchanged and to minimize the latency. The existing mechanisms are not so suitable for 3G/UMTS and WLAN interworking.

In this paper, we propose a secure vertical handoff policy between 3G/UMTS and 802.11 WLAN networks. To achieve this goal, our scheme is proposed to create a secure communication channel from UMTS to WLAN. Also, a security vertical handoff scheme from WLAN to 3G/UMTS is presented. On the other hand, we propose a robust authentication protocol which can perform efficient localized re-authentication procedure and provide non-repudiation service. Our scheme refers to Keyed-Hash Message Authentication Code (HMAC)0, Hash-chaining techniques0, Challenge/Response and Symmetric key Encryption which mention how to withstand the replay attack, guessing attack, impersonation attack and WEP (Wired Equivalent Privacy) weakness attack.

The summary of these articles will be presented in the following sections: The proposed our mechanism will be presented in Section 2. Moreover, the security analysis and performance of the proposed scheme will be mentioned in section 3 and section 4. Finally, we will make the conclusions and come up with some future research directions in section 5.

2   Proposed Mechanism

In this section we propose a new authentication mechanism based on challenge/response, HMAC and one-way hashed chain. Our protocols greatly improve the security and the communication performance.

2.1   Network Architecture

The network architecture as shown in Fig.1 is considered for 3G/UMTS and WLAN interworking in this study, MN denotes mobile node, H-AAA denotes home AAA server of a mobile user MN, and F-AAA denotes foreign AAA server of the WLAN that a MN wants to visit. The F-AAA and the H-AAA belong to separate providers called AAA Brokers; those should be the association between the H-AAA and the F-AAA. The AAA Brokers sets up reliable security associations and routes AAA messages to the H-AAA.

Our authentication model is based on Salgerelli's work. The authentication model directly corresponds to network architecture in previous section. Fig.2 illustrates the various network entities involved in the authentication procedure. In order to authenticate and/or protect data in transit between X and Y, a security association $A_{X,Y}$ should be set up and can be defined as the combination of the nodes' identity

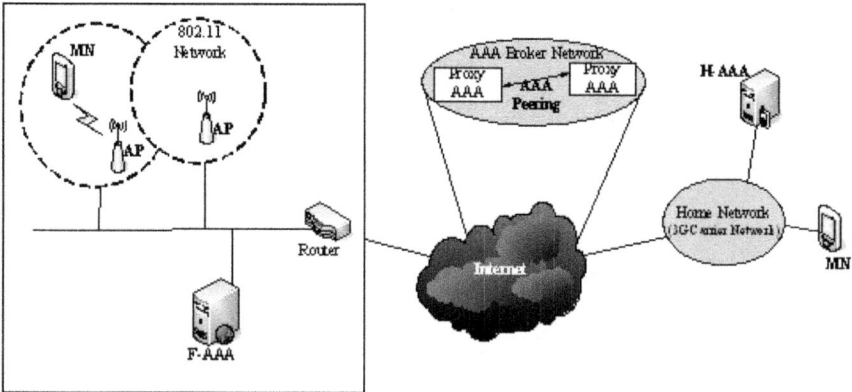

Fig. 1. The network architecture for 3G/UMTS and WLAN interworking

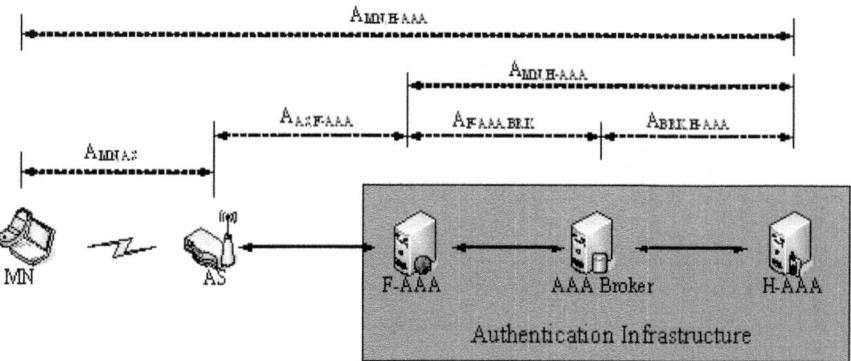

Fig. 2. The authentication model

information(e.g. IMSI, NAI), some form of cryptographic key(e.g. public keys, pre-shared symmetric key), and information on cryptographic algorithms to be used. Each AS maintains a preconfigured security association $A_{AS,F\text{-}AAA}$ with its F-AAA server, other $A_{X,Y}$ same meanings. In the 3G/WLAN interworking, F-AAA and H-AAA may belong to separate service providers, and then an association has to be set up via an AAA broker or pair-wise relationship should be setup part of roaming agreement.

2.2 Protocols

The characteristic of our mechanism is that it doesn't need the security channel, so every node passes itself legal information of authentication to the H-AAA verity. There are four proposed protocols in our proposal: the full authentication protocol, the WLAN AS fast re-authentication protocol, the 3GPP F-AAA network fast re-authentication protocol, and the 3GPP H-AAA network fast-authentication. Table.1 shows the notations of the proposed protocols.

Table 1. The Notations of the proposed system

IMSI:	International Mobile Subscriber Identity
PID_A:	Pseudonym Identity of A
ID_A:	Real Identity of A
TID_A:	Temporary Identity of A
ASID:	Unique identity of Authentication System
k:	A Secret Key pre-shared between the H-AAA and the MN
f:	A Secret Key pre-shared between the H-AAA and the F-AAA
Ks:	A Secret Key produced between the H-AAA and the MN at authentication time
K_{AB}:	A Session key between the A and the B
RAND:	A random seed/value.
MAC_{AB}:	Message Authentication Codes Function between the A and the B
$E_k()$:	A symmetric function with key k
$PRF_k()$:	A Pseudo Random Function with key k
$f_k()$:	Produce K_S function with key k
Hash():	One way hash function
AHC_A:	Authentication Hash-Chain value of A

1. The MN sends an EAPOL start to AS after the WLAN association process.
2. The AS response an EAPOL-EAP request/identity to the MN.
3. The MN generate a random seed $RAND_M$, and computes $MAC_{HM}=HMAC_k(RAND_M,IMSI)$
4. The MN send the EAP Response/Identity message to AS, which involves ID_H, PID_M, $RAND_M$, and MAC_{HM}.
5. The AS sends the EAP Response/Identity message to F-AAA, the *ASID* append to the message.
6. F-AAA computes $MAC_{HF}=HMAC_f(RAND_F,ID_F)$, in order to make the MN easy to verity H-AAA legally.
7. The F-AAA sends the EAP Response/Identity message to H-AAA.
8. The H-AAA first checks whether the MN access profile is available. If not, the H-AAA was rejected by the MN.

   — The H-AAA uses the pre-shared key and the received $RAND_M$, $RAND_F$, ID_F, *IMSI* to verity MN and F-AAA legally.
   — If verity failed, the will be rejected. Otherwise, the H-AAA generates random seed $RAND_H$ to compute $k_s = f_k(RAND_M \oplus RAND_H)$.
   — The H-AAA generates a new temporary identity of MN, with TID_M have replace PID_M for next time of full authentication protocol.
   — The H-AAA computes the first authentication hash-chain value *xAHC* of the H-AAA and the F-AAA. In order to make the MN easy to re-authentication by the H-AAA and the F-AAA, and keep track of the MN spent based on *xAHC*. Show as follows:

$xAHC^1_H = HMAC_{Ks}(ID_H)$
$xAHC^1_F = HMAC_{Ks}(ID_F)$

— After generating the authentication hash chaining, the H-AAA computes *xAUTH* purpose to avoid falsity message.
— The H-AAA computes the authentication hash-chain value $xAHC^i_H$ and $xAHC^j_F$, in order to make the MN easy to re-authentication by the H-AAA and the F-AAA(the *i* and *j* indicates the hash time; and it can be adjusted on demand). Show as follows:
$xAHC^i_H = Hash^i(xAHC^1_H)$
$xAHC^j_F = Hash^j(xAHC^1_F)$

— The H-AAA computes the session key between the MN and the F-AAA, shown as follows:
$K_{MN-F} = PRF_{Ks}(xAHC^i_H)$

— The H-AAA computes $xMAC_{FH}$ for the purpose of the F-AAA avoid falsity message from the malice attacker.
— The H-AAA keeps TID_M and *Ks*, which have replaced PID_M and *k* for next time of full authentication protocol.

9. The H-AAA sends the EAP success message to the F-AAA.
10. The F-AAA preserve $xAHC^j_F$, K_{MN-F} and TID_M after receiving the EAP success message. Among $xAHC^j_F$ is the hash-chain value when MN and AS process re-authentication protocol, K_{MN-F} is a session key between the MN and the F-AAA; TID_M will not be using PID_M at the time of full-authentication next-time, in order to be anonymous.

— The F-AAA proves whether $xMAC_{FH}=?MAC_{FH}$ is equal from the H-AAA. If the F-AAA is not with the secret key pre-shared *f*, it will fail to verity.
— The F-AAA computes $xMAC_{FA}$ for the purpose that make MN avoid falsity message from the malice attacker.
— The F-AAA computes the session key between the MN and the AS as shown follows:
$K_{MN-AS} = PRF_{K_{MN,F}}(xAHC^j_F)$

11. After the F-AAA forwards successful authentication message to the AS.
12. The AS preserve the K_{MN-AS}, TID_M for the ease of transmission between the MN and the AS.
13. The AS forwards the EAP success message to the MN.
14. The MN obtains the $RAND_H$ from the H-AAA and the $RAND_M$ producted when MN requests for authentication. Then computes to the secret key K_S produce between the H-AAA and the MN of authentication time, shown as follows:
$K_S = f_k(RAND_M \oplus RAND_H)$

— The MN generates a new temporary identity $TID_M = Hash(RAND_M \oplus RAND_H, IMSI)$.
— The MN computes the first authentication hash-chain value *xAHC* .
— The MN computes the authentication hash-chain value $xAHC^i_H$ and $xAHC^j_F$.
— The MN computes the session key K_{MN-F} .
— The MN computes the session key K_{MN-AS} .

- The MN verity $xAUTH$ in order to avoid falsity message from the malice attacker.
- The MN computes $xMAC_{FA}$ for the purpose that make the MN avoid falsity message from the malice attacker.
- The MN keeps TID_M and Ks which have replace PID_M and k for next time of full authentication protocol.

15.   In this step, the MN and the H-AAA successfully authenticate each other.

2.3   Fast Re-authentication Protocol of the F-AAA

Here we depict the detailed successful re-authentication of the F-AAA. The MN and the F-AAA share a session-key $K_{MS,F}$ which made the re-authenticate key. In the step of the n-th re-authentication, j is limited for the number of F-AAA re-authentication times, and $j-n$ number of re-authentication times once left. When the MN accesses the F-AAA which belongs to the 3GPP visit network, the authentication mechanism is also based on the hash chaining technique. The MN presents its identity TID_M, and the MN computes $AHC^{j-n}{}_F$, then sends the result to the F-AAA. After this F-AAA verifies the $Hash$ $(xAHC^{j-n+1}{}_F)=?AHC^{j-n}{}_F$; If passing, it means the F-AAA has authenticated the MN. The $AHC^{j-n}{}_F$ is stored for the next authentication and for the non-repudiation evidence.   Afterwards,   the   F-AAA   responses   to   a   challenge $xMAC_{FA}= \boldsymbol{HMAC}_{K_{MN,F}}$ $(xAHC^{j-n}{}_F,\ ASID^*$), and computes new session key $K_{MN\text{-}AS}$ $= \boldsymbol{PRF}_{K_{MN-F}}$ $(xAHC^{j-n}{}_F)$. On the other hand, the $xMAC_{FA}$ and $K_{MN\text{-}AS}$ are sent to the WLAP AS; the AS keeps the $K_{MN\text{-}AS}$ which is used as dynamic WEP key, and forwarded the $xMAC_{FA}$ to the MN. The MN first verifies the $xMAC_{FA}$. If passing, it means the MN has authenticated the F-AAA server. Next, the MN derives the $K_{MN\text{-}AS}$ $= \boldsymbol{PRF}_{K_{MN-F}}$ $(xAHC^{j-n}{}_F)$. Eventually, the mutual authentication has been successfully completed and the WEP key has been confidentially delivered.

2.4   Fast Re-authentication Protocol of the H-AAA

This is a roaming reference model. When the MN accesses the H-AAA which belongs to the 3GPP visit network, the authentication mechanism is also based on the hash chaining technique. The Fast Re-authentication protocol of the H-AAA is just the same as the Fast Re-authentication protocol of the F-AAA. The only difference is that the Authentication Hash-Chain Value is added to $AHC^{i-m}{}_H$, and the access control is charged by the H-AAA server. By using the $AHC^{j-n}{}_F$ and $AHC^{i-m}{}_H$ sent to the H-AAA, the re-authentication method is based on the hash chaining technique result to the mutual authentication and key agreement can be achieved.

2.5   Fast Re-authentication Protocol of the AS

This case is under the non-roaming reference model, so the authentication traffic is routed through the New AS and Old AS. The MN computes $Ticket$ in order to help Old AS prove whether New AS is a legal node. The MN produces and offer the random value $RAND$ to the New AS computes the New Session Key $K_{MN\text{-}AS^{**}}$ so that it can take precautions of the backward to security attack.

Because both sides have agreements of roaming, the other side shares the private session key which can decrypt message of encrypt. The New AS forwards the request message to the Old AS, then the Old AS verifies *Ticket*; if unsucceding, it will reject to serve. Otherwise, represent authentication of the New AS is legal node and produces new random key K_{RAND}. The Old AS responses to a challenge *Ticket$_2$* and computes new session key K_{MN-AS*}, making use of private session key K_{AS-OLD} to encrypt K_{MN-AS*} and old session key K_{MN-AS} to encrypt K_{RAND}. Then it produces new session $K_{MN-AS**}$ so that the New AS makes XOR operation with K_{MN-AS*} and *RAND*. With that, The New AS forwarded *Ticket$_2$* and encrypt K_{RAND} to the MN. The MN decrypt message obtains K_{RAND} at first, and verifies *Ticket$_2$*. If passing, it means the MN has authenticated the New AS. Next, the MN produces the new session $K_{MN-AS**}$. Finally, the mutual authentication has been successfully completed and the WEP key has been confidentially delivered.

3   Security Analysis

In this section, we will show our mechanism can preclude several attacks, according to Byzantine insiders, which indicates the network elements belong to independent service provider that are not trusted fully because it have a direct or indirect security association between each other. The Security Analysis as shown in Table 2.

- Prevent Guessing Attack: In full authentication protocol, the Secret Key Pre-shared k between the H-AAA and the MN, are for authentication purpose. Therefore, it is possible for an attacker to reveal the Secret key Pre-shared k from the known information. However, the k is impossible to derive it during a reasonable time which is at least 128bits. Utilizing one time password of AHC^{i-m} and AHC^{j-n} to upgrade session key in fast authentication, it is invalid to obtain session key K_{WEP}.
- Prevent Replay Attack: In full authentication protocol, it is the situation where an attacker intercepts $\{ID_H, PID_M, RAND_M, MAC_{HM}\}$ sent by the MN in step4 and uses it to masquerade as the MN to send the authentication request next time. Though $RAND_M$ is generated by the MN, the malice attacker don't knowing the Secret Key Pre-shared k between the H-AAA and the MN, and it can't respond the correct MAC_{HM} and *AUTH* to the H-AAA and the MN both. On the other hand, the authentication hash chaining value *AHC* of fast re-authentication will be used only once, to replay the *AHC* will not pass theauthentication.
- Prevent Impersonation Attack: The malice attacker attempts to impersonate the MN to access the WLAN. In full authentication protocol, $MAC_{HM} = HMAC_k(RAND_M,IMSI)$ is encrypted with a pre-shared secret k; hence without secret key k, it can't impersonate the MN. In fast re-authentication, the attacker cannot compute $xAHC^i_H=Hash^i(xAHC^1_H)$ or $xAHC^j_F=Hash^j(xAHC^1_F)$ to impersonate the MN, because the Pre-shared Secret Key k is only known by the MN-self and the AHC^1 has been securely sent to the H-AAA by the MN in full authentication. In this case, the attacker can't compute backward the authentication hash chaining value *AHC*.
- Prevent WEP weakness attack: The WEP key congenital disadvantage in the gold key IV value is not enough and easy to analyze and explain for the Brute-Force

attack in length,since the WEP key is also renewed in each full authentication of fast re-authentication protocol. Therefore, our mechanism can overcome the weakness of the original WEP.

- Prevent Forward Secrecy and Backward Secrecy to possible attacks: One session key/secret key will not lead to the compromise of the past session key/secret key and the corresponding transmission because one key follows the form of randomness, the one-way property of hashing chains and the session key pre-shared between each other. Thus, each session key/secret key is random and independently, and is fairly controlled by the MN and AAA Server or AS. It can prevent Forward/Backward secret attack then accomplishes the resistance to the known-key attack, the impersonate attack, and the replay attack.

- Legal evidence for use-bill: In the billing process, the AS and F-AAA have to submit all latest hash chain values sent by the MN after each full authentication to H-AAA. $xAHC$ will record the usage of MN so that WLAN ISP and the 3G ISP will charge H-AAA for fees according to $xAHC$. Because of having one-way characteristic of hash chaining function, the ISPs is unable to compute to the $xAHC^{i-n-1}$ value so that it is also unable to cheat H-AAA with incorrect data of the usage of the evidence, then reach both sides' mutually beneficial fairness.

- Mutual Authentication: The $xAHC_H$ and $xAHC_F$ hidden in $xAUTH$ is resulted from computing the AAA Server Identity. The MN will fail to authenticate if there is no legal AAA Server. According to the principle of Transitive, when the authentication between MN and H-AAA, H-AAA and F-AAA, F-AAA and AS all succeed, the one between MN and AS will success, too. The MN will prove legal node of the AS, if the mobile node computes to MAC_{FA} equals with $xMAC_{FA}$ from the H-AAA.

- Secret Key Establishment: The first secret key K_s is produced after the H-AAA and the MN accomplish full authentication. By $RAND_M, RAND_H$ and k compute K_s which needn't pass K_s to the MN, the MN will computes K_s by itself. The main purpose for this is to improve its security, which will replace the secret key pre-share k in the full authentication protocols next time.

- Non-repudiation: Our mechanism will complete secret key k with registering in advance. To put $RAND$ and ID in the Message Authentication Codes Function can produce MAC value, then will can use MAC to verify the legitimacy of both sides with by its characteristic of Challenge & Response

- Message Integrity: Guarantee mainly the content in the course of transmission has not been falsified. Our mechanism check out the equality between MAC and $xMAC$; so does between $AUTH$ and $xAUTH$, in order to confirm the integrality of the message.

- Protect Transmit Session Key: The Session Key $K_{A,B}$ is transmitted to other communication apparatus under the protection of the symmetric function, preventing $K_{A,B}$ from being stolen in the course of transmission.

- Perfect User Anonymity: H-AAA and MN will figure out TID_M, and TID_M will replace PID_M for next time of full authentication protocol. Only the issuer (MN or H-AAA) is able to produce the temporary identifier TID_M. Our scheme, different with EAP-SIM and EAP-AKA, is not transmitted for each time when the temporary identifier is not available; it adopts the dynamic way to produce TID_M. Therefore, perfect anonymity is achieved.

Table 2. The Security Analysis comparison of our mechanism and other mechanism

	EAP-AKA	W-SKE	IDKE	Our Mechanism
Prevent Guessing Attack	x	x	x	○
Prevent Replay Attack	x	○	○	○
Prevent Impersonation Attack	x	○	○	○
Prevent WEP weakness attack	○	x	○	○
Prevent Forward/Backward Secrecy attacks	x	x	x	○
Legal evidence for use-bill	x	x	x	○
Mutual Authentication	x	x	△	○
Secret Key Establishment	○	x	x	○
Non-repudiation	x	x	x	○
Message Integrity	○	○	x	○
Protect Transmit Session Key	x	x	x	○
Perfect User Anonymity	x	x	x	○

○:Achieved △:Incomplete —:No propose X: No Achieved

Table 3. The Performance Analysis comparison of our mechanism and other mechanism

Round Trip Time	EAP-AKA		W-SKE		IDKE		Our Mechanism	
	FA	RA	FA	RA	FA	RA	FA	RA
$T_{F-AAA,H-AAA}$	2	0	1	No	No	0	1	0
$T_{F-AAA,AS}$	4	3	2	No	No	1	1	1
$T_{MS,AS}$	5	4	3	No	No	2	2	2

FA: Full Authentication RA: Fast Re-Authentication RTT: Round Trip Time

4   Performance Analysis

In this section, we will evaluate the efficiency of our mechanism in terms of authentication latency in more details. Let $T_{F-AAA,H-AAA}$ denote the one trip latency between H-AAA and F-AAA, $T_{F-AAA,AS}$ denote the one between F-AAA and AS, and $T_{MS,AS}$ denote the one between MS and AS. According to the number of authentication time, we can see that $T_{F-AAA,H-AAA} > T_{F-AAA,AS} > T_{MS,AS}$. Table.3 shows The Performance Analysis comparison among our mechanism, EAP-AKA, W-SKE and IDKE. The authentication latency of our full authentication is $2T_{F-AAA,H-AAA} + 2T_{F-AAA,AS} + 4T_{MS,AS}$, EAP-AKA is $4T_{F-AAA,H-AAA} + 8T_{F-AAA,AS} + 10T_{MS,AS}$; W-SKE is $2T_{F-AAA,H-AAA} + 4T_{F-AAA,AS} + 6T_{MS,AS}$; but IDKE doesn't point out this method. Moreover, in terms of fast re-authentication, our scheme is $2T_{F-AAA,AS} + 4T_{MS,AS}$; EAP-AKA is $6T_{F-AAA,AS} + 8T_{MS,AS}$; IDKE is $2T_{F-AAA,AS} + 4T_{MS,AS}$; while W-SKE doesn't mention it .

5   Conclusions and Future Works

In our mechanism, we discuss about the security and authentication protocol for WLAN and 3G/UMTS interworking. EAP-AKA, W-SKE and IDKE have been examined, and shown the security weaknesses of W-SKE, the in-efficiency of EAP-AKA, and integrate localized re-authentication of IDKE. Moreover, we have figured out a new authenticated key exchange protocol. We propose a robust authentication protocol which can perform efficient localized re-authentication procedure, provide non-repudiation service, solve the problems of losing packages, shorten the authentication time delay and greatly improve the security. In our future work, we expect to do a more in-depth research focused on the handover mechanism, roaming management, packet forwarding and transmission in the future days.

References

1. 3GPP TR 22.934: Feasibility study on 3GPP system to Wireless Local Area Network (WLAN) interworking, Release 6 (2003)
2. 3GPP TS 22.234: 3GPP system to Wireless Local Area Network (WLAN) Interworking, System description, Release 6 (2004)
3. 3GPP TS 33.234: 3G Securtiy: Wireless Local Area Network (WLAN) interworking security, Release 7 (2006)
4. Buddhikot, M., Chandranmenon, G., Han, S., Lee, Y.W., Miller, S., Salgarelli, L.: Integration of 802.11 and Third-Generation Wireless Data Networks. In: Proceedings of the IEEE INFOCOM 2003 (2003)
5. Zhu, J., Ma, J.: A New Authentciation Scheme with Anonymity for Wireless Envioronments. IEEE Member (2004)
6. Salgrelli, L., Buddhikot, M., Garay, J., Patel, S., Miller, S.: Efficient Authentication and Key Distribution in Wireless IP Networks. Bell Laboratories, Lucent Technologies. IEEE Wireless Communication (2003)
7. Kambourakis, G., Rouskas, A., Kormentzas, G., Gritzalis, S.: Advanced SSL/TLS-Based authentication for secure WLAN-3G interworking. Communications 151 (2004)
8. Prasithsangaree, P., Krishnamuthy, P.: A new authentication mechanism for loosely coupled 3G-WLAN integrated networks. In: IEEE Vehicular Technology Conference (2004)
9. Tsen, Y.M., Yang, C.C., Su, J.H.: An efficient protocol for integrating WLAN and Cellular Networks. In: International Conference on Advanced Communication Technology (2004)
10. IETF Draft: IETF internet draft EAP-SIM authentication (2003),
    http://www.ieft.org/internet-draft-haverinen-appext-eap-sim-10.txt
11. IETF Draft: Extensible Authentication Protocol Method for 3rd Generation Authentication an Key Agreement (EAP-AKA). RFC 4187 (2006)
12. Lamport, L.: Password Authentication with Insecure Communication. Communication of ACM 24(11), 770–772 (1981)
13. Krawczyk, H., Bellare, M., Canetti, R.: Keyed-Hashing for Message Authentication. RFC 2104 (1997)

A Framework of a Recommendation System Utilizing Expert Groups on a Social Network

Tzong-Shyan Lin and Chun-Cheng Lin[*]

Department of Industrial Engineering and Management,
National Chiao Tung University, Hsinchu 300, Taiwan
cclin321@nctu.edu.tw

Abstract. A social network is used as a mechanism to link people together to solicit and relay recommendations from one another. However, in a large social network where most people would have hundreds of acquaintances and millions of people within the social network, relying solely on the recommendations obtained through a search that involves a significant number of people within a network, which may not be the most practical and economical option. A solution to this is to limit the number of people between two people within a social network, between the person soliciting a recommendation and a person potentially providing a recommendation. To compensate for the potential loss of recommendations as a result of the limit, a mechanism to compliment the recommendation system, known as expert groups, is created. Expert groups are a collection of people with a common expertise in a common knowledge area and a certain degree of like-mindedness. People within these expert groups can provide recommendations on issues within the common knowledge area. The proposed framework uses software agents to model the behavior of people when soliciting recommendations and providing recommendations.

Keywords: Recommendation system, social network, expert group, trust score.

1 Introduction

Until the emergence of social networks, seeking recommendation over the internet usually involves posting a question on a bulletin board system or newsgroup system. Then other users can then post recommendations of their own in response to the request. With all the wide variety of recommendations, it comes difficult for the requestor to choose which recommendation to accept. A few systems publicize all previous posts made by the user on his or her public profile that can be reviewed in an attempt to determine the validity of the recommendation by a particular user. But this is quite time consuming and in many cases, the "correct" recommendation is dependent on biased factors such as personal preferences.

Social networks creates essentially a mapping of real world personal relationships on a computing platform that can be analyzed, and all interactions between individuals on social networks can be stored and utilized in the future to determine the level of

---

[*] Corresponding author. Research supported in part by NSC 98-2218-E-009-026-MY3.

R.-S. Chang, T.-h. Kim, and S.-L. Peng (Eds.): SUComS 2011, CCIS 223, pp. 297–306, 2011.
© Springer-Verlag Berlin Heidelberg 2011

trust and similarity of preferences. When replies to solicitations for recommendations are sent by a user to other users over the social network are received, the usefulness of each received recommendation can then be evaluated based on past interaction. After following a recommendation, the user would provide input into the social network the recommendation which the action was based upon and whether the user was satisfied with the results of the action. A recommendation leading to satisfaction with results, upon which it was based, increases the level of trust the user has towards the individual providing the recommendation [7]. Over time and repeated interactions, it is expected that users with similar preferences and tastes would be linked together on the social network via paths of high trustworthiness.

In the real world, people with an interest in a certain domain area often actively communicate with each other to exchange new ideas, perspectives, and various types of information related to the domain area. But the commonality among these people is not only determined by a shared interest in a domain area, but also by a shared fundamental perspective of issues within the domain area. Members of groups that differ significantly in their shared fundamental perspectives in a certain domain area usually find it difficult to agree on the assessment of issues related to the domain area. Note that people who find it difficult to agree on the assessment of issues related to a particular domain may find it easy to agree on that related to another domain of interest. People with an interest in a certain domain area are often viewed by other people that do not belong to that domain area as experts of that domain area. When a person is in need of a recommendation of a topic, the request for a recommendation may be directed to an expert of the relevant domain area known by the requestor. If the expert is sufficiently confident to give a recommendation, the expert will reply to the requestor with a recommendation directly.

The objective of this proposal is to integrate the described phenomenon into a recommendation system on a social network. It is hoped that through integrating this phenomenon, not only can users receive a higher ratio of recommendations that lead to satisfying results [2], but also through the identification of groups of people with shared interest and fundamental perspectives in the domain area, they can be utilized to help market products or services. A possible method to do so may be to offer products or services to people belonging to groups that have been identified to be potentially highly receptive of the products or services for free or at steep discounts. It is hoped that people belonging to these groups would be highly satisfied with the products or services that were offered to them and would recommended them to other users on the social network that are inquiring about the products or services.

2   Related Works

Recommender systems were created to link sellers of products with customers that have a high probability of showing interest in the product. Further improvements focus not only on finding customers that have a high probability of showing interest in the product, but also has a high probability of liking the product after the product is purchased and consumed.

Most implementations of recommender systems are usually centralized systems operated by companies selling their products or other entities on their behalf [6,10].

There are two main approaches when designing recommender systems. *Content-based approaches* suggest product by matching profiles of people with characteristics of products and services. The other approach is *collaborative filtering*, which focuses on measuring the similarity of preferences between people and recommends what other people who have similar preferences have already chosen. In both methods, however, people who are potential customers have little influence in the process, and in fact have little influence in how they are perceived by system [4,5]. While it is true that people are often allowed to change their personal profiles, they do not have control how their profile is interpreted by the recommender system.

The use of bulletin board systems created an opportunity for people to receive recommendation from other people. However, it is often difficult to determine validity and reliability of the suggestion. Recently, the emergence of social networks allows the possibility of receiving recommendations and evaluates them based on their degree of trust. While the issue of trust in the computing community traditionally refers to the application of cryptography involving security systems, in recent years, it has expended to include the reliability of commercial and social activities by various entities [8,9]. It is with this expanded role of trust in which this framework is based upon.

3   Description of Proposed Model

We propose a model of autonomous agents connecting other autonomous agents forming a social network [3]. The social network is used by the autonomous agents to solicit recommendations concerning purchases. It is expected that each agent only connects to a very small number of agents relative to the total number of agents on the social network [1,2]. Every connection represents a pair of agents that are acquainted with one other. Each of the two agents in the pair maintains a trust score of the other agent. An agent only assigns a trust score to other agents that it is acquainted to. It does not assign a trust score to agents that would require each agent to have a certain degree of global knowledge and defeat the purpose of a network of agents [11].

The agents in this social network make iterative decisions on whether to purchase a certain item. If the agent does not have previous experience with the item in question, it will request its acquaintances to provide recommendations on whether to purchase the item. When acquaintances of the agent receive the request to provide recommendation, it would return a recommendation if it had previous experience with the item. If it does not, it would solicit recommendations from its other acquaintances. The recommendation returned would be either "like" or "not like".

Whether an agent would "like" or "not like" an item after it is purchased is dependent on minimal conflicts between the attributes of the item and attributes that form the preferences of the agent. The heterogeneous nature of agent preferences results in agents on the social network having diverse preference attributes. While each agent has a fixed configuration of preference attributes that can be used to determine the likeability of an item after it is purchased, the preference attributes cannot be used to assist an agent in making the purchase decision.

Some agents in the social network may be part of an expert group. An expert group consists of like-minded agents experienced in a certain item category. Agents belonging in an expert group are not required to provide recommendations for all items within an item category. When the agent receives a request to provide recommendation for an item within an item category corresponding to a relevant expert group in which the agent is a member of, the agent can forward the request to other members of the expert group instead of other acquaintances when it cannot provide the recommendation itself. Other agents within the expert group capable of providing a recommendation would return a recommendation. The formation of expert groups that each specialize in a specific item category and consisting of like-minded agents is expected to provide recommendations that can closely match the preferences of its member agents and their highly trusted acquaintances.

3.1   Attributes, Items, and Item Categories

There exists a fixed finite set of attributes used to define the characteristics of items and preferences of agents. Each attribute either exists or does not exist within a subset of attributes that represents the characteristics of items and preferences of agents. A subset of the full set of attributes is associated with each item to distinctively define the characteristic of the item. When two or more items share the same subset of attributes, they are all items of the same kind. It is assume that the attributes are correct and can be objectively observed during consumption by the agent.

Items represent a fixed predefined set of physical objects, services, and digital goods considered for purchase. When it is decided that an item is to be purchased, it is then purchased and consumed by the agent. While items representing physical objects can be either perishable goods that disappear from existence when consumed or non-perishable goods that still remain in existence after being consumed, it is assumed that the Agent is able to determine whether it likes the item after it is consumed for the first time. The consumption of items representing to be services is assumed to be completed by an agent in a reasonable amount of time. While the proposed framework in its current form does not explicitly distinguish whether items represent physical objects, services, and digital goods, it should be noted that these can also be incorporated into attributes that define the characteristics of items.

Item categories are groups of items which are predefined and fixed. When given an item category, the items within the item category can be determined with minimal effort as the relationship is predefined. Conversely, when given an item, the item categories in which it is part of can also be determined with minimal effort as the relationship is predefined as well. It should be noted that an item can belong to multiple item categories. Conceptually, items in each item category should share some common characteristic. However, within this framework, since items categories and items within each category are predefined, no mechanism exists to define or to authenticate the shared attributes of items within each item category.

3.2   Agents and Preferences

All agents are created at the same time when the social network is initiated. Agents are not inserted and removed when the social network is in operation. The basic roles of the agents are: 1) Provide or relay suggestions on whether to purchase items. The suggestion on whether to purchase an item is based on whether the agent making the suggestion likes the item. 2) Make decisions on whether to purchase an item. If it is decided that an item is to be purchased, after it is purchased and consumed, it will know whether it likes the item or not. 3) Evaluate the perceived trustworthiness of neighboring agents connected on the social network.

Each agent has its own preferences that determine if it likes or does not like an item when it consumes the item. A preference of an agent consists of two sets of attributes to reflect that the agent likes and does not like. Attributes in the two sets are subsets of the full set of attributes explained above. Each attribute can exist in either the "like" set or the "not like" set, but not both for a particular agent. An attribute can exist in neither of the two sets for an agent as well, reflecting the fact that the agent is indifferent for that particular attribute. Within the proposed framework, agents cannot utilize the two sets of attributes that define its preferences when making a decision on whether it should purchase an item. Rather, it is utilized when the item is consumed to determine whether the agent likes or does not like the item. After the agent consumes an item and knows whether it likes or does not like the item, it can maintain an internal data entry of the result that can be used in future purchase decisions. Obviously, if the item is liked, then in the future the agent will purchase the exact same item again when given the opportunity. Conversely, if the item is not like, then in the future, the agent will refrain from purchasing the same item again.

When an agent consumes an item, the attributes of the item are compared to the "like" set of attributes and "not like" set of attributes. For every attribute of the item that is within the "like" set of attributes, it would score "+1". For every attribute of the item that is within the "not like" set of attributes, it would score "-1". After summing up the scores received to calculate the total score, if the total aggregated score is a non-negative number, then it is determined that the agent likes the item. Conversely, if the total aggregated score is a negative number, then it is determined that the agent does not like the item that was just consumed.

3.3   Acquaintances and Trust Scores of Acquaintances

Agents within this framework consist of interconnected autonomous agents on a social network. Within the social network, agents are nodes of the network while the connections between agents on the network are edges of the network. Edges on the network are bidirectional in nature, allowing agents on both sides of each edge to communicate to the agent on the other side. Each agent is only connected to a very small number of agents relative to the total number of agents on the social network. These connections are defined to be fixed and do not change during the operation of the social network. Acquaintances are two neighboring agents connected on the social network. Each agent assigns a trust score to all of its acquaintances independent of the trust score assigned to it by its acquaintances. An agent cannot assign trust scores to non-acquaintances even though it may receive advice initiated by a non-acquaintance, as this would require each agent to have a global view of all agents on the network which defeats the purchase of a social network.

A trust score between 0 and 1 (non-inclusive) is assigned by each agent to each of their acquaintances. The higher the trust score, the higher the degree of trust an agent has on the acquaintance corresponding to the score. The lower the trust score, the lower the degree of trust an agent has on the acquaintance corresponding to the score. Initially, a neutral trust score of 0.5 assigned, and would be reassigned as agents gain or lose trust in the acquaintance corresponding to the score.

When making decisions on whether to purchase an item, the agent would request recommendations from its acquaintances. Recommendations from acquaintances with higher trust scores would have a greater probability of being accepted by the agent making the purchasing decision, while recommendations from acquaintances with lower trust scores would have a lower probability of being accepted by the agent making the purchasing decision. If the recommendation is relayed by the acquaintance instead of given by the acquaintance, the cumulated product of trust scores assigned by agents relaying the recommendation through the social network to acquaintances in which the recommendation was given or received from is also provided to the agent receiving the recommendation by the acquaintance. In the latter case, the cumulated product of trust scores is used as the trust score in determining the probability of the recommendation received being accepted.

After the agent decides to purchase and consume an item, it would return the results of whether it actually "like" or "not like" the item to acquaintances from which it received recommendation from, including both those who sent their own recommendations and those who simply relayed their own recommendations. Those acquaintances that simply relayed recommendations passed on to them will relay the results received to its acquaintances from the corresponding recommendations were received. The main purpose for returning the results of purchasing and consuming the product is to allow agents to adjust trust scores of their acquaintances.

3.4   Expert Groups

An expert group consists of like-minded agents with significant experience gained by consuming items within a certain item category that can provide recommendation to each other. Agents are not required to be a member of an expert group, but it can be a member of multiple expert groups. Member agents of an expert group do not automatically become acquaintances with each other due to being members of the same group, although some member agents may coincidently be acquaintances with each other. Expert groups are implemented through expert group objects. An expert group objects receives a request for recommendation on a certain item that is within the item category that corresponds to the expert group and relays the request to all other agents that are members of the expert group. If any agents in the expert group had previous experience consuming the item for which the recommendation is being requested for, it would respond with either a "like" or "not like" to the expert group object which will then relay the recommendation back to the requesting agent. A request for recommendation received by an agent through the expert group object is not relayed to the agent's acquaintances if the agent is not able to provide the recommendation itself. The expert group object will tally the number of "like" and "not like" responses received from agents within the expert group and return the higher of the two back to the member agent that sent the request for recommendation to the expert group object. In the event of a tie, the response returned will be "not like". This is because a recommendation that could induce an action to purchase and consume an item should be more than a recommendation that induces non-action.

It should be stressed that member agents of the expert group do not communicate with each other unless the communicating pair happens to also be acquaintances, rather the intra-group communication are communicated though the expert group object.

After the requesting agent receives one or more recommendations, if it decides to purchase and then consume the item, it will report back to the expert group object after consuming the item on whether it "like" or "not like" the item. If the requesting agent is only relaying the request, it would only report the results of consuming the item received from acquaintances which it had assigned a relatively high trust score and the trust score received with the relayed results are above a certain level. When an export group object receives the result after consuming an item based on recommendations from other member agents of the expert group, it will store the recommendation and result pair as well as the member agent that requested the recommendation and member agents that provided the recommendation so that it will became the basis in which expert groups are adjusted. These adjustments are intended to better group like-minded agents together.

3.5   Social Network and Search for Recommendations

Autonomous agents form the nodes of the social network and can communicate with other agents via the bidirectional edges of the social network. The purpose of communications between agents within the social network is to enable the following: 1) Request recommendation for the items considered to purchase and consume; 2) Receive recommendation for the items considered to purchase and consume; 3) The result of whether the agent "like" or "not like" item is sent to the other agents that contributed to the recommendation, if the agent decides to purchase and consume the item after receiving the recommendation.

When an agent requests recommendation for an item considered to purchase, it would utilize an expert group if it is a member of an expert group for a category with the item. If the agent is not its member or no recommendation is received from the expert group, then the request is sent to all its acquaintances. Upon receiving such a request, an acquaintance would return a recommendation if it had prior experience in consuming the item; otherwise, it would attempt to obtain a recommendation from an expert group if it is a member an expert group for an item category with the item. Otherwise, the request is sent to all its acquaintances except for the one which the request is received from. Note that agents need to record all requests that it has received previously and refrain from re-processing the request had the same request been processed previously to prevent the request from traveling in an endless loop on the social network. If a request eventually reaches an agent that can provide a recommendation either by itself or from its expert group, then the recommendation would follow the same path in which the request had travelled through but in the reverse direction back to the agent that made the request. Essentially the request for recommendation is a depth-first search on the social network.

Since the size of social network can actually be quite large with each node (agent) typically being linked to more edges than most other types of networks, it is essential to place a limit on the maximum distance a request can be relayed to from the originating node (agent). Otherwise, in the worst case scenario, a single request for recommendation would travel to every single node on the social network. This level of loading can not only overwhelm the network, but would require the agent requesting recommendation having to wait for a long time to be sure that recommendation have been received. In this framework, we set the maximum distance to 20. Upon receiving the recommendations, the agent decides whether to purchase and consume the item. If it is decided that the agent will purchase and consume the item, the results of whether the agent "like" or "unlike" the item will be returned to all those who provided the recommendation via the same path on the social network in which the recommendations were sent, but in the reverse direction. Agents along the path can utilize the results that were received and the recommendation made as a basis on adjusting the trust scores of its acquaintances.

3.6   Decision Making

The recommendations received by the agent that requested recommendation of an item are either "like" or "not like". If the agent decides to follow the "like" recommendation, it would purchase and consume the item, and then gives it experience with consuming the item. After consuming the item, the agent can then determine if it likes the item and remember this. In the future, if the agent is asked to provide a recommendation for this same item, it will respond with a "like" if the agent had liked the item when consuming it, else it would respond with a "not like" if the agent did not like the item. If deciding to follow the "unlike" recommendation, the agent would refrain from purchasing and consuming the item. Hence, it still does not know if it actually likes the item and if asked to provide a recommendation, will not be able to. Agents will attempt to obtain recommendation from an expert group in which it is a member of first, if possible. Only when it cannot obtain recommendation from an expert group does it send request for recommendation to all its acquaintances. If no recommendations have been received, then by default, the agent will purchase and consume the item. While this behavior may appear to be irrational, it is necessary to do so to populate the social network with a least a few agents with experience for every item in existence during the early periods when the social network is operated.

After all the recommendations have been received from acquaintances, the individual trust scores for each recommendation received is summed together to calculate the "total trust score". The probability of each recommendation being chosen by the agent is the trust score of the recommendation as a percentage of the total trust score. The reason for assigning a probability of being chosen to each recommendation rather than always choosing the recommendation with the highest trust score or choosing the recommendation with the highest aggregated trust score is to ensure that the recommendation for a certain item does not gravitate significantly towards "not like", and in later stages agents would not get any opportunity to actually try it because by accepting a "not like" recommendation, the agent does not attempt to find out for itself whether it actually likes it or not.

3.7   Evaluating and Updating Trust Scores of Acquaintances

This section discusses how and when trust scores are updated to reflect the change in perception of acquaintances by agents over the course of time though interactions with one another. In human society, gaining the trust of others not only takes time but requires repeated interaction with them. Unfortunately, the destruction of trust can happen suddenly with a single event and may be difficult to recover. A social network is a computer model of certain aspects of human interaction. In this social network model, this phenomenon is reflected to a certain extent in how trust scores are adjusted. Below we show how a trust score is increased and decreased by one unit:

When a trust score is to be increased by one unit, let t_x be the current trust score and t_{x+1} be the new trust score: $t_{x+1} = (\sqrt{t_x} - t_x)/2 + t_x$. When a trust score is to be decreased by one unit, let t_x be the current trust score and t_{x+1} be the new trust score: $t_{x+1} = t_x/2$. The agent requesting a recommendation on whether to purchase an item will increase the trust score assigned to all acquaintances that provide it with the correct recommendation by one unit only when it actually consumes the item. Conversely, the agent requesting a recommendation on whether to purchase an item will decrease the trust score assigned to all acquaintances that provide it with the incorrect recommendation by one unit only when it actually consumes the item.

Agents along the relay pathway from the agent requesting the recommendation to the agent providing the recommendation will increase the trust score assigned to the acquaintance providing the correct information by one unit when the acquaintance receiving the relayed recommendation has already been assigned a trust score of 0.9 or higher. Conversely, agents along the relay pathway from the agent requesting the recommendation to the agent providing the recommendation will decrease the trust score assigned to the acquaintance providing the incorrect information by one unit when the acquaintance receiving the relayed recommendation has already been assigned a trust score of 0.9 or higher.

A recommendation for an item is determined to be correct when it is the same as the perception of the agent that requested the recommendation after purchasing and consuming the item. When the perception of the agent that requested the recommendation after purchasing and the consuming the item is different than the recommendation given, then the recommendation is determined to be incorrect.

3.8   Formation, Modification, and Destruction of Expert Groups

An expert group is formed when two neighboring agents that have assigned each other a trust score > 0.5 and each have experienced (purchased and consumed) ≥ 10% of all items within a common item category. An agent will join an existing expert group as experienced ≥ 10% of all items of item category corresponding to an expert group in which a mutually trusting (trust score > 0.5) neighboring agent is already a member of the expert group. If two expert groups of the same item category shares > 30% of its members, the two expert groups will merge into a single expert group.

When there exists 5 or more member agents of an expert group in one of the following situations on more than 12 out of the past 20 rolling instances that involve either providing recommendation for an item different from the recommendation given by the expert group, or when requesting recommendation or relaying a request for recommendation for an item in which the result after experiencing it was different than the recommendation provided by the expert group object from an acquaintance that had been assigned a trust score of 0.9 or higher, the 5 or more member agents are then placed in a new expert group of the same item category. An expert group should be destructed when it provides incorrect recommendations to more than 12 out of the past 20 rolling unique members of the expert group that have experienced the item.

The above strategic rules are expected to ensure that expert groups consist of not only member agents that have significant experience within a common item category, but also they are like-minded in their preferences for items within the common item category corresponding to the expert group. The expert group object will maintain the historic data required to enforce the strategic rules and should be consistently monitoring to ensure the strategic rules are enforced.

References

1. Jennings, N.R.: On agent-based software engineering. Artificial Intelligence 117(2), 277–296 (2000)
2. Kim, M., Seo, J., Noh, S., Han, S.: Reliable social trust management with mitigating sparsity problem. Journal of Wireless Mobile Networks, Ubiquitous Computing, and Dependable Applications 1(1), 86–97 (2010)
3. Macal, C.M., North, M.J.: Tutorial on agent-based modeling and simulation. Journal of Simulation 4(3), 151–162 (2010)
4. Massa, P., Avesani, P.: Trust-aware collaborative filtering for recommender systems. In: On the Move to Meaningful Internet Systems: CoopIS/DOA/ODBASE, pp. 492–508 (2004)
5. Massa, P., Avesani, P.: Trust-aware recommender systems. In: Proc. of 2007 ACM Conference on Recommender Systems, pp. 17–24. ACM Press, New York (2007)
6. Montaner, M., López, B., de la Rosa, J.L.: A taxonomy of recommender agents on the internet. Artificial Intelligence Review 19(4), 285–330 (2003)
7. Pujol, J.M., Sangüesa, R., Delgado, J.: Extracting reputation in multi agent systems by means of social network Topology. In: Proc. of First International Joint Conference on Autonomous Agents and Multiagent Systems, pp. 467–474. ACM Press, New York (2002)
8. Sabater, J., Sierra, C.: Reputation and social network analysis in multi-agent systems. In: Proceedings of First International Joint Conference on Autonomous Agents and Multiagent Systems, pp. 475–482. ACM Press, New York (2002)
9. Sabater, J., Sierra, C.: Review on computational trust and reputation models. Artificial Intelligence Review 24(1), 33–60 (2005)
10. Sarwar, B., Karypis, G., Konstan, J., Riedl, J.: Analysis of recommendation algorithms for e-commerce. In: Proc. of 2nd ACM Conference on Electronic Commerce, pp. 158–167. ACM Press, New York (2000)
11. Walter, F.E., Battiston, S., Schweitzer, F.: A model of a trust-based recommendation system on a social network. Autonomous Agents and Multi-Agent Systems 16(1), 57–75 (2008)

Quality-of-Service in Wireless Personal Area Networks

Teng-Hui Wang, Ming-Yi Shih, and Der-Jiunn Deng

Department of Computer Science and Information Engineering,
National Changhua University of Education, Taiwan
oncememory0723@yahoo.com.tw, {myshih,djdeng}@cc.ncue.edu.tw

Abstract. IEEE 802.15.4 standard defines the physical layer and medium access control layer protocols for low-rate wireless personal area networks (LR-WPANs). In IEEE 802.15.4 LR-WPANs, quality-of-service is supported by using the guaranteed time slots (GTS) to transmit real-time packets since a LR-WPAN device doesn't need to contend the channel in the GTS. In the PAN coordinator, requests of GTS are allocated based on the first-come-first-service policy. However, with the increasing of multimedia applications, this original design has suffered from the lack of priority mechanism to support the transmission of real-time packets. In this paper, we propose a non-preemptive priority-based polling scheme for the GTS allocation in IEEE 802.15.4 LR-WPANs. The proposed scheme can ensure that the connections which have higher priority can transmit real-time packets quicker. The simulations show that the proposed scheme can achieve more GTS allocations, higher throughput, better bandwidth utilization and lower packets access delay time.

Keywords: IEEE 802.15.4, LR-WPANs, GTS, QoS, Priority.

1 Introduction

The IEEE 802.15.4 standard [1] defines the physical (PHY) layer and medium access control (MAC) layer protocols for low-rate wireless personal area networks (LR-WPANs). One of the well-known implementations in IEEE 802.15.4 LR-WPANs is wireless sensor networks (WSNs). The wireless sensor networks have many applications, such as medical treatments, traffic transport systems, military tracing, and industry, etc. A wireless sensor network is composed of many small-sized sensor devices which can monitor the physical and environment conditions continuously, and most of the sensor devices are working with limited power.

IEEE 802.15.4 standard has the characteristics of low power consumption, low cost hardware, low-data-rate transmission, and short range communication. The medium access control (MAC) protocol used in the IEEE 802.15.4 LR-WPANs is superframe structure. There are 16 equal-sized slots in the superframe, and the first slot is used as the beacon frame especially. Beacon frame has the following functions: (1) starting a super frame; (2) announcing the existence of a

R.-S. Chang, T.-h. Kim, and S.-L. Peng (Eds.): SUComS 2011, CCIS 223, pp. 307–316, 2011.
© Springer-Verlag Berlin Heidelberg 2011

PAN coordinator; (3) synchronization between the PAN coordinator and other devices; (4) informing pending data, such as superframe duration, beacon duration, allocation for guaranteed time slots (GTS), destination address, etc. The remainder slots are divided into contention access period (CAP) and contention free period (CFP) to transmit packets.

The contention access period uses the *carrier sense multiple access with collision avoidance* (CSMA/CA) scheme as contention access mechanism, while the contention free period uses a contention-free policy to transmit packets for satisfying the quality-of-service (QoS) requirements. Contention free period is composed of some pre-arranged slots, called guaranteed time slots (GTS), which can be used for real-time packets transmission. When a device wants to transmit packets in the contention free period, it will send a request of GTS allocation to the PAN coordinator. After receiving the request, PAN coordinator will allocate a GTS for this device based on the first-come-first-service (FCFS) policy. When the request is accepted, the device would transmit its packets in the allocated GTS. The superframe structure is shown in Fig. 1.

However, with the increasing of multimedia applications, this original design has suffered from the lack of priority mechanism to support the transmission of real-time packets. For example, intelligent transport systems in the traffic application, safety management for nuclear power plants and surveillance of enemy tracks in the military application, etc. Data such as these information must be real-time and have the highest priority, so the original design in the IEEE 802.15.4 standard has been not suitable at all under these circumstances.

To overcome this problem, many literatures have proposed some schemes for priority connections. In [2], the authors adopted one clear channel assessment (CCA) for high priority connection. Although this scheme reduced the delay time for high priority connection, it may increase the collision rate tremendously for data frame and ack frame since it only perform one CCA. In [3], the authors changed three important variables: *BE*, *CW* and *NB* under different situations, they assigned different values according to the connection's priority. However, it would increase the collision rate and average delay time since it changed the maximum and minimum backoff exponent. In [4], the authors have presented a novel back off strategy by using gaussian distribution to enhance the QoS mechanism, but it is too complicated to implement in IEEE 802.15.4 LR-WAPNs. Huang et.al has proposed a new GTS allocation scheme, called AGA scheme

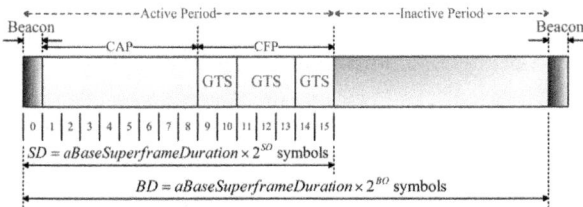

Fig. 1. Superframe structure

[5], which considered the latency and fairness. In [6], the authors used a knapsack problem to get the optimal GTS allocation. But above studies [5, 6] didn't emphasize the aspect of priority. A novel and smart scheme for enhancing the quality of service in IEEE 802.11 standard has been proposed in [7], which inspired and motivated us very well. In [8, 9], they have derived the performance of the beacon-enabled mode in IEEE 802.15.4 standard, which can be used to analyze the performance for our proposed scheme in the future works.

In this paper, we propose a non-preemptive priority-based polling scheme for the GTS allocation based on the IEEE 802.15.4 standard. In the proposed scheme, it can immediately start the CAP or CFP according to the polling token buffer is empty or not. And the proposed scheme can achieve better bandwidth utilization since we add an admission control scheme. Furthermore, simulations show that the proposed scheme can achieve more GTS allocations, higher throughput, and lower packets access delay time.

The remainder of this paper is organized as follows: Section 2 introduces the management of GTS in the IEEE 802.15.4 standard. In Section 3, we describe the proposed scheme. Section 4 demonstrates some simulation results. Finally, we conclude this paper in Section 5.

2 Preliminary

In the contention free period, quality-of-service (QoS) is supported by using guaranteed time slots (GTS) to transmit real-time packets since a LR-WPAN device doesn't need to contend the channel in the GTS. GTS is managed by the PAN coordinator, and it only can be used for communication between devices and the PAN coordinator. The management of GTS includes allocation of GTS and deallocation of GTS, which will be described at the following subsections in detail.

2.1 GTS Allocation

If a device wants a GTS to transmit real-time packets, it will send a request of GTS allocation to the PAN coordinator which contains the information of starting slot of GTS, desired length of GTS and associated device address. When the PAN coordinator receives this request, it will send an acknowledgment frame to this device for confirming its receipt. After that, the PAN coordinator will check if there is an available capacity during this superframe according to the following two conditions:

(1) Number of allocated GTSs ≤ 7.
(2) Current length of CAP - Desired length of GTS $\geq aMinCAPLength$ (440 symbols).

If this request satisfies above two conditions, the PAN coordinator will allocate a GTS based on first-come-first-service (FCFS) policy, and then it will reduce the current length of CAP according to the desired length of GTS. Furthermore, the PAN coordinator will make a decision within $aGTSDescPersistenceTime$

superframes (4 superframes). Note that all GTSs should be placed contiguously at the contention free period. After deciding to allocate this GTS, the PAN coordinator will save the message including the starting slot of GTS, allocated length of GTS and associated device address in the beacon frame. Devices would get these information by synchronizing with the PAN coordinator after receive acknowledgment frame. If the PAN coordinator cannot decide the GTS allocation in four superframes, then it's failed for this request of GTS allocation. Device would send out a new request of GTS allocation at next superframe time.

2.2   GTS Deallocation

If a device misses the beacon at the beginning of a superframe, it will not use its GTSs until it receives a beacon correctly. Then the device would consider deallocating its GTSs. Firstly, the device will send a request of GTS deallocation to the PAN coordinator, and then the PAN coordinator will send an acknowledgment frame to this device for confirming its receipt. Then, the PAN coordinator will deallocate this GTS, and increasing the length of this deallocated GTS at current CAP length.

3   Proposed Scheme

In this section, we present the proposed scheme in detail. We first develop a channel access model to depict the data access procedure, and then we will illustrate the admission control mechanism for the proposed scheme. Finally, we describe the proposed scheme how to transmit packets. As a side note, the proposed scheme only considers the beacon-enable mode.

3.1   Call Admission Control

The main issue in real-time packets transmission is how to transmit packets in time without any additional delay time. As mentioned before, IEEE 802.15.4 LR-WPANs use contention free period to transmit the real-time packets with fewer access delay time. The PAN coordinator is the primary controller of determining which connection can get the allocation of GTS. In the follows, we propose a packet transmit-permission policy for the IEEE 802.15.4 LR-WPANs to enhance the priority mechanism. As we will see later, the proposed scheme is efficient and easily implement in the present IEEE 802.15.4 standard.

The channel access model considers the LR-WPAN device to be in one of four states: "*Idle State*", "*Request State*", "*Ready State*" and "*Transmitting State*". Devices with empty buffers are in the idle state initially. When the real-time packets arrive to the buffer, it will enter the request state. When a device in the request state, it will send a request of GTS to the PAN coordinator through the CSMA/CA mechanism at the beginning of contention access period. When the request transmits successfully, it will proceed to the allocation process; otherwise, it will retransmit this request until it transmits this request successfully.

The proposed process of allocating a GTS will be described at the next subsection. When the request of GTS is allocated successfully, this device would first check if it has received the detailed information of this GTS allocation. If it has received this information, it will enter the ready state; otherwise, it will deallocated this GTS first and then goes to the request state to transmit another request of GTS. Device in the ready state will periodically listen to the PAN coordinator to check if it has been polled. Once a device is polled, it will enter transmitting state to transmit real-time packets in the allocated GTS. After transmitting real-time packets, the device will check if these packets have the signal of End-of-File. If it has received the End-of-File signal, the device will enter the idle state to wait for other real-time flow. Otherwise, the device will go back to ready state and wait for the PAN coordinator polling it again. Note that the PAN coordinator will continuously poll devices which have been allocated a GTS until all these devices have transmitted real-time packets completely. The state transition diagram is shown in Fig. 2.

It's worth to note that an admission control mechanism is used in the proposed scheme before a device entering the allocation process. When there is a new coming request arrives, this request will affect the delay time of other requests which have lower priority. In other words, this request will be affected by the requests which have higher priority. Let $\sum_{k=1}^{i-1} \lceil \frac{\gamma_k}{\gamma_i} \rceil \times T_{tran}$ be the total packet transmitting time of those requests who have higher priority, where γ means the packets transmitting rate, and T_{tran} means the transmitting time of a real-time packet. Therefore, $T_{tran} + \sum_{k=1}^{i-1} \lceil \frac{\gamma_k}{\gamma_i} \rceil \times T_{tran}$ means the maximum waiting time (or maximum tolerant time) of request i. Before a request entering CFP, we will check if its maximum waiting time less than its delay time σ_i and $\frac{1}{\gamma_i}$. This condition holds means that the delay time of this request wouldn't be affected by the higher priority requests when this request joins into the polling list.

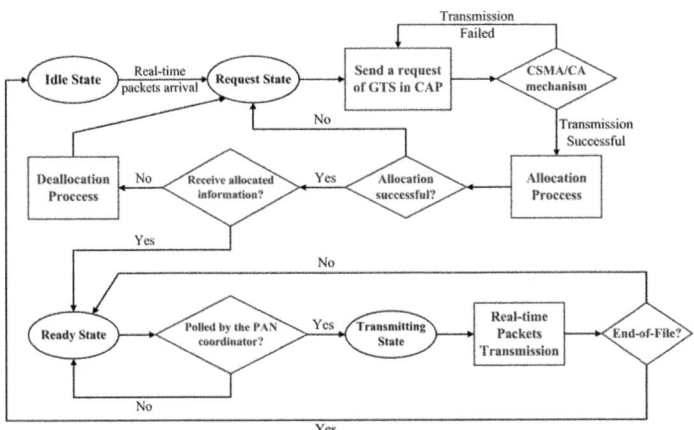

Fig. 2. State transition diagram

Therefore, any request which satisfies this condition can ensure that transmitting real-time packets would not increase any extra delay time and it can be admitted to enter CFP. This condition is our admission control mechanism.

3.2 Packet Transmit-Permission Policy for Real-Time Flow

In the proposed scheme, each request of GTS for real-time flow has the following two parameters (γ, σ), where γ is the packets transmitting rate and σ is the delay time. We take the delay time as the measurement of priority. The smaller delay time means that this real-time flow has to transmit packets quicker, so real-time flow that has the smallest delay time has the highest priority. Detail steps of this policy are described as follows.

Step 1
Any device who wants to use the GTS to transmit real-time packets will send a request of GTS allocation to the PAN coordinator by using a slotted CSMA/CA mechanism at the beginning of the contention access period. For each real-time flow, its polling token is generated in the PAN coordinator if any request of GTS allocation arrives. Once a token is generated, the PAN coordinator will immediately start the contention free period.

Step 2
The PAN coordinator scans the token buffers of real-time flows according to the preset priority order. If a token is found, it removes one from this token buffer and then polls this device.

Step 3
When a device is polled by the PAN coordinator, it will start to transmit its real-time packets from transmitting state and the PAN coordinator will generate the next token for this real-time flow if the device has not been received the End-of-File signal.

Step 4
When an End-of-File signal from a real-time flow is received, the PAN coordinator will remove the polling token of the real-time flow from the polling token buffer.

Step 5
If there is no token found in all token buffers, the PAN coordinator will end this contention free period and begin next superframe by transmitting a beacon of next superframe. And the PAN coordinator will start the next contention free period interval if any token is found by observing the token buffer continuously.

4   Performance Evaluation

In this section, we evaluate the performance of the proposed scheme and provide a comparison with the IEEE 802.15.4 standard.

Table 1. Default attribute values used in simulations

Attributes	Meaning and Explanation	Default Value
aBaseSuperframeDuration	minimum length of active period	960 Symbols
aMinCAPLength	minimum length of CAP	440 Symbols
SuperframeDuration	length of superframe duration used in the simulations	61440 Symbols
BeaconDuratuin	length of beacon duration used in the simulations	122880 Symbols
macMinLIFSPeriod	length of long interframe space (LIFS)	40 Symbols
macMinSIFSPeriod	length of short interframe space (SIFS)	12 Symbols
aTurnaroundTime	maximum turnaround time	12 Symbols
aUnitBackoffPeriod	length of forming the basic time period used by the CSMA/CA algorithm.	20 Symbols
L_{CCA}	length of one CCA	8 Symbols
γ	packets transmitting rate	62500 Symbols/s
σ	delay time	68.48~498.56 ms
T_{tran}	time of transmitting a real-time flow packet	16 μs
L_{ack}	length of a ack frame	12 ~32 Symbols
$L_{real\text{-}time}$	length of a real-time flow	50000~100000 Symbols

4.1 Simulation Environment

The simulations model is built in an event-driven custom program which was written by the C++ programming language, and each simulation runs at least 50 times. All the simulations are conducted in Windows 7 on an Intel Core 2 Duo 2.53 GHz CPU notebook with 2 GB memory.

To simplify the complexity of simulations and highlight the behavior of the CFP, we suppose that the requests of GTS through the CSMA/CA mechanism always transmit successfully and the symbols transmitting rate is CBR in our simulations. Default values used in the simulations are listed in Table 1. The values for the simulation parameters are chosen carefully in order to closely reflect the realistic scenarios as well as to make the simulation feasible and reasonable.

4.2 Simulation Results

In Fig. 3, we compare the number of GTS allocations with the proposed scheme and original scheme in IEEE 802.15.4 standard. Note that the number of GTS allocations in the proposed scheme and original scheme increase quickly when the load is light but increase slowly when the load is heavy. As expected, the proposed scheme always has higher allocation times than the original scheme. It shows that our proposed scheme is better than the original scheme.

Fig. 4 depicts the throughput of the proposed scheme and original scheme. As shown in the figure, throughput of the proposed scheme and original scheme both increase when the load becomes heavier. And the proposed scheme always

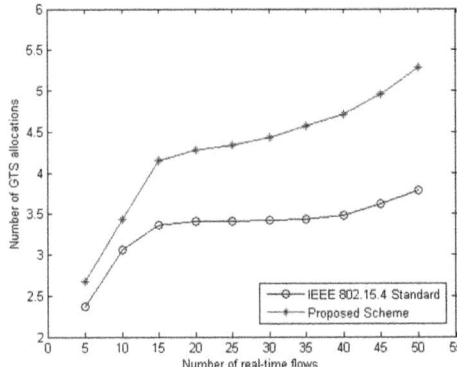

Fig. 3. Number of GTS allocations versus number of real-time flows

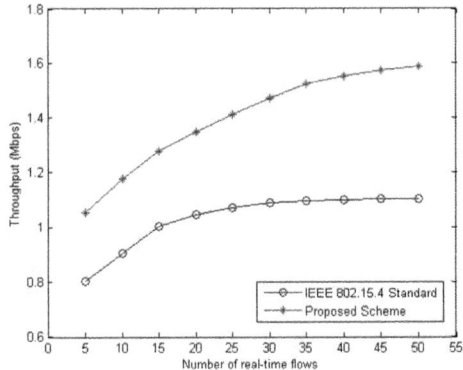

Fig. 4. Throughput versus number of real-time flows

has higher throughput than the original scheme. It reveals that the proposed scheme can achieve better performance than the original scheme.

Fig. 5 indicates the bandwidth utilization of the proposed scheme and original scheme in IEEE 802.15.4 standard. Bandwidth utilization is the percentage of the bandwidth actually being used in the total bandwidth. We can see that bandwidth utilization of the proposed scheme and original scheme both increase when the load becomes heavier. And bandwidth utilization of the proposed scheme is always higher than original scheme. It provides the evidence that the proposed scheme can use the bandwidth more efficiently than the original scheme.

Fig. 6 compares the average access delay time with the proposed scheme and original scheme. The average access delay time of the proposed scheme and original scheme both increase when the load becomes heavier. As the figure shows, the average access delay time of the proposed scheme is always less than the original scheme because that the proposed scheme sorts the delay time in advance and the real-time flows whose delay time are higher than the maximum

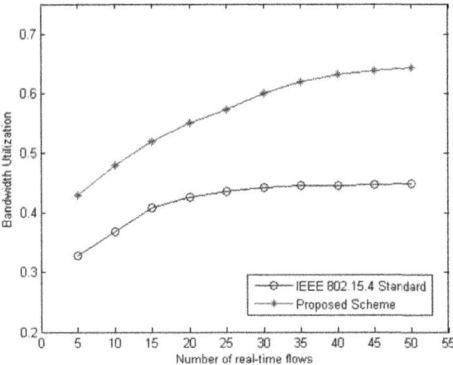

Fig. 5. Bandwidth utilization versus number of real-time flows

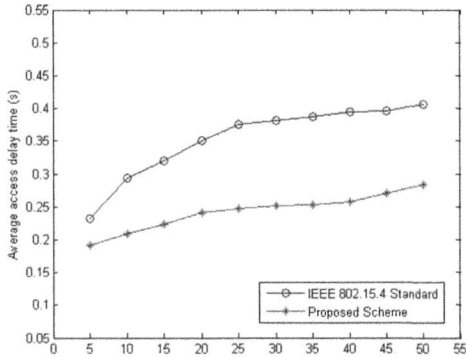

Fig. 6. Average access delay time versus number of real-time flows

waiting time would not be admitted into the CFP. Therefore, the average access delay time of the proposed scheme is lower than the original scheme.

5 Conclusion

Recently, applications in IEEE 802.15.4 LR-WPANs have a tremendous development and the design of priority scheme has been the major problem. Although IEEE 802.15.4 standard has supported the quality-of-service (QoS), it still has the problem of sacking priority mechanism. In this paper, we has proposed a priority based scheme in the IEEE 802.15.4 standard to extend the QoS support. The proposed scheme is better than the original scheme which uses the first come first service policy. And the proposed scheme is simple, efficient, and easy

316 T.-H. Wang, M.-Y. Shih, and D.-J. Deng

to implement. Simulations show that the proposed scheme achieves more GTS allocations, higher throughput, better bandwidth utilization and lower packets access delay time than the original scheme.

References

1. IEEE Standard 802.15.4 Working Group: IEEE Standard for Information Technology Part 15.4: Wireless Medium Access Control (MAC) and Physical Layer (PHY) Specifications for Low-Rate Wireless Personal Area Networks, LR-WPANs (2006)
2. Kim, T.H., Choi, S.C.: Priority-Based Delay Mitigation for Event-Monitoring IEEE 802.15.4 LR-WPANs. IEEE Communications Letters 10(3), 213–215 (2006)
3. Koubaa, A., Alves, M., Nefzi, B., Song, Y.Q.: Improving the IEEE 802.15.4 Slotted CSMA/CA MAC for Time-Critical Events in Wireless Sensor Networks. In: Workshop of Real-Time Networks (2003)
4. Youn, M., Oh, Y.Y., Lee, J., Kim, Y.: IEEE 802.15.4 based QoS support Slotted CSMA/CA MAC protocol for Wireless Sensor Networks. In: International Conference on Sensor Technologies and Applications (2007)
5. Huang, Y.K., Pang, A.C., Hung, H.N.: An Adaptive GTS Allocation Scheme for IEEE 802.15.4. IEEE Transactions on Parallel and Distributed Systems 19(5), 641–651 (2008)
6. Shrestha, B., Hossain, E., Camorlinga, S., Krishnamoorthy, R., Niyato, D.: An Optimization-Based GTS Allocation Scheme for IEEE 802.15.4 MAC with Application to Wireless Body-Area Sensor Networks. In: IEEE International Conference on Communications, ICC 2010 (2010)
7. Deng, D.J., Yen, H.C.: Quality-of-Service Provisioning System for Multimedia Transmission in IEEE 802.11 Wireless LANs. IEEE Journal on Selected Areas in Communications 23(6), 1240–1252 (2005)
8. Buratti, C.: Performance Analysis of IEEE 802.15.4 Beacon-Enabled Mode. IEEE Transactions on Vehicular Technology 59(4), 2031–2045 (2010)
9. Pollin, S., Ergen, M., Ergen, S.C., Bougard, B., Perre, L.V.d., Moerman, I., Bahai, A., Varaiya, P., Catthoor, F.: Performance Analysis of Slotted Carrier Sense IEEE 802.15.4 Medium Access Layer. IEEE Transactions on Wireless Communications 7(9), 3359–3371 (2008)

Hybrid Service Integration Engineering: Implications from a Game-Story-Combined Mobile Social Game

Toshihiko Yamakami

ACCESS
Toshihiko.Yamakami@access-company.com

Abstract. The content business has witnessed a turning point toward service engineering. Information was a precious resource in the past, however, that is not so true anymore. Content providers need to address the issue of how they position themselves in terms of their standpoint on servicization. Mobile social games are increasingly attracting attention from the viewpoint of revenue-generating engines. The massive revenue-generating capability of mobile social games has accelerated the advances in service engineering. The author focuses on a mobile social game called "Peony Garden" and discusses the implications of servicization in the mobile content.

1 Introduction

The era of Information has changed the meaning of information in the content business. When information was a scarce resource, providing information was the mainstream of the content business. The mass media born in the 20th century has inherited this DNA from its glorious success for decades.

The content landscape has drastically changed by advances in the information and communication technologies. Information is not a scarce resource anymore. The massive quantity of information stored on the Internet has drastically decreased the value of information.

At the same time, the value of services has increased. As long as the end users appreciate the value of services, there will be an increasing opportunity to generate revenue. One example is the mobile social game market in Japan. The major SNS providers started providing open platforms in late 2009. Within one and a half years, it has created a 100 billion yen market.

The author focuses on a game called "Peony Garden" and discusses the meaning of service engineering in this era of abundant high-speed information and communication technologies.

The author examines the extension of Gamenics theory to general service engineering from the implications of the analysis.

R.-S. Chang, T.-h. Kim, and S.-L. Peng (Eds.): SUComS 2011, CCIS 223, pp. 317–325, 2011.
© Springer-Verlag Berlin Heidelberg 2011

2 Purpose and Related Works

2.1 Purpose of Research

The aim of this paper is to identify the factors that drive the success of mobile social games.

2.2 Related Works

Mobile social games have some unique factors like ubiquity and high community-oriented-ness.

Ubiquity helps to maintain motivation. Ahtinen discussed the possibilities of mobile wellness applications in reference to their ubiquity and technological capabilities [1].

High community-oriented-ness provides the suitability of game-based learning of social norms. Early focus on multi-player games on mobile handsets was discussed by Paul [6]. Hildmann discussed game-based learning of social norms [3].

Various approaches have been taken in the mobile social games in order to cope with capability constraints. Ivanov discussed a summarization technique for mobile social album sharing [5].

Gamenics is a massive body of know-how related to the user interfaces that were first created by Nintendo for the Japanese videogames market. Isbister summarized Gamenics theory in an interview with Professor Saito, the inventor of Gamenics theory [4] (Chapter 23.1).

Febretti discussed the difference between usability and playability with regard to long-term engagement [2].

Yamakami presented a community-based stage model in order to explain the evolution of the mobile content business in Japan [7].

Past literature did not capture the service engineering aspects of mobile social games with a departure from legacy categories.

The originality of this paper lies in its identification of a new concept of "hybrid service engineering," in the context of mobile social service engineering with an extension to Gamenics theory.

3 Industrial Landscape

3.1 Stage Model of Mobile Business

In the last century, many content providers depended upon their competence in dealing with the scarcity of information resources. It was time-consuming to refine the quality of information,

This preciousness of information has been lost gradually through the rapid advances in information and communication technologies. The costs for storing and copying digital information have drastically dropped during the past decades. This leverages the need to convert information delivery services into user-experience-oriented services.

The transitions in the evolution of business models are depicted in Fig. 1. The original paradigm of the Internet was just a replacement of information transfer using a digital method. At the early stage, the Internet was just a pile of unstructured information.

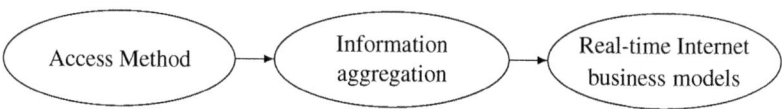

Fig. 1. Transition of Business Model towards Real-time Internet

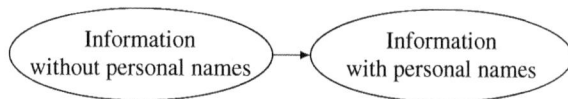

Fig. 2. Trend of Information with Personal Names

The emergence of the ubiquitous high-speed Internet and inclusion of social networks have leveraged the real-time Internet business models that include a wide rande of social factors.

These are driven by the trend depicted in Fig. 2. In 1990's, almost no one in the Internet cared who wrote the web pages, because information was uploaded by the persons who were not the original authors in many cases. The emergence of real-time human networks has driven the emergence of information with personal names, which has impacts on business model engineering.

In the past, information had no links to personal names. People did not care who wrote the pages of Yahoo!, Wiki pages, and so on. Information is something can be copied by anyone, so its sources were of no concern. For the most part in the early days, the person who uploaded a piece of information was a good-will engineer without a name, and not the original author.

Quantity changes the quality. The bandwidth used for Internet traffic has grown at a blistering pace.

The human network of information, with Twitter, and Facebook, and so on, has grown and outnumbers other traffic like Google now.

The real-time Internet was imagined to be something like video Internet, broadcast Internet in the early days. Also, after the emergence of ubiquitous computing, it was imagined to be something like the Internet of things, with millions of interconnected sensor devices.

At this point, we have to agree that the current state of art of the Internet has brought with it a new definition of the real-time Internet, which is an Internet with billions of people interacting in a real-time manner with twitterers and communicating via SNS services.

This new real-time Internet had brought a massive impact on Internet business model engineering. Social services like Twitter and Facebook still have some way to explore their revenue-generating engines. They should be free services because no one will invite others to join paid services. This is a weak point of the business models of social services. However, in areas adjacent to these social services, a new trend of revenue-generating engines has emerged. One example is a social game vendor, such as Zynga, which leverages the power of social networks for their revenue-generating engines. Another example is a social commerce service, such as Groupon, which leverages the power of social networks for its coupon commerce.

Information is heavily laden with personal names, with human contexts and human emotions.

3.2   Example of Peony Garden

"Peony Garden" is a popular social game in Japan. It is a multiple ending story where the story is influenced by a sequence of choices that the reader makes as the story develops. One of the characteristics of this game is that a mini-game is associated with it to earn the points required to read more of the story. The story is split into pieces, and some game points earned in mini-games are required to read each piece. Therefore, it is a *game-story-combined* mobile social game.

This game is free, however, some of the option items can also be purchased. If a user would like to read the next piece of story beyond the number of game points earned, the user can purchase a ticket to read it.

Interestingly, although, it is that it is highly possible that no one would pay for the story or a mini-game, the combination of story, mini-games and social aspect makes the revenue-generation possible.

The design of this game is depicted in Fig. 3. This is interesting because it artificially inserts the time-consuming prefix games before the main content. It makes the consuming process of content more complicated with insertion of gaming experience. The game itself is not essential, however, the combination makes the new value for its content.

3.3   Gamenics Theory

Games can provide some clues for these new challenges to revenue-generation. Gamenics is one of these clues. The theory demonstrates that we need to explore the time-dimensional control in games in order to cultivate an increased mind-share in end users.

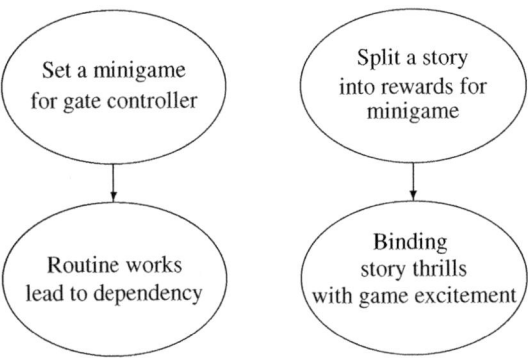

Fig. 3. The game design of Peony Garden

Gamenics is the massive body of know-how related to the user interfaces that were first created by Nintendo for the Japanese videogames market. Professor Akihiro Saito coined this word "gamenics", which is a portmanteau combining the word "game" with the "nics" of "electronics" and "mechanics." Gamenics is different from game design. Game design makes a game interesting, and gamenics is what communicate this to the player. Professor Saito argued that any complicated system can be operated, even by children, with the help of Gamenics. Gamenics is the method of teaching users how to play. The uniqueness of Gamenics theory is that it focuses on the dimension of time. Gamenics suggests that increased complexity should be provided together with the joy of mastering new operations or know-how as the user increases the understanding of the game, Incremental achievements strengthen the learning, therefore, kids can master a very complicated operation over a span of time. For this, There is much know-how regarding how successive frustration-achievement cycles should be presented to a user in order to achieve this learning process.

This massive know-how was derived through decades of struggling over how to facilitate user learning with very limited hardware capabilities, using detailed tuning of software. This is understandable considering the decades of evolutionary history of game consoles. Game consoles were invented in the U.S, however, after game consoles were equipped with software tuning, the main battlefield was shifted from the U.S. to Japan.

In other words, Gamenics theory is the know-how of software-tuned learning systems. It consists of structured decision branches with four rules:

- Intuitive user interface
- Understanding operations without a manual
- Game direction toward being addicted to and the effect of incremental learning
- Externalization of the game

It is a collection of know-how about how game design leads users to get into a game. Gamenics is unique in its handling of the time dimension in the user interface, much different from universal design theory or affordance theory.

Saito described how ordinary children all over the world can play a Nintendo game without reading the Japanese manuals The game, Dragon Quest, contains 1500 different pieces of information, including locations, monsters, items and tactics. However, children of the age 10 easily absorb and manage all of these pieces of information. It is said that the typical English speech of a President of the United States is composed from a 500-word English vocabulary. When the appropriate methodology is undertaken, any child can say a President's speech without difficulty.

There are several basic rules behind Gamenics theory. A "game" is fundamentally a process that creates a virtual stress and an opportunity to remove this stress. During the removal of a stress, people experience a happy feeling. This is the driving force for a game.

The position of Gamenics theory within the scope of game design is illustrated in Fig. 4.

Gamenics theory places an emphasis on time-dimensional control in the learning process. It assumes user evolution over a span of time to add complexity and to stimulate the joy of learning and achievement. These time-dimensional and learning-centric methods are key to Gamenics theory.

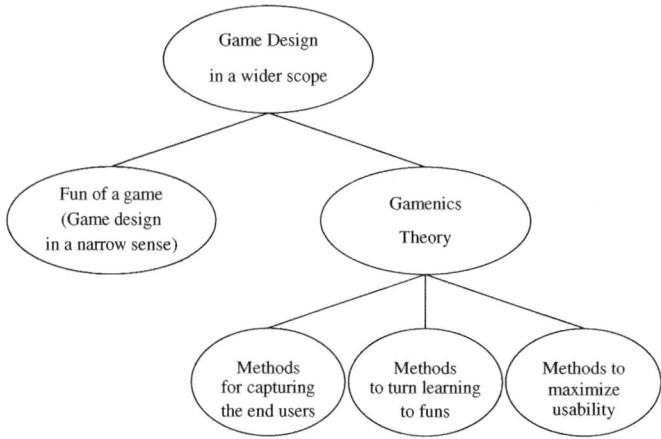

Fig. 4. Overview of game design including Gamenics theory

Saito claims that the unique feature of the Gamenics theory is its time-dimensional considerations which make it unique compared to Affordance theory and Universal design theory.

3.4   Why We Have to Extend Gamenics to Hybrid Service Engineering

Gamenics is a step forward in controlling the time-dimensional management in game design. The social dimension is captured in the 4th rule of Gamenics, however, it must be further enhanced in view of the emergence of massive social games. The social dimension is becoming an increasingly important aspect of game design in the era of real-time Internet.

And, Gamenics is not clear in two aspects: (a) dependency management, and (b) expectation management. Both factors are crucial to game design. In order to highlight the service engineering aspect of Gamenics theory, it is important to focus these two aspects when implementing of four rules of Gamenics theory.

The most important reason to extend Gamenics theory is that we need a broader sense of service engineering even when utilizing game design. Information and other content including games are parts of service engineering. Standalone categories do not make sense when the service providers focus on what a service is.

Hybrid service engineering is a framework whereby multiple pieces of content are reconstructed to create a service utilizing enhanced Gamenics theory with a focus on dependency management and expectation management.

3.5   Hybrid Service Engineering

Mobile social game design consists of five different factors:

The media business has been in trouble since the emergence of the Internet. Most of the mass media business such as TV, radio, magazines and newspapers witnessed their glory days from the early to the middle of the 20th century. During those success

Table 1. Five factors of mobile social game design

Item	Description
Routine work	Monotonous routine work that facilitates regular gaming from addiction
Skills	Minor skills to achieve small goals, e.g. finger actions
Chances	Dependency on luck
Tactics	Mid-term and long-term strategies
Social relationship	Greeting exchange, support, trust, social rewards, social recognition, . . .

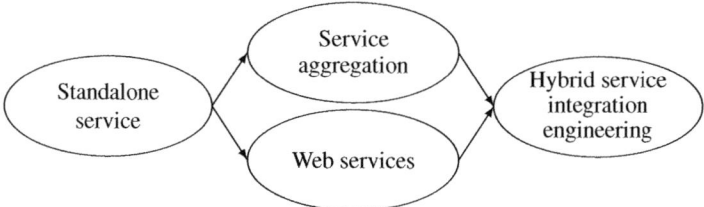

Fig. 5. Transitions of service engineering

days, information was a rare resource. When information was scarce, providing the information itself was an important service.

Radical advances in information and communication technologies brought with them the new paradigm of services. When there is ambient information that cannot be processed by end users, simply providing information does not make a useful service anymore. Therefore, we have to develop a new methodology to explore servicization in an era of ambient information.

Servicization is an industrial shift from product manufacturing to service development. As the user satisfaction shifts from ownership of a product to use experience of a service, servicization has come to a main focus of many industrial sections. The author coined the new concept "Hybrid Service Engineering" in order to extend Gamenics to the broader sense of servicization.

Hybrid service engineering is a concept that explores the time-dimensional management of user mind-share using social and time dimensional extension of Gamenics.

The transitions in the evolution of service engineering are depicted in Fig. 5. The user satisfaction depends on how content are presented not just as information but as services. One of the techniques to enable this is time-dimensional control, as presented in the game "peony garden".

4   Discussion

4.1   Advantages of the Proposed Approach

Service science was a term introduced by IBM to describe the study, design, and implementation of services systems. It was initiated in IBM laboratories in 1993, and widely known around 2004 with the margining industrial and academic attention to management of services. Service science provides people in the service industries with the quantitative skills necessary to model key decisions and performance metrics associated with services. Service science in the past did not focus on the time-dimensional management, dependency management and expectation management well.

Hybrid service engineering focuses the service engineering utilizing extended Gamenics theory to reflect the lessons learned from the mobile social games. It deals with the time dimensional management of a combination of multiple services and content that creates new values for users.

Hybrid service engineering is a framework in which holistic service engineering is performed with a departure from the legacy content categories. Simply providing information or providing games is not sufficient to build a service anymore. Given the ambient information and content available on the Internet, service engineering needs to focus how each item of content can be integrated into a service while managing dependencies and expectations. These factors are critical in mobile services because mobile users are easy-come and easy-go.

4.2 Limitations

This research is a qualitative study. Quantitative measures for verifying multiple aspects in the hybrid service engineering discussed in this paper remain for further study.

Acceptance of mobile social games is an ongoing transitive prolegomenon that requires further observation with regard to game design and playability.

Detailed research models of mobile social games and their verification are beyond the scope of this paper.

Different games have different target users. This paper does not address the diversity of mobile social games.

Japanese mobile social games are different from Facebook games in terms of the identity and trust structure. Detailed study of Japanese-specific regional factors is beyond the scope of this paper.

5 Conclusion

Ambient information on the Internet has impacted the content industry by eliminating the scarcity of information resources upon which many content providers based their core competence, and diminishing that source of revenue. The content industry needs to address this issue and explore new revenue-generating opportunities.

At the same time, the Internet itself has witnessed a turning point from the massive collection of past information to the massive collection of current ongoing personal information.

This has brought about new business opportunities such as Zynga and Groupon.

The mobile social game market in Japan has been growing rapidly, reaching more than one billion US dollars in the one and a half years since OpenSocial acceptance in late 2009. That rapid growth has brought a wide range of trials with new mobile content as games.

The author discussed the implications of "Peony Garden" a popular mobile social game in Japan. This game represents a new paradigm of service engineering that does not depend on the legacy concepts of games and e-books.

With the examination of the game design principles of this game, the author proposes a new framework of "Hybrid service engineering," in order to extend Gamenics theory to service integration in the context of mobile social games.

Hybrid service engineering is a paradigm for service engineering in the current context of ambient information and highly-interactive services.

Hybrid service engineering extends Gamenics theory with dependency management and expectation management. The author believes that this conceptual framework scan serve as a vehicle of new media services that are a departure from the fixed legacy content categories of the past.

References

1. Ahtinen, A., Huuskonen, P., Häkkilä, J.: Let's all get up and walk to the north pole: design and evaluation of a mobile wellness application. In: Proceedings of the 6th Nordic Conference on Human-Computer Interaction: Extending Boundaries, NordiCHI 2010, pp. 3–12. ACM, New York (2010), http://doi.acm.org/10.1145/1868914.1868920
2. Febretti, A., Garzotto, F.: Usability, playability, and long-term engagement in computer games. In: Proceedings of the 27th International Conference Extended Abstracts On Human Factors in Computing Systems, CHI 2009, pp. 4063–4068. ACM, New York (2009), http://doi.acm.org/10.1145/1520340.1520618
3. Hildmann, H., Uhlemann, A., Livingstone, D.: Simple mobile phone-based games to adjust the player's behaviour and social norms. Int. J. Mob. Learn. Organ. 3, 289–305 (2009), http://portal.acm.org/citation.cfm?id=1552242.1552247, doi:10.1504/IJMLO.2009.026314
4. Isbister, K., Schaffer, N.: Game Usability: Advancing the Player Experience, illustrated edn. Morgan Kaufmann, San Francisco (2008)
5. Ivanov, I., Vajda, P., Lee, J.S., Ebrahimi, T.: Epitome: a social game for photo album summarization. In: Proceedings of the 1st ACM International Workshop on Connected Multimedia, CMM 2010, pp. 33–38. ACM, New York (2010), http://doi.acm.org/10.1145/1877911.1877921
6. Paul, S.A., Jensen, M., Wong, C.Y., Khong, C.W.: Socializing in mobile gaming. In: Proceedings of the 3rd International Conference on Digital Interactive Media in Entertainment and Arts, DIMEA 2008, pp. 2–9. ACM, New York (2008), http://doi.acm.org/10.1145/1413634.1413641
7. Yamakami, T.: A stage view model of development of mobile data services: Implications from mobile data service and business model evolution in japan. In: ICSSSM 2010, pp. 205–210. IEEE Computer Society, Los Alamitos (2010)

A Driver's Physiological Monitoring System Based on a Wearable PPG Sensor and a Smartphone

Yuan-Hsiang Lin[1,*], Chih-Fong Lin[1], and He-Zhong You[2]

[1] Department of Electronic Engineering,
National Taiwan University of Science and Technology, Taipei, Taiwan
[2] Graduate Institute of Biomedical Engineering,
National Taiwan University of Science and Technology, Taipei, Taiwan
{linyh,M9802132,M9823013}@mail.ntust.edu.tw

Abstract. In the course of driving, sudden disease outbreak often cause traffic accidents. In this study, we designed a wearable photoplethysmography (PPG) sensor module based on a Programmable System on Chip (PSoC). It transmits PPG signal to a smartphone via Bluetooth. On the smartphone, a heart rate (HR) detection algorithm is implemented. When the abnormal HR is detected, the smartphone will use the sound and vibration to warn the driver. At the same time, physiological data and GPS location are also be transmitted to the remote server (remote health care center) via the 3G mobile network, so that the staff on the center can monitor the newest information and understand the driver's driving status. In order to reduce motion artifact, LED and silicon photodiode are put into the separate magnetic ring and use the transmission method to measure PPG signal on earlobe. The results show the difference in heart beats between the ECG method and our method there is 0 in all driving behaviors test. It shows this new PPG sensor can prevent motion artifact effectively in driver's physiological monitoring.

Keywords: Physiological monitoring system, PSoC, smartphone, PPG, wearable sensor.

1 Introduction

In the course of driving, sudden disease outbreak often cause traffic accidents. In the past studies, many people measure physiological signals in the car such as ECG, EMG and respiratory signal [1]. However, these methods need to hang on many physiological measurement sensors and wires on the body so that the drivers may feel inconvenient and even affect their driving behaviors.

In 2009, Jonannes Schumm et al integrated the ECG measurement system into the backrest of the airplane seat [2]. As this ECG system is unobtrusively integrated into the seat, it does not disturb the user, but it is sensitive to body movements and is only capable of measuring the ECG while the user is leaning on the back. In 2010, Heung-Sub Shin et al present the car driver's condition monitoring system that designed by

---

[*] Corresponding author, IEEE member.

R.-S. Chang, T.-h. Kim, and S.-L. Peng (Eds.): SUComS 2011, CCIS 223, pp. 326–335, 2011.
© Springer-Verlag Berlin Heidelberg 2011

using ECG and PPG sensors to obtain physiological signals on the steering wheel [3]. These methods use non-wearable sensor which are convenient for measuring on driving, but it ignores the driver's driving behavior. If the driver can't always hold the steering wheel, then the physiological signals can't be measured. In 2007, Lei Wang et al design the earpiece PPG sensor [4]. The device is encapsulated with multiple LEDs and photodiodes based on a reflective PPG design. The ear measuring method is more suitable than previous measurement, just like the Bluetooth headset, but the motion artifact is still the most serious problem. In 2010, Ming-Zher et al also use wireless earpiece to measure PPG signal on the earlobe [5] and reduce motion artifact to get higher accuracy by adaptive noise cancellation [6], but the elimination of noise are also limited.

Recently, smartphones are very popular and have great computing capability and communication capability. Moreover, most of the drivers are used to wear a Bluetooth headset on the road. If the physiological sensors can be built into the wireless headset and use the smartphone to process the data, then the size of the measuring device and wires on the body will be greatly reduced. Although there are many ways to measure physiological signals for drivers, but the most devices can't real-time alert the driver to rest or emergency contact a remote server when the driver's physiological signals are abnormal. Therefore, this study designed a wearable PPG sensor module based on a PSoC and can transmit signals to a smartphone by Bluetooth. In order to reduce motion artifact, the physiological sensors are put into the magnetic ring and are used to measure the PPG on the earlobe. When the abnormal physiological signals are detected, the smartphone will generate a feedback to alert user. It is expected to reduce traffic accident when the abnormal physiological signals occur.

2   System Description

In this study, we develop a wearable real-time physiological monitoring system based on the smartphone. This system consists of three parts, including a wearable sensor module, a smartphone and the remote server. Fig. 1 shows the system block diagram. The sensor module can be worn on the earlobe. It includes an optical sensor which uses transmission method for PPG measurement, a three-axis accelerometer (G-sensor) and a PSoC. The signal acquisition and analog circuits are designed by PSoC. The G-sensor is used to detect the head status. Furthermore, the data transmission interface between the sensor module and the smartphone is using Bluetooth.

The PPG data are transmitted to the smartphone in real-time and the smartphone is used to perform digital signal processing include FIR digital filter and compute the physiological parameters such as HR. The PPG waveform and HR information are shown on the display of smartphone. If the abnormal physiological signal is detected, the smartphone will use the sound alarm and vibration alert to warn the driver. At the same time, physiological data and GPS location are also be transmitted to the remote server (remote health care center) via the 3G mobile network, so that the staff on the center can monitor the newest information and understand driver's driving status. Therefore, the driver can find the best solution at the first time.

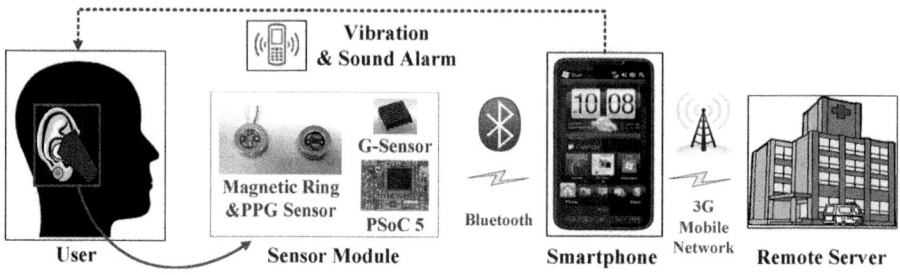

Fig. 1. System block diagram

2.1   Sensor Module

The sensor module can be divided into PPG sensor and microprocessor module.

PPG Sensor. The PPG sensor is composed of an IR LED (infrared light emitting diode), a silicon photodiode, and a 3-axis G-Sensor (ADXL335). All devices are using SMD components to implement in order to reduce hardware size, so that it is comfortable to wear on the earlobe. In order to reduce motion artifact, we use the transmission method to measure PPG signal on earlobe. Besides, LED and silicon photodiode are put into the separate magnetic ring. Fig. 2 shows the optical sensors and magnetic rings. The two magnetic rings can attract together to clamp the earlobe. This structure not only makes LED light directed beam to the receiver, but also makes the sensor contact with the earlobe become more stable and can reduce motion artifact.

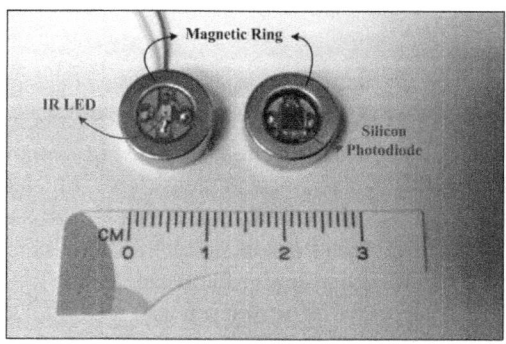

Fig. 2. PPG sensor and magnetic rings

Microprocessor Module. PSoC 5 is a main chip for our microprocessor module. It includes a Cortex M3 processor, OPAs, multiplexers, ADCs, DACs, GPIOs and UARTs. The PPG signal is processed by a high-pass filter (cut-off frequency is 0.48Hz), a low-pass filter (cut-off frequency is 4.82Hz), and an amplifier (gain is 120) through internal OPAs. Then, the processed PPG signal and G-Sensor signals (Ax, Ay, Az) are fed into internal 4-to-1 multiplexer. The output signal of the multiplexer is connected to the internal 8-bit ADC and convert to digital signals. The sample rate is 100Hz for each channel. Finally, the processed signals are sent to UART, which is connected to a Bluetooth module for data transmission. The Baud rate is 9600. Fig. 3 shows the detail hardware block diagram. Orange blocks are internal blocks of PSoC.

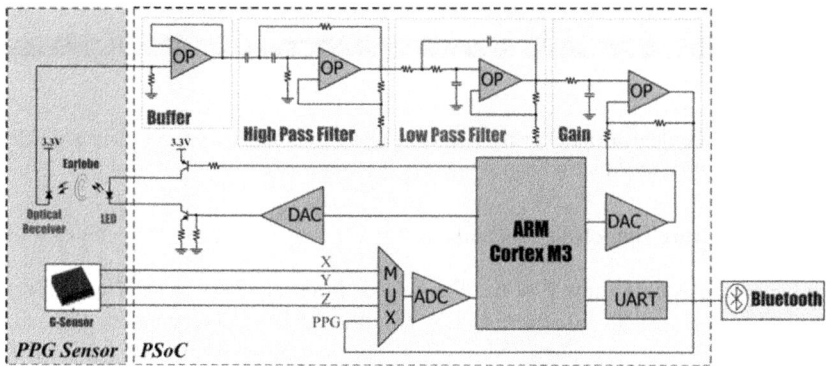

Fig. 3. Hardware block diagram

2.2   Smartphone Platform

On the choice of mobile phones, we choose HTC HD2. It uses windows mobile 6.5 operating system and contains a 1GHz processor and 448MB RAM. We use Microsoft Visual Studio 2008 C# .Net for smartphone application program development. Fig.4 shows the software flow chart on the smartphone platform.

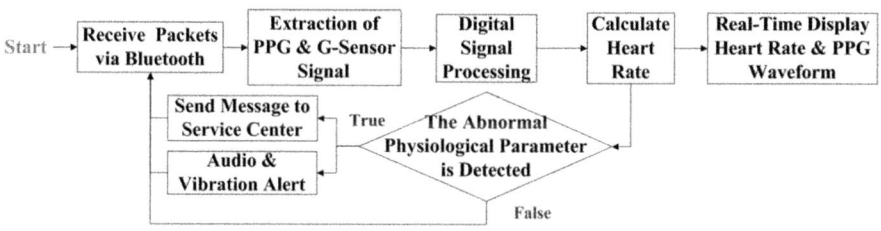

Fig. 4. Software flow chart on the smartphone platform

First, it receives and unpacks the data packets via Bluetooth module. Second, through signal processing to calculate the HR, and then shows the PPG signal waveform and HR on the LCD display of smartphone for users to observe. After the signal analysis, the system will use vibration or audio to alert drivers to take a rest or to find out medical service immediately when the abnormal physiological parameter is detected. Fig. 5(A) is the physiological monitoring interface. It can show the PPG waveform and HR information on smartphone. Fig. 5(B) shows the setting interface, it can set alert conditions and feedback methods for alert. Fig. 5(C) is the alert interface when the abnormal physiological signal is detected.

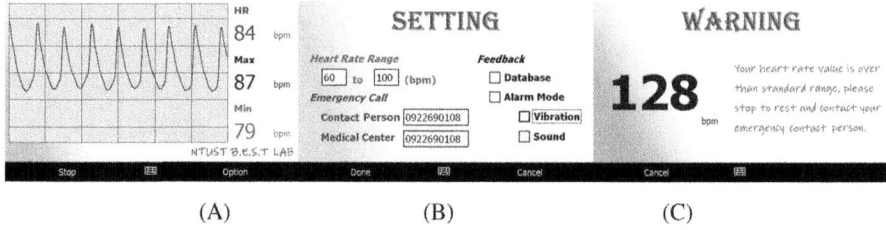

(A)   (B)   (C)

Fig. 5. (A) Physiological monitoring interface. (B) Physiological setting interface. (C) Alert interface when abnormal physiological signal is detected.

2.3 Heart Rate Detection Methods

The heart rate is determined by the Peak-Peak Interval (PPI) of PPG waveform. PPI calculation is shown in Equation 1. The n_{th} PPI (PPI_n) is determined by the n_{th} peak index (P_n) and the n-1$_{th}$ peak index (P_{n-1}) and sampling frequency. 'S' means the sample rate of PPG signal and heart rate is calculated by Equation 2.

$$PPI_n = \frac{P_n - P_{n-1}}{S}. \tag{1}$$

$$HR_n = \frac{60}{PPI_n} = \frac{60 \times S}{(P_n - P_{n-1})}. \tag{2}$$

Signal Process. In order to calculate HR, we must get the exact peak location of PPG waveform. Fig. 6 shows signal processing steps for PPG peak detection.

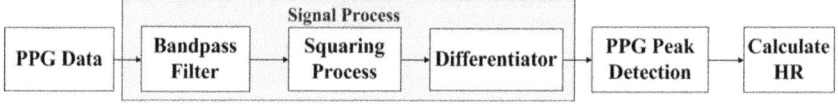

Fig. 6. Signal processing steps for PPG peak detection

Fig. 7 shows PPG signal processing steps. Signal processing steps include bandpass filter, squaring process and differentiator. Fig. 7(A) is an ECG signal as a reference. Fig. 7(B) is the original PPG signal. First, in order to attenuate noise, the signal passes through a digital bandpass filter that cutoff frequency is 0.8Hz and 4Hz. Fig. 7(C) shows the output of this filter. The next process after bandpass filtering is squaring. We use the squaring to enlarge the signal characteristic. Fig. 7(D) shows the output of the squaring. After the squaring is differentiation. Information about the slope of the PPG signal is obtained in this derivative stage. We use this slope to detect the position of the PPG's peak. Fig. 7(E) shows the output of the differentiation.

Peak Detection. We utilize the slope feature and set a dynamic threshold to detect the PPG's peak. When the PPG slope value is larger than this threshold, then PPG peak position can be detected on the first slope value which is less than or equal to 0. Fig. 8(A) shows the slope feature of PPG signal after the differential process. The beginning of detection, *Flag* is set to false. When the slope value is larger than the threshold, the *Flag* is set to true and this slope value is recorded to the buffer. When the *Flag* is true and slope value is smaller than or equal to 0, then we can get the PPG's peak index (position) in this moment. Afterwards we take out the maximum slope value from the buffer and use it to update the new threshold. We can calculate the peak to peak interval after the peak index is obtained. Finally, we clean the buffer and restart to detect next peak. Fig. 8(B) shows the flow chart of the peak detection.

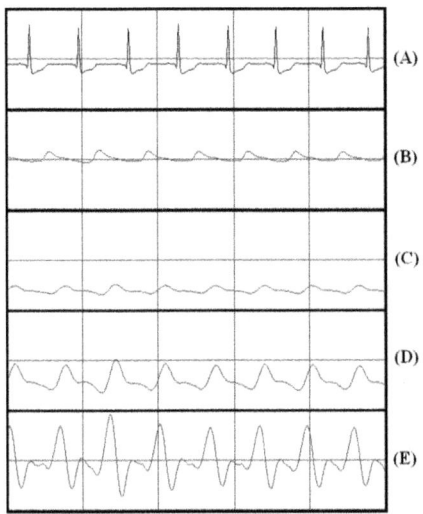

Fig. 7. PPG signal processing steps. (A) ECG signal as a reference. (B) Original PPG signal. (C) Output of bandpass filter. (D) Output of squaring process. (E) Results of differentiator.

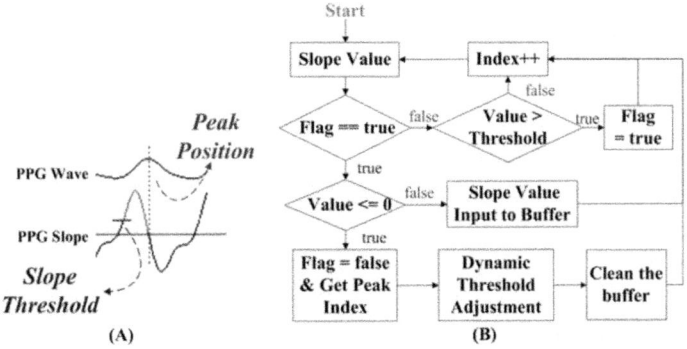

Fig. 8. (A) The slope feature of PPG signal. (B) The flow chart of the peak detection.

Dynamic Slope. Threshold Adjustment and Peak-to-Peak Period Estimation. The dynamic slope threshold is updated with the previous maximum slope value of PPG waveforms. The initial threshold value, we can select a small threshold to ensure that the first peaks can be detected. Each period we can get a maximum slope value, so that we can use this maximum slope value to multiply a coefficient to generate a new threshold for detecting the next PPG peak. According to the Equation 3, the n_{th} threshold (T_n) is determined by the previous maximum slope value (S_{n-1}) and coefficient value (T_C). In this study, this coefficient value is 0.35.

$$T_n = S_{n-1} \times T_c. \tag{3}$$

In addition to dynamic threshold adjustment, we also set a time window to reduce the occurrence of error peak detection. The time window is also dynamic adjusted by previous PPI. PPI_L is the minimum time window, and PPI_H is maximum time window. PPI_L and PPI_H are calculated by Equation 4 and Equation 5. If we detected a peak point and the new PPI is smaller than PPI_L, then this point will be considered that is an error and ignore it. If we can't detect any peak in this maximum time window, then the threshold should be initialized to initial threshold. Fig. 9 shows the dynamic slope threshold adjustment and the time window.

$$PPI_L = PPI_{n-1} \times 70\% \tag{4}$$

$$PPI_H = PPI_{n-1} \times 130\% \tag{5}$$

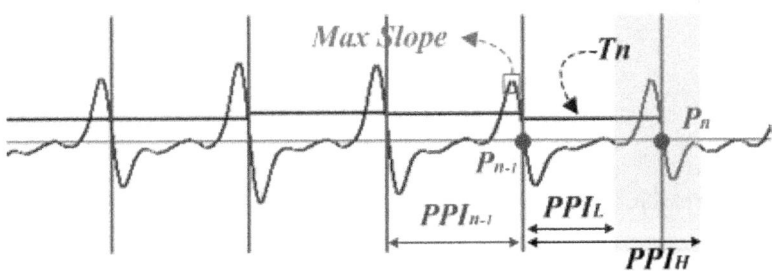

Fig. 9. Dynamic slope threshold adjustment and the time window

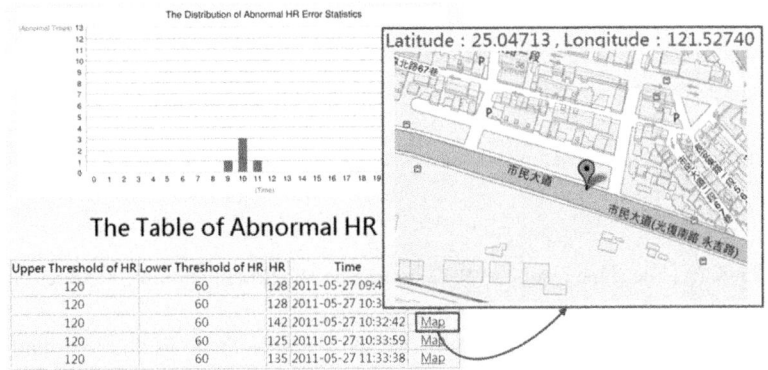

Fig. 10. The database management web page and the GPS coordinates show on Google Map

2.4   Remote Server

The smartphone can real-time transmit the abnormal HR value and GPS coordinates to the remote server by 3G mobile network. On the server, we use MySQL database and PHP web page to read the information. It can also use the Google API chart to show the abnormal state, and use Google Map to show the driver's position. Therefore, the staff in service center can monitor driving conditions quickly and clearly via the web page. The database management web page for the abnormal HR statistics is shown in Fig. 10. When click the "Map" of the database, the GPS coordinates can be shown on Google map.

3   Results

The accuracy of HR detection will describe in following. In the past, motion artifact is the most common problem on wearable PPG system. Therefore, our verification methods focus on the behaviors that may cause motion artifact when the driver wears this device. The common behaviors for the driver such as talking, watching left and right side mirrors, and head shaking. Therefore, we design a five-minutes testing procedure (Table 1). Test procedure has 10 stages, each stage has 30 seconds, includes rest (stage 1, 3, 6, 8, 10), reading the article and read out the sound (stage 2). In the stage 4 and stage 5, system will sound at the second and fourth second of every five seconds, it repeats six times in both stage 4 and stage 5. The tester who heard the first sound need immediately to turn his head to see right/left side (mirror direction), and immediately return back to front when the second sound. In stage 7 and stage 9, the tester need to continuous shake head for 30 seconds.

Table 1. The test procedure of five minutes

Stage	Time(mm:ss)	Behavoir
1	00:00 ~ 00:30	Rest.
2	00:30 ~ 01:00	Reading the article and read out the sound.
3	01:00 ~ 01:30	Rest.
4	01:30 ~ 02:00	See the mirror on right side
5	02:00 ~ 02:30	See the mirror on left side
6	02:30 ~ 03:00	Rest.
7	03:00 ~ 03:30	Continuous head shaking (left and right).
8	03:30 ~ 04:00	Rest.
9	04:00 ~ 04:30	Continuous head shaking (up and down).
10	04:30 ~ 05:00	Rest.

In this test, we measure PPG signal by our self-made sensor module. At the same time, we use ECG signal to verify the heart beats. There are 5 people were tested, each person records 4 times and each time records 5 minutes. Tester is requested to sit on the chair in all test stages. The range of all testers' HR is from 62 to 100 bpm. The results show the difference in heart beats between the ECG method and our method there is 0 in all driving behaviors test. Table 2 shows the heart beats of both methods.

Table 2. Heart beats of both ECG and PPG methods

Tester	n	Method	Stage 1	Stage 2	Stage 3	Stage 4	Stage 5	Stage 6	Stage 7	Stage 8	Stage 9	Stage 10	Total
A	1	PPG	50	49	49	48	50	51	50	50	50	50	497
		ECG	50	49	49	48	50	51	50	50	50	50	497
		Diff.	0	0	0	0	0	0	0	0	0	0	0
	2	PPG	48	47	48	47	47	47	48	47	46	48	473
		ECG	48	47	48	47	47	47	48	47	46	48	473
		Diff.	0	0	0	0	0	0	0	0	0	0	0
	3	PPG	47	45	46	47	45	46	45	48	45	45	459
		ECG	47	45	46	47	45	46	45	48	45	45	459
		Diff.	0	0	0	0	0	0	0	0	0	0	0
	4	PPG	49	48	49	49	48	48	48	48	48	48	483
		ECG	49	48	49	49	48	48	48	48	48	48	483
		Diff.	0	0	0	0	0	0	0	0	0	0	0
B	1	PPG	31	36	32	32	31	31	33	33	33	32	324
		ECG	31	36	32	32	31	31	33	33	33	32	324
		Diff.	0	0	0	0	0	0	0	0	0	0	0
	2	PPG	33	34	33	33	31	32	34	35	34	33	332
		ECG	33	34	33	33	31	32	34	35	34	33	332
		Diff.	0	0	0	0	0	0	0	0	0	0	0
	3	PPG	34	35	33	31	31	32	31	32	34	33	326
		ECG	34	35	33	31	31	32	31	32	34	33	326
		Diff.	0	0	0	0	0	0	0	0	0	0	0
	4	PPG	33	35	33	33	32	33	33	33	35	32	332
		ECG	33	35	33	33	32	33	33	33	35	32	332
		Diff.	0	0	0	0	0	0	0	0	0	0	0
C	1	PPG	38	40	38	35	36	36	37	38	39	38	375
		ECG	38	40	38	35	36	36	37	38	39	38	375
		Diff.	0	0	0	0	0	0	0	0	0	0	0
	2	PPG	38	39	39	36	35	39	37	38	38	39	378
		ECG	38	39	39	36	35	39	37	38	38	39	378
		Diff.	0	0	0	0	0	0	0	0	0	0	0
	3	PPG	39	39	41	39	39	41	39	41	40	41	399
		ECG	39	39	41	39	39	41	39	41	40	41	399
		Diff.	0	0	0	0	0	0	0	0	0	0	0
	4	PPG	38	42	39	37	38	39	38	39	41	40	391
		ECG	38	42	39	37	38	39	38	39	41	40	391
		Diff.	0	0	0	0	0	0	0	0	0	0	0
D	1	PPG	36	39	38	37	37	38	40	37	41	38	381
		ECG	36	39	38	37	37	38	40	37	41	38	381
		Diff.	0	0	0	0	0	0	0	0	0	0	0
	2	PPG	38	41	36	41	40	40	43	42	42	39	405
		ECG	38	41	36	41	40	40	43	42	42	39	405
		Diff.	0	0	0	0	0	0	0	0	0	0	0
	3	PPG	34	35	36	34	36	34	38	34	38	33	352
		ECG	34	35	36	34	36	34	38	34	38	33	352
		Diff.	0	0	0	0	0	0	0	0	0	0	0
	4	PPG	36	38	35	34	34	32	36	34	36	34	349
		ECG	36	38	35	34	34	32	36	34	36	34	349
		Diff.	0	0	0	0	0	0	0	0	0	0	0
E	1	PPG	42	44	43	40	40	41	41	42	42	42	417
		ECG	42	44	43	40	40	41	41	42	42	42	417
		Diff.	0	0	0	0	0	0	0	0	0	0	0
	2	PPG	41	43	40	41	40	41	41	40	42	42	411
		ECG	41	43	40	41	40	41	41	40	42	42	411
		Diff.	0	0	0	0	0	0	0	0	0	0	0
	3	PPG	42	42	41	39	40	42	39	40	42	40	407
		ECG	42	42	41	39	40	42	39	40	42	40	407
		Diff.	0	0	0	0	0	0	0	0	0	0	0
	4	PPG	41	41	39	38	40	40	39	40	40	39	397
		ECG	41	41	39	38	40	40	39	40	40	39	397
		Diff.	0	0	0	0	0	0	0	0	0	0	0
Total		PPG	788	812	791	771	770	783	790	791	806	786	7888
		ECG	788	812	791	771	770	783	790	791	806	786	7888
		Diff.	0	0	0	0	0	0	0	0	0	0	0

4   Discussion and Conclusion

We test the sensor module's current consumption in two conditions. One is for data transmission rate of 100 byte/sec that is only transmitting PPG data. The total current consumption of our sensor module is 77.357 mA, includes the 23.629 mA current consumption of Bluetooth module. Another is for data transmission rate of 600 byte/sec that is including 3-axies data of G-Sensor, PPG data, one start and one stop characters. Total current consumption of this sensor module is 88.714 mA, includes the 34.129 mA current consumption of Bluetooth module. It still has space to reduce current consumption by changing LED control method and perform data compression.

In the Bluetooth transmission test, the transmission error rate is 0 in the open space within 10 meters, so it's no problem to transmit physiological signal in the car. In the 3G mobile network transmission tests, we use smartphone to transmit the packets to the remote server per second for 1000 times continuously. The average packets transmission time of 1000 times is less than 350ms, so that it can achieve the purpose of real-time transmission.

In this paper, we present a smartphone based physiological monitoring and alert system for driver to monitor their HR in real time. When the abnormal HR is detected, smartphone will automatically warn driver to achieve the real-time alert function. Besides, remote health care center can also monitor the newest driver's status and location via the 3G mobile networks. Therefore, the driver can find the best solution at the first time. It is expected the traffic accidents caused by the abnormal physiological signals can be reduced via the real-time alert function. We also proposed a new PPG sensor structure that is combining the sensors with magnetic rings to reduce motion artifact. Experiments have shown that this system can monitor driver's HR and has not been affected by the motions caused by general driving behaviors.

References

1. Healey, J.A., Picard, R.W.: Detecting stress during real-world driving tasks using physiological sensors. IEEE Transactions on Intelligent Transportation Systems 6(2), 156–166 (2005)
2. Schumm, J., Setz, C., Bachlin, M., Bachler, M., Arnrich, B., Troster, G.: Unobtrusive Physiological Monitoring in an Airplane Seat. Personal and Ubiquitous Computing 14, 541–550 (2010)
3. Shin, H.S., Jung, S.J., Kim, J.J., Chung, W.Y.: Real time car driver's condition monitoring system. In: IEEE Sensors 2010 Conference, pp. 951–954 (2010)
4. Wang, L., Lo, B.P., Yang, G.Z.: Multichannel Reflective PPG Earpiece Sensor With Passive Motion Cancellation. IEEE Transactions on Biomedical Circuits and Systems 1(4), 235–241 (2007)
5. Poh, M.Z., Swenson, N.C., Picard, R.W.: Motion-Tolerant Magnetic Earring Sensor and Wireless Earpiece for Wearable Photoplethysmography. IEEE Transactions on Information Technology in Biomedicine 14(3), 786–794 (2010)
6. Widrow, B., Glover, J.R., McCool, J.M., Kaunitz, J., Williams, C.S., Hearn, R.H., Zeidler, J.R., Dong, E., Goodlin, R.C.: Adaptive noise cancelling: Principles and applications. Proceedings of the IEEE 63(12), 1692–1716 (1975)

Rectangular Cartogram Visualization Interface for Social Networks

Shun-Yu Jhong[1], Chun-Cheng Lin[2,*], Wan-Yu Liu[3], and Weidong Huang[4]

[1] Dept. of Computer Science, Taipei Municipal University of Education, Taipei 100, Taiwan
[2] Dept. of Industrial Engineering and Management, National Chiao Tung University,
Hsinchu 300, Taiwan
cclin321@nctu.edu.tw
[3] Dept. of Applied Natural Resources, Aletheia University, Tainan 721, Taiwan
[4] CSIRO ICT Center, Australia

Abstract. Social networks link people together, among which a lot of factors influences their complexity. To our understanding, so far most visualization interfaces for social networks have not reflected any of their factors. Therefore, this paper tries to solve such a problem by rectangular cartograms, which is a kind of geographical visualization interface using rectnaguls to represent regions in a map. Besides the relative position of each rectangle can reflect the actual geographical related positions, one of the main feastures of rectangular cartograms is that the area size or the shape of each rectangle can reflect the information of its corresponding region, e.g., the population in that region. This paper proposes a layout approaph for rectangular cartograms with area labeling for social networks, in which each region has a minimum-width constraint for accommodating a text label. As a result, this paper applies a genetic algorithm to finding the area-labeling rectangular cartogram with minimum width under some constraints to meet the practical use in social networks. By doing so, we can visualize the labeling text on each rectangle and observe the information represented by its area size or shape at the same time. Furthermore, the proposed approach is applied to visualizing the distribution of the Facebook popularity of an enterprise in Taiwan. From the cartogram, the text label on each region can be read directly and the relation among regions as well as the popularity can be visualized, so that the enterprise can improve the regisons with poor popularity by the help from the regions with high popularity.

Keywords: Rectangular cartogram, area labeling, map labeling, social network.

1 Introduction

As social networks are social structures consisting of people, link people together, and are influenced by many factors, e.g., values, concepts, regions, and so on, they play an important role on sociology, anthropology, computer science, etc. In addition, their importance can be found in many applications, e.g., the frameworks proposed by Facebook and Google. Facebook applies the concept of social networks to linking

* Corresponding author. Research supported in part by NSC 98-2218-E-009-026-MY3.

R.-S. Chang, T.-h. Kim, and S.-L. Peng (Eds.): SUComS 2011, CCIS 223, pp. 336–347, 2011.
© Springer-Verlag Berlin Heidelberg 2011

people together and constructing the networks of groups so that real-time sharing effects can be achieved, and developing games using those groups. The engineerings employed by Facebook also use the concept of social networks to establish a world map by using the locations of users over the world. On the other hand, Google applies the concept to Google Buzz, which focuses on the users with Gmail accounts, incorporating information with daily life by sharing photos and movie chips, so that daily life is not restricted to only the neighorhood. In light of the above, it is of importance to develop the visualization tools for social networks. The visualization of social networks are common in the literature, but most of those studies focused on drawing abstract graphs consisting of vertices and edges underlying social networks. For example, Shi et al. [7] designed the visulization of a social network that are working, which is a chaleging task but meets the basic requirement. They used HiMap to create the visualization interface, and its feature was to incorporate image group and hierarchy division to draw social networks. Zhu et al. [14] proposed a so-called concept visualization approach, facilitate the understanding of the concepts in social networks. However, those kinds of visualization cannot reflect the information of any factor of each node in social networks. As a result, this paper applies rectangular cartograms that can reflect the information of the factor represented by each region, and hopes to provide an effective way to visualize social networks.

Rectangular cartogram [1,6,12] is a kind of cartogram. In general, since the size of each region in a cartogram may not necessarily reflect its real area, theshape and adjacency among regions cannot remain. However, the judgement of a good cartogram is reconizable via another aspect. As a whole, there are four types of cartogram. The standard cartogram is contiguous area cartogram, which deforms each region so that its size reflects its real area exactly and its adjacency is preserved. There exist a lot of literature on this type of cartogram (e.g., see [7]). The second type is non-contiguous area cartogram [9,10], in which each region preserves its correct shape, but can represent its corresponding geographical value by scaling its size, so that some adjacencies among regions may not be connected. Those scaled regions are sometimes placed at its original position to increase the recognition. The third type of cartogram is based on circles, which were proposed by Dorling [4]. The forth type of cartogram is the rectangular cartogram proposed by Raisz in 1934 [10]. The strength of using rectangles is the good estimation of the area size of each region, in comparison to the other types of cartograms. However, the shapes of rectangles are not easy to be reconized, and the diversified posibility of representation are constrained. In the literature, there also exist some works incorporting the first and forth types of cartograms, and also a few works on rectilinear cartograms [2].

Heilmann et al. [8] applied rectangular cartograms to the USA president election. Based on USA population census, they proposed two algorithms for rectangular cartograms that represent the proportion of the area of each state in USA. The regions with different colors belong to different parties, whose votes in the election of USA president can be visulized according to their area. de Berg et al. [3] used rectangular cartograms to produce a game, which applied geometry to build a large rectangle with many rectangles with fixed size. When the length and width is modified, the other is modified accordingly. van Kreveld et al. [13] proposed an algorithm for rectangular cartograms, which uses a precise formula depending on the adjacency among regions, and established rectangular cartograms by the existing algorithms from VLSI layout design. Furthermore, they characterized a class of rectangular cartograms that can be calculated efficiently. From the literature, there were studies on rectangular cartograms that use area size to represent geographical locations or use colors to distinguish different information, but, to our understanding, there was no study on rectangular cartograms with area labeling. As a result, this paper takes the area labeling into account to design rectangular cartograms.

In this paper, we consider the following two settings: 1) consider the information that are not reflected in the visualization interface of social networks, e.g., the popularity of a node to the other nodes; 2) place text area labeling inside the contour of each region in rectangular cartograms. This paper proposes an approach for rectangular cartograms that considers the above two settings (e.g., see Figure 1). Since each region in rectangular cartograms is required to be labeled by a predescribed text, it has a minimum drawing width. Hence, we apply a genetic algorithm to find the minimal-width rectangular cartogram reflecting the information of factors under the minimum-width constraint of each region. Furthermore, the proposed approach is applied to visualizing the distribution of the Facebook popularity of an enterprise in Taiwan. From the rectangular cartogram, the text label on each region can be read directly and the adjacency relation among regions as well as the popularity of each region can be visualized, so that the enterprise can improve the regisons with poor popularity by the help of those with high popularity.

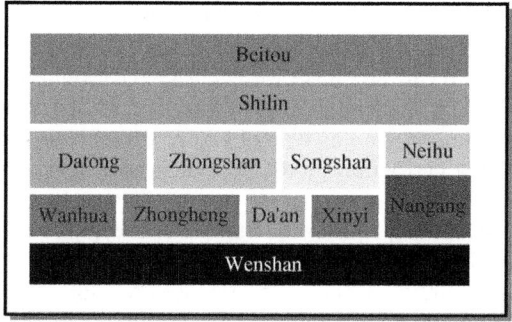

Fig. 1. Illustration of an area-labeling rectangular cartogram

The organization of this paper is stated as follows: Section 2 describes the settings of our concerned problem. Section 3 proposes our approach for the described problem, and gives the details of the proposed genetic algorithm. Section 4 gives an experimental result applied to the visualization of the distribution of the Facebook popularity of an enterprise in Taiwan. Section 5 concludes our work with some lines of future work.

2   Problem Setting

This paper extends the problem setting proposed by Heilmann et al. [8] to describe ours. The problem setting of our concerned problem is stated as follows: Given a map with n regions $\bar{P} = \{\bar{p}_1, ..., \bar{p}_n\}$, in which all the regions are corresponding a geographical variable vector $Z = (z_j)_{j=1,...,n}$ (where $z_j \geq 0$ and $\sum_{j=1}^{n} z_j = 1$), our problem is to determine a feasible rectangular cartogram $P = \{p_1, ..., p_n\}$ that is corresponding to the topology. Such a feasible solution is required to meet the following constraints:

- P is planar,

- each region $p \in P$ is a rectangle,

- each region $p \in P$ is a neighbor of at least one different region $p' \in P$.

A cartogram is feasible if it meets the above constraints. Let the set of all the feasible cartograms be denoted by M.

The quality of a rectangular cartogram P is evaluated from the following two aspects: 1. whether $\bar{P}$ can be recognized easily in P should be evaluated; 2. the geo-spatial data values given by Z should be reflected by the areas of the regions in P. General speaking, those requirements are in conflict with each other. Based on the two aspects, we apply the following criteria to evaluate the quality of P. Those criteria are respectively corresponding to objectives or constraints of our concerned problem. They are described as follows:

- Area : The quality of P is measured by the area error $A(P) = A(P, Z)$ with

$$A(P) := \frac{1}{n} \sum_{j=1}^{n} \frac{|\varepsilon_j - z_j|}{z_j},$$

where $\varepsilon_j := a(p_j) / \sum_{k=1}^{n} a(p_k)$; $a(p_j)$ is area of a region p_j in P.

- Empty space: Rectangular cartogram P may contain "hole" or empty space that comprises those areas which are completely surrounded by filled space. Therefore, the quality of P can also be measured by the empty space error $E(P)$ with

$$E(P) := \frac{A_t(P) - A_f(P)}{A_t(P)},$$

which is equal to the ratio of unoccupied space $(A_t(P) - A_f(P))$ over $A_t(P)$. $A_t(P)$ represents the space surrounded by the boundary of P. And, $E(P)$ is normalized to the interval $[0,1]$.

- Area labeling: In area labeling, each text label is placed inside the contour of the area of each region. Since each text label consists of some letters, the region has a minimum width to accommodate the text label. Hence, the criteria of area labeling is defined as follows:

$$L(P) := \frac{1}{n} \sum_{j=1}^{n} \frac{|l(p_j) - l(\bar{p}_j)|}{l(p_j)}$$

where $l(p_j)$ is the width of $p_j \in P$; $l(\bar{p}_j)$ is the width of the area labeling text on $\bar{p}_j \in \bar{P}$.

● Drawing width: The width of the whole rectangular cartogram is denoted by $W(P)$.

According to the above criteria, the objective of our concerned problem is defined as follows:

$$F\,(P) = (A(P), W\,(P)).$$

Since one of the main features of a rectangular cartogram is to use the area of each region to represent its geographical variable value, we require to make $A\,(P)$ as small as possible. In addition, in order to use the whole screen space, we require $E\,(P)$ to be zero. Although the rectangular cartogram is one of the representations of maps or topologies, so far there have been no rectangular cartograms designed for area labeling. Hence, it is of interest to investigate the algorithm for rectangular cartograms with area labeling. In this paper, we will design a minimal-width rectangular cartogram that takes into account the following two settings: 1) each region has to reflect its geographical variable value, and 2) the width of each region is large sufficient to accommodate the text label attached to it so that there are no overlapping labels and regions. As a result, our concerned problem for rectangular cartograms is characterized to find a feasible rectangular cartogram P in M with

$$\text{Min } F\,(P) \tag{1}$$

$$\text{s.t. } P \in M, E\,(P) = 0, L(P) \geq 0 \tag{2}$$

3   Area-Labeling Rectangular Cartogram

This section proposes the algorithm for producing the rectangular cartogram for the problem with objective (1) and constraints (2). Since we require each region to be wider than a minimum width so as to accommodate the text label attached to it, we can visualize the relationship among regions and the geographical variable values that are reflected, as shown in Figure 1. The proposed algorithm is given in Algorithm 1.

Each step in Algorithm 1 is explained as follows. The input of the algorithm is a map. In Steps 1 and 2 in Algorithm 1, as shown in Figure 2, we find the bounding box R enclosing all the regions, and then find the centroid of each polygonal region in the map. Then, Step 3 collects the geographical variable value of each region to be used in the genetic algorithm in Step 4.

Algorithm 1. AREA_LABELING_CARTGRAM()

Input : a map
Output: a rectangular cartogram of the map that soloves the problem with objective (1) and constraints (2)

Step 1: find the bounding box R enclosing all the regions in the map
Step 2: find the centroid of each polygonal region in R
Step 3: collect the geographical variable value of each region
Step 4: take the information obtained by the above steps as the input of the proposed genetic algorithm

---

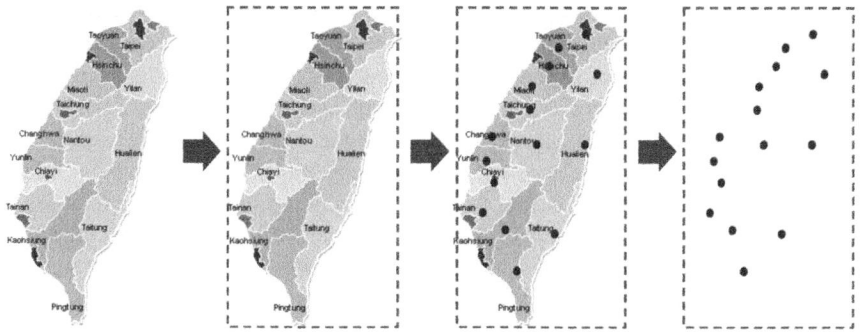

Fig. 2. Illustration of finding the centroid of each polygonal region in a map

In Step 4 of Algorithm 1, we use genetic algorithm for the rectangular cartogram problem with objective (1) and constraints (2). For solving the concerned problem, the objective of our genetic algorithm is to find a rectangular cartogram with minimal width so that each region in the cartogram reflects its geographical variable value as much as possible. In what follows, we give the details of the main components in our proposed genetic algorithm.

3.1   Solution Representation

Assume that there are n regions in the map. We apply horizontal cuts or vertical cuts (in which horizontal cuts respect y-coordinates, while vertical cuts respect x-coordinates) to slice the bounding box R into n regions. In our genetic algorithm, we use a chromosome to represent a feasible rectangular cartogram. Each chromosome is represented by a binary string, in which 0 represents a horizontal cut, while 1 represents a vertical cut. Note that we assume that each cut is sliceable (see Figure 3). Therefore, the ordering of the genes in the chromosome determines the ordering of all the cuts, and we can use the ordering to draw a rectangular cartogram, as shown in Figure 3.

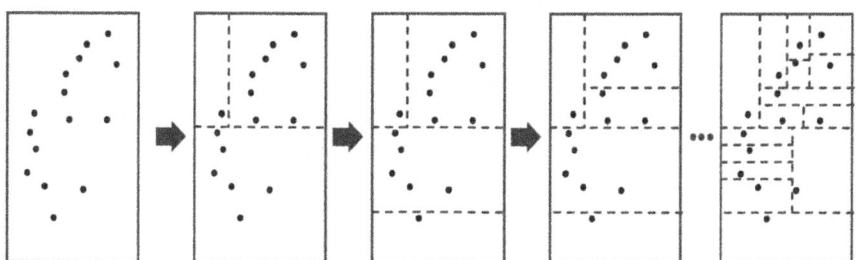

Fig. 3. The process of how to use the chromosome 0100111101000 to establish the corresponding rectangular cartogram

After the ordering of all the cuts is determined, in order to meet the requirements of our concerned problem, we make each region reflect its geographical variable value as follows. From the first three steps in Algorithm 1, we have n centroids to represent n regions in the map, and the centroid of each region p_i has a geographic variable value z_i. The criterion of cutting is based on the cumulative sum of geographic variable values. First, according to the ordering of cutting to determine the use of either a horizontal or a vertical cut, we scan all the centroids from bottom to top or from left to right, and we sum up the geographical variable values of scanned centroids. We stop at the centroid when the cumulative sum is greater than 1/2, and then use an interpolation formula to determine the precise position of the cutting.

The interpolation formula is explained as follows. Consider a rectangle that contains a number of centroids. Without loss of generality, we apply a horizontal cut on this rectangle. Let the centroids (region) with the minimal and the maximal y-coordinates be denoted by p_i and p_j, respectively. We scan the centroids from bottom to top, and suppose that we stop at the centroid p_k where the cumulative sum of geographic variable values is greater than 1/2. Then the y-coordinate of the horizontal cut is equal to

$$y(p_{k-1})+(y(p_k)-y(p_{k-1}))\cdot\frac{\sum_{t=i}^{k-1}z_t}{\sum_{t=i}^{j}z_t} \qquad (3)$$

In addition, there is a boundary condition, where the cumulative geographic variable value of the first centroid exceeds 1/2. When the condition occurs, we apply the following formula to represent the y-coordinate of the horizontal cut:

$$y(p_i)+(y(p_{i+1})-y(p_i))\cdot\frac{z_i}{\sum_{t=i}^{j}z_t} \qquad (4)$$

According to the above two formulas, we can use $(n-1)$ cuts to slice the bounding rectangle R into n rectangles.

3.2   Generation Definition

We first define the first generation in our genetic algorithm. A generation has 100 chromosomes, each of which has $(n-1)$ genes, corresponding to $(n-1)$ cuts. In the initial generation, each chromosome is a binary string generated randomly, in which 0 represents a vertical cut, while 1 represents a horizontal cut. In addition, each chromosome has a fitness value, which is calculated as follows: Since a chromosome determines a rectangular cartogram, the width $l(p_i)$ of each rectangle p_i can be measured. Also, since we require rectangle p_i to be as least wider than $l(\bar{p}_i)$, the fitness of the chromosome is defined as the maximal scaling factor of each rectangle as follows:

$$\max_{1\le i\le n}\{\frac{l(p_i)}{l(\bar{p}_i)}\} \qquad (5)$$

In other words, the fitness represents the scaling factor of the rectangular cartogram with respect to this chromosome. Note that in order to meet the requirements of the concerned problem, our genetic algorithm is to find the minimal-width rectangular cartogram among all. Therefore, we sort the 100 chromosomes in the generation according to their fitness values, and preserve the chromosome with the best fitness to the next generation. The other 99 chromosomes in the current generation are processed by the selection operator in the next subsection. Figure 4 is the flow chart of our genetic algorithm.

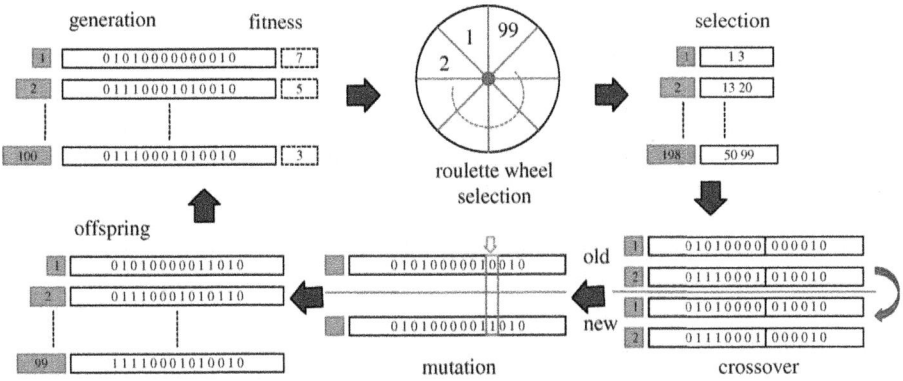

Fig. 4. Flow chart of our proposed genetic algorithm

3.3   Selection

The selection operator applies the roulette wheel approach, which is explained as follows: Suppose that in the current generation there are three chromosomes with fitness values 5, 3, and 2, respectively. The sum of fitness is 10. Hence, the probabilities of the three chromosomes are 5/10, 3/10, 2/10, respectively, i.e., 0.5, 0.3, 0.2. Hence, their cumulative probabilities are 0.5, 0.8, and 1, respectively. Then, we generate a random number in the interval [0, 1]. If the number falls between 0 and 0.5, the first chromosome is selected; else if the number is between 0.5 and 0.8, the second chromosome is selected; otherwise, the third chromosome is selected. That is, if a chromosome occupies a large ratio of the wheel, it has a high probability to be selected. The operator uses 99 chromosomes for selection, and generates 198 chromosomes. Then each pair of the 198 chromosomes is fed into the crossover operator, mentioned in the next subsection.

3.4   Crossover and Mutation

As for the crossover operator, we generate a random integer number i between 1 and $(n - 1)$, and then swap the i-th to the $(n - 1)$-th genes of one chromosome with those of the other chromosome. After crossover, one of the two chromosomes remains to mutate with an a priori probability. Suppose that the mutation probability is 10%. We generate a random float number between 0 and 1. If the number is less than 0.1, the mutation is executed. We randomly selected one of the $(n - 1)$ genes of the chromosome. If the gene is 0, then it is changed to 0; otherwise, 1. After the 198 chromosomes experience crossover and mutation, only 99 chromosomes remain. Plus the chromosome with the best fitness obtained in the previous subsection, the next generation includes 100 chromosomes, which will be sorted in this iteration. After several generations, if the best fitness is not modified or the maximal number of iterations is achieved, then the chromosome with the best fitness is the output of our genetic algorithm.

4   Implementation and Experimental Results

The section provides implementation and experimental results of our proposed algorithm. The experimental result is a rectangular cartogram applied to the distribution of popularity of the Facebook of an enterprise with marketing in Taiwan. This section has three subsections: The environments and data of our experiments are given first, and then some experimental results on the distribution of popularity of Facebook of the enterprise is given.

4.1   Environments and Data

Our algorithm is implemented on a Windows XP PC with 3.0 GHz Dual Core CPU and 4GB memory in Java language, which is portable over all platforms. The data of the popularity of the Facebook of an enterprise is simulated. Figure 5 gives the Taiwan map as well as the topology of cities in Taiwan. Figure 6 gives the popularity (i.e., the number of joining the enterprise's Facebook) in each city in Taiwan.

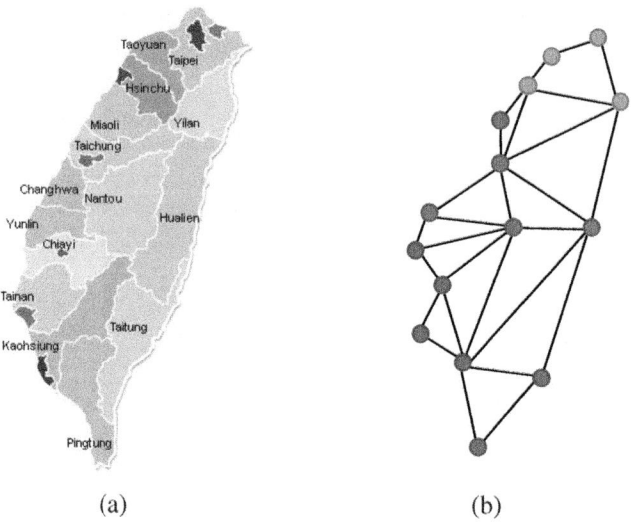

(a)   (b)

Fig. 5. (a) Taiwan map and (b) its underlying topology, in which each node represents a city and each edge represents their adjacency

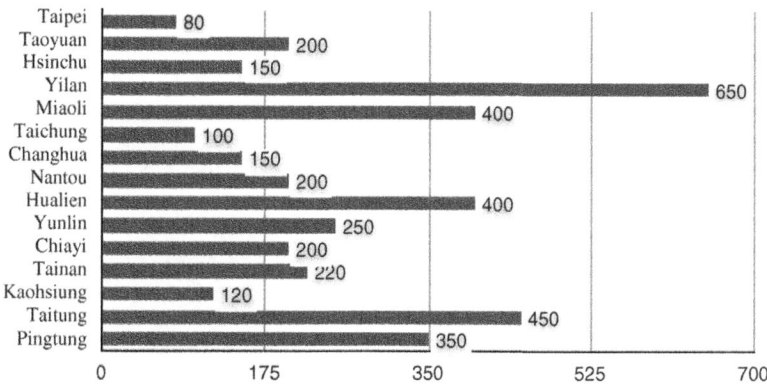

Fig. 6. The popularity of the Facebook of an enterprise in each city in Taiwan

4.2   Environmental Results

We apply our rectangular cartogram approach to the distribution of the popularity of the Facebook of an enterprise with marketing in Taiwan, as shown in Figure 7. The features of such a rectangular cartogram include 1) the area of each rectangle in this cartogram is proportional to the number of joining the enterprise's Facebook in the city represented by that rectangle; 2) the rectangular cartogram has a minimal width under the constraint of each rectangle with enough width accommodating its corresponding text label, so that we can observe the name of each retangle directly. In practice, when an enterprise is making decision, it can apply the area-labeling rectangular cartogram to visualize the relationship of adjacency and the relationship of popularity. For example, we can see from Figure 7 that the popularity of Taipei accounts for the least proportion, while Yilan, its adjacent city, has a large popularity, which implies that the enterprise should apply the adjacency marketing to increase the popularity, or dispatch the employees in Yilan to assist the branch in Taiwan to raise their popularity.

Furthermore, Figure 8 is the rectangular cartogram that adds colors to Figure 7, in which Taiwan is distinguished into three divisions. Each division has a color, so that an additional variable can be presented in this rectangular cartogram. By Figure 8, aside from using the rectangle area to reflect the popularity of the corresponding city, we also observe the divisions from colors, e.g., the enterprise have three administers A, B, C for the three division colored by orange, blue, and red, respectively. From Figure 8, the popularity of Taipei in the division supervised by administrator A is very small, which reflects that the number of the customers in Taipei joining the Facebook of the enterprise is few, as compared to Yilan. Hence, the enterprise should be alarmed from the rectangular cartogram to enhance the popularity of Taipei branch, and hence should ask administrator A to execute the task.

Our proposed method still has some constraints, and can be improved in the future. We apply the genetic algorithm for the tool of solving our problem, but we do not evaluate the efficiency and complexity of the algorithm. Hence, some basic components in the genetic algorithm still can be improved, e.g., the definition of chromosome, the crossover and mutation. In addition, since the general problem of designing minimal-width rectangular cartograms is NP-hard, we may try to find the polynomial time algorithms for some simplified versions, i.e., we consider the following two constraints: 1) when the width of each rectangle has a lower bound two; 2) the width of each rectangle is restricted to two or three. It is reasonable to apply the above two constraints in practice, because 2-letter or 3-letter labeling is very common.

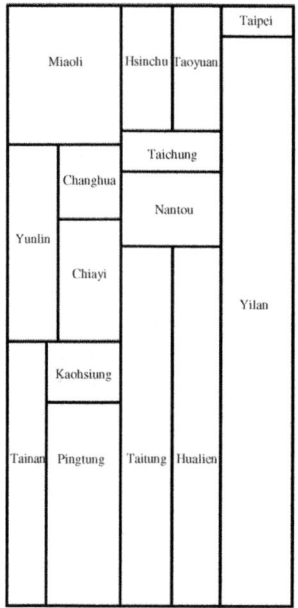
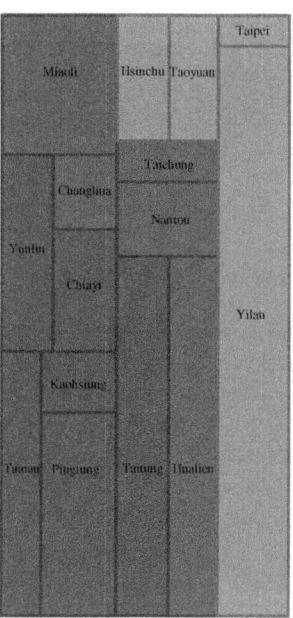

Fig. 7. Our experimental result for the data in Figure 6

Fig. 8. Our experimental result that adds colors to Figure 7

5   Conclusion

This paper has proposed an approach for rectangular cartograms that take into account area labeling, and applies the approach to visualizing the distribution of popularity of the Facebook of an enterprise with marketing in Taiwan. By selecting the information of the Facebook of the enterprise, we created a rectangular cartogram interface for the enterprise, which shows the information of popularity of its Facebook as well as area labeling at the same time. By using our method, it is guaranteed that the text label in each rectangle of the rectangular cartogram does not overlap each other. After calculation by our genetic algorithm, an optimal scaling factor of the rectangular cartogram can be obtained. By doing so, it can be recognized easily to visualize which city has the highest popularity for the Facebook of the enterprise.

Our future work is to conduct a comprehensive evaluation on the performance of our proposed approach, and evaluate the time complexity of our genetic algorithm with a variety of parameters. In addition, we will also consider dynamic rectangular cartograms, and apply them to mobile devices, coupled with GPS. It would be of interest to develop the applications with interaction.

References

1. Biedl, T.C., Genc, B.: Complexity of octagonal and rectangular cartograms. In: Proc. of 17th Canadian Conference on Computational Geometry, pp. 117–120 (2005)
2. de Berg, M., Mumford, E., Speckmann, B.: Optimal BSPs and rectilinear cartograms. International Journal of Computational Geometry and Applications 20(2), 203–222 (2010)
3. de Berg, M., van Nijnatten, F., Speckmann, B., Verbeek, K.: Rectangular cartograms: the game. In: Proc. of 25th Annual Symposium on Computational Geometry, pp. 96–97. ACM Press, New York (2009)
4. Dorling, D.: Area Cartograms: Their Use and Creation, Concepts and Techniques in Modern Geography, vol. 59. University of East Anglia. Environmental Publications, Norwich (1996)
5. Fabrikant, S.: Cartographic variations on the presidential election 2000 theme (2000), http://www.geog.ucsb.edu/~sara/html/mapping/election/map.html
6. Florisson, S., van Kreveld, M.J., Speckmann, B.: Rectangular cartograms: construction and animation. In: Proc. of 21st Annual Symposium on Computational Geometry, pp. 372–373. ACM Press, New York (2005)
7. Gastner, M., Newman, M.: Diffusion-based method for producing density-equalizing maps. Proceedings of the National Academy of Sciences 101(20), 7499–7504 (2004)
8. Heilmann, R., Keim, D.A., Panse, C., Sips, M.: RecMap: Rectangular map approximations. In: Proc. of 10th IEEE Symposium on Information Visualization, pp. 33–40. IEEE Press, Los Alamitos (2004)
9. Olson, J.: Noncontiguous area cartograms. Professional Geographer 28, 371–380 (1976)
10. Raisz, E.: The rectangular statistical cartogram. Geography Review 24, 292–296 (1934)
11. Shi, L., Cao, N., Liu, S., Qian, W., Tan, L., Wang, G., Sun, J., Lin, C.-Y.: HiMap: Adaptive visualization of large-scale online social networks. In: Proc. of PacificVis 2009, pp. 41–48 (2009)
12. Speckmann, B., van Kreveld, M., Florisson, S.: A linear programming approach to rectangular cartograms. In: Proc. of 12th International Symposium on Spatial Data Handling, pp. 527–546 (2006)
13. van Kreveld, M., Speckmann, B.: On rectangular cartograms. Computational Geometry: Theory and Applications 37, 175–187 (2007)
14. Zhu, B., Watts, S., Chen, H.: Visualizing social network concepts. Decision Support Systems 49(2), 151–161 (2010)

Author Index